Shock Waves

Shock Waves

Eastern Europe after the Revolutions

John Feffer

Montréal/NewYork

BLACK ROSE BOOKS No. V181
Hardcover ISBN: 1-895431-47-6
Paperback ISBN: 1-895431-46-8

Canadian Cataloguing in Publication Data

Feffer, John
Shock waves: Eastern Europe after the revolutions

Includes bibliographical references and indes.
ISBN 1-895431-47-6 (bound)
ISBN 1-895431-46-8 (pbk.)

1. Europe, Eastern—Politics and government—1989— . 2. Europe, Eastern—Economic conditions—1989— . I. Title.

DJK51.F44 1992a 320.947 C92-090631-1

Cover design by Nancy Adams

Mailing Address

BLACK ROSE BOOKS
C.P. 1258
Succ. Place du Parc
Montréal, Québec
H2W 2R3 Canada

BLACK ROSE BOOKS
340 Nagel Drive
Cheektowaga, New York
14225 USA

A publication of the Institute of Policy Alternatives of Montréal (IPAM)

Printed in Canada

Table of Contents

Introduction

Part One: The Past as Prologue

Part Two: After the Revolutions

Conclusion

To my parents:
who taught me how to struggle and why

Acknowledgements

This book has been a collaborative effort. I relied on the help and wisdom of hundreds of men and women in the countries through which I traveled. I have cited many of these people in this book, but in comparison to their guidance, citation seems a pale recompense. I only hope that when they visit the United States I can repay their kindness. For their personal help, I would particularly like to thank Elzbieta Bohomolec, Bogdan Lapinski, Abel Soriano and Bogusia Pienkowska, Ryszard and Maria Holzer, Michaela Sikorova and Vasek Novotny, Jaime Walker and David Crawford, Fred Abrahams, Mara and Nicolae Savitiu, Florentina and Valentina Hristea, Zoja Skusek and family, and Olga Melnikova. The names and contacts provided by Joanne Landy and the Campaign for Peace and Democracy., Jenny Yancey and Dan Siegal of New Visions, Victoria Brown, Tom Conrad, Virden Seybold, Bogdan Denitch, and Peter Jarman were greatly appreciated.

I am also deeply grateful for the assistance I received stateside from the American Friends Service Committee. Special thanks to Michael Simmons and the East-West Program for entrusting me with the task of traveling in the region; Michael's faith in me and this enterprise sustained me through many a trying time. Thanks also to Corinne Johnson for supporting this project with patience and care, and for reading over an early draft of this book with a keen editor's eye. Hazel Keys provided critical logistical support that smoothed over some potentially tricky situations. Thanks also to Bruce Birchard for helping out during a remarkable one-week tour of Moscow.

At the manuscript stage, I received able assistance from Steve Chase and the entire South End Press collective. I would also like to thank the readers who took time out of their busy schedules to comment on individual chapters: John Bell, Matei Calinescu, Manuela Dobos, Adrienne Edgar, Andrew Feffer, Joanne Landy, Gerry O'Sullivan, David Ost, Vladimir Tismaneanu, and James Ward. The mistakes that have managed to survive such a thorough vetting process are mine and (unfortunately) mine alone. Since some of the material in this book made its first appearance in *Z, Commonweal, New Politics,* and *Peace and Democracy,* my thanks also go out to all of these publications for permission to use this material here.

Finally, I would like to thank: Julie Drizin for sheltering me during the time I composed this book; Kip Voytek for invaluable technical assistance; my new colleagues at World Policy Institute for giving me a job and, more importantly, an extraordinarily supportive work environment; my Philly friends for catering to my restaurant habit; my more distant friends for bearing with the "struggling writer" shtick; my family for encouraging my most outlandish dreams.

John Feffer
New York City—March 1992

Preface

In the past seven years, more by accident than design, I have been in some very interesting places at some very interesting times. During the first summer of *perestroika* in 1985, I was studying Russian in Moscow, paying less attention to my drills in gerund formation than to the Gorbachev-led experiment taking place outside the classroom. It was early on in the Soviet reform effort, and the dimensions of the struggle were still unclear. At street-level, the average Muscovite demonstrated little enthusiasm for the impending shake-up, preferring instead to grumble about the restrictions on vodka introduced during the anti-alcoholism campaign. Moscow intellectuals were deeply skeptical despite early stirrings of *glasnost*. Grumbles and cynicism notwithstanding, the Soviet Union was on the eve of another revolution, and to be present at the scene was exhilarating.

This revolution in the Soviet Union literally could not contain itself. Ripples could be felt at the furthest reaches of Soviet influence. By 1988, signs of ferment from below indicated that the communist nations of Europe might take *perestroika* one step further. In the vanguard of change, the democratic opposition in Hungary chomped at the political bit, and the Solidarity trade union in Poland was re-emerging from a long slumber with two pivotal strikes. Even in the more doctrinaire East Germany, government censorship of official Soviet magazines revealed the communist leadership's increasing isolation—from its neighbors as well as from its own population. The Soviet Union may have been the story of 1985-87 but Eastern Europe was clearly going to be the next locus of rapid change in the communist world.

Late in January 1989, I arrived in Warsaw to start work at the Polish Academy of Science, my address book filled with the coded phone numbers of prominent dissidents in and around Solidarity. Within several days of my arrival, Poland became the politically "in" place to be. The Polish government announced that roundtable negotiations with the still illegal trade union would begin the following month. The country's internal cold war was about to thaw; two seemingly irreconcilable enemies had taken an unprecedented step into the unknown. Not long after the government's groundbreaking announcement, I discovered that my sponsor at the Academy was no mere member of the Polish Communist Party. As of the beginning of that year, he had become a member of the Politburo and would shortly be chosen by the Party to be the chief government negotiator on political issues in the roundtable talks. There I was, Solidarity contacts in one hand and Party contacts in the other.

Poland was changing rapidly that year, and again I would be extraordinarily fortunate to be on hand to watch this new theater of upheaval and compromise. Indeed, I had front row seats for the drama of early 1989 to witness both the willing suspension of disbelief surrounding the roundtable talks and the show-stopper triumph of Solidarity in the semi-free elections that followed. Regretfully, I left the region that August before the drama had really peaked. As change swept through the other capitals of Eastern Europe, I was stateside, sadly forced to watch the revolutions televised.

Governments fell in 1989, but that was only part of the story. In 1990, Eastern Europe faced monumental tasks of political and economic transformation. Once again I was able to witness the process firsthand. From March to November 1990, I traveled throughout Eastern Europe—from Gdansk to Sofia, from Berlin to Riga—on behalf of the American Friends Service Committee, an international Quaker organization. My mandate was broad: to get a general sociopolitical feel for what was going on. My job was to travel and talk.

Instead of trying to track down the Havels and Walesas, I interviewed the people behind the scenes: journalists, sociologists, workers, feminists, ministry appointees, and poet-protesters. I talked with a Leipzig pastor who appealed for nonviolence during the East German revolution, a Warsaw feminist fighting to stop a law criminalizing abortion, and a Czech Jew who interviewed Yasser Arafat for a newly independent daily. I met with Hungary's first political lobbyist as well as a Romanian taxi driver dreaming of work in South Africa. I drank coffee with a Bulgarian political scientist interested in rock and roll and Orthodox theology, and ate lunch with a Slovenian peace activist who specialized in guerrilla graffiti parties in the early hours of the morning.

Through these interviews, I hoped to acquire a sense of Eastern Europe, an overall understanding grounded in the details of individual lives and specific locales. I wanted to get behind the headlines, to go beyond the glossy photos of the Berlin Wall's collapse and the video stills of the executed Ceausescus. I wanted (perhaps a bit naively) to watch history unfold, not in a book or on a screen, but there in front of me as I drank pilsner in Prague, rode the dimly lit Bucharest subway, and climbed to the castle district of Zagreb.

Pursuing this goal, I stumbled into some intriguing places. I attended an Alcoholics Anonymous meeting in a monastery outside Warsaw and wandered into a summer camp on a Hungarian lake for a political party whose 22 parliamentary representatives averaged 28 years of age. Outside Bucharest, I visited a camp for "irrecuperables"—120 children with mental and physical handicaps cared for by a staff of two. I attended a first-time meeting between independent Bulgarian and Romanian trade unionists and a strategy session for the East German political movements that had led the revolution in 1989 only to lose the election in 1990. I watched the Socialist (formerly Communist) Party building burn in Sofia late one night in August, only days after I had been inside interviewing the party member in charge of "public relations." I toured the massive Ursus tractor plant in Warsaw, saw the horrible grandeur of Ceausescu's Civic Center, and stood in the crowd pressed tightly together in the courtyard of Prague's Castle hoping to catch a glimpse of Vaclav Havel during his presidential inauguration. As I traveled, I didn't always know what I was doing, and I certainly didn't know what everything meant. But the exhilaration I had felt in Moscow in 1985 and Warsaw in 1989—the thrill of immediacy—propelled me forward.

Only later, after I had returned from my trip and had begun to think more generally about Eastern Europe, did this book begin to take shape. I wanted the project to cover the countries I had visited but wondered whether it was still possible to treat Eastern Europe as a region. Was anything to be gained by writing a book on this collection of countries rather than a more modest study of one in particular? After all, the very term "Eastern" Europe was falling out of favor. Into this single category fell the former German and Russian territories of Poland, portions of the Austro-Hungarian empire, Balkan Bulgaria, and, that exemplar of heterogeneity, Yugoslavia. Eastern Europe was a territorial Frankenstein monster, stitched together from bits and pieces of dead empires and animated for a time by Soviet power. With the virtual end of Soviet influence, perhaps this creature had been put to rest and the region would truly witness a "return to diversity."

In the end, I decided that the category of Eastern Europe is still useful. The countries traditionally included in the region—(East) Germany, Poland, Czechoslovakia, Hungary, Romania, Bulgaria, Yugoslavia, Albania—have shared similar experiences, particularly over the last 45 years. Thus, during the current, often unpredictable period of reform, these countries will continue to behave in many similar ways. One can indeed construct a composite Eastern European country based on these commonalities. As a tribute to British novelist Malcolm Bradbury's satires of this area of the world, let's call this imaginary country Slaka.[1]

The new government of Slaka wants to privatize a large number of the state's enterprises but doesn't know how to assess their value. Furthermore, the Slakan public possesses only a small percentage of the money needed to buy these assets. Slaka also suffers from a shortage of experienced and honest politicians capable of taking over the reins of power. The new Slakan leaders want to forget the years of "international socialist solidarity" and join the European Community as quickly as possible. In Slaka, the environmental situation is abysmal, the issue of the secret police remains explosive, many of the same hated bureaucrats sit in the same offices, ethnic tensions are boiling to the surface, foreign policy is dominated by concerns of German strength to the west and Soviet disintegration to the east.

Slaka, of course, remains a fiction and cannot fully embody the myriad differences among the countries of the region. But Slaka's usefulness as a construct demonstrates that Eastern Europe remains a collection of shared concerns if not an actual region with precise geographic boundaries.

Treating Eastern Europe as a region has its drawbacks. As journalist Timothy Garton Ash—the region's de Tocqueville—has noted, "virtually all general writing about 'Eastern Europe' is either a catalog or, if analytically more ambitious, extrapolates from the one or two countries the author knows best."[2] This book will try to squeeze through this analytic Scylla and Charybdis, avoiding the equal horrors of a boring catalog and an erroneous extrapolation. The reader should ideally acquire from this book a general sweep while retaining a sense of each country's particularity.

I have divided this book into three very unequal parts. Although the Eastern Europe of 1989 captured the world's attention, I have decided to focus on those events primarily in the introduction. The newspapers and several fair-to-excellent books have already covered this ground.[3] I am more interested in providing background material so that the reader can understand why 1989 happened in the way it did. Therefore, in the second section I look at the historical and geographical factors that shaped the eastern parts of Europe before they officially became "Eastern." The Soviet model—political, economic, military, social—is described, as well as the process by which it was first imposed on Eastern Europe and then deposed by the region's inhabitants.

The third and largest section addresses post-revolutionary Eastern Europe. Each chapter in this section focuses on a specific problem of reform: political development in (East) Germany, economic reform in Poland, the new Czech and Slovak foreign policy, the Hungarian environmental movement, the Romanian secret police, ethnic conflict in Bulgaria, and the future of federal structures, if any, in Yugoslavia. Each chapter will show how these concrete issues fit into the given country's overall reform process and will compare and contrast the handling of similar problems in other Eastern European countries. In other words, I will look at how, say, the environmental movement in Hungary catalyzed the entire democratic opposition and then at how the environmental situation in Hungary compares with the regional picture.

Weaving through the text are the book's three themes: Europe, modernization, and revolution. Europe is the oldest story here, involving the peoples of its eastern regions in a millennial narrative of "civilized" versus "uncivilized." Integration in the West and escalating nationalism in the East are not, as some imagine, entirely contradictory tendencies; rather, they are both byproducts of a historical process of identity-building shaped by external and internalized threats. Modernization is a more recent project, associated with the progressive application of technology to economic systems to bring about social change. Eastern Europe's current "leap forward" encounters not only the inherent challenges of modernization but also the contemporary criticisms of the overall project of technological and industrial progress. Temporarily obscuring issues of culture and economics, the revolutions that erupted in 1989 altered Eastern Europe's political environment. These revolutions initiated changes in both leadership and government policy. To what degree are these new programs borrowed from previous regimes or imported from the West? Naturally, the revolutions have been institutionalized (the fate of all revolutions). But in this process have the original impulses of the revolutionaries been irremediably compromised?

This book is not simply descriptive, however, a mirror carried along the roads of Eastern Europe. In attempting to tie together the book's three themes, I will raise some provocative points concerning the rapidity of the transition to a market economy, the development of new political elites, the apparent decline of socialism, and the consolidation of European identity. The revolutions of 1989 promised a future free from the defects of the previous regimes. Although the revolutionaries were less certain about alternatives, they generally hoped to avoid the defects of other systems as well (technocracy, social injustice, environmental degradation, amoral foreign policy, or ugly nationalism). To a greater or lesser extent, the revolutionaries accomplished their goal of breaking politically with the past. But in attempting to implement innovative alternatives, they have been less able (or less willing) to escape deeper economic and cultural determinants. What happened overnight to East Germany—loss of autonomy and incorporation into the West—is happening over a longer period of time for the rest of the region: the abandonment of one model and the uncritical acceptance of another.

1989 may have opened up a world of possibilities for Eastern Europe, but the 1990s have seen those possibilities quickly vanish. Joy has given way to disillusionment; hope has been replaced by despair; idealism has been eroded by cynicism; unity has been destroyed by discord. Some of the disappointment is temporary, some of the broken promises inevitable, some of the post-revolutionary compromises unarguably necessary. But, as I will attempt to demonstrate, alternatives have failed in Eastern Europe in the 1990s for less predictable, less mundane, and frequently less excusable reasons.

With other parts of the world in even more serious disarray, what can justify continued interest in Eastern Europe by any but the impassioned specialist or obsessed enthusiast? Eastern Europe remains important for historical, geopolitical, and empirical reasons. Throughout history, the world has ignored events taking place in eastern and central Europe at great cost. The deterioration of the Habsburg empire in the 19th century continually threatened the European order until finally, in the 20th century, its territorial feuds precipitated World War I. Inter-war dictatorships that fed on underdevelopment and envy facilitated the extension of Nazi power and the outbreak of World War II. Reforms and revolutions in the post-war period intermittently challenged the rough superpower consensus on the division of Cold War Europe until 1989, when that consensus collapsed with the Berlin Wall. Present developments in the region—for example, the Yugoslav conflict—will have tremendous impact on overall European integration (which is creating an entity more powerful economically than either the United States or Japan). Though a relatively small and impoverished region, Eastern Europe will still play a geopolitical role in this regard.

Moreover, issues such as market reform, ethnic conflict, and environmental protection are not peculiar to Eastern Europe but are being debated in one form or another in virtually every country in the world. How do we balance efficiency and social justice, industrialization and environmental protection, the freedoms of the majority and the rights of the minority? Both developing and industrialized countries have much to learn about handling these conflicts, and Eastern European governments may, with a little luck, perseverance, and assistance, develop innovative and potentially exportable solutions.

It is this last point which saves this book from being an exercise in pessimism. While many of the alternatives discussed or attempted in Eastern Europe—participatory politics, worker self-management, moral diplomacy—have subsequently been ignored, overshadowed, or abandoned, they may nonetheless return when enthusiasm for hyper-capitalism dims.

Some qualifications. Seven months of travel around a particular region does not necessarily bestow upon the traveler automatic or complete understanding of the countries visited. Although I saw much during my journey, there is much I didn't see (including an entire country, Albania, not discussed in this book). I have tried to fill in some of the gaps with previous experience and additional research. Also difficult is writing a book about a rapidly changing subject. I have attempted to cover this canvas at great speed with broad strokes, and so the paint may drip at certain points (but the contemporary reality of Eastern Europe, to my mind, resembles more a Jackson Pollock than a Vermeer). Although well-researched, this is not a scholarly work. This book focuses on current events and thus aspires to journalism's highest goal—a first draft of history. The pulse of this work, then, emanates from the text, not the footnotes. For clarity, the alphabets of Eastern European languages have all been transliterated into English. My apologies, especially to the people whose names appear in these altered forms.

A final note. The first three chapters of this book cover historical ground. As a Polish friend once told me, North Americans are perhaps the only people in the world who say "that's history" to refer to the unimportance of an object or event. But history permeates the everyday life of most Eastern Europeans. The 1956 revolution is just yesterday for many Hungarians, the 1795 partition that wiped their country from the map for 123 years is a matter of daily concern for many Poles, and the 1389 military defeat at Kosovo still stirs the hearts of many Serbians. Understanding the Eastern European present involves an understanding of its past. A reader fixated on current affairs may skip ahead, but only at the risk of losing some of the flavor of the enterprise.

MAP BY JERRY ALEXANDER

Introduction

The revolutions of 1989

You lose, you lose, you lose, you lose, and then you win.

—Rosa Luxemburg

In retrospect, historical outcomes always seem inevitable. The revolutions of 1989, viewed from the secure knowledge of the present, had to have happened. Gorbachev was steering the Soviet Union in a new direction, protests were building throughout Eastern Europe, the communist governments in the region were looking shakier and more isolated each day. This bloc was about to burst apart. It was just a question of when.

But on June 4, 1989, when the Berlin Wall was still an implacable presence, with Nicolae Ceausescu still comfortably ensconsed in his Romanian personality cult, and the revolutions of the fall a hot summer away, nothing seemed inevitable. True, from the Polish point of view, a new era was beginning. Voters throughout the country were turning out for their first (partially) free national elections in four decades, and the newly legalized Solidarity was heading for a resounding victory. But that same day, on the opposite side of the world, another historical path was being followed. The Chinese government had decided to put down the Beijing Spring with force, sending troops and tanks into Tiananmen Square, killing hundreds, and extinguishing for the time being not only revolution but democratic reform as well.

Even the Poles, in their post-election elation, eyed the Chinese "solution" warily. As they celebrated their own electoral victory that June, Poles remembered their experience with martial law eight years earlier: the defiance, the repressions, the move underground, the ineffectual foreign response. It had happened once. Why not again? The opposition in Poland had been repressed so many times that its pessimism, bordering on paranoia, seemed reasonable when measured against this historical background.

If the Poles still harbored lingering fears, so much greater were the worries of their neighbors. The words "Tiananmen Square" would be the negative reference point, the worst-case scenario for the emerging opposition movements in the region in the fall of 1989. The possibility that any of the collapsing governments might use force—the truncheon of last resort—certainly diminished the "inevitability" of the radical change even as that change was occurring at breakneck speed. The proponents of change had lost before. In some countries, they had lost dozens of times. But in 1989, they were poised, finally, to win. And when the "Tiananmen Square" scenarios were finally pushed safely into the "might have been" and change became irreversible, the feeling was exhilarating. For people who had learned, as Polish literary critic Stanislaw Baranczak put it, to "breathe under water," resurfacing in those first heady revolutionary moments was a narcotic like no other.[1]

The beginning of 1989 found Eastern Europe divided into roughly three groups. Poland and Hungary were in the forefront of reform. The communist governments in both countries had decided that to win public approval for an austerity package of economic reforms they would permit a degree of political pluralism and power-sharing with the opposition movements. In the second category were the damage controllers: East Germany and Czechoslovakia. Dismissive of the political and economic reforms favored by their reformist neighbors, the communist governments of the GDR and Czechoslovakia were more interested in controlling opposition than in repressing them outright (though explicit repression did happen too). These governments preferred to purchase the support of their populations with consumer goods and treated with great skepticism the flowering of *glasnost* and *perestroika* in the Soviet Union. In the third category, as the Stalinist holdover, Romania maintained a well-developed police state that waged an internal war against its population. Straddling these categories, the Bulgarian Communist Party was rather schizophrenic, adopting reformist programs based on Gorbachev's *perestroika* and yet violently repressing its ethnic Turkish community. In Yugoslavia, an Eastern Europe in miniature, all three categories were represented as each republic prepared to strike off in different directions.

The differences among these countries in 1989 were not something new. Eastern Europe had never been the undifferentiated ring of satellites referred to in Cold War shorthand as the Soviet "bloc." Regional animosities underscored the heterogeneity. Romania and Hungary clashed politically over ethnic and territorial issues; Bulgaria and Yugoslavia feuded over Macedonia; Poland and East Germany continued to trade complaints over their common border and adjacent territorial waters. This was no happy family of socialist nations. This was a region whose leaders were forced to settle for unhappy compromises for fear of the geopolitical implications of a rancorous divorce.[2]

This era of unhappy compromises—among communist states as well as between the governments and the political oppositions—came to an abrupt end in 1989. Ironically, the new age was heralded by a compromise—between Poland's Communist Party and the outlawed Solidarity trade union movement. In the years after martial law, Solidarity's membership and influence had declined significantly, in part because its moderation irritated younger, more militant workers. Those workers took the lead in 1988, spearheading two key strikes. Meanwhile, in the fall of that year, after continued economic decline, a new communist government led by Mieczyslaw Rakowski came to power declaring that the Party had two choices: institute reform now or be surprised by revolution later. With the Party leaning toward rapprochement and the workers raising their voices, the electrician from Gdansk who had vaulted to the leadership of Solidarity in 1980 returned to the spotlight. In December 1988, Lech Walesa formed the Citizens' Committee, a group, largely intellectuals, brought together to negotiate with the communist government in the roundtable talks announced at the beginning of 1989.

These talks lasted a mere eight weeks, but in that short time Polish history was rewritten. Formerly implacable enemies sat down together to draft an agreement legalizing Solidarity and establishing a timeline for the first partially free national elections in over four decades. What had seemed for so long to be an unbridgeable gap between a communist government and a non-communist opposition was, albeit with many mutual reservations, gradually bridged. Governments and opposition movements in neighboring countries could look to Poland for inspiration in negotiating out of corners as they had once looked with a mixture of pity and fear at how both sides in Poland had negotiated themselves into them in 1980-81.

Hungary was the first country to follow suit. Throughout the spring of 1989, a series of events—an unofficial celebration of the 1848 revolution, an alternative May Day—demonstrated the depth of public support for change. In June, the reburial of Imre Nagy, the martyred leader who stood up to the Soviets in 1956, brought out 250,000 Hungarians and was treated to an eight-hour television broadcast. (At a similar commemoration the previous year considered unlawful by the government, the police quickly dispersed the few hundred brave demonstrators.)[3] Begun nine days after the success of Solidarity's Citizens' Committee in the Polish elections, the Hungarian roundtable negotiations legalized underground parties as in Poland but also laid the groundwork for entirely free elections in 1990.

An informal competition had begun between the two countries: who would be in reform's absolute vanguard? Poles could boast of

Solidarity and its decade-long struggle; Hungarians emphasized that their revolution was being accomplished not only nonviolently but virtually without strikes or mass demonstrations. Poland sponsored the first roundtable talks; Hungary would schedule the first entirely free elections. By the time Hungary issued its final roundtable document, Poland had again moved into the lead when Tadeusz Mazowiecki formed the first non-communist government in Eastern Europe. The Polish government in September 1989 was no longer controlled by the Polish Communist Party. The options for opposition movements had just widened: not simply power-sharing on a junior basis but power-controlling.

It is not hard to imagine the shock and horror with which the governments of East Germany, Czechoslovakia, Bulgaria, and Romania viewed these deviations and heresies. Yet, throughout the changes of the first half of 1989, they maintained an "it-can't-happen-here" attitude. After all, these more orthodox regimes had not permitted massive trade unions in their midst as in Poland or well-developed semi-official movements of civil society as in Hungary. This security proved illusory indeed. The misplaced confidence of these communist leaders certainly contributed to triggering the revolutions of the fall. Their refusal to reform left revolution the only alternative.

The first country to join Poland and Hungary in the camp of radical reform was East Germany. Pastors from the Lutheran Evangelical Church, the largest religious denomination in the GDR, had been conducting peace vigils in the southern city of Leipzig for the better part of the 1980s. In the fall of 1989, these vigils gave birth to the Monday demonstrations which, in the context of the Polish changes and the emigration of GDR citizens, rapidly grew in size. The hemorrhaging of the GDR that August and September amounted to tens of thousands of people. Meanwhile, police repression of nonviolent protesters increased in several cities. The aging East German communist leader Erich Honecker decided that it was time for a Chinese solution. Honecker notified the army, and preparations were made for confrontation in Leipzig. An isolated government willing to use force to compensate for declining legitimacy squared off against an overwhelming majority of the population.

Honecker's order to use force on October 9 in Leipzig was ultimately countermanded. The demonstration proceeded peacefully. A civic group, New Forum, formed in mid-September, took advantage of the large turnout to call for negotiations with the government. By October 23, demonstrations in Leipzig had swelled to 200,000 people. The chants, which at the height of the exodus were "we want to go," had changed to the infinitely more provocative "we want to stay." Although travel restrictions to the West were lifted on October 20, the rallies continued to grow. The determination of the East German protesters caught the communist leadership by surprise.

But the biggest surprises were yet to come. On November 7, the entire political leadership of the GDR resigned. Then, while the new communist government was still adjusting to the situation, the mayor of East Berlin gave an order on November 9 that was subsequently misinterpreted. He asked the border guards at the Berlin Wall to allow people to cross over for that night only in order to relieve some of the political pressure. The border guards opened the Wall that night—and never closed it again. From that moment on, with the Wall no longer separating East from West, the pace of change quickened. Roundtables proliferated at all levels throughout the country, the hated security police (Stasi) were neutralized, and national elections were planned for the following spring.

As the Polish government prepared for roundtable negotiations at the beginning of 1989, the Czechoslovak government was busy arresting 800 opposition activists, among them playwright and dissident Vaclav Havel. Later, as Poles were anticipating their first semi-free elections, one of Havel's plays made its Warsaw debut. Communist Prime Minister Rakowski attended the opening night performance while Havel himself was still sitting in jail. The night East and West Germans danced on the Berlin Wall, toasting each other with champagne, Czechs and Slovaks did some soul-searching. First Poland, then Hungary, now East Germany: why not here? Czechs and Slovaks would soon answer their own question. A week after the fall of the Berlin Wall, police confronted a line of students marching toward the center of Prague. The students placed their candles at the feet of the riot police and calmly sat down on the street. After a tense stand-off, the police attacked with truncheons, breaking arms and legs and sending many students to the hospital. As the attack of Birmingham police on Black school children had galvanized the US Civil Rights Movement in 1963, the beating of unarmed young people pushed Prague workers and intellectuals into further non-violent action.

The following Monday, 300,000 people massed in Wenceslas Square to listen to playwright Havel publicly proclaim the very messages for which he had been repeatedly jailed. A general strike was planned, an opposition movement was united under the name Civic Forum, and demands were presented to a government as taken aback by the protests as Honecker and his cronies had been a month earlier in East Germany. In the space of six weeks, the demonstrators executed a "velvet" revolution—peaceful, nonviolent, often humorous—that toppled the communist government, installed an interim government with Vaclav Havel as its interim president, and instituted roundtable negotiations that would detail the elections to come that following spring.

Bulgarian leaders had now seen enough. Sufficiently warned, Party reformers replaced long-time ruler Todor Zhivkov in November, initiating limited changes from above. Too little, too late. For a country that had had no significant opposition movement for four decades, a broad-based coalition of protesters came into existence with surprising speed. Within a week of Zhivkov's ouster, 50,000 people were demonstrating in Sofia pressing for further change. Various opposition movements pulled together in December to form the Union of Democratic Forces and to prepare for eventual elections. But in Bulgaria, as in Yugoslavia, the legalization of parties outside the Party would have to wait until early 1990.

Entering the last month of 1989, it looked as though the convulsions in Eastern Europe had subsided. Two countries remained relatively unaffected by the changes, Romania and Albania, Eastern Europe's truly disadvantaged. Albania wouldn't undergo any substantial change until 1990. In Romania, meanwhile, Nicolae Ceausescu and his Communist Party, considering their positions secure, expected to live out the century in the leader's proclaimed Years of Light. They were not given the chance to revise their estimates.

The Romanian revolution began in Transylvania, home of the mythic Dracula and, more importantly, a sizable Hungarian minority. An outspoken ethnic Hungarian pastor, Laszlo Tokes, was removed from his church by the Romanian authorities, touching off large-scale demonstrations in the regional capital, Timisoara. The Tiananmen Square scenario, which had been successfully averted in every other Eastern European country, quickly became reality for Romania. A combination of security police and army personnel killed hundreds of people in Timisoara. Undaunted by early reports of thousands massacred, protesters took to the streets in Bucharest. When Ceausescu appeared at the balcony of the Party building to greet the crowds at an orchestrated pro-government rally on December 21, he heard the chants of opposition activists for the first time. The surprise on his face was clearly visible. Four days later, on Christmas day, Ceausescu and his wife were dead, executed after a cursory trial by order of a provisional government. The reports of tens of thousands killed have since been amended—896 killed, 2,100 injured. Other events of those revolutionary days, however, remain mysterious. Evidence has subsequently surfaced of a coup planned by dissidents within the uppermost ranks of the Party, the military, and the security forces. Meanwhile, the composition and intentions of the National Salvation Front, the coalition which took over the reins of power after the December revolution, are still opaque.

* * *

1989 was Eastern Europe's year of living dangerously. It began with relatively sedate negotiations and ended with bloody revolution. In between came a series of more or less "velvet" transitions. The pace and suddenness of the changes seemed to indicate that they had come from nowhere. Newspaper coverage emphasized the singularity of the events of 1989, their almost ahistorical character. But the revolutionary changes certainly had their sources, whether in the region's history of opposition and reform or in the developing context of East-West relations.

The "great man" theory of history has often been the recourse of hurried journalists and conservative historians. While certainly the Caesars, Napoleons, and Washingtons have had their impact on history, excessive attention paid to their personal roles often obscures the roles of other actors and underestimates the impact of structural and collective forces. With this caveat established, however, the role of Soviet leader Mikhail Gorbachev in the changes in Eastern Europe must be recognized. Upon coming to power in 1985, Gorbachev received what could only be considered a lukewarm reception in the West.[4] Even as he consolidated control within the Party and began the political and economic reforms that would shake up and eventually destroy the Soviet Union, Gorbachev was still treated with great suspicion by Western politicians, journalists, and Sovietologists.[5]

Regardless of the domestic future of the post-Soviet Union, Gorbachev's reforms in foreign policy have changed the direction of European and world history. Not only did Gorbachev resurrect Khrushchev's doctrine of "separate paths to socialism," but he, unlike Khrushchev, held to the principle. Khrushchev encouraged reform in Eastern Europe only to step backward in 1956 and order Soviet troops to put down the Hungarian experiment. By contrast, Gorbachev spoke of "separate paths to socialism" as early as 1986 and watched in 1989 as the countries of Eastern Europe took very separate paths indeed, and none of them toward a stated goal of socialism.[6]

In fact, Gorbachev did more than simply watch. Domestically he pushed through reforms, especially in the area of cultural freedom, that inspired movements in Eastern Europe to demand similar changes. Not content to work by example, Gorbachev took an interventionist stance as well, actually accelerating changes along his western border. He telephoned Party members in Poland to "encourage" them to compromise.[7] In October 1989, as demonstrations swelled in East Germany,

Gorbachev deliberately underscored his previous position in a speech in Finland, declaring that "the Soviet Union has no moral or political right to interfere in the affairs of its East European neighbors."[8] It marked, as his government spokesperson phrased it, the replacement of the Brezhnev Doctrine (which justified Soviet intervention into the affairs of neighboring powers) with the "Sinatra Doctrine" (which allowed countries to do things "their way"). Two days before the initial student demonstration in Czechoslovakia in November, Gorbachev gave high-level advice to the Communist Party there: change, or else.[9]

Although he was important, one man did not change everything. Gorbachev removed the struts from beneath the communist parties in Eastern Europe, leaving them vulnerable but not necessarily on the verge of collapse. Western economic institutions also contributed to weakening the various governments by saddling them with large debts and encouraging them to leave the Soviet bloc.[10] The CIA funneled money and equipment covertly to anti-communists in the region through such organizations as the National Endowment for Democracy and even enlisted the Vatican's assistance in the case of Poland.[11] But toppling these governments still remained the task of public movements.

Were the events of 1989, strictly speaking, revolutions? With the exception of Romania, the changes were accomplished with little bloodshed. In Poland and Hungary, the handover of power took place through negotiations that stretched over many months. Even in the GDR, Czechoslovakia, and Bulgaria, where the negotiations were collapsed into a shorter period, the communist authorities gave up power, involuntarily perhaps, but without a military struggle. Still, I will refer to these momentous events as revolutionary. They were, after all, sudden political ruptures in which movements from below succeeded, however imperfectly, in removing internationally recognized governments.

Although sudden, these revolutions were not simply conjured from air. Groups of workers, intellectuals, students, and artists had been chipping away at the power of the communist parties for years. They had lost on innumerable occasions and, perhaps because of these losses, were not considered to be legitimate threats to the prevailing order in Eastern Europe. Yet, against all odds, as the Hollywood wordsmiths like to say, these groups finally succeeded.

But before turning to the struggles of these opposition figures and their post-revolutionary challenges, we should take a step back. Where exactly is Eastern Europe and what brought it to the revolutionary crossroads of 1989?

Part One

The Past as Prologue

Chapter 1

History and geography

The people of Central Europe...cannot be separated from European history; they cannot exist outside of it; but they represent the wrong side of this history; they are its victims and outsiders.[1]

—Milan Kundera

The center of Europe is not Paris, or Berlin, or even Prague. Assuming the European continent to extend from the Atlantic Ocean to the Ural mountain chain, the geographic center of Europe is to be found in what was once the Soviet Union. The navel of the continent the ancient Greeks called the "land of the setting sun" rests somewhere in the Carpathian mountain region of Ukraine.[2] A map with Ukraine at the center therefore reveals that "Eastern" Europe is not eastern at all but in fact certifiably central.

Not that the attributive "Eastern" has ever possessed a precise geographic meaning. It has always been more a cultural designation used to refer to sections of Europe not considered 100 percent European, whether because of religion, economic development, ethnic composition, or political temperament. Indeed, Eastern Europe is so often portrayed as being "apart" from the West—a region both grey and backward, historically and culturally in the hinterlands—that it is often surprising to be reminded that Luther nailed his 95 theses to the door of a church that would later stand in East Germany, that Copernicus studied and worked in Poland, that Kafka wrote his distinctive German-language novels in Czechoslovakia, that the first subway system on the European continent was built in Budapest in 1896, that Bucharest was once known as Little Paris, that rich cultural communities flourished before World War II in a great central European swath from Vilnius (Lithuania) and Lvov (Ukraine) through Chernovtsy (Ukraine) to Timisoara (Romania) and Novi Sad (Vojvodina). Eastern Europe has thus been central to the grand European narrative, not merely a jumble of "noises-off."

Artificially bracketed off from Europe, "dragged Eastward" in Czech writer Milan Kundera's phrase,[3] this compact region straddling the center of the world's second smallest continent is nevertheless distinctive.[4] Prague and Budapest are significantly different from Madrid and Amsterdam on the one hand, and Moscow and Tbilisi on the other. To understand this unique region that would eventually become Eastern Europe, we have to plunge first into European history. We need to examine the European idea, its role in establishing a cultural identity for the entire continent and in propelling the region ahead of all global rivals. A section on both Western and Eastern European history in the modern age will establish the necessary context for understanding the great 20th-century upheavals of modernization and revolution.

The invention of Europe

Europe, for the average North American, is a tangle of history, a confusion of parliamentary factions, a bewildering assortment of economic mechanisms with the deceptively simple label of the Common Market. Europe is highbrow culture and expensive summer vacations, pricey restaurants and a profusion of museums. Europe is strong left-wing parties and extensive social welfare systems. Europe is poorly paid migrant labor, outlying regions of agrarian poverty, and perennial outbursts of xenophobia. Europe is the rise and fall of colonialism and the heart of what some lovingly and others sneeringly refer to as Western Civilization.

However multifaceted, Europe today often assumes the status of a cultural and geographic given, a fundamental and unchanging reference point in intellectual discussions. But in fact the idea of Europe emerged over time, its cultural attributes invented and reinvented through the centuries, its borders constantly shifting to include and exclude different peoples. Indeed, the development of the European idea can be understood as a series of comparisons designed to elevate Europe at the expense of other continents, other cultures.

Before Europe had even taken shape as a continent, much less an idea, the ancient rivalry between the Greeks and the Persians initiated the process of comparison. The Greek worldview, which has been subsequently adopted by all claimants to "Western" heritage, held that Asians were, as a rule, either flowery (Aeschlyus) or servile (Aristotle).[5] At this stage, "Asian" style was measured against Greek, not European, standards. Even later, under the Romans, most of Europe remained an imperial backwater dotted with occasional garrison towns, a land of dark forests, mist-enshrouded islands, and mysterious tribes.[6] With their skeptical philosophies and superior military technologies, Greeks and Romans considered themselves the beacons of civilization. To the extent that they looked elsewhere for cultural inspiration, it was not to Europe with its Normans, Celts, and Goths but to Egypt, Phoenicia, and the Near East—the places from which Greece derived much of its culture, the domains where Alexander the Great later extended his empire, the regions which over the centuries would enhance Hellenism.

The rise of Christianity in the heart of the Roman empire and its survival into the Middle Ages (5th to 13th centuries) after Rome had been repeatedly sacked signaled the next step in European consciousness. Here was a religious phenomenon independent of Greece and Rome that relied not on sites and states for its authority, but on a text. And unlike the comparably text-driven Judaism, the new religion emphasized a proselytism that would expand its influence far beyond the Holy Land, particularly to the nearby European continent. Acutely aware of religious comparisons to Judaism and geographic comparisons to Israel that might put them in an unfavorable light, early Christians in Europe found proof in the story of Noah's three sons of the superiority of their faith *and* their continent. Suddenly, as Denys Hay explains, a qualitative divide opened up between Europe and Asia:

> Europe was the land of Japheth, of the Gentiles, the Greeks and the Christians; Asia was the land of Semitic peoples, glorious in that they had produced the patriarchs and prophets, the chosen people and Christ himself; but—as the land of the circumcised adherents of older laws—condemned to an inferiority which was stated in the scriptures: "God shall enlarge Japheth and he shall dwell in the tents of Shem."[7]

Medieval Christians replaced the contrast of Greek and Persian with a Christian-infidel dichotomy. Of the numerous "infidels" bearing down upon the medieval Church, none proved more influential than Islam, for it was this highly sophisticated civilization which put military pressure on the southern flank of Europe and pushed the centers of Christendom northward.[8] When Islamic culture in the Abbasid dynasty (750-1258) was at its glorious height, Europe was still, by conventional comparison, a barbarous land.[9] Yet the idea of Europe gained strength by opposition to its alleged inferior. Significantly, the first recorded use of the adjective "European" came in a chronicle of the Battle of Tours (732) when Charles of Martel defeated the advancing Moslem forces.[10] When the Frankish leader Charlemagne (742-814) established the Holy Roman empire, the predominantly Christian, northern sections of the continent began to take on the familiar contours of "Western European civilization"—an outline that rather resembles the European Community of the 20th century.[11] For the remainder of the Middle Ages, Christianity, through the Crusades that began in 1098 against the Islamic caliphate, would claim the highest allegiance of the heirs of Charlemagne.[12]

Before the critical 16th century, European culture was derivative, built upon new technologies imported primarily from politically and economically advanced China (printing, papermaking, gunpowder) and reliant on the intellectual contributions of Islam (philosophy, medicine, mathematics). After 1500, however, Europeans became "cultural creditors."[13] This rapid turnaround stemmed in part from a continent-wide recovery from two devastating plagues, the Black Death that carried off 40 percent of the European population between 1348 and 1377 and the Hundred Years War that pitted Britain against France and accounted for a significant decline in their respective populations from 1337 to 1453.[14] The loss of friends and family took a heavy toll on public morale; the decimation of the workforce sharply impeded economic progress.

Just as the economies of the countries began to recover, an unforeseen development unleashed a new source of expansionist energy that would eventually bring Europe untold wealth: the "discovery" of the New World. The voyages of Columbus, Vespucci, and Magellan at the turn of the 15th century came at a particularly opportune time. Plagues behind them, the various European powers could transmute the precious metals of the New World into a new global position. No longer would China and India—with their rich art and exotic cinnamon—represent the height of civilization in the minds of Europeans. The scepter would pass to the Portuguese, Spaniards, French, British, Dutch, Italians, and Germans. At first relying on treasure-laden galleons rather than man-o-wars, the *nouveau riche* European powers used gold escudos and silver pieces of eight to pay for the penetration of Asian markets and subsequent control of the spice trade.[15]

The Renaissance in culture (roughly 1350-1650) provided the necessary ideological touch. Prior to the rebirth of classicism in the 14th century, learning was tightly controlled by a Church often ambivalent toward the "pagan" Greeks and Romans; the Carolingian, Byzantine, and Abelardian mini-renaissances were simply exceptions that preserved some small amount of ancient thought. Although the Middle Ages were not quite the cultural black hole so often presumed, the insular and generally anti-materialistic Church fathers did not provide a cultural atmosphere conducive to intellectual and commercial expansion.

Following the lyrical lead of Dante and Petrach, controversial thinkers such as Da Vinci, Erasmus, and Copernicus revolutionized the Old World. The Renaissance humanists scoured the Ancients for links between the emerging European philosophies and the glories that were Greece and Rome. Though often critical of the Church, these writers and scientists were nonetheless religious and conceived of civilization and

Christianity as inseparable. After the fall of Trebizond in Asia Minor in 1461, Europe had become the exclusive domain of Christianity (however weakened by dissent and division the Church might have been). In the minds of the Renaissance thinkers, then, no other land competed with Christian Europe for the mantle of the Hellenic tradition. Whereas high civilization once radiated from Athens and Rome, the "humanizing" influences would, from the Renaissance on, be assumed to emanate from the new cultural capitals of Europe: Paris, London, Madrid, Lisbon, Amsterdam—not Byzantium or Alexandria or Baghdad or any of the other former centers of Hellenism and contemporary centers of Islamic culture. Factors that complicated the passing of the Graeco-Roman heritage directly to the Renaissance Europeans were conveniently ignored. The Church's role in suppressing the classics and the part played by Islamic and Jewish scholars in preserving and improving upon these works were routinely forgotten. The Asian and African contributions to Hellenic culture were systematically undervalued. When Europeans of the time admitted that the sources of their culture might be non-European, they argued that they had borrowed to make better.[16]

What was the precise relationship between extension of empire on the one hand and the discovery of cultural roots on the other? Did the unearthing of "sophisticated" ancestors in some sense justify the subjugation of "primitive" coevals? "Europeans become conscious of the idea that the conquest of the world by their civilization is henceforth a possible objective," writes Marxist theorist Samir Amin of this critical period. "They therefore develop a sense of absolute superiority, even if the actual submission of other peoples to Europe has not yet taken place."[17] Europe discovered New and Ancient Worlds alike in the Renaissance period; the interplay between the two worlds in legitimizing feelings of cultural superiority would greatly influence the growth of the European idea.[18]

Many cultures define themselves in opposition. The ancient Jews, for example, developed specific dietary and behavioral codes, recorded in the books of the Torah, in part to distinguish themselves from surrounding tribes. Europe too defined itself according to challenges at its borders. Even before the appearance of the New World and the resurrection of the Ancient World, Europe acquired partial identity by uniting against the Islamic "infidel" trying to gain a foothold in Spain, the Hungarian tribes that reached as far as France, and the Normans sweeping south in their fleets. From the 8th to the 14th centuries, these conflicts defined Europe as predominantly Christian, with Latin as the *lingua franca*. So strong was this cultural unity that many of the non-Christian challengers eventually adopted the religion and value-systems of the peoples upon whom they had so recently descended.

One group singularly uninterested in becoming Christian was the Turks. The fall of Constantinople to the Ottoman empire in 1453 spelled the official end of the eastern half of the former Roman empire. By seizing Belgrade in 1521 and taking control of large sections of Hungary after 1526, the Ottoman empire established itself as a power in Europe, one not opposed to joining with French Catholics and German Protestants against the Austrian Habsburgs. Despite their political skills, the Turks failed to capture Vienna in 1529 as the Habsburgs used the defense of Europe to rally the European powers, a gambit that obscured more mundane territorial objectives.[19] Stopped at Vienna but still controlling most of the Balkans, the Turks posed such a threat to 16th-century Europe that one contemporary French poet suggested relocating all of European society to the New World far from Islam's reach.[20] European culture was thus identified in contrast to an alien force, not by its attachment to a particular landmass.

Unity against the Ottoman empire waxed and waned according to the proximity of the Turkish approach. "European identity," one historian writes, "remains strong only as long as the threat (or alleged threat) to Europe remains strong, and disintegrates as soon as the immediate incentive becomes less urgent."[21] The Ottoman empire declined rapidly after the 17th century, and Western Europe would not find such unity again until the Cold War produced a similar atmosphere of fear 250 years later.

* * *

The emerging European self-consciousness—shaped by Christianity, enhanced by Graeco-Roman pedigree, validated by imperial extension, and clarified by external threat—provided an opportunity for the various parts of the continent to emerge from the Renaissance in one conceptual piece divided in myriad ethnic and familial ways. These divisions spawned numerous conflicts (Seven Years War, Thirty Years War, Eighty Years War) that prevented any conclusive European unity.

Despite these bloody disputes, however, Europe witnessed a "miracle" after the Renaissance. During the 16th and 17th centuries, Europe jumped ahead of competing empires (the Mughal in India, the Manchu in China), an event that still puzzles scholars today. Projecting later trends backward, Paul Kennedy attributes European success to a "combination of economic laissez-faire, political and military pluralism, and intellectual liberty."[22] E.L. Jones stresses environmental and geographic factors (fewer natural disasters, distance from the Asian steppes, proximity to Islamic culture and later to the Americas).[23] It was the concentration of the population, argues Peter Gunst, and the consequent intensification of agriculture.[24] According to the more radical view, the riches of Africa, Asia, and the New World, acquired ruthlessly by European powers and invested prudently by European bankers, fueled the unprecedented development.[25]

Whatever the combination of these factors, however, the European "miracle"—and the healthy jolt it applied to the emerging European identity—is still only half the story: the western half. Read any US textbook on European history and you'll get a bucketful of information on the French, British, Dutch, Spanish, Portuguese, Austrians, Germans, and Italians. But where are the Poles and Czechs, the Croatians and Slovenians, the Hungarians and Romanians, the ethnic Turkish and Gypsy populations?[26] High school students are more likely to memorize the French kings than the heirs of the Jagiellonian throne, though the United States contains at least as many Polish immigrants as French.

This emphasis on the western half of Europe is in part for economic, in part for cultural reasons. The industrial revolution, which produced a capitalist system that would eventually cover the globe, began in Western Europe. Capitalist societies will naturally be interested in studying their origins, however superficial that study might be at times. On a cultural level, the Western bias is of a piece with the Eurocentric "discovery" of the New World, the exclusive attention paid to Greek and Roman civilization, the relative neglect of Asian, African, and indigenous American cultures. History is, in US textbooks at least, seen through a European prism; when it comes to peoples East of the Oder River, even that prism is half-obscured. No wonder that North Americans are generally surprised to discover that the Hungarians and Romanians are two very different peoples, neither Slavic. No wonder that most North Americans were surprised to discover, only as civil war tore it apart, that Yugoslavia consisted of several very distinct ethnic groups.

Europe is neither a natural nor a neutral category: it was constructed in such a way as to elevate some and disparage others.[27] Against external threats, Europe was an invention at least as important as the crossbow. Domestically, the European category engendered a continental hierarchy. The traditional history of "Western" Europe that figures so prominently in the textbooks nonetheless raises many themes important to the development of Eastern Europe. For those readers who snoozed during European History 101, then, a quick run-down.

European history, Western-style

The "European miracle" had already established Western Europe as the globe's new core power when, in the waning years of the 18th century, the French revolution cleaved European history in two, dividing the world of the *ancien regime* from the brave new world of the modern era. In the revolution of 1789, the aspirations of a rising middle class and a continually wretched peasantry confronted the interests of the ruling aristocracy. Feudalism had seemed, until that point, an inviolable grid locking peasants and landowners into a generally rigid and stable society. But the emergence of a new capitalist order led by traders, salesmen, and craftsmen—the burghers—issued a challenge to feudalism. The Enlightenment values of science, progress, and reason, coupled with the burghers' demands for political and economic freedoms (that would primarily benefit themselves), became the cries of French revolutionaries. Their appeals for liberty and equality spread throughout Europe, emboldening both the middle class and the disenfranchised, and paralyzing the nobility with fear.

In France, revolution led to counter-revolution and the eventual dictatorship of Napoleon Bonaparte. Under Napoleon's leadership, French military forces moved out across Europe at the beginning of the 19th century, ranging as far as Russia and the Balkans, and attempting to control virtually everything in between. Biting off more of Europe than he could properly digest (and nibbling at other continents as well), Napoleon was defeated and exiled by 1812. He escaped from Elba for a reign of 100 days only to fail again at Waterloo in 1815.

During the course of what would eventually be Napoleon's final defeat, the great European powers of Britain, Austria, Russia, and Prussia met in Vienna to discuss the new European order. Orchestrated by the chief Austrian negotiator Prince Metternich, the Concert of Vienna was a victory of reaction. The *anciens regimes* had a unique opportunity to consign the French revolution to the proverbial dustbin of history, and they apparently relished the task.[28] France was, by virtue of its revolutionary inclinations and imperial pretensions, locked out of the new order; the empire of the Habsburgs, meanwhile, received new life after almost being divided out of existence by Tsar Alexander and Napoleon; and unquestionably a European power, Russia consolidated its territorial gains. Revolution, so the diplomats reasoned, had been contained by imperial consensus and shrewd diplomacy: after centuries of bloodshed the continent was about to embark upon a 100-year experiment in *detente*.

But the "poison of French ideas" lived on, despite the best efforts of the monarchs and their diplomatic servants. Although the European continent was relatively free of war in the 19th century, overreaching ambitions still stirred otherwise conservative leaders, and revolutionary impulses continued to emerge from below. The Greeks revolted against their Ottoman rulers in 1821 and gained their independence in 1829.

Rebellions broke out in 1830, first in France, spreading to Belgium, Switzerland, Italy, Germany, and Poland.

But it was 1848, the so-called "spring of nations," when the ideals expressed during the French revolution bore greatest fruit. As in 1789 and 1830, the outbreak of rebellion began in France, and it was pure *deja vu:* the establishment of a second republic which gave way to a Second Empire and a second Napoleon (prompting Marx's famous gloss on Hegel that history occurs twice, once as tragedy, then as farce).[29] Emboldened by the French republicans, the populations of Italy, Germany, and even Austria revolted against the order forever associated with Metternich. Popular uprisings similar to the 1789 revolution also occurred in Switzerland, Belgium, and Britain.[30] The greatest activity took place in the Austrian empire as Hungarians, Croats, Czechs, and Poles all fought to re-establish "nations."[31]

In the meantime, Western Europe embarked on an unprecedented economic experiment that would raise it from *a* global power to *the* global power. The industrial revolution, set into motion in the 1830s, fundamentally changed the organization of people's lives. The Concert of Vienna may have represented a victory for reaction at the diplomatic level, but a radical economic development, given perhaps its most dramatic expression during the French revolution, was sweeping through society. "A blind faith in spontaneous progress had taken hold of people's minds," writes economic historian Karl Polanyi, "and with the fanaticism of sectarians the most enlightened pressed forward for boundless and unregulated change in society. The effects on the lives of the people were awful beyond description."[32]

With the enclosure of public lands, the creation of a labor market through the Poor Law Reform Act, the implementation of the gold standard, and the mythologizing of the self-regulating market, capitalism transformed 19th-century Europe, providing an economic base for the new liberal states and forging the standard for global modernization. The market did not, as *laissez-faire* enthusiasts past and present have claimed, spring into autonomous existence. At every point in development, the state shaped these emergent markets, a process we will return to in later chapters.[33]

In the post-1848 world, as high finance began to knit together capital internationally, empires continued to fight one another: the Russians against the French and Turks in Crimea during 1854-56, the French against the Prussians in 1870. Empires also made secret agreements (for instance, over the long-awaited division of the Ottoman empire). In 1861, Italy was created by the revolutionary Garibaldi and the monarch Victor Emmanuel, while a decade later Bismarck united Germany "by blood and iron." As the century drew to a close, old and new empires began to jostle one another more vigorously, national aspirations became more acute, and popular uprisings acquired a cyclical character. Important advances in industry had expanded the economic power of European nations, leading them to look for increased raw materials and new markets overseas. The age of colonialism channeled imperial pressures (that would in the next century engulf the continent in violence) into an external thrust. The European idea was being exported at great speed and often with great ferocity. Writes historian Geoffrey Bruun, "one-fifth of the land area of the globe and one-tenth of its inhabitants were gathered into the expanding domains of the European conquerors within a generation, a rate of imperialist encroachment unsurpassed in history."[34] As with the detente of the Cold War era, the long peace of the Concert of Vienna could be maintained only by the export of war and conflict to the non-European hinterlands.

But even the safety valve of colonialism could not forestall conflict in Europe. On the eve of World War I, the tensions—among empires, among nations, and among peoples—were so pronounced that a minor event at the periphery of a decrepit empire ignited the most horrendous conflict the world had witnessed to that point.

* * *

At this point, in most major accounts of European history, Eastern Europe gains prominence, indeed becomes inescapable. After all, World War I began in the Austro-Hungarian empire, in Sarajevo, the capital of Bosnia-Herzogovina (later part of Yugoslavia). For most of modern history, however, Eastern Europe had been a barely tolerated understudy in the European drama: conquered by a series of empires, taken from Napoleon and given to Metternich in 1815, repressed in 1848, ignored during the Age of Imperialism, and brought to the world stage after the carnage of World War I only to be relegated to a sideshow once again after the renewed bloodletting of World War II. The global importance and morbid fascination of these two world wars and of the last 45 years of communism have rendered Eastern European history prior to the 20th century comfortably distant, more often than not encapsulated in the true but banal phrase "for longstanding historical reasons."

To understand the current situation, we need to dig deeper. We need to address themes covering the particular history of Eastern and Central Europe, those parts of the continent which had been traditionally divided between the Austro-Hungarian, Prussian, Russian, and Ottoman empires. Five general trends should be kept in mind: historic backwardness, the pervasiveness of ethnic and territorial disputes, the influence of authoritarian and statist tendencies in general, the absolutism of the

Habsburgs in particular, and an unfortunate vulnerability to external aggression.

Europe of the East

Emerging from the Middle Ages, the peoples of Eastern and Central Europe were in no perceptibly inferior position with regard to their continental brethren to the west. The Renaissance produced great achievements in Poland, Bohemia, and Hungary, including the founding of the famous universities at Krakow and Prague in the 14th century. Geography, however, constrained regional development. Unusually susceptible to invasions, Eastern and Central Europe suffered a great deal from Western encroachment, particularly the *Drang nach Osten* ("push to the East") of the Germans. First the Ostrogoths in the 4th century, followed by the Zipsers and Saxons of the 12th century, and finally the Teutonic Knights of the 13th century, Germans spread destruction and later culture to a region to which they would return with even more devastating consequences in the 20th century. Meanwhile from the east, the Mongols swept through on several occasions, though without succeeding in gaining much of a foothold anywhere but Russia. After the 14th century, however, Turkish invasions from the south proved most destabilizing. Against the backdrop of these invasions, the Jagiellonian dynasty (1490-1526), which brought together Poland, Lithuania, Bohemia, and Hungary in a monarchy of the three seas (Baltic, Black, Adriatic), constituted a brief and rare middle European unity.[35]

Just at this point of greatest unity, as Hungarian historian Ivan Berend has pointed out, the peoples of Eastern and Central Europe acquired their "latecomer"status:

> At the turn of the fifteenth and sixteenth centuries, however, when the West began its spectacular and successful transformation into a modern world, the countries of Central and Eastern Europe fell behind disastrously. The rebirth of rigid feudal structures, or the introduction of them in places where they had not existed in their proper form before, refeudalized Central and Eastern Europe at a time when Western Europe had set out on the path of capitalist development.[36]

A look at an economic map of Europe circa 1500 confirms Berend's assessment. Whereas the Netherlands and northern Germany were centers of banking, wool, and linen, the realms of Eastern and Central Europe offered only copper and some silver mines.[37] In other words, the region produced few finished products and didn't gather sufficient currency from sales to warrant an extensive banking system. Industry and finance, the twin engines of capitalism, would propel Western Europe into the modern era, leaving the East as perhaps Europe's first colonial territories, a Third World of the 16th century providing raw materials for the industrialists back west, a testing ground for bankers and financiers to practice what they would later perfect in more distant lands.[38]

This was the flipside of the European "miracle"—the Eastern European non-miracle. The region slipped firmly into the "periphery," to use Immanuel Wallerstein's core-periphery distinction, and suffered from a terms-of-trade disparity that would later characterize North-South relations.[39] Although certain areas managed to escape regional stagnation, notably Bohemia (part of the future Czechoslovakia), the pattern established in the 16th century continued through to the 20th. When sections of Eastern Europe managed with considerable sacrifice to reach the levels achieved by the first industrial revolution, the wealthiest countries of northwestern Europe were busy on their second leap forward into steel and chemicals. Predictably, as Eastern Europe struggled with this second revolution, the West was already well into the computer and information age. Worse still was the position of the Balkan countries. By the start of the 20th century, this section of Eastern Europe remained almost exclusively agricultural and worse, one crop countries: Greek raisins, Bulgarian tobacco, Romanian corn. When these crops maintained market value, the countries eked out an existence; otherwise they faced bankruptcy.[40]

Why didn't Eastern and Central Europe simply industrialize themselves out of the corner like their more advanced Western neighbors? There were several reasons. In terms of the prevailing geopolitics of the modern era, it was not in the interest of the western imperial powers—France, Britain, Prussia—to encourage development in a competing region. The Habsburg empire, which covered most of Eastern and Central Europe, was already severely weak by the beginning of the 19th century; the other participants in the Concert of Vienna saw little reason to provide economic assistance to a failing imperial power. Meanwhile, within the Habsburg lands, a combination of vested interests prevented modernization. In the northern regions of Germany, Poland, Hungary, and the future Czechoslovakia, the aristocracy and nobility—the *ancien regime* of the East—were not interested in encouraging the development of a middle class which could, as in the French revolution of 1789, eventually unseat them. The eastern *declasse* nobility, which in the West drifted toward cities and created an urban middle class, more frequently remained in the rural and small town environment.[41] Where absolutism did not replace feudalism, as in Poland, foreign powers rushed in to fill the void; where absolutism succeeded, for instance under the Habsburgs, it managed to cling to existence into the 20th century.[42] Liberal institutions failed to take hold; Eastern Europeans did not achieve the status of citizens.[43] In the southern regions, rural landlords comfortable with their limited and anachronistic feudal power prevented the disruptive and quite radical forces unleashed by industrial capitalism.[44] Large peasantries accustomed to servitude within the Ottoman empire occasionally rose up against their masters in bloody jacqueries, but never could the peasants provoke any more than limited land reform.

A third factor behind underdevelopment was the lack of Protestantism's ethic of delayed gratification, sociologist Max Weber's favored cause for the genesis of capitalism.[45] Predominantly Catholic, the Habsburg empire severely discriminated against Protestant populations, particularly in the Czech lands (which managed, despite repression, to develop economically). A final factor that assumed greater importance in the 20th century was the disproportionate concentration of ownership of the limited financial and industrial sector of Eastern and Central Europe in the hands of Germans and Jews. German and Jewish middle and upper classes were to one degree or another assimilated into Eastern and Central European society. When these peoples virtually disappeared from the region after World War II (Hitler and his allies exterminated 6 million Jews; the Allied victors expelled 12 million Germans), the region took a large cultural and economic step backward.

Historic backwardness should not be viewed as an iron law, nor should it be equated with biological deficiency. Put into proper perspective, however, "latecomer" status does much to explain what happened in Eastern and Central Europe in the 20th century. As Berend points out, "the Central and Eastern European countries' feeling of being pushed to the periphery prepared the ground for the revolt against liberalism, the free-market economy, parliamentary democracy and the rationalism of the Western world."[46]

Indeed, an underdog ethic is ingrained in the region's collective memory: Eastern and Central Europe, as Eduardo Galleano describes Latin America, has "specialized in losing."[47] While another culture might use military loss as a spur to collective action ("Remember the Alamo!"), Eastern and Central Europe place their historic losses at the mournful center of a tradition: Kosovo (Serbs lose to Turks in 1389), Mohacs (Hungarians lose to Turks in 1526), the Battle of White Hill (Czech Protestants lose to Habsburg Catholics in 1620). A similar valuation of loss can be found in the Shi'ite Moslem tradition. Tracing their origins to the defeat of Mohammed's son-in-law Ali by the Sunnis, the Shi'ite sense of marginalization has translated into both a championing of the underdog and a strong tendency toward fundamentalism.[48] For Eastern and

Central Europe, memories of loss and underdevelopment have also reinforced an anti-modern sensibility.

Discussion of Eastern and Central Europe as a region in moth balls inevitably returns to the Habsburgs, the family whose holdings at one time or another stretched from Spain to the Ukraine, from Belgium to Bosnia. The Habsburg dynasty, which began in 1273 with the crowning of Count Rudolph, grew more from well-placed inter-dynastic marriages (and their well-timed offspring) than from territorial grab. In the early 16th century, under Charles V, the Habsburgs acquired the German provinces (the Holy Roman empire) as well as Spain and its New World possessions. The imperial breadth was deceptive: "Charles's empire was less than the sum of its parts," one historian notes.[49] Indeed, ownership of virtually the entire European continent lasted less than half a century. By the middle of the 16th century, the more familiar Habsburg empire emerged: Austria, Hungary, portions of Germany, and Bohemia. The empire gradually acquired parts of Poland, Romania, and the southern Slav lands to add to its "prisonhouse of nations." The 1848 revolution in Hungary demonstrated the powerful national aspirations of the Magyars, but it wouldn't be until 1866, when the Austrians lost to the Prussians at Koniggratz, that the Habsburg eagle became double-headed and the empire acquired a new name: Austro-Hungarian.

The post-Stalinist tendency has been to romanticize the rule of the Habsburgs, particularly its last, long-lived emperor Franz Josef.[50] "Better Franz Josef than Josef Stalin," writer Jacques Rupnik declares.[51] Certain Habsburg leaders do stand out as liberalizers, notably Joseph II (1780-90), who emancipated the empire's serfs and extended certain rights to Jews.[52] But Joseph II ruled with an exceptional benevolence during his short reign. Brutally suppressing Protestants, peasants, and populists, the Habsburgs were perhaps the chief brake on Eastern and Central European progress for several centuries. Hungarian-born historian Oscar Jaszi, looking back from the pre-Stalinist days of the 1920s, had a particularly jaundiced view of the empire where he once lived and worked:

> Nobody can deny that the warlike absolutism nowhere took such rigid and uncouth forms as in the Habsburg empire where not only all military operations were strictly withdrawn from the control of the parliamentary corporations, but the economic life, the administration, the judiciary itself was put under a rude military control.[53]

The Habsburgs set precedents in the region for such unappetizing policies as censorship, restriction of civil liberties, martial law, religious intolerance, ethnic repression, enrichment of elites, ubiquitous snooping—even personality cults. Emperor Franz Josef, whose circle of fawning servants went to the extreme of producing counterfeit newspapers leaving out facts that might disturb the emperor, called for the printing and distribution of such pamphlets as "What Emperor Francis Joseph Did For His Peoples."[54] While these criticisms could certainly be levelled against other European emperors and imperial orders of the day, countervailing pressures from the middle classes eventually established in western countries the bourgeois state of law. Wary of an independent middle class, the Habsburgs relied on Church, army, and bureaucracy to defeat revolution and keep absolutism in place.[55]

At least the Habsburgs did not export their model to other continents. While the Western European powers acquired territories throughout Africa, Asia, the Middle East, and Latin America, the Austro-Hungarian crowns only made tentative forays against their neighbor-in-decrepitude, the Ottoman empire. This relative non-participation in the age of colonialism merely reinforced the empire's second-class status. Whether the lack of imperial extension hampered economic growth in Eastern Europe is difficult to conclude definitively (though, by contrast, British economic power was clearly enhanced by naval power and the mercantile exchange that brought raw materials in and sent finished goods out).[56]

While other imperial powers divided the world, the Austrians and Hungarians spent their imperial energies trying to keep the home empire—a melting pot the Habsburgs neither managed nor intended to create—from spinning apart. The Austro-Hungarian empire was a multicultural but unhappy mosaic of Albanians, Austrians, Bosnians, Croats, Czechs, Germans, Gypsies, Hungarians, Italians, Jews, Macedonians, Poles, Romanians, Ruthenians, Serbs, Slovaks, Slovenians, Turks, and Wallachians.

> To suppose that this part of the Continent was once a near-paradise of cultural, ethnic, and linguistic multiplicity and compatibility, producing untold cultural and intellectual riches, has been part of the Western image in recent years...When in truth Central Europe, from the Battle of the White Mountain down to the present, is a region of enduring ethnic and religious intolerance, marked by bitter quarrels, murderous wars, and frequent slaughter on a scale ranging from pogrom to genocide.[57]

This reputation rested on the expulsion of over 30,000 Czechs during the Thirty Years War, the brutal suppressions of Italian and Hungarian freedom struggles in 1848, the acceptance, even encouragement, of the Polish nobility's killing of Ruthenian peasants, the perennial discrimination against Slovaks, and the short-sighted annexation of Bosnia.

The history of the Habsburg lands from the early part of the 19th century until the dissolution of empire after World War I is rife with separatist movements and attempts by one country to regain territory lost at some point in history to another country. Romania and Hungary have long battled over the Transylvania region; Italy and Austria have struggled over border territory; prior to World War I, southern Slavs had frequently attempted to consolidate their territory into a Yugoslavia (land of "southern Slavs"). Meanwhile, Poles were struggling to regain nationhood after being wiped off the map in 1795 in the third partition between Prussia, Russia, and Austria; Czechs were likewise trying to establish a nation; the Ruthenians (eastern Ukrainians) were, in a spirit of pan-Slavism, hoping for a chance to ally with the Russians.[58]

The Habsburgs spent a good deal of money and firepower keeping all these peoples together, not in a marriage of equals but in a family ranked in importance under a single monarch. Outside threats such as the encroaching Ottoman empire provided one consolidating influence.[59] But increasingly, movements for autonomy within the empire required more sophisticated strategies than raw repression (which was nonetheless still used until 1914). In 1848, for instance, the Hungarians presented such a challenge that a dual monarchy was eventually established, elevating the Magyars in 1867 to co-imperial powers. Meanwhile, the Czechs and Croatians were given greater autonomy, partly to keep the Slovaks and Serbs in line.

Indeed, the Austro-Hungarian lands brought together peoples with such antagonistic interests that the frequent anticipations of imperial collapse simply obeyed probability theory. True, various "centripetal" forces kept the status quo intact: the military, the Church, the police. If the French revolution had never happened, if the Greeks and Belgians hadn't built their own states, if the Germans and Italians hadn't unified disparate territories under one government, then perhaps these centripetal forces might have kept the Austro-Hungarian empire together. Pressures from both within and without, however, doomed the empire to be a multinational anachronism in an age of nation-states.

World War I brought the contradictions of the Habsburgs into sharp relief.[60] The origins of the conflict lay with the empire's invasion in 1878 of Bosnia-Herzogovina, which had been until then under Ottoman yoke. Occupying and then annexing territory in the land of the southern Slavs was a particularly risky maneuver. Slovenians, Croatians, and Serbs were willing to put aside any mutual distrust in order to unite against the Habsburg threat: either to create a Yugoslavia or at least transform the Austro-Hungarian empire from a dual to a triple monarchy. The Balkan wars, 1912-13, which weakened both the Ottoman empire and Bulgaria, inflamed tensions even further. In 1914, when a Serbian nationalist assassinated the Austrian heir to the throne in Sarajevo, the capital of Bosnia-Herzogovina, the Habsburgs declared war on Serbia. The European powers signed up on either side of the conflict. With Serbia went Russia, France, Britain, and later Japan and Italy. Austria and Hungary were joined by the Germans and later Turkey. War against an external enemy did not unify the Habsburg empire as it had done previously against the Ottomans.[61] Undone by its own divide-and-conquer policies, the Habsburg realm imploded.

Some have offered rather grand reasons for the outbreak of World War I ("the ultimate cause of the war was the moral bankruptcy of Western civilization").[62] But severe ethical lapses in the Western world aside, World War I was the direct result of a dying empire unwilling to accept its decline (the parallels with the post-Cold War world are intriguing, for both the Soviet Union and the United States).

It was not simply the Habsburg empire which dissolved in the bloodletting (ten million dead) of World War I. The 19th-century order finally collapsed in 1918 as the German, Russian, and Ottoman empires expired as well. Europe had not had such an opportunity to completely reorganize itself from the top down since 1815. For Central and Eastern Europe, the possibilities were breathtaking. The aspirations of 1848—the spring of nations—were finally realizable. The revolutionary ideals of 1789 could brush aside the static, conservative, and stifling values of the Austrian and Hungarian crowns. Power vacuums on this scale often produce utopian hopes.

But they equally often produce dystopian realities. Although the new nations carved out of the fallen empires rapidly instituted new parliamentary systems and attempted land reform, the reforms could not adequately address the problematic legacies of the old system. "The old stable patriarchal system," Jacques Rupnik writes, "was breaking down without sufficient provisions for integration of large sections of society into the new democratic system. They—the peasantry, but also many members of the intelligentsia—became vulnerable to the appeal of right-wing radical demagogues."[63] While only 34 percent of the population in more industrially developed Czechoslovakia was involved in agriculture, Bulgaria was fully 80 percent agrarian in the inter-war years, with the rest of the countries falling somewhere in between.[64] For a heavily agricultural region mired in illiteracy, the liberalism associated with urban industrial powers was difficult to manufacture overnight.

Although the rising tide of reaction in the inter-war years could find numerous historical precedents, liberalism was not an entirely unknown concept in the region. During the period of the "Noble Republic" (1569-1795), the Polish parliament, acting in the interests of the *szlachta* or Polish nobility, set out to create a rule of law. But the idealistic *liberum veto,* which allowed any one noble to block a piece of legislation, quite literally paralyzed parliamentary activity: during one 30-year period in the 18th century, for instance, only one session of parliament managed to pass any legislation at all.[65] This occasional political paralysis notwithstanding, the Polish parliament's experience is framed by two remarkable documents, the 16th-century "Act of Tolerance" providing guarantees of universal religious freedom and the 18th-century constitution which proved to be a model for the rest of Europe.[66]

Intermittent attempts to establish more humanistic and egalitarian societies were also made in other countries over the centuries. But these traditions could not prevent the emergence after World War I of strong-arm leaders, statist models, and even several distinct varieties of fascism.[67]

The single exception, under the leadership of philosopher Tomas Masaryk, was the new creation of Czechoslovakia (combining predominantly Protestant Czech lands and predominantly Catholic Slovakia), which maintained a liberal tradition: an open culture, an expanding market, a tolerant political space, and a serious land reform enfranchising the poorer agrarian population. Masaryk, who has greatly influenced later Czech and Slovak intellectuals including Vaclav Havel, emphasized Czechoslovakia's place at the center of Europe. It was during his stewardship that Prague—where Mozart shaped the final sections of his opera *Don Giovanni*—became once again a cultural center in the inter-war years, home to novelists Franz Kafka, Karel Capek, and Joseph Roth.

Other countries in the region veered rightward. Poland ended 123 years of partition and dismemberment after World War I, only to have to fight for independence against the Soviets in 1920. General Josef Pilsudski, the one-time socialist from Lithuania, led Polish forces to victory in that war and then became his country's first president. By 1926, using political instability as a pretext, Pilsudski instituted martial law and went from president to *putschist*. In the 1930s, the military consolidated its power, directed an increasingly state-controlled economy, and intensified its anti-Semitic campaigns. On the eve of World War II, Poland was still a nation, but the state had lost any semblance of liberalism.

The collapse of monarchy in Hungary in 1918 led to tremendous polarization of opinion. A communist movement seized power in 1919 under Bela Kun, but could hold power for only four months. A proto-fascist regime under Admiral Horthy then seized the reins of power, christening the new order with the blood of hundreds of suspected supporters of the previous regime. The Horthyites held on to power through World War II, gradually accommodating their policies to the Nazi movement which had filled a similar power vacuum in neighboring Germany. Though the Horthy regime is best remembered for its repression and intolerance, Hungary also managed to industrialize to a significant degree during the inter-war period.[68]

Romania came out of World War I with a sizable increase in territory, courtesy of the 1920 Trianon treaty that had scattered sections of Hungary to its neighbors. Operating within a constitutional monarchy, several successive state governments initiated agricultural reform and attempted industrialization. But a powerful bureaucracy—"less competent than their Habsburg predecessors and often corrupt"—kept Romanian society locked in place.[69] An indigenous fascist organization—the Iron Guard—competed with a young monarch and fractious parties for influence in the 1930s. After the outbreak of World War II, the king turned to General Ion Antonescu to "rescue" Romania from Germany and Russia as well as from various domestic threats. After relying on its support, Antonescu smashed the Iron Guard, only later to incorporate key elements of its program: allying Romania with the Nazis during World War II and participating in the liquidation of Romanian Jews.

Having gained its independence in 1878 after 500 years of Ottoman rule, Bulgaria also established a constitutional monarchy. Since most Bulgarians were peasants, the agrarian parties played a critical role in the development of parliamentary politics. After World War I, the Peasant Party under Alexander Stamboliski used the land issue to win the 1919 elections. His government subsequently toppled in a coup in 1923. Stamboliski was then given over to be tortured and killed by the Macedonian separatist movement (IMRO), which then formed a government, unstable from its inception, that was succeeded by several military regimes that carried Bulgaria through the 1930s.

The dream of many southern Slavs—a united state—finally came true after World War I with the creation of the Kingdom of Serbs, Croats and Slovenes (Macedonians, Montenegrins, Bosnian Moslems, and Albanians were conspicuously left out of the tripartite arrangement). Serbia was the natural choice to lead the new state since Slovenian and Croatian armies—part of the Austro-Hungarian force—had been disbanded under the armistice agreement. But Serbia ruled with a mixture of corruption, repression, and favoritism, generating almost immediate political conflict among the three ruling ethnic groups. A royal dictatorship attempted to resolve a series of political crises from 1929 to 1934. After the king's assassination in Marseilles in 1934, a government supported by Slovenian, Bosnian, and Serbian parties took over but could not contain the growing Serbian-Croatian dispute. On the eve of World War II, tensions among the ethnic groups had intensified to such a degree that civil war would have erupted had not world war intervened. To be more accurate, civil war in Yugoslavia raged *during* World War II. Battle among Croatian fascists, Serbian nationalists, and communist irregulars probably took more lives than battle against either the Axis or the Allied powers.[70] First, the Ustasha fascists slaughtered countless thousands of Serbs, Jews, Gypsies, and suspected communists. Then, upon taking control of the country after the withdrawal of German and Italian troops, the communists wreaked bloody revenge.

Dictatorships and unstable governments were the rule in Eastern and Central Europe in the inter-war period. External threats only contributed to the instability. Tying together the new countries worried about the resurgence of Austria and Hungary, a system of foreign policy agreements sought to construct a buffer zone between East and West. The Little Entente brought together Czechoslovakia, Romania, and Yugoslavia. The Balkan Entente of 1930 included Greece, Yugoslavia, Romania and Turkey. One chief problem with these treaties was the countries which were excluded: Poland in the first case, Bulgaria in the second. More problematic: the countries of the region were simply not willing to come to each other's defense—they disliked one another too thoroughly.[71]

Given these collective problems, the security arrangements were woefully unprepared for the resurgence of Germany under Nazi leadership. The National Socialists in Germany had come to power in "normal" parliamentary fashion in 1933. Having eliminated his opponents by 1935, Adolf Hitler built a military-industrial complex unparalleled in Europe at that time. The corporatist state lifted Germany from the inflation and unemployment of the Wiemar republic and erased the ignominy of the World War I loss. Hitler set out to dominate Europe in the late 1930s, spurred by an expansionist and racist ideology that placed Germany at the center of the world and Germans at the pinnacle of a racial hierarchy (with Jews, Gypsies, and Slavic people at the bottom, joined by other social outcasts such as homosexuals and communists). In 1938, he annexed Austria and the Sudetenland section of Czechoslovakia heavily populated by Germans. Moves by both Poland and Hungary to seize coveted sections of Czechoslovakia on the heels of Hitler's intervention only emphasized the disunity of Central Europe. In 1939, Germany concluded a non-aggression pact with Stalin's Soviet Union, a secret protocol of which divided Poland between the two powers and gave the Baltic countries (Lithuania, Latvia, Estonia) and sections of Romania to the Soviets. The stage was set for World War II. On September 1, 1939, Germany launched its *blitzkrieg* on Gdansk and Warsaw. Poland fell after five weeks, but not without inflicting over 50,000 casualties on the German war machine.[72]

The Nazis proceeded to take over all of Eastern and Central Europe, acting either through direct administration (Poland, the Czech lands, Serbia), fascist collaborators (Slovakia, Croatia), or strategic allies (Hungary, Romania, Bulgaria). Reviving the *Drang nach Osten,* the Germans sought to enlarge their dominions through the extermination of Jews and Gypsies and Slavs. In addition to destroying life and property, the Germans also industrialized sections of the region to aid their war effort. Hungary, Czechoslovakia, and of course the future German Democratic Republic expanded capacity. Poland and Romania were allowed to languish. This strategy merely built upon previous trends in these countries and ensured that modernization after the war would yield different results throughout the region.

* * *

This brief survey of history—from the Greeks to the Nazis—cannot do justice to the rich political and economic complexities of European development. But it does set a necessary context for understanding the later history of Central and Eastern Europe. The creation of "Europe" established certain geographic boundaries and a constellation of cultural signifiers. The rise and fall of a united Church, the steady progression of the industrial revolution, and the ascendancy of colonial empires contributed to the definition of "Western European civilization," an image that alternately transfixed and enraged peoples in the European hinterlands. These attributes of a European culture would, after the 1989 revolutions, shape the development of the post-communist societies to a significant degree. Of equal importance, however, would be the particular historical features of Eastern and Central Europe—"latecomer" periphery status, ethnic and territorial rivalry, geographic vulnerability, and militaristic, reactionary regimes.

These historical attributes of East and West together formed an emerging identity for the region between Germany and Russia. After the failure of the Nazis to conquer the Soviet Union and their headlong retreat to Berlin, this region became "Eastern Europe." From 1945 until 1989, a new template was laid over the preceding European order: the Soviet model. In part a rebuke of Europe and European culture, this Stalinist model was also the latest in a long series of attempts to modernize Eastern Europe out of its predicament. The region was not so much wrenched from the European context as pushed along a much-heralded shortcut to modernity, a shortcut which in the final analysis turned out to be little more than a deadend, a shortcut which would leave Eastern Europe bloodied but still defiant.

Chapter 2

The Soviet model

> *I cannot accept your canon that we are to judge Pope and King unlike other men, with a favourable presumption that they did no wrong. If there is any presumption it is the other way against holders of power, increasing as the power increases. Historic responsibility has to make up for the want of legal responsibility.*[1]
>
> —John Acton

Imagine that you are the leader of a developing country in the 20th century. Your country relies heavily on agriculture for export, and what industry you have is antiquated and uncompetitive. Your labor force is underskilled and your economy depends disproportionately on the export of produce and raw materials. In other words, your country is at least a generation behind the more industrialized nations of the world.

You might well seek a method of catching up, of closing the gap, of winning membership in the club of history's most favored nations. Now imagine you can draw upon any economic model of modernization available, deciding whether transition should proceed gradually or rapidly, democratically or in an authoritarian manner. You must also take into consideration the various factors beyond your direct control, from potentially hostile armies on your borders to potentially indifferent bankers in the world's financial centers. Bearing in mind that the longer you wait the further behind you will fall (and the less tenable your leadership position will be), what policies would you seek to implement?

For both dictators and democrats, the riddle of modernization has proven uniquely problematic over the centuries. The industrial revolution blazed one trail, but it was both long and fraught with immense suffering. Would any leader consciously choose to initiate such cataclysmic change (particularly if its duration must be telescoped and its effects intensified)? But what other choice is there? Karl Marx, for instance, had no clear-cut answer, having spent the greater part of his life critiquing capitalism without successfully constructing a workable alternative to it. His successor, Vladimir Lenin, eventually decided that the best technique to modernize a society was capitalism, even if the desired outcome of the development was communism.[2] Stealing from the very theorists he later had executed, Soviet leader Joseph Stalin finally hit upon an alternative to the capitalist path of modernization and from that time on Stalin's conception of economic development came to be seen, for all intents and purposes, as communism. The Georgian dictator's novel contribution to economics entailed a form of high-speed modernization: an industrial stength version of the industrial revolution.

Why did Stalin depart not only from the then-current Western developmental model, but from the theories of his communist forebears as well? As we shall see, the choice was not simply economic; it had its political and social components as well, both in the Soviet Union and in Eastern Europe. Before we turn to the export of the Stalinist model, we need to understand this alternative path of modernization and the means by which Stalin hoped to drag the Soviet Union kicking and screaming into the 20th century.

A great leap forward?

In 1928, 80 percent of the Soviet population was agrarian.[3] A country supposed to exemplify a new proletarian spirit contained very few proletarians indeed. The Bolsheviks had inherited an economically backward country and in their first decade in power, had not succeeded in closing the gap between Russia and the West. The Soviet Union had by this time already gone through two radically different economic programs since the Bolsheviks overthrew the liberal Kerensky government in a second revolution in November 1917. Under the pressures of civil war between the Red Army of revolution and the White Army of counter-revolution, Lenin had instituted War Communism, a particularly draconian system involving expropriation at gunpoint and nationalization by fiat. After the Red Army triumphed in 1920, Lenin introduced the New Economic Policy (NEP) as the basis for a mixed and largely market-driven economy. War Communism proved critical in maintaining the regime in power. Although NEP signalled an important relaxation of controls, it still did not propel the Soviet Union into the community of developed nations. Nor did features that built upon the revolutionary enthusiasm of workers (such as the *subbotnik*, or extra Saturday of work) generate the competitive edge.

Soviet theorists in the 1920s were divided on the question of economic reform. The gradualists preferred the continuation of a reformed NEP together with the preservation of a revolutionary link between peasants and workers—as represented in the Soviet symbol of the hammer and sickle. Another group, led by Leon Trotsky, favored a massive state-directed swing of resources toward industry at the expense of the peasantry. Stalin first sided with the gradualists in order to discredit Trotsky and his followers but then, obeying the laws of opportunism rather than ideology, switched to the heavy industrializers in order to eliminate the gradualists. Having dispatched both camps of potential opponents, Stalin took the kernel of Trotsky's position and added several tyrannical touches of his own.[4]

1929 was the critical year. With his Politburo opponents ousted or powerless, Stalin proceeded to model the entire Communist Party in his own image, setting into motion the first of what would be a series of purges reaching into virtually every niche of Soviet society. At the same time, he established the Five Year Plan, the cornerstone of centralized planning and the command economy. Collectivization—the elimination of private farming—accelerated that year. The rationales behind both economic moves were the same: to industrialize an essentially agrarian country, compress the several centuries of industrial revolution into a mere generation, and concentrate power at the center.[5] To accomplish this Herculean task, Stalin relied on the economic virtues of centralized planning, the massive transfer of capital from countryside to industry, and a repressive hold over the Soviet population.

Not one distinct policy, centralized planning was, rather, a range of often very different directives sharing a common point of origin—the state. These policies affected pricing, investment, inter-enterprise sales, foreign trade, labor relations, quality control, product development, accountability, monetary and fiscal policies, and so on. Gosplan—the Soviet planning bureau—handled an enormous number of prices annually, and later, in the information age, with computers at least a decade behind the West. The center controlled the key resources; the remaining commodities were handled by the lower planning echelons.[6]

Statistical challenges aside, the command economy has traditionally boasted several advantages over the market economy, in theory and occasionally in practice. Because the central government controls all economic levers, it can quickly redeploy raw materials, managerial talent, and the labor force. A command economy can also take advantage of "economies of scale" (if one widget costs 2¢ to make, 100 widgets will cost slightly less than $2, 1,000 widgets substantially less than $20, and so on). The command economy further aims for the full employment of both resources and labor which, in theory, creates a prosperous economy. Finally, centralized planning was designed to offer a degree of protection from the unpredictable cycles of capitalism. When Stalin engineered the Soviet alternative, the West was experiencing its most devastating economic downturn, the Great Depression of the early

1930s. The manifold problems of centralized planning to be discussed in later chapters—inefficiency, lack of incentives, ecological hazards, and consumer shortages—were not so evident at the time as they are today.[7]

Stalin's answer to the riddle of modernization was not simply to centralize planning, however. He also had to locate the capital that the central government could use. Since the Soviet economy was primarily agrarian, this capital had to come from the agricultural sphere. Soviet economists began to formulate—in the doublespeak of the late 1920s—a theory of "primitive socialist accumulation" which grew into the policy of collectivization. Soviet farmers were stripped of their private lands and forced to join collectives or state farms. The state took control of the agricultural profits. Those farmers who refused were either shot or sent to prison camps (in certain areas, such operations precipitated or aggravated famines that killed millions). While the capital needed for modernization was thereby drained from the countryside, many former peasants followed the money flow to cities and the new industrial mega-sites. Food, now controlled by collective farms and the state, could more quickly be directed to feed the new industrial working class. The Soviet Union was quickly being proletarianized.

The choice to centralize planning and collectivize agriculture also served political ends. By forcibly reorganizing the countryside, Stalin managed to eliminate any bourgeois challenges from large landowners, the political base of outlawed parties with lingering agrarian influence, and the potential of a more general peasant uprising. The centralization process destroyed many promising economic alternatives as well: cooperatives, worker-owned and managed factories, innovative mixtures of free enterprise and state control. Stalin successfully replaced the orthodoxy of the market with the orthodoxy of his own version of communism and, in so doing, solidified his own political position.

The Stalinist version of modernization was not a project confined to the economic sphere. Clustered around centralized planning were a number of political, military, cultural, and social issues which could, collectively, be termed Stalinism. The military-industrial complex, for instance, grew like a poisonous weed, protected and nurtured by the priority that heavy industry received from the Soviet center. In this symbiotic relationship, the military was ensured a steady supply of tanks, airplanes, and ammunition in return for its steadfast support for privileging heavy industry over light industry, foodstuffs, consumer goods, and agriculture. To force economic transformation on a largely unwilling population, Stalin further restricted political debate and expanded the Soviet security apparatus. The Party had eliminated dissent from its ranks in the 1920s, and Stalin further emphasized this trend by subordinating the Party to his own personal political line. Potential and imagined threats were systematically thwarted with the help of an extensive security apparatus whose traditions extended back to Ivan the Terrible's dreaded *oprichnina* of the 16th century. Intellectuals were forced to conform to the straitjacket of "socialist realism." The Russian Orthodox Church was alternately harassed and coopted into a close state relationship.

Stalinism was the closest the Soviet Union came to pure totalitarianism, in which the state breaks down the barrier between public and private spheres to control not only the outward flow of social life, but the inner lives of individuals as well. Most Soviet leaders were simply content to preserve their own power, but Stalin's peculiar mixture of paranoia and ruthless adherence to a theoretical model translated, in practice, into a police state, a personality cult, and the sacrifice of an entire generation for the sake of superpower status. Nevertheless, an agricultural backwater in 1928, the Soviet Union managed to draw abreast of the major industrial powers by Stalin's death.

There is an unfortunate tendency to apply a cost-benefit analysis to the Stalinist project: on one side of the balance sheet fall the victims, and on the other side the tangible results. Of course there were sacrifices, the argument runs, but in the space of a decade, an isolated agricultural nation rapidly became an industrialized world power. The Soviet omelet required its broken eggs—no social pain, no economic gain. Historical necessity subordinated means to ends. But Stalin's project cannot be evaluated simply on the basis of economic criteria or the fallacious reasoning by hindsight that whatever was "successful" was "right."[8] By the same argument, the economic benefits of slavery, of fascism, of austerity capitalism could be used as thin justifications for fundamentally immoral policies. Separating economics from the social fabric and treating it as a value-free instrument allows such a Machiavellian rationality to shape public policy.

After the devastation of World War II, the Soviet model and its economic virtues offered Eastern Europe a certain degree of inspiration, however. Communist ideology did persuade certain groups in the region. But most East Europeans held sufficient reservations concerning the other aspects of Stalinism to prevent them from voting for communist parties *en masse* in the first post-war elections. Ultimately, Stalinism came to the region much as it had come to the Soviet Union: imposed from the top. Political, economic, and moral arguments were ultimately unnecessary in the face of brutal force and the calculations of geopolitics.

The dawn of the Cold War

In the late 1930s, Eastern European countries were, with the exception of Czechoslovakia, ruled by authoritarian governments. The authoritarianism that came to power in Germany by popular vote in 1933 was, however, of a very different character. Not content simply to tyrannize on the home front, Hitler and his National Socialists insisted on extending German boundaries and eradicating those races they considered inferior. Eastern Europe was the first region to absorb German advances, putting the authoritarian leaders there in a quandary. As first Poland, then Belgium and France fell to the Germans in 1939-40, Eastern European countries seemed to have few alternatives. Britain appeared ready to collapse under the German air attack. The United States had yet to enter the war. Despite some pan-Slavism among the populations, alliance with the Soviet Union was out of the question: the monarchs and dictators of the region perceived communism as too grave a threat. For purposes of alliance, Germany was, if not the moral choice, at least an alternative more in keeping with the ideologies of the right-wingers. When the Nazis launched Operation Barbarossa in 1941 to subdue all of the Soviet Union, they also revived the Habsburg technique of divide and conquer to exploit territorial and ethnic rivalries and neutralize opposition in Eastern Europe.[9]

Allied commanders on the western front watched with a good deal of apprehension as Hitler's forces pushed deep into the Soviet territory in 1941, reaching as far as the suburbs of Moscow. Although some shared Winston Churchill's pox-on-both-their-houses philosophy, these military commanders knew that once Hitler pacified his eastern flank, he would turn his entire attention back to the west. Yet, proposals to open up a southern front with an Allied invasion of the Balkans—which would have relieved some pressure on the Soviet military—were constantly postponed in favor of an invasion of France (the eventual D-Day invasion of Normandy in 1944). The timing was critical. In 1943 the Soviet Union stopped the Nazis at Stalingrad and broke the siege of Leningrad. Then, with the help of Allied materiel assistance, the Soviets pushed the German armies back through Europe, liberating Poland, Hungary, Bulgaria, Romania, parts of Czechoslovakia, Yugoslavia, and Austria, and arriving in Berlin several steps ahead of the US and Western European troops. Liberators, keepers.

Or so it appeared. In fact, negotiations had been going on since 1943 between representatives of Churchill and Stalin over the issue of post-war control of Eastern Europe. In the hallowed tradition of the 1815 partition of Poland and numerous secret plans to divide the Ottoman empire, the representatives of the Great Powers apportioned the spoils beforehand. A final under-the-table agreement in 1945 gave Stalin Hungary, Romania, and Bulgaria while keeping Greece in the Allied camp. Yugoslavia was to be divided equally.[10] Formal agreements divided both Germany and Austria into four zones controlled by Soviet, French, US, and British forces.

The incorporation of Eastern Europe into the Soviet camp was not entirely accomplished in either formal or informal discussions. Rather, the process took place in a succession of stages in a worsening Cold War climate. Had the United States and the Soviet Union not split into two irreconcilable camps, Eastern Europe would have perhaps enjoyed greater autonomy. The bi-polarism implicit in both Stalin's and Churchill's worldviews, and explicit in the breakdown of the Alliance, did not permit neutrality for the majority of the strategically located Eastern European countries.

Why the seeming inevitability of the Cold War stand-off? Miscalculations on both sides certainly facilitated the division.[11] But roots of conflict extend deeper into the history of US-Soviet relations. For example, in the aftermath of World War I, both President Wilson and the new Soviet leader Lenin recognized that the old European order—led by the colonial powers—was coming to an end. The war had destroyed four empires, but it weakened the victors as well, notably Britain and France. In the service of both abstract principle and concrete national interests, Lenin and Wilson advocated the new concept of "self-determination"—the struggles of peoples against foreign control and intervention—in order to facilitate the decline of the old colonial powers. A rare consensus was achieved between the soon-to-be superpowers; although vastly different in many regards, Wilson's 14 points and Lenin's revolutionary decrees, Wilson's League of Nations and Lenin's Communist International (Comintern) shared the same language of anti-colonialism.[12]

World War II dispatched the colonial order that World War I had weakened. Britain had fallen into debt paying for the war effort, in essence ceding its empire to the United States. France, exhausted from its occupation, would hold on to its colonies in Africa and Asia for little more than a decade. Germany and Italy lost their colonies as spoils of war. Self-determination, whether fueled by liberal or revolutionary impulses, would eventually create a politically autonomous, if economically dependent, Third World.

Having hastened the exit of the colonial powers from the world stage, the United States and the Soviet Union were left to determine the new world order. Conceivably, they might have chosen a form of condominium or joint rule. Ideology need not have prevented such an arrangement. Stalin was known for his opportunism (e.g., a treaty with Hitler); Roosevelt seemed to favor a continued alliance (though Truman was more ideologically inclined against the USSR). There was one major sticking point: Europe. An emerging superpower could simply not resist control of what had recently been the world's most industrialized region.[13] Stalin and Truman were fated to butt heads in the center of Europe (and Eastern Europe was uniquely fated to suffer for it).

The creation of the two spheres of influence had both its overt and covert sides. The christening of the divide was left to the virulently anti-Soviet Churchill and his "Iron Curtain" speech of 1946. The Soviets followed suit with Andrei Zhdanov's "two camp" pronouncement of 1947 and the resurrection of the Comintern under its new name of Cominform. Accusations and counter-accusations were traded, positions were hardened, and the enemy images of Germans and Japanese quickly dissolved into the Cold War stereotypes of Western imperialists and Red infiltrators. The two sides were indeed consolidating control over their respective spheres.

This shift from alliance to antagonism was facilitated by a change in the composition of the US foreign policy establishment. Between 1945 and 1948, the "soft-liners" associated with Roosevelt were rapidly replaced with a cohort of analysts—George Kennan, Charles Bohlen, and Dean Acheson—whose positions were either "hard" or "hardening." Acheson in particular had the job of molding Truman, a new president unversed in foreign policy and unsure of what stand the United States should take toward the USSR. The goal was a global capitalist system dominated by the United States.[14]

With the new hard-line attitudes came an enormous increase in covert operations. In Western Europe, the US government and its intelligence arm, the OSS (Office of Strategic Services, the forerunner of the CIA), poured money into anti-communist parties competing in post-war elections throughout the region. More questionable was the recruiting of former Nazis, particularly from areas then under Soviet control. Not only did these new recruits provide valuable information, they often served as covert operatives smuggled back into their former countries to destabilize and overthrow the governments. US-backed coup attempts in Romania (1947) and Albania (1949-50), counterinsurgency in Greece (1947), and a program of parachuting anti-communist operatives into Ukraine (1949) served as models for later US ventures, for instance with anti-Castro Cubans in the ill-fated Bay of Pigs invasion of 1961.[15]

As the new policy establishment prepared the United States for its new position as "world police force," it also developed a sophisticated "good cop/bad cop" routine. The covert operations constituted the "bad cop" side, conveniently obscured from the public eye. The "good cop" side—the Marshall Plan (1947) and the Berlin Airlift (1948)—was better advertised. US largesse, in the form of large infusions of dollars into the ravaged Western European economies and supplies parachuted into a blockaded West Berlin, did more to strengthen a nascent Atlantic Alliance and establish the United States as the dignified contrast to presumed Soviet treachery. But even the seemingly more acceptable aspects of US Cold War actions had their negative consequences. A participant in the OSS's intelligence operations in Europe but better known as containment's formulator, George Kennan took a critical stance toward US foreign policy after the initial propaganda offensive of the early Cold War years. As historian John Lewis Gaddis explains, Kennan

> regarded several of [the US government's] major actions between 1948 and 1950—the formation of the North Atlantic Treaty Organization, the creation of an independent West German state, the insistence on retaining American forces in postoccupation Japan, and the decision to build the hydrogen bomb—as certain to reinforce Soviet feelings of suspicion and insecurity, and, hence, to narrow opportunities for negotiations.[16]

Kennan assumed, of course, that the United States was interested in negotiating, a diplomatic skill forced into early retirement by the Truman administration.

The Soviet Union was, paradoxically, both more interested in negotiations and more blatant in manipulating its new sphere of influence. With the exception of Yugoslavia and Albania, where indigenous communist movements immediately established one-party states, the newly liberated countries of Eastern Europe began the post-war era with coalition governments. In this "inclusionary" stage, the Soviet Union encouraged communist parties in the region to participate in elections and take every possible ministerial post, but dissuaded them from seizing power in coups (even when, as in Hungary, the Party was eager to do just that).[17] Stalin was not, at this stage, opposed to negotiations with the enemy—his geopolitics had always been flexible.

Because the Stalinist model sat uncomfortably with the initially liberal post-war governments in the region, the "inclusionary" stage was almost by definition unstable. Stalin was willing to permit a degree of political instability in the region, however, if it served greater geopolitical purposes, namely preserving a working relationship with the West. But as the Cold War climate worsened, Stalin turned away from appeasing the West.

Saddling the cow

The policies crafted in the Soviet Union after 1929—rapid industrialization, central control of the economy, a new oligarchic politics, the elimination of all potential dissent from society—had been designed to build socialism in one country. With the Cold War intensifying, Stalin exported his model to Eastern Europe in order to create a more unified and dependable defensive zone. As such, he moved away from the "inclusionary" policies of the immediate post-war period to embrace first the strategy of "bogus" political coalitions in the region before settling finally on the "exclusionary" position. Whatever flexibility Stalin had possessed—and however self-serving it might have been—that willingness to negotiate disappeared as the US position hardened. And that was not good news for Eastern Europe.

Bogus coalitions in the region discredited authentic dissent and forced alternative left parties, both socialist and social democratic, to toe a communist line. At this stage, the parties which participated in the coalition did so in name alone. The coalition had simply become an extension of the Communist Party.[18] The exclusionary policy represented the abandoning of coalitions, bogus or otherwise, and strengthened orthodoxy within the communist parties as well. So-called national communists who supported both communism and a degree of independence from Moscow would, Stalin realized, cause more problems than waffling social democrats or conservative Christian democrats. He therefore fed the newly constituted communist parties with a stream of "Moscow" communists whose allegience to the Soviets surpassed any national considerations. The Moscow communists employed intimidation, fraud, and violence to wrest power from other communist factions and other parties.

In Poland, the Soviet army and the Polish underground eventually seized control from the Nazis. While still battling anti-communist Polish units, the Soviets created a Moscow-supported communist government in the town of Lublin. After substantial disagreement between the Lublin government and the pre-war government in exile in London, the leader of the latter, Stanislaw Mikolajczyk, returned to Poland to participate in a coalition government from June 1945 to January 1947. Then, after a suspicious election, the Polish Communist Party seized control. Purges and deportations eliminated major sources of domestic unrest. The Party began to implement the Soviet-style economic reform, "fitting a cow with a saddle" as Stalin put it with characteristic crudity.[19] But key elements of the Stalinist project never took hold in Poland. By the early 1950s, for example, the government simply gave in to public resistance to collectivization, and Polish agriculture returned to predominantly private hands.[20]

East Germany did not immediately come into existence after World War II. The Soviet Union, from 1945 until 1949, called for a united Germany and was willing to make concessions for a demilitarized neutral space in the center of Europe. Moves by the United States, France, and Britain in their zones—stalling the de-Nazification program, preparing the three zones for eventual entry into a Western alliance—prompted the Soviet Union to do likewise in its own zone. The Soviets had been extracting what was left of the Nazis' economic base as unofficial reparations since the war's end.[21] When a communist government was established after a suspect referendum in 1949, the capital flow eastward began to taper off. Still, it took several years for an East German identity to emerge. As one specialist has commented, "The GDR state was an afterthought."[22]

In 1945, Czechoslovak citizens favored the Communist Party over all others (communists received 40 percent of the vote in Czech lands, 30 percent in Slovakia). A coalition led by the pre-war social democratic leader Edward Benes ruled from 1945 until 1948. The communists continued to maneuver behind the scenes, outflanking the Slovak Democratic Party and intimidating its national coalition partners into keeping to an increasingly doctrinaire line. A cabinet coup in 1948 brought in communist leader Klement Gottwald, who rapidly transformed the country into a Soviet satellite. Purges of dissidents from the Party continued into the 1950s.

The coalition effort lasted in Hungary until 1948, when the Communist Party disbanded its bogus coalition. Three years earlier, the communists managed 17 percent in a free election, with the agrarian-based Smallholders Party garnering the majority of votes. Assisted by Soviet troops that had yet to withdraw after the war, the Hungarian communists diluted the smallholders' power through imagined plots and harassment. After absorbing a broken Social Democratic Party, the communists began to implement the Soviet model.

In the Balkans, true coalition governments lasted for a shorter time, though the bogus coalitions limped along from 1945 to late 1947. In Romania, Soviet occupation forces and Moscow communists at first determined the political course of the country. The communist front coalition, the National Democratic Front, organized elections in 1946, won primarily through intimidation, and used the suspect results to legitimize increased communist control. While explicitly destroying all potential centers of resistance connected with the fascist and anti-communist past, Romanian communists also recruited key fascists into the party.[23] National communists, who were jailed in other Eastern European countries, managed to cooperate with the Moscow communists in destroying the vestiges of radical nationalism. These national communists, primarily of ethnic Romanian stock, then turned around and used anti-Semitism and anti-Hungarianism against their former allies (many of whom were ethnically Jewish and Hungarian).

In Bulgaria, a similarly organized coalition, the Fatherland Front, bullied its way to victory in 1945 elections. Although capitalizing on long-standing pro-Russian sentiment and strong coalition partners, the Fatherland Front "won for itself one of the worst records of terrorism of the postwar period."[24] It is estimated that 100,000 people were killed during Bulgaria's Stalinist period.[25] Squeezing out the opposition peasant and social democratic parties and executing the main leader of the opposition, Nikola Petkov, the Front began to implement the more familiar aspects of the Soviet model when it officially seized control at the end of 1947.[26]

Although its Communist Party followed the Bolshevik path to power most closely, Yugoslavia would also be the first country to challenge Soviet control in the post-war years. There were no coalition governments in post-war Yugoslavia, no free elections, no attempts to provide a liberal facade to the West. On the other hand, because Josip Broz Tito's partisans had fought successfully against German and Italian forces, the communists did have a certain degree of true support in post-war Yugoslavia. A key policy disagreement with Stalin led to Yugoslavia's ouster from the Soviet bloc in 1948 and Tito's development of a unique path to socialism. It was, however, an anomaly in the region.

* * *

To understand how communism came to Eastern Europe, it would be a mistake to focus simply on the manipulations from above, whether by the Soviet Union or the Allies. Communism did receive support from the various populations throughout Eastern Europe, to a greater (Czechoslovakia) or lesser (Poland) extent. While the Stalinist model was indeed imposed from above, communism as an ideology struck some responsive chords in the public. Timothy Garton Ash eloquently elaborates this response:

> Many reasons led sensitive and educated men and women to embrace those incredible, utopian claims of ideology: from the experience of social injustice, racial prejudice, and bigotry under prewar regimes to the indescribably terrible Central European experience of war, occupation, and Holocaust. These reasons cannot be summarized or synthesized, for they are not only reasons but motives, drives, compounds of fear and longing, "of eros and of dust," hunger for power, lust for destruction, vulgar ambition, but also desperate responses to such suffering as the human spirit simply will not acknowledge to be senseless.[27]

Bracketed off from the powerful forces promulgating it, communism was frequently presented as little more than a tool for achieving a better, more humane society. The same combination of idealism and ignorance of vested interests had, several years earlier, inspired the community of US scientists working on the atomic bomb. While some scientists were driven by ambition or hatred of the enemy, others were, as Richard Rhodes has pointed out, "working also paradoxically believing they were preparing a new force that would ultimately bring peace to the world."[28] Communism too was seen by many as the bearer of peace and, after centuries of economic backwardness in Eastern Europe, prosperity as well.

Communism was also the ideology of the liberators. Soviet expulsion of the Nazis from the region certainly raised the USSR's credibility. True, this "liberation" was not unmitigated. Poles, in particular, had reason to be suspicious of their new benefactors. The Soviets had nearly captured Warsaw in 1920, had divided Poland in 1939 with the Nazis, had killed several thousand Polish officers in 1940 at Katyn Forest in Byelorussia, had deported two million Poles to Siberia and Kazakhstan during 1939-40 (half of whom had died one year later).[29] In 1944, the Soviet army halted just outside Warsaw, thus allowing the Nazis to suppress the Poles' heroic uprising. Chasing the Nazi troops westward through other parts of Eastern Europe, Soviet troops did their own share of raping and looting. Nevertheless, after the brutality of Nazi and fascist regimes, the allure of an explicitly anti-Nazi country, especially one that had also suffered immensely as a result of the war, cannot be underestimated.

Running deeper than pro-Sovietism were currents of pan-Slavism. In 1848, at the Slavic Congress in Prague, two important elements of this new transnational ideology emerged: a unique historical mission of Slavs in Europe and the necessity of defending Slavic integrity in the face of German expansionism.[30] When the Germans again threatened the region in World War II, pan-Slavism enjoyed a renaissance with the convening of the first congress of the Pan-Slav Committee in 1941 (which, as historian Stephen Borsody points out, was not simply a communist front organization).[31] Although pan-Slavism had proven rather weak in Poland (i.e., forging precious little solidarity between Polish nobles and Ruthenian peasants), further south the sentiment grew stronger. It intensified desires for a unified Yugoslavia and even led the future Czech president Tomas Masaryk to propose a corridor through Hungary that would link northern and southern Slavs.[32] Because of the role Russia played in guaranteeing Bulgarian independence, pan-Slavism linked these two countries as well, inspiring in part communist leader Todor Zhivkov's unappetizing proclamation that "Bulgaria and the Soviet Union will act as a single body, breathing with the same lungs and nourished by the same bloodstream."[33] But as the repressive measures accompanying the imposition of the Soviet model became clearer, pan-Slavism was gradually overwhelmed by anti-Sovietism.

Also facilitating the adoption of the economic component of the Stalinist model were the pre-World War II historical precedents. Since the end of the 19th century, most Eastern European governments favored centralized control of economic development, including import quotas, direct state investments, and agricultural subsidies. These centralized policies inevitably identified heavy industry as the spur for development, though these industries remained for the most part concentrated in certain regions.[34] Even primarily agrarian Poland saw its future in the factory during the inter-war period. Statist policies were accentuated by inter-war regimes and subsequently by the corporatist states established by Nazi and fascist regimes during World War II.[35]

Other features of the Stalinist system had their precursors as well. As mentioned in the previous chapter, Prince Metternich had created an espionage network throughout the Habsburg empire and beyond its borders in order to halt the continued decline of imperial power. The Bach system of absolutist bureaucracy, instituted after the 1848 revolutions and named for the Habsburg's minister of interior, created—in the words of 19th-century political theorist Adolph Fischhof—"a standing army of soldiers, a sitting army of officials, a kneeling army of priests and a creeping army of denunciators."[36] The Soviet model could clearly feed on the absolutisms of the past.

Stalin was certainly more paranoid and destructive than Metternich, and the Soviet model generated more conformity and collaboration than the Bach system. State-directed economies prior to the imposition of Stalinism in Eastern Europe were also capitalist, even though emphasizing government intervention. Precedents do not determine historical outcomes; they simply create contexts and underscore particular trends. Furthermore, the presence of historic precedents and the experiences of Nazism and pan-Slavism do not imply that Eastern Europe had to adopt the Soviet model. Soviet "encouragement" was necessary, not only to establish communism but also the particular brand developed by Stalin at the end of the 1920s. The cow, in other words, did not invite the saddle.

For all its anti-Soviet rhetoric, the West also facilitated this imposition, more by its intransigence than its so-called appeasement. Given Stalin's "inclusionary" tactic in the early stages of the Cold War, the Soviet Union might have been persuaded to continue its support of popular fronts in the region. Had diplomacy triumphed over militancy, Soviet troops might have withdrawn from the region and Eastern Europe might have enjoyed an Austrian or Finnish neutrality. Except for mostly ridiculous attempts at espionage and the propaganda of various radio broadcasts, the West abandoned Eastern Europe because it had decided *pro forma* that negotiations with Communists were useless.

In the absence of skillful Western diplomacy, Stalin consolidated control over his sphere. That control would not, however, go unchallenged in the post-Stalinist period in Eastern Europe. Some of those challenges came from below, some from the national governments, some even from the Soviet Union itself. Eventually every aspect of the Stalinist model—its oligarchies, security police ruthlessness, cultural propaganda and prohibitions, finally even its version of modernization—would come under fire. Stalinist shock therapy in the immediate post-war era killed many people and ruined many lives in Eastern Europe. Such harsh medicine, though designed to make Eastern Europe dependent on the Soviet Union, was also intended to make the region stronger, more able to compete economically in the modern age. But Stalinism succeeded only in strengthening the resolve of most East Europeans to find a viable alternative. Denied an opportunity to challenge Stalinism legally, the opposition movements and reformers we will meet in the next chapter worked to ensure that the policies of the Soviet leader would not go down in history as justified.

Chapter 3

From above and below

I would rather bark like a dog than speak the language of the foreigners.[1]

—Czech noble

Stalin lived, imposed his model on Eastern Europe, then died. Revolution broke out in Hungary in 1956, in Czechoslovakia in 1968, and in Poland in 1980. Then came Gorbachev. Finally a new era dawned in 1989, people awoke as if from a dream, the Wall fell, and the Stalinist model finally crumbled in its entirety. *Voila,* the Cold War in fast forward.

This condensed version of the last 45 years in Eastern Europe does not, needless to say, capture the ebb and flow of reform and revolution in the region. Spanning the Cold War gap between Stalin and Gorbachev, numerous top-down restructurings and popular uprisings from below chipped away at the communist system of one-party rule, centralized planning, and security police surveillance. By 1989, Stalin's model had been hollowed out by his communist successors and non-communist detractors alike.

This hollowness was often referred to, in the lingo of specialists, as a "legitimation crisis": the communist rulers could not ultimately fulfill the expectations generated by their own propaganda.[2] No longer reliant solely on the raw repressions of the Stalinist period, such governments sought political legitimacy through rigged elections, economic stability through high growth and external borrowing, and social support through egalitarian rhetoric. Whatever the legitimacy gained initially by these policies, communist governments gradually drifted toward crisis, attempting to fine tune from above when protest erupted from below. The events of 1989 did not come from nowhere. Both the Gorbachev-style reformers and the successful oppositionists had their forebears. Although tensions had long been waxing and waning, emphasis in the 1980s was clearly on the wax rather than the wane. The Soviet model—a distinctly foreign tongue to many in the region—was to be a short-lived *lingua franca.*

Reform from above

The Soviet Union had only a brief period of complete control over Eastern Europe, perhaps only several months. The last true coalition government lasted until February 1948 when Czechoslovak communists seized control in a coup. In June of the same year, Yugoslav communists were expelled from the Soviet bloc: the first major challenge to Moscow's presumed status as capital of the communist world. The "nationalism" of the Yugoslavs would soon affect every Communist Party in the region, providing a model for reform-from-within and subverting any notion that the Eastern European countries were mere satellites whose orbits would never deviate from course. Political scientist Charles Gati writes,

> Without Yugoslavia it is impossible to understand what the likes of the Hungarian Imre Nagy and the Polish Wladyslaw Gomulka were to do in the mid-1950s or what the Czechoslovak Alexander Dubcek would do in the late 1960s. Tito established a precedent for autonomy and, later, reform in the communist world—in Soviet eyes, a very dangerous precedent at that time.[3]

Tito was accustomed to setting precedents. A footsoldier in World War I and an early communist, Tito formed partisan units to combat the Nazis after the German invasion defeated the king's troops in 1941. During World War II, Yugoslavia was split into several parts, with the fascist Ustasa ruling in Croatia and the newly absorbed Bosnia-Herzogovina, a Nazi puppet controlling Serbia, the Italians attempting to administer Montenegro and part of Slovenia, and the Bulgarians trying to subdue Macedonia. The key players, however, were two major underground armies—Tito's communists and Draza Mihailovic's Serbian royalists—that ranged throughout the country. Tito's ability to attract support from across Yugoslavia and his successes against the Germans and Italians prompted the Allies to switch support to him in 1944. Willing to eliminate domestic challenges ruthlessly, Tito managed to consolidate power rapidly in the immediate post-war period.

Friction with Stalin was inevitable. Tito was not a Moscow communist lacking a popular base. Half-Croatian and half-Slovenian, based in Bosnia-Herzogovina during the war, and determined to reestablish Belgrade (Serbia) as the capital of a new Yugoslavia, Tito was uniquely able to stitch Yugoslavia back together again. He had even, in the final days of the war, established control over Macedonia, Montenegro, Kosovo, and, through proxy, Albania as well. After the war, with Yugoslavia the most powerful Balkan nation, Tito won part of the Istrian peninsula from Italy (though failed to annex Austrian Carinthia). In other words, Tito was quickly transforming Yugoslavia into a regional power.

When Stalin called Yugoslav leaders to task for dispatching military units to Albania and considering a Balkan union with Bulgaria, Tito and his top advisers chose to defy the interference in their internal affairs.[4] Stalin tried to outmaneuver Tito but failed, leaving Yugoslavia's expulsion from the Soviet bloc in 1948 the only recourse.

A decade before the Sino-Soviet split, Yugoslavia destroyed the conception of Moscow as an invincible communist monopole. Tito could genuinely represent another communist path. In the early years after 1948, however, the Yugoslav alternative surfaced in neighboring countries only in pejorative contexts, as false accusations leveled against purged communists: the epithet "Titoist" carried as much negative weight as "Zionist" or "Trotskyist."[5] Rapprochement between Belgrade and Moscow was slow in coming. When Yugoslavia applied for membership in the regional organization of planned economies in 1949, it was rejected pointblank.

How then did Yugoslàvia survive the propaganda assault, the economic blockade, and a potential military onslaught from the Soviet Union? External factors were perhaps the most important. On the one hand, Stalin was not willing to hazard an attempt at subduing an entire unfriendly country so soon after World War II and so soon into the Cold War. On the other hand, Western aid in the 1950s ($2 billion in outright grants) provided critical support during the period of economic isolation.[6]

The Titoist heresy was the first indication that Stalinism in its purest form in the region would not substantially outlive Stalin himself (though severe repression would later reappear in the region, most dramatically under Ceausescu in Romania and Zhivkov in Bulgaria). In the Soviet Union itself, liberalization occurred rapidly after Stalin's death in 1953, catching the United States by surprise ("We have no plan," President Eisenhower remarked after Stalin's death. "We are not even sure what difference his death makes").[7] Under the stewardship of Georgi Malenkov, the Soviet Union dramatically recast its foreign policy objectives, exemplified by the 1955 negotiated withdrawal of Soviet troops from Austria. Fixed in its conception of a divided Europe, the United States failed to negotiate with the new Soviet leaders a neutral and demilitarized Europe.[8]

Nikita Khrushchev's dramatic speech to the 20th Party Congress in 1956, denouncing key aspects of the previous regime elevated de-Stalinization to an official policy. The Stalinist model was redesigned to give greater authority to a cadre of communist officials, with a loosening of economic controls and a cultural thaw also introduced. The Soviet model of modernization, devised in the late 1920s, was forced to adapt to the realities of the 1950s and 1960s.

Khrushchev's denunciations of Stalinism, both a statement of principle and a useful technique to discredit his opponents within the Party, reverberated throughout Eastern Europe. Of chief importance were Khrushchev's thoughts on "separate paths to socialism." Suddenly the Yugoslav transgression was forgiven. Moscow had not only relinquished its unchallenged control but had recognized the loss. At the same time, the Moscow communists who had guided Eastern European communist parties to power in the post-war period discovered that their links to the Soviet Union had become a liability. The national communists who had emphasized more indigenous brands of communism (such as Gomulka in Poland) were rehabilitated. Instead of appealing to Bolshevik or even pan-Slavic values, these national communists stressed the particular histories of their countries, whether Bulgaria's medieval origins or Poland's legendary battles with the Teutonic knights. Nationalism didn't disappear from the region during the communist era; it merely took a new form.

From top-down Stalinism to top-down reform, Eastern Europe played follow-the-Soviet-leader in the mid-1950s, experiencing a thaw similar to the one breaking out in the USSR. In Poland, the national communists waged a successful campaign against the more Stalinesque Party leader Boleslaw Bierut. Forced collectivization ended. Stalin's name was removed from the plaque on the building he had given to Warsaw—the Palace of Culture and Science, a wedding-cake structure in the very center of the city. In Romania, self-criticism (the code-word at that time for de-Stalinization) began in 1953 when the new Party leader Gheorghe Gheorghiu-Dej closed forced labor camps, initiated a cultural liberalization, and weeded Moscow communists from the Party.[9]

Generally bypassed by these tumultuous changes, Czechoslovakia suffered until 1968 under the rule of Antonin Novotny, a by-the-book Stalinist who had perversely resisted liberalization. His replacement in 1968, Alexander Dubcek, attempted a reform from within, the famous "socialism with a human face." Instituting multi-candidate elections for Party posts and legalizing non-communist associations, Dubcek charted a course back to the humanist and progressive roots of communism. The students, intellectuals, and workers who participated in the Prague Spring were not revolutionaries but reformists on a grand scale, committed to the values of the pre-Stalinized Czechoslovak Communist Party. This was Eastern Europe's first and last real attempt to fulfill the promise of the early communist ideal. The Soviet invasion, helped by troops from the GDR, Poland, Hungary, and Bulgaria, put an end to the experiment.

Although ruthless in Prague, the Soviets nonetheless permitted radical reform in the region, as long as it remained in the economic sphere and didn't challenge fundamental political and foreign policy dogma. Given the crudity of the Stalinist jump-start of the economies of Eastern Europe, a restructuring of centralized planning was inevitable. Indeed, as the 20th century advanced, substantial accommodations to the international economic system could not be avoided. But just as the problems of the command economy were diverse, so too were the recipes for reform: a pinch of market, a touch of centralized efficiency, a trace of worker participation, and mixed with Western capital throughout.

With its much celebrated New Economic Mechanism, Hungary went with the pinch of market. Responding to disgruntled workers and consumers, the government of Janos Kadar in 1968 allowed private enterprise on a small scale, freed prices, and decentralized enterprise decisions.[10] The market had entered through the back door under the acceptable labels of "liberalization" and "decentralization." Nicknamed "goulash communism," the Hungarian model produced a standard of living higher than that in neighboring countries (and when the reform stalled in the early 1970s, foreign borrowing kept this standard artificially buoyed).[11] The relative lack of shortages in Budapest and the comparative contentment of Hungarian citizens proved a powerful recommendation for the Kadar strategy of grafting consumerism onto the communist ideology and creating a new class of rural entrepreneurs to satisfy demands for produce.[12]

After a series of student protests and worker revolts, a new Polish government under Edward Gierek introduced a series of reforms in 1970 intended to dynamize the economy—to create a bigger pie that would yield larger slices for everyone. Though the reform combined both greater centralization (of large economic organizations known as WOGs) and decentralization (of enterprise decisions on prices), the key innovation was the discovery of deficit spending: higher imports and larger loans from the West.[13] Reform of the Polish economy would approach this centralization dilemma from different angles but the loans would remain a constant feature—buying more imports to satisfy consumer demands, purchasing comfortable lifestyles for Gierek's technocrats, and sponsoring harebrained investments such as the production for export of thousands of golf carts which were never sold. In the wake of Solidarity, more thoroughgoing market reforms were attempted, including greater enterprise autonomy and self-financing leading to potential bankruptcy.[14]

The GDR and its New Course represented the other pole of reform. The first changes came in 1953 when collectivization pressures eased and the expropriation of private property ceased.[15] In the 1970s, the GDR moved toward greater centralization with its *kombinate*—large enterprises that gave the GDR a regional and occasionally global edge in micro-optics and electronics. Enormous firms such as Carl Zeiss Jena were held up as examples of the anti-minimalist ethic: more, the GDR maintained, is indeed more. Similarly orthodox in orientation, the Romanian government wielded increasingly draconian control over the economy in the 1980s under Ceausescu's intensified export strategy. Bulgaria extended social protection and raised wages in the agricultural sphere in 1957 but waited until the late 1970s before the New Economic Model pushed the country in the direction of decentralization.[16]

Hungary and Poland experimented with the market, introducing it in cautious amounts in their economies. For the GDR, Romania, and Bulgaria, however, the market was anathema, evidence of Western decadent imperialism. Yugoslavia meanwhile devised a self-styled third way, "self-management," that attempted to thread between the tight organization of central planning and the chaos of the market. On the one hand, enterprises were given greater autonomy, and market principles began to govern inter-enterprise relations. On the other hand, through enhanced participation in semi-autonomous workers' councils, workers in an enterprise became more involved in industrial decisionmaking and profited, at least theoretically, from an enterprise's success. It was an experiment in workplace democracy where "despite not being the owners of the resources, a worker can manage, work, dispose of resources and assume full economic responsibility for the results achieved."[17]

While the language of self-management was absorbed into the economic rhetoric of other Eastern European countries *(samorzad* in Poland, *autoconducerea* in Romania), the radical content of the institutions was diluted by the communist governments. In Yugoslavia, too, the spirit of self-management evaporated over time. One critic notes that "Yugoslavs show a lack of interest in self-management institutions, a faulty knowledge of the way they work, and a seeming disregard for the consequences of their action."[18] As the Yugoslav economy eventually became mired in corruption and imprisoned by inflation, principles of self-management were ignored. But even before these economic failings, the lack of political democracy in Yugoslavia made this "third way" a dubious alternative.[19]

Prior to Gorbachev's implosive reforms, the final challenge to communism coming from within its own ranks was Eurocommunism. Unique in that it united dissident communist parties from both blocs, Eurocommunism issued a challenge to Moscow that recalled Tito's original heresy.[20] Communist parties which had seen such promise in Dubcek's cause—of communism correcting its deviations and proceeding on to its promised goals—decided that, in the end, Tito had been right: a third path between Washington and Moscow was unavoidable. Predictably, neither Moscow nor Washington felt entirely comfortable with this offspring of detente. As Santiago Carrillo, the leader of the Spanish Communist Party, remarked: "[W]hen Kissinger agrees with some of the Soviet comrades in affirming that Eurocommunism does not exist...this confirms that Eurocommunism exists and is in good health."[21]

But as detente fell, so fell Eurocommunism. Increased polarization between East and West did not permit the emergence of a Eurocommunist middle ground. In the years after 1976, Yugoslavia and Romania maintained their independent positions, West European communist parties generally continued the program of revisionism, and the "loyalists" maintained their loyalty (although both Hungary and Poland were taking steps in the 1980s toward a more autonomist position).[22]

* * *

The retreat from Stalinism—as in the cases of Khrushchev or Tito—sometimes resulted from political infighting. More frequently, change from above was designed to forestall or coopt growing dissent. Economic reform often promoted "pacification through consumption";[23] cultural thaws released some intellectual steam before the valves were tightened again; political shake-ups replaced the unpopular with the unknown. Throughout the period of reform from above, certain sacred cows might have been attacked, but they were never slaughtered. The leading role of the communist parties was preserved; the allergy toward political pluralism was never overcome. When the countries of Eastern Europe seemed in danger of sliding down this slippery slope of bourgeois liberalism, the Soviet Union intervened to maintain orthodoxy.

In Hungary in 1956, Czechoslovakia in 1968, and through the proxy of military *putsch* in Poland in 1981, the Soviet Union influenced the pace of reform in Eastern Europe. Although Moscow could never dictate the fine details to Eastern European parties after national communists succeeded Moscow communists, it could function as a fuse that would cut the current of reform when it exceeded a certain limit. As Timothy Garton Ash pointed out prior to the 1989 revolutions, the Soviet fuse changed over time:

> In response to the three major post-war East European challenges, the Soviet Union has each time hesitated longer—days with Hungary in 1956, months with Czechoslovakia in 1968, more than a year with Poland in 1980-81. It has gone to increasing pains to disguise its intervention—unilateral in 1956, multilateral [Warsaw pact] in 1968, Polish "internal" in 1981.[24]

The threat of Soviet military intervention would all but disappear in the Gorbachev period, although homegrown repression by the communist parties in the region could not be ruled out as the final challenge to the grassroots opposition.

Revolt from below

Opposition to the imposition of Soviet control flared up sporadically throughout Eastern Europe in the years after World War II. But it was chiefly in Poland where protest came in a military form. Elements of the Home Army, an underground force that waged a limited but highly successful campaign against the Nazis, continued to fight for complete Polish independence after the war's end.[25] Although decimated during the Warsaw uprising of 1944 (as the Soviets waited on the right bank of the Vistula), the Home Army spawned further guerrilla movements that fought until 1947.[26]

With the exception of the Polish fighters, initial opposition to the Soviet model had a parliamentary cast. Peasant, social democratic, and church-based parties competed in post-war elections of varying degrees of openness and participated in coalition governments all destined to be collapsed into one-party states. When the parliamentary option disappeared, institutional and legal alternatives disappeared with it. In this period of "pure" Stalinism, alternatives within the Party evaporated, and even dogmatic communists worried about purges and the possibility of execution. This was the beginning of emigration, the move overseas, as well as the exile within. For those who remained in Eastern Europe and who opposed the government, survival depended on a retreat from organized social activity which lasted, in some countries, for nearly the entire 45 years of communist rule.

But after the death of Stalin, another option became available. Groups of people with similar interests gradually drifted together or were propelled by particular events into organized protest. Initial opposition came from two sectors—workers and intellectuals. Later, in the 1970s and 1980s, revolt from below cut across class lines by linking protest to particular issues: ecology, national identity, disarmament, religious freedom. By 1989, the various threads would coil into an oppositional force whose unity was as unprecedented as it was short-lived.

Workers

The first important revolt of workers in a workers' state came in 1953 in East Berlin.[27] It was the year of Stalin's death and the birth of the East German economic reform. This economic New Course, although signaling a relaxation of certain state controls, provided precious little for workers. Borrowing a page from the capitalists' book, the government raised the norms in the piece-rate system, forcing workers to produce more output per hour for the same pay. Occasional strikes had occurred prior to 1953, but now, with Stalin dead and norms raised, the revolt of June 1953 spiraled to a higher level of opposition. Begun by construction workers in East Berlin, the strikes quickly spread to other professions and other cities and, though garnering little support from intellectuals, required several days for Soviet troops to quell.[28] This first use of Soviet troops since World War II sent a clear warning to other "friendly" neighbors in the Soviet sphere of influence.

Workers in Poznan, in the former German territories of Poland, were the next to launch a viable challenge to communist authority. Responding to declining living standards, the workers at the Stalin Engineering Works took to the streets in June 1956. Seventy-four workers and militia died during these "Bread and Freedom" riots, precipitating a change in party leadership and producing an October thaw under the reform communist Gomulka.[29] Intellectuals largely benefited from the 1956 reforms; workers would be forced by circumstances to return to the streets in later decades.

Peaceful demonstrations of Hungarians in solidarity with the workers of Poznan eventually turned into an insurrection that defied the categories of reform from above and protest from below. After a group of insurgents had gone from peaceful demonstrations in support of changes in Poland to uprooting a Stalinist statue in the center of Budapest, to seizing weapons from a passive army, the Hungarian revolt from below became a national movement for self-determination: the famous 1956 uprising. Former Politburo member Imre Nagy was brought back to lead his country out of crisis. Keeping in close touch with Moscow, Nagy embarked on a policy of economic change and political rehabilitation that fulfilled many of the aspirations of the revolutionaries. As political scientist Ivan Volgyes points out, these activists

> wanted to re-establish Hungary's independence, to create a truly democratic state, to maintain the social advances made since 1945, and to ensure all the freedoms theoretically guaranteed in the Hungarian Constitution years earlier. They did not want to turn Hungary into an anti-Soviet base, to restore the old order, to

> re-establish capitalism in its pre-war form, or to throw the Communists in jail.[30]

The maneuvering space between the revolution from below and Moscow's dictates proved too narrow for Nagy. He eventually sided with the revolutionaries. His announcement of Hungary's withdrawal from the Warsaw Pact only a year after the pact was formed prompted Soviet military intervention.

Apart from several coal miner strikes in Romania and periodic strikes in Yugoslavia, the locus of workers' opposition in Eastern Europe after 1956 would be in Poland. In the cities along the Baltic coast in 1970, workers revived the spirit of Poznan by challenging the government's proposed price increases. Several workers were shot by police in the subsequent crackdown, and the '56 reformer Gomulka lost his position to Edward Gierek, who guided the Polish economy into greater dependency on the West. In 1976, further worker protests in Radom and Warsaw resulted in arrests and prompted the creation of KOR, the Workers' Defense Committee, the first bridge in the opposition between workers and intellectuals.[31] Risking imprisonment themselves, KOR members worked on behalf of dismissed and jailed workers, creating in the process a new type of oppositional network, and demonstrating the usefulness of organized protest, however modest. By 1980, another round of proposed price increases produced another worker response, this time in the Baltic port of Gdansk. A recently dismissed shipyard electrician and veteran of the 1970 protests, Lech Walesa climbed over the gates of the Lenin Shipyard, first joining and then leading the Gdansk strike. The shipyard workers would eventually join with other striking workers, notably Silesian coal miners, to create the independent and world-famous Solidarity labor union.

Ten million strong in a country of less than 40 million, Solidarity represented a breakthrough for Eastern European opposition on a number of levels. The movement's sheer size and unity across specialities set a precedent for worker protests. From the outset, Polish workers transcended narrow demands for wage increases by articulating a comprehensive economic and political program that could be put on the negotiating table with the authorities. Finally, Solidarity brought together workers and intellectuals under a single umbrella.[32] The KOR activists, with new additions such as medieval historian Bronislaw Geremek and editor Tadeusz Mazowiecki, did not prepare workers' consciousness or shape an inchoate grassroots movement. Rather, as historian Lawrence Goodwyn persuasively argues, the workers guided the movement, frequently overcoming the hesitancy of the intellectuals.[33] By 1989 the situation had changed: Geremek would become the head of Solidarity's parliamentary faction, Mazowiecki would become Poland's first non-communist prime minister in over four decades, and the workers would be left with all the pain and none of the glory.

Intellectuals

The very words "Central Europe" conjure up a cultural atmosphere both rich and refined: Freud, Kafka, Curie, Ionesco, Mucha, Celan, Brancusi, Ebner-Eschenbach, Mahler. In this land of the imagination, the *intelligentsia* represented a class which has no direct equivalent in Western Europe or the United States.[34] While two world wars and imposed Stalinism certainly have taken their toll on the *intelligentsia,* that pre-war tradition has nonetheless survived. Contrary to the stereotype of a grey and rigidly conformist culture, Eastern Europe has produced a brilliant mixture of intellectual products in the post-war era—the critical works of Miklos Haraszti and Milovan Djilas; the novels of Stefan Heym, Christa Wolf, Gyorgy Konrad, and Bohomil Hrabal; the poetry of Mircea Dinescu and Blaga Dimitrova; the plays of Vaclav Havel and the experimental theater of Jerzy Grotowski; the philosophy of Leszek Kolakowski and the Praxis group; the economic theory of Janos Kornai and Ota Sik; the films of Milos Forman and Andrzej Wajda; the music of the Leipzig Symphony Orchestra and the rock band Plastic People of the Universe; the theater and painting of Tadeusz Kantor; the socialist surrealism of Poland's Orange Alternative. The list is seemingly inexhaustible.

The relationship between intellectuals and the communist state was tempestuous. Initially, many intellectuals, including writers such as Bertolt Brecht, Milan Kundera, and Tadeusz Konwicki, enthusiastically enlisted in the ranks of Eastern European communism. Many others were imprisoned, censored, or fired from their academic positions for their heterodox views. Of the latter, some chose exile and established reputations in the West. Others took non-intellectual jobs or kept their true beliefs hidden in order to maintain jobs in the academies. In the early years of communism, intellectual revolt could not survive for long outside the party. Most effective criticisms were delivered within party congresses or official professional circles.

Since the state attempted to control cultural norms, intellectuals could not operate in an independent public space. As Hungary's Miklos Haraszti noted in his celebrated essay *The Velvet Prison,* "The edifice of art is built out of the very barriers put before it by the state. We skillfully reshuffle the formations around the walls of the house of art. We learn to live with discipline; we are at home with it."[35] While state-controlled culture might have been a "velvet prison" for many cultural figures in the region, others such as Czech playwright Vaclav Havel crossed over the line of polite criticism and endured stays in real prison on behalf of their commitments.

The break with communism came at different times and in different ways for East European intellectuals. The first wave consisted of the revisionists. "Sooner or later," former Marxist intellectual Leszek Kolakowski writes, "obedience proved to be unbearable and irreconcilable with intellectual claims, and those among the intellectuals who did not completely renounce obedience and attack the doctrine from the outside but rather attempted to improve it from the inside, were especially destructive."[36] Of this latter group, Hungarian intellectuals were particularly influential. Intellectual guidance of the 1956 uprising—through the Writers' Association, the Petofi Circle, and the shock troops of energetic students—was anti-Soviet but not for the most part anti-Marxist.[37] Milovan Djilas' *The New Class* (1957) combined the *intelligentsia's* traditional horror of bureaucracy—a la Gogol and Kafka—with its new-found distaste for communist privilege. Jacek Kuron and Karol Modzelewski wrote an open letter to the Party in 1963 that contrasted the exalted theory and the impoverished practice of Polish communism. But these were critiques from within the Marxist tradition, not unlike Trotsky's dissection of Stalinism's defects.

These last attempts of intellectuals for reform from within—the revisionists' project—would find final expression in the Prague Spring. In Dubcek's experiment with socialist humanism, intellectuals rallied with great vigor to the cause of remodeling state and party, in a reprise of the enthusiasm of many Soviet intellectuals in the aftermath of the Bolshevik revolution. While the Soviet invasion of Czechoslovakia accelerated the growth of Eurocommunism in the West, it also dashed intellectual hopes that East European communism could be reformed internally. Except for a group of East German activists, opposition intellectuals would no longer talk of "socialism with a human face." For opposition intellectuals, 1968 spelled the end of politics as usual. Deprived of the reform-from-within option, these intellectuals came to embrace what Hungarian novelist Gyorgy Konrad would later call anti-politics. The Party had so poisoned the political sphere that committed intellectuals had to renounce politics altogether, turning instead to "civil society." This latter concept, drawn from a long line of theorists from Rousseau to Gramsci, emphasized social and cultural organizations independent of state interference. As Polish dissident Adam Michnik strategized in his essay "The New Evolutionism," these institutions of civil society would gradually grow stronger, take back social space previously ceded to the state, and achieve the revolutionary demands of political pluralism and cultural freedom at the incremental pace of reform.[38] The communist party would lose more and more responsibilities, eventually becoming a figurehead, not substantially different from the English queen.[39]

One organization to symbolize this new form of opposition in Eastern Europe was Charter 77 in Czechoslovakia. Established in 1977 by philosopher Jan Patocka, this "group" simply called on the Czechoslovak government to honor the protocol on human rights that it had signed in Helsinki along with the Soviet Union, the United States, Canada, and 32 European countries. A modest collection of anti-politicians, Charter 77 came to represent the aspirations of all those who, as Vaclav Havel put it, wanted to "live in truth." As its founding statement declared, "Charter 77 is not an organization...[it] does not constitute an organized political opposition. It only supports the common good, as do many similar organizations that promote civic initiative in both the East and West."[40] Here was the prototypical anti-political structure, one that explicitly rejected both politics and structures. It would champion above all the notion of civil society and, in so doing, greatly influence other intellectual movements in the region, from the democratic opposition in Hungary to the emerging human rights activists in Poland, Bulgaria, Romania, Yugoslavia, and the GDR.[41]

Religion

Central and Eastern Europe has traditionally been a land split by religious controversy. Martin Luther preached in a church in Wittenberg that would later become part of East Germany, Jan Hus led a band of Bohemian reformers against the Catholic Church in the 15th century, the Bogomils spread an anti-materialist heresy throughout the Balkans in the early part of the millenium. The Catholic Habsburgs consistently persecuted Protestant sects. The Ottoman empire conducted Islamization campaigns in the Balkans and then, after its withdrawal and collapse, left behind ethnic Turks who were in turn subjected to repression. From the East, the Russian empire tried to impose its brand of orthodoxy. Lacking an empire or even a nation, Jews suffered discrimination at the hands of different faiths at different times.

Atheism became official state policy in the region after World War II, but it was only in Albania that religion was explicitly outlawed. Elsewhere, after the universal repressions of the Stalinist years, the communist governments adopted critical but usually indifferent attitudes. Even that indifference frequently dissipated when the authorities realized to what advantages religion could be shaped. Christian, Jewish, and Islamic leaders were often brought into a close relationship with state authorities through the creation of state-sponsored religious councils. Both sides benefited from the arrangement. The state could rely on the churches for social control while the religious institutions, invoking centuries-old survival techniques, proceeded to safeguard their power base. As Poland's Cardinal Stefan Wyszynski characterized the delicate position: "The Church in Poland does not intend to fight with the system or the State...if we expect anything, it is above all wider margin and freedom for the Church. Certainly we shall not misuse it against the Nation or the State."[42]

Despite this comfortable relationship between two upholders of the status quo, various movements within the religious communities were able to challenge the party line. In Poland, where over 90 percent of the citizens consider themselves Catholic, church institutions became overtly political during the 1956 thaw. One stream formed Catholic political parties (Znak, Pax, Christian Social Association) which then maintained an occasionally critical position in Parliament. Another stream remained outside party politics, establishing the only truly independent newspaper in Eastern Europe, Krakow's *Tygodnik Powszechny,* and the influential KIK, or Club of Catholic Intellectuals.[43]

During later movements from below, notably 1970 and 1976, Polish workers used religious symbols and themes to make political statements. When granted an opportunity to erect a monument to workers who had fallen in previous years, Solidarity placed an enormous structure in front of the Lenin Shipyards of Gdansk: three towering crosses crucifying three anchors. Visits by the Polish Pope in 1979 and 1983 also contributed to the general atmosphere of change, the first trip providing a religious basis for oppositional activities, the second offering solace and inspiration in the closing days of martial law. The murder of Polish priest Jerzy Popieluszko in 1984 by security police violated a longstanding and informal arrangement between Church and state, only deepening the ties between Church and opposition.

After the early state campaign against organized religion, the East German Evangelical Lutheran Church gradually accepted its position in socialism, as opposed to being *for* or *against* socialism.[44] When politics could no longer be freely discussed in public, the Lutheran Evangelical Church often provided the space and the opportunity for interchanges that in more democratic countries would have taken place in party headquarters or town halls. Although the Church here too had an official relationship with the state, individual pastors frequently pursued independent lines. As the novelist Stefan Heym quipped in 1982: "In East Germany today the clerics are now talking like revolutionaries while the functionaries are talking like priests."[45] One of those revolutionary clerics, Reiner Epplemann (who ironically would later serve as the GDR's defense minister), conducted "Blues Services" with a distinctly anti-militaristic message that appealed especially to young people.[46] By 1982, Epplemann and others had issued the Berlin Appeal calling on both blocs to remove their nuclear weapons from Europe and all occupying forces to be withdrawn from Germany. This evenhanded appeal resulted in Epplemann's immediate arrest.[47]

Many religious leaders were active in East Germany's peace movement in the early 1980s, challenging military service and education within the GDR and cultivating contacts with Western peace and religious movements.[48] During the 1989 revolution, church leaders continued to play a role. "Without the Church, the changes would have taken longer," Peter Zimmermann, a Leipzig theologian instrumental in the demonstrations, has said. "The changes probably would have been violent and might have resulted in a civil war."[49]

Particular religious leaders in other countries provided inspiration to popular movements. Vaclav Maly and Frantisek Cardinal Tomasek in Czechoslovakia and Laszlo Tokes in Romania attracted the enmity of the authorities by taking prominent positions on human rights and religious freedoms. In Hungary, elements of the religious community worked with the peace movement, encouraging discussions of both pacifism and conscientious objection to military service.[50]

Peace, human rights, and ecology

In the early 1980s, the presence of Soviet SS-20 intermediate-range missiles in Eastern Europe and US Pershing II and Cruise missiles in Western Europe galvanized an enormous peace movement in the West. Less well-known were the peace movements in the East. Putting their regime's stated commitment to peace into practice, these movements in Eastern Europe worked closely with Western European movements such as END (European Nuclear Disarmament), IKV (Dutch Interchurch Peace Council), and CODENE (Committee for Nuclear Disarmament in Europe) in calling for the removal of nuclear arsenals from Europe by *both* blocs. The East German peace movement, with church connections and the help of West German Greens, was perhaps most prominent and encompassed the campaign for alternative military service, Dresden's Peace Forum, peace protests in Jena, and women's peace groups in East Berlin.[51] The contradiction between the GDR government's espousal of peace and its arrests and expulsions of peace activists further decreased its political legitimacy.[52]

The Dialogue group in Hungary also challenged the authorities on the peace issue, joining with other, smaller groups to recapture the language of peace that had been corrupted through banal and substanceless repetition by both superpowers (the North American "Peace through strength" and nuclear "peace-keeper" missiles; the Soviet "struggle for peace").[53] Independent peace demonstrations also broke out in several Yugoslav cities. Poland's Freedom and Peace (WiP) challenged compulsory military service on pacifist grounds. Even Charter 77, though carefully disavowing that it was a peace movement, maintained close contact with Western peace organizations because of similar values and a comparable civic spirit.[54]

At the intersection of peace and human rights, the grassroots movements East and West had perhaps the most successful cooperation. Peace activists from the West, in organizations such as the US Campaign for Peace and Democracy/East and West, brought the anti-militarism message east and insisted on including the human rights abuses of the Soviet system on the agendas of Western peace organizations. The cooperation across borders by citizens and non-governmental organizations was not always untroubled. But movements from below nonetheless played a central role in ending the Cold War.[55]

The degraded natural environment of Eastern Europe inevitably spawned Green and proto-Green movements in the region. In some countries, notably Hungary, environmental topics even served as a substitute for explicit political debate. In 1980, the Polish Ecological Club was founded in Krakow and attracted support from Solidarity and other civic groups. The churches in the GDR also joined ecological issues to their peace appeals. It was the Chernobyl accident in the fall of 1985, however, that really awakened Green consciousness. Fallout from the nuclear reactor accident outside of Kiev in Ukraine spread throughout Eastern Europe, contaminating crops and endangering vulnerable populations. As a consequence, particularly outspoken anti-nuclear power protests broke out in Poland, East Germany, and Yugoslavia.[56]

National and transnational movements

Nationalism did not disappear from Eastern Europe during the Cold War. Although communism has at its core an internationalist philosophy, communist governments in Eastern Europe frequently appealed to national values for additional legitimacy. It is no accident that many of the communist political fronts were named for the "fatherland." Organizations put into place after domestic crackdowns, such as Poland's Patriotic Movement for National Renewal (PRON) from 1982, used a rhetoric derived more from pre-World War II national traditions than Marx's internationalist aims.

Nationalism was not the exclusive property of the communists. Movements from below rooted in pre-communist national traditions posed a great threat to the communist order.[57] Perhaps realizing the immense energy that nationalism could kindle, communist governments in the region were careful to isolate and destroy these nationalist heresies. Sometimes these movements, such as the Confederation for an Independent Poland (KPN), argued for national independence for the country as a whole. Sometimes movements emerged calling for the independence of "swallowed" nations: Croatia, Slovakia, Transylvania. Or ethnic peoples struggled for rights independent of nationhood, for instance ethnic Turks in Bulgaria, or Gypsies throughout the region. Although the events of 1989-90 have fulfilled the goals of groups such as KPN, the "national" question remains unresolved in the region, cropping up in debates over ethnic rights (as in Bulgaria) or bloody conflicts over state structure (as in Yugoslavia).

While communists borrowed nationalist language from their previous opponents, some opposition movements incorporated into their activities the internationalism of the communists. The *intelligentsia* is often called cosmopolitan since it values membership in an intellectual community that cuts across national boundaries. Demonstrating this cosmopolitan spirit, the intellectual activists in Eastern Europe frequently met in the 1970s and 1980s—covertly, discreetly, sometimes in the West or through Western intermediaries. Charter 77 and KOR activists met on several occasions, members of the democratic opposition in Hungary maintained contacts with opposition activists in Romania, and Yugoslav activists took advantage of their relative freedom of movement to visit with their counterparts abroad. In the 1980s, in particular, the traffic among movements increased as organizations closely followed the appeals, arrests, and activities of one another in an informal network that played a critical role in preparing for the revolutions of 1989.

The nationalism historically so strong in the region appeared to be almost non-existent at this level of contact. In the Polish tradition of "for your freedom and ours," Solidarity had truly demonstrated its internationalism by reaching out to other nascent opposition movements in the region, as well as strongly condemning apartheid in South Africa and the jailing of Chilean unionists. A 1988 Charter 77 appeal in solidarity with the people of Romania, sponsored as well by Polish, Hungarian, and Soviet activists, replaces nationalism's exclusivity with an extraordinary empathy: not merely for one jailed dissident or one beleaguered movement, but for an entire oppressed people.[58]

* * *

In 1985, the two varieties of reform collided. From above, in the Soviet Union, Gorbachev was forcing reform upon a largely unwilling party structure. It was a classic case of reform forestalling revolution. If we don't transform the apparatus, Gorbachev told his colleagues, Soviet society will slide further into stagnation and our positions will become that much less tenable. Closely following economic reforms in Hungary and Yugoslavia, mindful of the trade-off between economic reforms and political freedoms in Poland, and seeing in the East German and Bulgarian parties a reflection of the most stubborn elements of his own, Gorbachev reversed the Soviet role in Eastern Europe from a brake on reform to its chief proselytizer. It is no contradiction, then, that East German youth chanted Gorbachev's name at a rally in 1987 along with "Down with the Wall." Gorbachev's moves since 1985 emboldened leaders in Poland and Hungary to liberalize, leading to the roundtables of 1989. More importantly, the Soviet leader gradually withdrew support from hardline leaders, creating the political space for the opposition movements described above to mobilize support on a large scale.

Some in the West have argued that the Star Wars (SDI) approach led to the end of the Cold War, that extravagant military outlays by the United States provoked similar Soviet expenditures which broke the Soviet economy and led to a deterioration in military control of Eastern Europe.[59] Star Wars certainly made Soviet military expenditures more expensive in the 1980s. But Star Wars did not produce Gorbachev or fashion his program. Nor did Star Wars create the opposition movements in Eastern Europe. While certain US virtues may have inspired these grassroots activists (the Constitution, Martin Luther King, the peace movement), highly sophisticated military technology of highly questionable utility provided little impetus.

This is not to suggest that cycles of East-West relations did not affect developments in the region. The creation of the Warsaw Pact in 1955 was in part a reaction to the acceptance of West Germany into NATO, only ten years after the end of the war. The Suez crisis of 1956 provided a cover for the Soviet invasion of Budapest. The Kennedy and Johnson administrations' touting of "flexible response" that justified US participation in conventional war in Europe led to the stationing of Warsaw Pact troops in Czechoslovakia.[60] Detente in the Nixon years created a climate in which Eurocommunism could flourish. Heightened East-West hostilities in the early Reagan years narrowed the options for Polish authorities coping with the Solidarity movement. Here, though, the fallacy of the SDI argument becomes apparent: hardline politics adopted by both blocs during the height of the Cold War generally produced nothing but hardline responses. Furthermore, the influence of Western economic institutions on Eastern European governments did contribute to the instability that eventually led to revolution. Both multilateral organizations such as the IMF and particular Western governments encouraged economic and political trends that pushed Eastern Europe further from the Soviet model. Capital provided to the region's governments throughout the 1970s came with strings attached; when recession hit in the 1980s, the international economic community began to pull these strings more vigorously.[61]

These various factors—reforms from above and protests from below, economic and political crises within the region, Western economic manipulation, Gorbachev's ascension to power in the Soviet Union, detente in US-Soviet relations—overdetermined, to borrow a term from sociology, the revolutions of 1989.

* * *

The philosophies of the various opposition movements shaped the strategies and concerns of the revolutionary period. Those movements steeped in nonviolence managed to bring about radical changes without the loss of life. The experiences of peace and Green activists led many of the revolutionary movements to call for an end to the military bloc system and an immediate cleanup of environmental hazards. Workers who maintained faith in enterprise self-management would try to apply this belief to post-communist economics. Human rights activists would carry over a concern for individual liberties and moral principles. Never given a chance to encounter the compromises of politicking, the underground movements maintained a certain abstract purity in their beliefs. Such oppositionists turned out to be successful revolutionaries. But when the revolutionaries tried to translate their philosophies into public policy, the results, as we shall see in the following chapters, have been decidedly mixed.

Centuries of occupation, marginalization, and economic underdevelopment have shaped Eastern Europe's relationship to European culture. Stalin provided an economic model to bring the region into the modern age. The opposition movements challenged the communist political order. The following chapters will look at the new political, economic, and cultural models being implemented in Eastern Europe, the degree to which they have roots in the history described in the previous chapters, the manner by which they are being encouraged from outside, the mechanisms through which they are being imposed from above, and the way they are being challenged once again from below.

Part Two

After the Revolutions

Chapter 4

East Germany... A shortcut to democracy

These parties are too good to receive any votes.

—Security guard at the House for Democracy

In East Berlin's high-rent district, not far from the showpiece Grand Hotel and the historic avenue Unter den Linden, the orchestrators of East Germany's revolution sat in their House for Democracy. Once the East German Communist Party's regional headquarters, the building had become home to the small, citizen-based parties and movements that had led the fight against the communist authorities. In 1990, that grand year of newly minted pluralism and first-time free elections, the House projected all the exuberance of an East European opposition: frenetic and haphazard, fresh and exciting, poor yet noble. And diverse. The conservative Democratic Awakening attracted the jacket-and-tie crowd. Activists from the Marxist United Left favored the bearded and crumpled look. Bespectacled Greens and feminists from the Independent Women's Association planned election strategy in cluttered offices.

In 1990, on the eve of East Germany's first (and only) free national elections, the House for Democracy seemed very much like Solidarity headquarters in Warsaw or Civic Forum's building on Wenceslas Square in Prague. Opposition nerve center. The heart of the struggle. The eyes and ears of the new political generation.

But the House for Democracy was none of these things. Having indeed led East Germany through its revolution, the groups and movements that filled the House would after the elections occupy but a small corner of the new Parliament. For all its similarities to the headquarters of its victorious counterparts throughout Eastern Europe, the House for Democracy was really at the fringes of East German politics. The foreign media, covering the first entirely free election in the region, emphasized by omission the House's marginality: newspaper reporters were more frequently seen around the corner at the headquarters of the election winners, the Christian Democratic Union (CDU). More resembling a bank or a consulate than a party headquarters, the CDU's building oozed wealth and status with its posters of Chancellor Helmut Kohl on the walls inside and the BMWs and Benzes parked on the street outside. Occasionally a reporter might wander back over to the House for Democracy to research an ironic profile highlighting the movement's journey from revolutionary center to electoral periphery.[1]

Such irony did not sit well with the inhabitants of the House. Both the election campaign and the election results had left them with a bitter taste of party-run pluralism. "We wanted to construct an alternative to Stalinism and capitalism," Thomas Klein of the United Left said, "but there was not enough political clarity and foundation for such an alternative." Reinhard Weisshuhn of the Initiative for Peace and Human Rights was more emphatic: "Before we had a single party dictatorship. Now there is a multi-party dictatorship." Petra Wunderlich of the Independent Women's Association expressed anger at the political infighting that had cost them the parliamentary seats promised by their coalition partner, the Greens.[2]

The residents of the House for Democracy who held the most electoral promise were grouped in Alliance '90: a coalition of the five-year-old Initiative for Peace and Human Rights, and the two most prominent groups to emerge during the East German revolution, New Forum and Democracy Now. Alliance '90 received only 3 percent of the vote in the GDR elections, enough to send representatives to the new parliament but not exactly a mandate from the grassroots.

How did this happen? How did revolutionary leaders become electoral losers in little over four months?

It might seem perverse to begin a tour of Eastern Europe with a country that no longer exists, and even odder to focus on a political movement that polled so poorly in this former country's only free and independent national elections. An examination of Alliance '90, however, highlights the critical choices facing political movements in Eastern Europe during its transition: democratic spirit versus democratic procedure, movements versus parties, civil society versus technocracy, principle versus compromise. The fate of Alliance '90 illustrates most visibly the dissipation of the revolutionary spirit in Eastern Europe. What happened to the East German coalition as an organization is ultimately what has happened to the revolutionary components of all the popular front movements throughout the region. As for the national disappearance of East Germany—absorbed into Western Europe from one day to the next—that too may anticipate trends for the region as a whole.

The golden age

For supporters of a single "Fatherland," the unification of East and West Germany could not have been smoother. The Berlin Wall fell in November 1989; less than one year later, Berlin was officially one city, Germany officially one country. The death of East Germany, according to one observer, received an "obituary without tears."[3] For the leaders of East Germany's grassroots movements, however, these watershed events in their country's brief independent existence—territorial unification with West Germany in October 1990, monetary union the previous July, national elections the March before that—were not entirely positive developments. Even the collapse of the Berlin Wall was not an occasion for unrestrained celebration.

For the activists who would eventually form Alliance '90, the fall of the Wall marked the end of the revolution's golden age, begun scarcely a month earlier with the first unharassed demonstration in the southern city of Leipzig. During this month, all dreams of an East Germany independent and democratic seemed possible. After West Germany poured through the hole in the Wall and into the consciousness of the East, the mood shifted, the political agenda of the opposition changed, and even the chants of the demonstrators underwent a subtle grammatical alteration: the *das Volk* (a People) of a democratic popular movement became the *ein Volk* (one People) of a nationally inspired unification. "As soon as the border was opened, the revolution was over," reported one movement leader.[4] Or put another way, the *first* revolution was over and the *second*, orchestrated in large part by West Germany, was about to begin.

During the first revolution, the golden age of newly experienced freedoms, the civic movements enjoyed their greatest support. The most prominent of these movements, New Forum, was founded in the middle of September 1989 by a collection of long-time dissidents, former communists, peace activists, pastors, and disaffected academics. New Forum was something entirely new for East Germany: an organized, mainstream movement of dissent. With a new non-communist government in Poland and the communists giving ground in Hungary, a new potential for change had opened up in the GDR. New Forum tried to tap this potential, as co-founder Jens Reich pointed out, by reaching out from the marginal dissidents to the "more respectable middle-aged generation."[5] The more orthodox dissidents, New Forum co-founder Barbel Bohley argued at the time, "have to learn that something has happened in society that does not necessarily have anything to do with them. They laid the foundation stone for it but it has to do with people's own experiences."[6] Bohley's criticism of the dissident community's isolation from the temper of the times would ultimately come back to haunt her and her group.

New Forum gained its fame not from a clearly-stated program but chiefly from denunciations by the communist government. For East German demonstrators massing in the tens and hundreds of thousands on the streets of Dresden, Leipzig, and Berlin, this critical stance offset any lack of specific information about the group. The ignorance of the demonstrators was entirely warranted; even New Forum members were hard-pressed to describe the group's aims. Their "Founding Appeal" called for "more and better consumer goods," but questioned "growth at any price," supported the GDR's entry into "international trade and commerce" but rejected debt dependence. The strongest and least equivocal statements articulated a pro-ecology stance and support for "the broadest public participation." But these were preferences, not concrete suggestions.[7] As Bohley confessed one month after New Forum's creation: "On the one hand, we reject the tutelage of the state, on the other we don't know how democracy really looks. Now some are calling for a program. We have to have patience."[8]

Patience is a virtue rarely cultivated in revolutionary situations. Many East Germans—30,000 that September alone—had already declared through emigration that they were not interested in waiting for domestic change.[9] Fleeing in large numbers, East Germans trekked eastward to go west—through Hungary into Austria, over the walls of West German embassies in Warsaw and Prague to get to the land that still lay inaccessible beyond the Wall. With an opportunity to stanch this flow with a positive platform for rapid change, New Forum maintained a frustrating silence. In lieu of programs, it issued proclamations. "Even more devastating," writes one sympathetic critic, "was the opposition's intellectual weakness, as it tried to cover up for its lack of professional expertise with empty and forced incantations about the need for a 'Third Way.'"[10] Without concrete political and economic suggestions, the opposition groups sounded, as Garton Ash put it, "vague, inchoate, uncertain. The alternative offered by West Germany was just so immediately, so obviously, so overwhelmingly plausible."[11]

In early December, with the Wall down and the Communist Party limping along in power, the government and the opposition met in a roundtable to hammer out an agreement on free elections. The opposition was represented by New Forum and six independent parties (Democracy Now, Democratic Awakening, the Greens, United Left, Free Democrats, Social Democrats).[12] With its revolutionary credentials, New Forum played an influential role in these negotiations. But the time for revolutionary movements had already come and gone; indeed, the time for roundtables had passed. Kohl had announced his ten-point plan for reunification at the end of November. The reunification taboo had crumbled with the Wall. Devoting their attentions to a new constitution and an elaborately worked-out social charter, the citizens' movements were preparing for a GDR that would have only temporary existence.[13]

With election guidelines established by the beginning of 1990, East Germans began to look for a West German-style party that could provide them with West German-style solutions. There was the relative latecomer, the Christian Democratic Union, wooed by Helmut Kohl away from its previous position in the Communist Party coalition. But the most popular choice in the early days of 1990 was clearly the Social Democrats who were thought most likely to take advantage of the presumably strong social ethic of East Germans.[14] With the experience and the finances of their West German partners, these new East German parties quickly put distance between themselves and the revolutionary movements. By February, polls showed the Social Democrats with a commanding lead, followed by the reformed and renamed Communist Party (the Party of Democratic Socialism), the Christian Democrats, and then all other movements and parties with less than 3 percent each.[15] As the March elections approached, however, the Christian Democrats were able to use the promise of rapid unification—and overnight prosperity for East Germans—to overtake the Social Democrats and win the contest handily.

The plausibility of the West German model and the vagueness of the New Forum platform were not the only reasons for this surprising outcome. The difference between the platforms of New Forum and the Christian Democrats, for instance, had less to do with plausibility than with power. New Forum called on East Germans to rebuild their society; the Christian Democrats called on West Germany to do the same job. Stated another way, the CDU offered things while New Forum offered ideas. A refrigerator in every home, a car in every garage—these promises are only more plausible than the dream of autonomy if the offering party has the perceived power to carry them out. That the CDU promises of instant wealth were exaggerated did not matter. East Germans were not accustomed to the bait-and-switch of capitalism. (After unification they would fall prey to every scheme cooked up by West German sharks, losing, according to one estimate, $2 billion alone in insurance rip-offs.)[16] Indeed, these CDU promises were the vaguest aspects of the entire campaign; unification was discussed not in terms of specifics but in terms of pace—fast or slow, next week or next year. When the parties offered concrete suggestions on other issues—such as demilitarization or liquidation of the secret police—the ideas had often originated with the citizens' movements.

The confrontation between "implausible" ideas and "plausible" materialism was not unique to post-revolutionary GDR. In the previous era, the communist government played the role of West Germany, responding to the 1953 uprising, for instance, by substituting economic progress for political freedoms. East Germans, from 1953 on, would struggle with the contradiction of relative prosperity and virtually no civil society. Long before laptops and Audis represented the rewards of unification, East Germans had accepted political dependence in exchange for a rising standard of living. Opposition based on "implausible" ideas was restricted to a relatively small circle of intellectuals drawn primarily from the ranks of the Communist Party itself. Bertolt Brecht, a leading Marxist supporter of the new regime, turned around in 1956 and called then Party leader Walter Ulbricht a dictator. Dissidents from within the Party—Wolfgang Harich, Robert Havemann, Christa Wolf—at various times tried to push for a "Berlin Spring." Popular songwriter Wolfgang Biermann, an early advocate of *glasnost,* was expelled from the GDR in 1977. These intellectuals managed to infuriate the state, but they had less success in appealing to the public at large. Compared to the undeniable economic growth sponsored by the communist government, the ideas of these dissidents might have appeared sadly abstract.

In the late 1970s, the most influential critique of East German communism came from Rudolf Bahro, an economist and former trade union official. When sections of his book *The Alternative in Eastern Europe* were published in a West German magazine, Bahro was promptly arrested, guaranteeing even greater interest in his manuscript in the West. Although most opposition movements had abandoned the rhetoric of "socialism with a human face" after the Soviet invasion of Czechoslovakia, Bahro maintained that, distortions eliminated, socialism could be perfected in East Germany.[17] Attacking the conservatism of ruling communist parties and calling for the creation of "space for public discussion of the 'burning questions of our movement,'" Bahro concluded that communism "is not only necessary, it is also possible."[18] These were critiques from within the system, taking communism to task not for any systemic problems but chiefly for its absorption of Western-style materialism and consumerism. Such a book, had it been written in Poland at that time, might have found an official publishing house; in more orthodox East Germany, however, *The Alternative* was grounds for expulsion.

Nourished by a burgeoning peace movement in the early 1980s and then the rise of Gorbachev in the USSR in 1985, the GDR dissident community managed to keep the Prague Spring flame burning, despite the turn away from reform socialism within the other Eastern European oppositions.[19] Canadian sympathizer Bruce Allen described this program as "a form of Democratic Socialism, freed by means of socialization and decentralization from the system of growth at any price and oriented towards an ecological humanism."[20] During the 1989 revolution, this vision translated into an independent East Germany that selected the best from the past 45 years—the guarantees of women's rights, a well-developed social safety net—and combined it with elements of Western-style grassroots politics. It was radical democratic politics influenced by Marxist humanism and post-Chernobyl ecological concerns. The plausible materialism of both Eastern communism and Western capitalism was not so much rejected as disdained.

Although modified by the concerns of a larger cross-section of the population, these theories and theorists guided the GDR's first revolution during the golden month before the fall of the Berlin Wall. This pre-Wall revolution, led by New Forum, might have established, after negotiations with or ouster of the communist authorities, an East Germany independent, democratic, and socialist. But this first revolution existed in a time-warp circa 1968, when a humane communism was still a popular option. However noble the aims, this initial revolution was doomed to disintegrate, like cave paintings that are effaced by exposure to modern air. Framed in the idealistic rhetoric of the GDR opposition, the platform conflicted with the ingrained materialism of the GDR population. Cast as populist, the philosophy did not attract enough people to maintain itself as a mass phenomenon. In weakening the communist leadership and ushering in an electoral age, the initial revolutionaries fulfilled their limited objectives and prepared for their own eventual failure.

The post-Wall revolution dispensed with theorists, weak, inexperienced, or otherwise.[21] It needed no *philosophes,* no intellectuals, no dissidents, and certainly no Marxists. It proceeded by practical example: the experience and influence of West Germany. As soon as the Wall fell in November, East German citizens went west, and West German political consultants rushed east. The citizens looked, the consultants talked, and each group, in its own way, achieved in several days what years of dissident work had failed to accomplish: an East German movement unified in its aims. New Forum and the citizens' groups were left without consultants and without constituency. Oblivious to the groups located at the House for Democracy, the Social Democrats and the Christian Democrats fought a war of promises and campaign budgets. Inflated in both departments, the Christian Democrats easily coasted to victory.

While the first revolution still lingered on within the platforms of the increasingly marginalized civic movements and during the discussions of the numerous regional and local roundtables, the trend toward consumerism and Western-style political parties was inescapable. Some activists prominent in the first revolution simply accepted the new state of affairs and enlisted in the second revolution as well. Hans Mislivitz, a pastor in a town outside Berlin, organized steelworkers and intellectuals during the golden age. By December 1989, however, Mislivitz had left the citizens' movement to join the Social Democratic Party. "It was also my idea to change society and attack the totalitarian structures," he said after the March 1990 elections. "But once this state broke down, we had to ask ourselves: who could take over responsibility and who could do this at a time when the majority of the people want re-unification?" Mislivitz realized that the noble ideals of the first revolution had to be squared with the popular desires generated by the second.

> We had to learn—and all the revolutionaries had to learn—that it was not only their creation. The deeper change came from the breakdown of the society and the breakdown of trust in the system. The citizens' movement multiplied this effect in a very necessary way, but you could not have a type of democracy based on an activist stance. The majority did not want to be activists or to be engaged—they wanted a new society but one that was very close to West Germany. You couldn't neglect it and say: "they all betray our nice revolution." Then you will simply become a memorial of that revolution. We have a great political responsibility to offer solutions to the people which they and not just we can use. We should not be avant-garde. This is an old type of revolution which leads into totalitarianism. That is the lesson of history.[22]

Despite numerous defections to the parties, the citizens' movements labored on after their first glorious month. While a second revolution shaped the political debate in East Germany in 1990, the initial revolutionaries struggled to elaborate their alternative.

Civil society versus technocracy

At a meeting two weeks after the March 1990 elections, New Forum was facing a seemingly irresolvable paradox. The movement was looking for candidates for local elections. The ideal candidate should have some political experience. But the only people with political experience had belonged to the Communist Party or affiliated movements. And New Forum billed itself as a clean break from the past. So it wanted candidates with "clean" records. But such people had no political experience. And people with no political experience were reluctant to run for political office.

Other countries solved the problem by accepting non-politicians as their representatives: Lech Walesa the electrician, Vaclav Havel the playwright, Zheliu Zhelev the historian, Arpad Goncz the writer. In a 1990 interview with the new magazine *Respekt,* Havel explained the attitude: "...the people who work the best and the most professionally are those who aren't themselves professionals. And the people who fulfill their duties the best are those whom it took a long time to talk into accepting their posts."[23]

But New Forum was not simply interested in persuading people to become politicians. Rather, it wanted to create a different kind of political system, one that valued civic participation over party professionalism, democratic accountability over administrative efficiency, *ethike* (ethical conduct) over *techne* (technical expertise). Parties and professional politicians represented both the communist *and* the capitalist solution. New Forum proposed in their place a more participatory model involving roundtables at every level of society. But such a model required a new group of politicized citizens skilled in movement organizing and roundtable negotiations. New Forum included many such people; it lacked, on the other hand, proto-politicians to run for office.

An astrophysicist from Potsdam, Helmut Domke worked for a number of years in peace and Lutheran Church circles. He also participated in the committee to dissolve Potsdam's Stasi (security police). Like many New Forum supporters, he found party politics wanting and the roundtables more consistent with active, thriving participatory democracy. "Roundtables are a remarkable feature of these transitions and they will end," he said regretfully in 1990.

> But the spirit of the roundtable should not be lost. It can be retained if roundtables can be organized for particular issues, where you can get a kind of consensus or broad acceptance necessary for a healthy society. The roundtable approach can be used in forming government decisions. It would be an interesting retention of our experience of the democratic process from the past year. This would be in order not to fall into a pure party democracy. Of course, the model of democracy in West Germany is much better than what we had here. But we would like to bring new elements into our new society.[24]

New Forum was caught in a peculiar predicament in 1990: espousing a political theory that the newly enfranchised citizenry did not support and participating in a political system for which it was ill-equipped both conceptually and financially. The roundtables, in spirit and practice, ended *and* New Forum failed at electoral politics. It could neither realize fully the first revolution nor engage successfully in the second. New Forum was caught midway between movement and party; it wanted both to remain in civil society and participate in the new power structure.

So frequently used in Eastern Europe, the concept of "civil society" has little currency in the United States (when used by one journalist in his dispatches, the expression was deleted by his editors because, they argued, readers wouldn't understand its meaning).[25] Simply put, civil society is a sphere of public activity independent of government.[26] Movements can maintain this independence; parties, however, orbit much closer around state power. New Forum never made up its mind, in part because the situation in East Germany was changing so rapidly. Since it never adequately defined its relationship to the state, New Forum was left with a rather amorphous platform. The citizens' movements were best known for sending hundreds of thousands of people to demonstrate in the streets. As exciting as those days had been, few East Germans wanted the future of the GDR to look anything like that. Unification and the Deutsche mark were compelling visions not only for the economic benefits that would potentially accrue to East Germans, but because they offered an assurance that the future would, in some ways, be just as stable as the communist past had been.

Instead of non-stop activism—a form of permanent revolution—most East German citizens preferred a less demanding solution: let the experts steer the course. Encouraged by West German politicians and their East German partners, this technocratic response—like the resurgent materialism—also had roots in GDR history. Between the 1950s and 1980s, the GDR, perhaps more than any other Eastern European government, perfected rule by experts. The members of the communist managerial class, like the "organization men" of US corporations in the 1950s, were team players who added their small contributions to the greater rationalized process.

Distinguished from the rest of the population by its privileges, this *nomenklatura* kept the relatively successful GDR economy running through technical proficiency, brute output, and careful negotiations with West Germany.[27] Economic problems were solved through fine-tuning the *kombinate*, the highly centralized system of enterprises. Politics in such a system was a necessary evil, resolving disputes among technocrats, not between citizens and the government. The state never consulted the public on critical policies; democracy would have disrupted the system's functioning. In the technocratic utopia, where all supposedly agree on the ends of social policy, there are no conflicts and thus no need for politics as we know it.[28] As long as the system "worked" (i.e., put food on the table), the non-experts permitted the experts to stage manage. When the ruling communists demonstrated inexcusable incompetence (and unprecedented weakness), the public balked, demanding a replacement of experts as much as a replacement of systems.

In the GDR's first revolution, the grassroots movement challenged many aspects of the previous technocracy: the false consensus, the economic tinkering, the substanceless political discussions, the spiritless populace, and the engrained materialism. Even as they offered an alternative, the movements themselves could not depart from certain technocratic assumptions. The members of the citizens' movements constantly asked themselves and colleagues in West Germany: Are we going about this revolution in the right way? Do we have enough expertise to propose alternative structures? Perhaps we should ask other people for advice.[29] Poland, Hungary, and Czechoslovakia had revolutionary precedents, dissident theorists, and, for a certain time after 1989, space independent from East and West. The East German revolutionaries could only navigate between their own inexperience and the quite obvious experience of West German consultants.

What was felt in the citizens' movement was more evident among the population at large. True, the average East German despised the Party, the Stasi, the *nomenklatura,* the official culture, the lack of autonomous social activity, and so on. While consciously criticizing the communist system, however, the GDR citizens also had internalized its reliance on experts, its overvaluation of Western models of testing economic efficiency, and its distaste for too much political participation from citizens. Therefore, when parties from the West entered the debate and offered, on a deeper level, a continuation of the technocratic policies of the past, the citizenry responded overwhelmingly. Even the Social Democrats, whose campaigning was inept and whose platform was even more amorphous than New Forum's, received over 20 percent of the vote. It was, after all, a party, and party status automatically conveyed expertise. Movements were almost by definition too inexperienced to lead a country through profound change.

Defeated in the March elections, and doing no better in the subsequent local elections, the civic groups arrived at a frustrating conclusion. The GDR possessed a unique opportunity to institute a brand new political model; few East Germans, however, were interested. Wolfgang Ullmann, a pastor and founder of Democracy Now who would be elected speaker of the East German Parliament, remained optimistic even in defeat. "Citizens' movements are very weak at the moment and their influence is limited. Their possibilities are limited," he said in 1990. "Parties are much more impressive and their impact is very strong as seen in the last election. But if you think about the future I am deeply convinced that it will be totally different. Really creative ideas—where do they come from? Not from the parties, but from us."[30]

The civic movements did put forward creative alternatives. But after the golden age of the first revolution and the triumph of the technocrats in the second, these alternatives would virtually evaporate.

The decline of alternatives

Although roundly defeated in the electoral arena, New Forum and its allies did succeed in shaping the way certain issues—the secret police, the military, and abortion rights—were handled by the East German government during its brief tenure of democratic rule. For instance, New Forum led the struggle against the infamous secret police known as the Stasi. Reportedly, 100,000 agents worked for the Stasi, with collaborators possibly numbering in the millions.[31] The organization collapsed with the communists, leaving behind 100 miles worth of files that had been kept on fully one-quarter of the GDR population. An estimated 20 percent of the information was destroyed during the revolutionary upheaval. To protect even more files from being destroyed after the revolution, grassroots committees sprang up all over East Germany. A national committee was also formed to handle the potentially explosive material. With so many influential people involved in the Stasi, it was not surprising to find a good deal of inertia, even outright hostility, within the upper echelons of German society to thorough de-Stasification.[32] The grassroots movements kept the Stasi issue prominent at a time when the new guardians of order would have preferred to handle the situation quietly. Moreover, New Forum's allegations of Stasi ties among high-level officials were not unfounded. The leader of the conservative Alliance of Germany, Wolfgang Schnur, was forced to resign shortly before the March elections when reports of his former Stasi connections surfaced. Later, after unification, former East German prime minister Lothar de Maiziere also resigned all party and government positions when his Stasi file showed up.

Another strongly-stated policy of New Forum was opposition to both NATO and the Warsaw Pact. While virtually every GDR party supported demilitarization (even the right-wing parties favored military cuts), Alliance '90 called for the dissolution of the bloc system and engaged in direct talks with the East German military on the issue. Many members of Alliance '90 had been members of the GDR peace movement and felt strongly about peace education and the issue of conscientious objection. Their views were translated into some brief but remarkable work by Reiner Epplemann in the Defense Ministry and Markus Meckel in the Foreign Ministry, both pastors and both active with the peace, religious, and human rights movements in the 1980s. With unification and Soviet acquiescence, however, the eastern part of Germany became part of NATO, geopolitics sweeping aside all talk of neutrality.

East German "uniqueness" was recognized, if only temporarily, on the issue of abortion rights. For 45 years, abortion had been legal and inexpensive for East German women. When unification became a distinct possibility, women in the GDR discovered that the West German law on abortion had some of the most restrictive provisions of any European legislation. Led by the Independent Women's Association and supported by the Social Democrats and the civic movements, the struggle to maintain the GDR law resulted in a compromise: the law would stay on the books in eastern Germany for two years. The Social Democrats and Liberal Democrats now support abortion on demand (during the first trimester); the SDP also favors removing abortion from the German criminal statutes altogether.[33]

Although making their voices heard on abortion rights and the Stasi, the civic movements failed to influence the course of economic reform. The theorists of the first revolution offered by way of economics an anti-materialist philosophy reminiscent of Rudolf Bahro. In *The Alternative in Eastern Europe,* he writes:

> Many intellectuals secretly consider it their own moral merit if (in Teilhard de Chardin's formula) they prefer "to know and to be, instead of to possess," whereas it is really the acme of their privilege to be able to live in such a way...The question is to create the objective conditions so that everyone can prefer "to know and to be, instead of to possess."[34]

The intellectuals dominant in New Forum and similar groups recognized the importance of increasing the number of consumer goods in the shops but disdained the consumerism that accelerated unification. They wanted to represent *civil* society, but not *bourgeois* society (in German, the word *burgerlich* contains both meanings). They did not want the revolution channeled exclusively into commercial impulses. But more than simply a producer of consumerism, raw capitalism was ecologically unwise, socially unjust, and morally suspect. If it hadn't been corrupted through association with decades of centrally-planned communism, democratic socialism might have been the logical alternative. But the civic movements did a poor job of "selling" such an alternative.[35]

On the question of economic reform, the civic movements were literally outclassed. The fall of communism in the GDR not only provided opportunities for acquiring political capital—as Helmut Kohl amply demonstrated—but capital also of the financial kind. Unification meant tremendous bonuses for West German business in particular. There, beyond the fallen Wall, was a mass of citizens eager to purchase precisely what had been denied them for 45 years. To sweeten the deal for West German firms, skilled workers living in the former land of communism could be hired for mere pfennigs.[36] What both West German business and East German citizens wanted to possess, the New Forum revolutionaries could not deny with fragile intellectual formulas.

Although East German citizens wanted the benefits of a market economy, few were eager to embrace the austerity and inequality that raw capitalism brings. The civic movements might have exploited this issue, but they were outflanked by the parties. The Christian Democratic Union did not, for instance, tout the unpleasant aspects of the market. Unification, the CDU insisted, would produce a prosperous eastern Germany virtually overnight. Left unsaid or substantially downplayed were the costs of unification. The CDU did not speculate on what would happen to the East German economy when exposed overnight to not only the West German economy, but the European Community (EC) and indeed the entire international economic system.[37]

The commonsense prediction would have been: high unemployment as uncompetitive enterprises go bankrupt, collapse of the domestic market with the influx of imports, deterioration of the export capability, rapid decline in the standard of living, and major tax increases in the western regions to pay for the bailout. In March 1990, an East German economist told me:

> The lowest estimate for joblessness under imposition of market conditions is 500,000. The highest is 4 million or roughly 40 percent of the workforce. Just look at the car industry. A couple weeks ago, you had to wait 15 years for a car. Now you can go to the store and get one immediately. These cars are not competitive. Everyone is waiting for Western German cars.[38]

He was right, of course: not only would the cheap and dreadful car, the Trabant, soon become a museum piece, but the entire East German economy would be transformed into an enormous anachronism.

The CDU hinted at these costs only *after* the elections, when Kohl announced a slowdown in unification. But even this belated acknowledgement was too optimistic, as Kohl had, in the words of *The Economist,* "wilfully underestimated the costs."[39] Having leaked some of the real story and discovered such caution out of place in the triumphal atmosphere surrounding unification, Kohl promptly disregarded his own statements and returned to preaching the gospel of the market. During financial union, when East Germans exchanged their currency for the good-as-gold Deutsche marks at a rate less than the CDU had originally promised, there were some grumbles, but few supported a reversal of the unification process. The collapse of the East German domestic market, on the other hand, produced more than mere grumbles.

The GDR economy had once been the pride of Eastern Europe. Its per capita gross national product, as estimated by the CIA, was twice that of Poland and nearly $2000 more than its nearest competitor, Czechoslovakia.[40] The GDR had achieved this position for several reasons. Its pre-World War II industrial infrastructure provided a base upon which to build after both the war's decimation and the Soviet Union's unofficial post-war reparations. Its unique geographic position also helped. Able to take advantage of cheap energy from the Soviet Union and backdoor access to EC trade through West Germany, the GDR led the region in exporting high technology, particularly electronics and micro-optics. Taking advantage of the *kombinate* system, the government was able to direct investments to what it considered the "cutting-edge" technologies. While the Poles were stuck with coal and ships that few countries wanted, and the Bulgarians were exporting agricultural products that brought a low yield on investment, East Germany provided technical goods that could be sold throughout the Soviet bloc and to the Third World for prices below Western market prices.

This situation began to change in the late 1970s. Adversely affected as were its neighbors by rising oil costs and global recession, the GDR weathered the crisis better than Poland or Romania. But instead of liberalizing its economy, the GDR moved toward greater centralization, towards theoretically more efficient *kombinate*. Some of the government's investment decisions—such as the computer megachip—absorbed tremendous funds and didn't produce the pay-off expected. Ironically, the GDR's historic economic success handicapped attempts at reform. As East German economist Bernd Beier pointed out:

> The big problem was that the GDR was always in the front of the Eastern European economies. If you tried to convince our top manager that we ought to turn things around, he would answer: "OK, you want to have what they—Poland and Hungary—have? They tried and they failed. So we shouldn't try any experiments."[41]

The East German economy swung from one extreme to the other. Once the bastion of economic conservatism, the GDR became the showcase in 1990 for one of the greatest economic experiments of the 20th century. Poland, as we will see in the next chapter, instituted its "shock therapy" of "overnight capitalism" in the beginning of 1990. But the pace of Poland's economic reform was lethargic compared to East Germany's sprint to the market. On July 1, the GDR truly switched to capitalism overnight when the financial union was concluded with West Germany. East German supermarkets eliminated their domestic products and restocked entirely with West German goods. Lines disappeared, and every citizen had Deutsche marks to burn. In half a year, East

Germans had gone from revolution to consumption. The promise of East German autonomy had been replaced by the promise of West German refrigerators. The revolution had been virtually forgotten or, as Eugen Weber has commented in a different context, the new consumer state had simply consumed its revolution.[42]

But there was a price to pay. With no internal market, East German industry ground to a halt, after industrial output had already declined 12 percent in the first six months of 1990.[43] As factories closed throughout the country, unemployment rose sharply, reaching 12 percent of the workforce by the fall of 1991. To hide the extent of the crisis, the government established a category of "reduced workshifts" which, for many workers, meant no work at all. Nearly 35 percent of the workforce fell into this category in September. With a declining German growth rate, rising inflation, and ballooning budget deficits, such large-scale unemployment is expected to last in the eastern lands well into 1993.[44]

Concerned with rising unemployment and a decreasing standard of living, East German workers and farmers took to the streets. Strikes and work actions convulsed trade after trade as the economic shocks spread through the industrial sphere.[45] Farmers competed not so much against West German produce but the perception that such produce was inherently superior because it had been grown in the West. Farmers and workers felt betrayed. As one trade union leader put it, "We didn't go out on the streets to help end the Communist regime just so we could lose our jobs and be thrown out on the streets."[46] Many eastern Germans thus decided to stop waiting for the East to catch up. Over 100,000 emigrated westward after the currency unification in July.[47] Capitalism had arrived in the GDR but it had not, contrary to the promises of Kohl, brought prosperity to all, or even most.

The economic issue underscored both how far behind politically and how prescient conceptually the civic movements had been. East Germans wanted to live better after the revolution, and Alliance '90 offered neither practical program nor pleasant myth. Instead it warned of the problems of the free market. Even when the first negative effects of the transition could be felt by the fall of 1990, these warnings failed to persuade. The CDU continued to string together promises, and the result was predictable: an overwhelming victory for Kohl in all-German elections in December 1990. In this first election in unified Germany, the civic groups allied with the Greens managed only 6 percent in the eastern regions, 1.2 percent overall, earning only eight parliamentary seats. Conventional politics is promises, and the civic movements had not learned or had deliberately decided not to learn this lesson.

After a year of turmoil, the movements trying to preserve some form of East German identity had little to celebrate. By July 1990, membership in New Forum had fallen by nine-tenths. Co-founder Bohley was crestfallen: "All of us feel East Germany has simply missed its chance to play a real part in the unification process. This is not the democracy we fought for. We are simply being devoured by the West. The terms of unity have been dictated by Bonn."[48] Only the liberal abortion measures had survived the unification process; everything else was disillusionment. As Christa Wolf remarked bitterly after East Germany had ceased to exist: "In all of my life I have never seen an atmosphere so foul. You don't throw 40 years of existence onto the rubbish heap...What we are going through now is a surrender, a disastrous collapse. We are losing many things that are worth crying over...I don't mind giving up the word 'utopia,' but I will not give up hope, goals, and dreams."[49]

After unification, East Germany was reduced in the minds of many Germans to sarcastic acronyms that translated into "Federal German Occupation Zone" and "Barrel Without Bottom."[50] The Trabant was gone, the Parliament disbanded, the former prime minister discredited because of Stasi ties, the economy of the five underdeveloped *lander* at a standstill. East Germany had been annexed as new federal states. The process had certainly been consensual, the rewards for many substantial, but the prices heavy as well. Autonomy was traded for a promise of security, and many eastern Germans still await the fulfillment of that promise.[51] "In the GDR we had the feeling we were trapped in a rigid system," comments artist Barbara Thalheim. "But now we find ourselves in one equally sterile, allowing no hope of changing it—and I feel the current system, based on the power of money, will be even more destructive."[52]

The GDR may inevitably have its revenge. Stripped of an independent identity, it will nonetheless influence the shape of Germany as a whole. Western German citizens, while responding with warmth and enthusiasm to events in the East and to unification in general, have now begun to realize the costs they will have to bear for their compatriots. Although the CDU won decisively in the all-German elections, the costs of unification will cut into its margin of victory in the future (and the inclusion of more social welfare-minded colleagues from the east will undoubtedly push the party pinkward). Kohl's announcement at the beginning of 1991 of a tax increase to pay for unification (and additional contributions to the Persian Gulf War) has not helped his party's position. Indeed, unification has left the CDU governing only two of the Western *lander* and a membership in the East that has declined from 130,000 to 50,000 by the fall of 1991.[53] Nestled now in the belly of the German beast, eastern Germany may lead to greater indigestion than Kohl ever imagined.

* * *

Civil society bloomed in East Germany in the fall of 1989. But over the course of the year, the *burger* as consumer replaced the *burger* as citizen. The activities of roundtables and public demonstrations, of colorful movements and ordinary citizens becoming political actors ended, and the putative democracy of the market took over. Democracy has been reduced to an annual trip to the polling station, a civic responsibility increasingly shirked in the absence of more substantial democratic institutions.

Movements such as New Forum fit imperfectly into this type of Western consumer-driven society. Their vision of decentralized democratic socialism required mass support, and the masses were not supportive. Somewhere down the road, as German unification fades into history, the New Forum model might return, in a tighter, more comprehensible, and more popular form. The defects of capitalism and party politics that the majority of Germans cavalierly ignored in 1989 may come back to haunt the now united country.

The initial revolutionary success of New Forum and its subsequent electoral failure offer one way of understanding the political developments in other Eastern European countries as well. In popular front organizations, the opposition movements successfully ousted the communist parties. With success, however, came the break-up of these popular fronts. The more radical elements became marginalized, in much the same fashion as their New Forum cousins were pushed to the fringes of politics more generally. Although the circumstances vary throughout the region, the results have been uniform—the decline of participatory politics and the adoption of a Western, party-driven model. The revolutionaries savored the collapse of communism but it is now the technocrats who are in the driver's seat.

The popular fronts

1989 was the year of the revolution; 1990 was the year of the election. But in that first year of formal democracy, Eastern European oppositions did not, as their first political task, construct pluralism. The communist parties had to be defeated—first in the streets through demonstrations and then through the ballot box. Since unity was necessary for achieving this goal, the oppositions turned to "popular fronts."[54] As interim structures, these coalitions allowed relatively inexperienced opposition movements to negotiate with and then compete on an equal basis against well-financed and still influential communist parties. Although variously composed, each front issued the same appeal: we must band together to fight the common enemy. Such coalitions—Solidarity's Citizens' Committee in Poland, Civic Forum in Czechoslovakia, Union of Democratic Forces in Bulgaria, Demos in Slovenia—were not parties but movements (the term "party" reminded them too much of *the* Party). Scorning party discipline, these fronts adopted vaguely articulated programs whose incongruities were concealed by resolute anti-communism. As intermediary organizations, the popular fronts linked underground oppositions to the multi-party systems that eventually replaced the standoff between communists and anti-communists. In the GDR and Hungary, this middle stage dropped out. Bulgaria, Romania, and Yugoslavia, meanwhile, are still stuck somewhere in the middle.

While the GDR took the leap into a full-blown pluralism because of external factors, Hungary dispensed with the popular front more for internal reasons. The country had too variegated an opposition and too weak and divided a Communist Party to sustain the "us-versus-them" dynamic that characterizes popular front politics. The more interesting political conflict in Hungary in 1989-90 was *within* the opposition, between the relatively more secular and intellectual Alliance of Free Democrats and the relatively more conservative and nationalistic Democratic Forum. The battle of these two exemplars of the divided Hungarian psyche produced an electoral campaign that many Hungarians described in less than glowing terms ("a dogfight!" spat one Green contemptuously in an interview). Alliance members accused the Forum of having collaborated with the former communists;[55] Forum supporters surreptitiously painted swastikas on Alliance posters (several prominent Alliance members are Jewish); Alliance members struck back, accusing the Forum of rabid nationalism, xenophobia, and anti-Semitism; Forum members responded that the Alliance's liberal economic program would throw Hungarians into desperate poverty. When the dust cleared, the Forum had won, chiefly because of its attacks on the Alliance's economic positions. After forming a government with the Independent Smallholders (an agrarian party with a pre-war tradition), the Forum managed to patch fences sufficiently with the Alliance to conclude an agreement that left Alliance member Arpad Goncz as president. The Hungarian elections were no mere contest between communists and anti-communists. Indeed, the two heirs of the Communist Party (reformists and hardliners) were almost forgotten amid the mud-slinging among opposition parties.[56]

Even with an opposition dominated by two strong parties, intriguing alternative parties also emerged in Hungary, chief among them the Alliance of Young Democrats (FIDESZ). Billed as liberal, radical, and alternative, FIDESZ aggressively campaigned on market principles, favored a radical political style, and supported alternative issues such as ecology and pacificism. The 22 FIDESZ parliamentarians, with an average age of 28 and with the youngest only 22, have made political debate in parliament very lively. This liveliness gained FIDESZ some ground in local elections in the fall of 1990, a success that leaves it currently one of the most popular Hungarian parties.

As explained above, a popular front did not lead the GDR opposition into the country's first free elections. Alliance '90 attempted to be such an umbrella organization, but the issue of unification and funds flowing into the Christian Democratic and Social Democratic parties from the West established a "pluralistic" model from the beginning. The relative inexperience of the GDR dissident community also contributed to the failure of a popular front. There was no Solidarity or Charter 77 in the GDR that could, once the communist government began to bend, sponsor a movement that the wider public would prefer to a Western-style party. On a superficial level, the pluralism of the GDR elections resembled Hungary's pluralism—several important opposition parties, a relatively marginalized post-communist party. But the GDR's pluralism was almost entirely imported while Hungary's was peculiarly its own.

For the rest of Eastern Europe, the elections of 1990 were not pluralistic. Rather, they pitted a communist bloc against an anti-communist bloc, with elections serving less as an opportunity for the trading of positions on issues than as a referendum on the previous 45 years. These fronts in general discouraged what was referred to as "excessive democracy" for fear of splits appearing within their ranks. The fronts attracted very diverse political activists who might have spent their considerable energies in ideological infighting, had the fronts' stated goals not been clear and had a communist victory not been perceived as all too possible. With the aim of defeating the Communist Party providing cohesion, Czechoslovakia's Civic Forum could bring together everyone from Trotskyist Petr Uhl to Friedmanite Vaclav Klaus. Poland's Solidarity hosted both radical trade unionists and radical supply-siders. Bulgaria's Union of Democratic Forces put social democrats and peasant utopians side-by-side. Even Demos in Slovenia had its radical nationalists, its temperate Catholics, and its social democrats. Like unstable atoms, these fronts could hold together only under very special conditions.

One of those conditions was intense pressure. No popular front had any previous experience with this kind of electoral politics. No front had more than half a year to prepare for elections. In short, the popular fronts had little time to disintegrate before election day. Just in case, however, these movements frequently compromised internal democracy to avoid any internal strife that might jeopardize their electoral chances. In Poland, for instance, a small national coordinating committee—Lech Walesa's Citizens' Committee—chose candidates for the 1989 national elections from its Warsaw office. In many cases, local candidates were completely ignored in favor of Warsaw's choice. Democratic procedures were fudged because the election campaign was limited and the Solidarity-backed candidates needed as much support from the center and as little disunity as possible to defeat the Communist Party candidates. Though the maneuver produced a convincing Solidarity victory—with the Citizens' Committee winning all but one of the contested seats in the 1989 election—the process created a good deal of rancor in the outlying regions. In winning the battle against the "enemy," Solidarity would sow the seeds of many internal battles to come.

Sometimes this expediency concealed less noble purposes. The limiting of political debate in Romania—in an election presided over by its major contestant, the National Salvation Front—did not result from any need to unify in the face of a powerful political adversary such as a communist party. The Communist Party in Romania had after all ceased to exist for all intents and purposes after the revolution. Rather, the NSF limited its opponents' access to media in order to enhance its own chances in the election. The results were even more overwhelming than anyone might have anticipated. The Front won over two-thirds of the vote, with its nearest competitor, the Democratic Hungarian Union, garnering a mere 7 percent. The support for the Front's presidential choice, Ion Iliescu, was even more overwhelming—85 percent. Instead of banding together in their own popular front, the opposition parties that faced the NSF were weak and disorganized. It would only be later, when popular fronts had all but disappeared from the northern tier countries, that the Romanian opposition would finally unite in such a coalition.

In other cases, oppositionists disregarded democratic procedure due simply to a lack of experience with democratic process. Activist Deyan Kironov told me that Ecoglasnost, one of Bulgaria's first opposition movements in the country, had carefully developed democratic procedures for its meetings and activities. Participating in the Union of Democratic Forces (UDF) coalition, however, Ecoglasnost was unable to transfer its organizational experience. Although heavily funded by the United States, the UDF lost the national elections to the Socialist (formerly Communist) Party in June 1990.[57] The Socialists had used the same tactic that the Democratic Forum had successfully employed against the Alliance of Free Democrats in Hungary: charging that its opponent's economic liberalism would throw the country into chaos. The maneuver worked again as the Socialists walked off with nearly half the votes, leaving the UDF with a little over a third. Even after this disastrous showing in the elections, Kironov told me, the UDF continued to conduct its sessions behind closed curtains, thinking perhaps that more expediency and less democracy would have served its cause better.[58]

Expediency was an internally divisive issue. A frequent charge levied against the popular fronts from outside was—"Who chose you as the leaders of the revolution?" There is no solution to this paradox of democracy. In lieu of formal elections, the popular front organizations derived their legitimacy in various ways—as organizers of mass rallies, as previously repressed underground organizations, as chief negotiators with the former communist governments. But inevitably there were challenges. After Civic Forum swept the elections in Czechoslovakia, for instance, the rival People's Party declared that "the elections were free, but they were not democratic. They were manipulated. The result is abnormal. One self-appointed dictatorship has been replaced by another."[59] But in the absence of any legal mechanisms to determine appointment, how could Civic Forum be anything but self-appointed? Revolutions are not preceded by elections to determine the revolutionaries. The inescapable fact was that Civic Forum and its Slovak sister organization Public Against Violence led the velvet revolution. The Christian Democrats, the People's Party, and other smaller groups only joined the fray at a later point. It was no surprise then that the two revolutionary coalitions captured nearly 50 percent of the vote, with their nearest competitor, the Communist Party, capturing only 14 percent.

The northern republics of Yugoslavia also held their elections in spring 1990. In Croatia and Slovenia, too, the choice came down to the former communists or the anti-communists. Demos in Slovenia and the Croatian Democratic Community (HDZ) in Croatia derived much of their support from their strong statements in favor of independence from Yugoslavia. But many of the intellectuals who had worked long years in the Slovenian and Croatian oppositions suspected that nationalist sentiment took precedence over democratic norms. Although establishing the electoral rules and parliamentary procedures of formal democracy, HDZ and Demos were not interested in developing a truly democratic culture. "One thing which is more or less obvious to us," sociologist Paule Gantor told me during my trip to Slovenia, "the path from the one-party system (basically totalitarianism) to a pluralist system (democratic elections and so on) is not such a one-directional path. After the elections, we still have problems with democratic institutions. Partly we are witnessing a new appearance of totalitarianism within the so-called democratic parties."[60] Another Slovenian intellectual agreed. "Demos, the coalition of some of the opposition parties, is now declaring itself the embodiment of the national interest," philosopher Tomaz Mastnak told me. "They have simply suspended the identities of the constituted parties on the one hand, and on the other hand they are very hostile to all the parties which are outside their coalition."[61] The Slovenian popular front Demos had established formal democracy only to discover that more substantive pluralism would destroy its own singular political position.

Although billed as revolutionary alternatives, the popular fronts discovered upon taking power that thorough revolutionary change requires a guillotine or its political equivalent. The new governments in the region were, in 1990, quite reluctant to dispatch all the people connected with the past regime. The experience of these officials was needed. The employee rolls—at the local government offices, the state companies, the army, and the police—changed little; most employees merely switched their allegiances. Promised a "thorough housecleaning by the new party in charge, Hungarians received only a 'light dusting,'" notes political scientist Rudolf Tokes.[62] However frustrating this continuity might have been to the average citizen, it was the concession the new leaders paid for stability.

I wasn't surprised therefore, on my return to Poland in 1990, to find little changed at the Ministry of Foreign Affairs. A new Solidarity government presided over Poland, but the Ministry seemed preserved in aspic. The same two somber men at the door demanded in even tones what my business was, and the same humorless guides escorted me to the entrance of the appropriate office, ostensibly to prevent any unnecessary fact-finding detours. In 1990, however, since the the new foreign minister was not a Communist Party member, it was decided that Ministry employees could not be Party members. Not surprisingly, 100 percent of the employees decided to remain outside the Party. Even the official I interviewed, the head of the third ministry in charge of the Americas, expressed little ambivalence concerning the about-face: "Those of us who worked here for a long time, even though we were Party members, have no problem working for a government which is, in the final analysis, anti-communist."[63]

Suppose a clean sweep had occurred and the thousands of employees—both skilled technicians and adept sinecurists—had been thrown out of their jobs. From what ranks would the newly elevated opposition movements find replacements? Opposition movements in the region did not have time to train an entire range of experts on foreign affairs, transportation, fiscal management, or environmental policy. Many of the spur-of-the-moment choices were indeed inspired, even poetic. The new East German government appointed pacifist pastor Reiner Epplemann as defense minister. Civic Forum chose a worker with impeccable blue-collar credentials, Petr Miller, for labor minister. Slovenia's minister of the army had been a draft resister. But while the choices for the top positions represented radical change, most of the positions extending downward in the bureaucratic pyramid were left untouched. In many respects, the events of 1989-90 resulted merely in the replacement of elites.

In Romania, Bulgaria, and parts of Yugoslavia, opposition movements did not immediately succeed with this first revolution. In Bulgaria, for instance, even the elites changed little as the Communist Party changed its name but maintained government power (though in general the reformers within the Party replaced the hardliners). Prior to the June 1990 elections, a student occupation strike at Sofia's university had been extraordinarily successful, scoring a hat trick by getting rid of the head of the television station, the communist president of the county, and even the embalmed body of Georgi Dimitrov from his mausoleum on September 9 Square. The subsequent elections were to have completed the revolution.

They didn't. In Sofia and many of the large cities, the opposition UDF won overwhelmingly. But the country as a whole supported the newly renamed Socialists. Crying "election fraud," some opposition stalwarts and many students from the university banded together for a 24-hour vigil. At the beginning, this "City of Truth" was huge—nearly 150 tents and thick crowds of people. A rainbow of movements were represented—ecological, trade union, religious. When I arrived in the middle of August 1990, the city was little more than a small village with a handful of tents and some rather dispirited staffers. These too would disappear after the burning of the Party building later that month.

But it would not be the end of the "uncompromising" opposition. Strikes throughout the fall of 1990 eventually led to the downfall of the Socialist government. Its replacement, however, represented what had long been a point of no compromise for the opposition UDF: a coalition government including Socialist and opposition ministers. But even that coalition would, after another round of elections, give way in late 1991 to a UDF government with a large Socialist opposition. The revolutionary standoff finally became a political confrontation.

* * *

What ultimately tore apart the popular fronts was neither their expedient detours around democratic procedure nor their reliance on the bureaucracies of the previous regimes nor the criticisms of their self-appointment as leaders of the revolutions. As pre-political organizations, the popular fronts were the perfect vehicles for former dissidents preparing for the first free elections. Once in office, however, and with the communist threat gone, popular fronts could simply no longer maintain cohesion. Popular fronts were undone by politics.

Schooled long years in the art of dissent, Eastern European revolutionaries thought in binary categories of totalitarian and anti-totalitarian. Their programs were routinely stated negatively. For all their courage, stamina, and wisdom, these revolutionaries were often profoundly uncomfortable with the classic political techniques of compromise and conciliation. During the communist era, compromise had acquired a distinctly pejorative tone, implying collaboration with evil rather than accommodation to political reality. Charter 77 was uncompromising in its insistence on improvements in the human rights realm. Solidarity was uncompromising in its insistence on legalization. But the old, uncompromising style had to change in 1989 as the communist authorities began to give up ground. It became a delicate balancing act: should Civic Forum participate in a coalition government, or demand the complete removal of the Communist Party from power? Should Solidarity accept the political compromise of the roundtable negotiations ensuring the communists 65 percent of the seats in the Sejm? Should Demos and HDZ accept the compromise of a continued federal Yugoslavia? How far should New Forum push the weak East German communist reformers who replaced Honecker?

Given the nature of compromise, naturally some elements of the opposition were disgruntled with the ultimate decisions. For instance, groups such as Fighting Solidarity and the Confederation for Polish Independence were incensed at Solidarity's participation in the 1989 roundtable—this was collaboration with the authorities, with the hated communists. Invited to participate in the roundtable, representatives of this "uncompromising" sector refused, expecting and even hoping the negotiations would fail, thereby discrediting Solidarity and advantaging their own splinter groups. But a new political era had begun, the roundtable succeeded, and Solidarity capitalized on its shrewd compromise.

Nevertheless, the early criticism of the popular fronts' "political" deals would return in an altered form. As Solidarity and Civic Forum took office, they endured more severe internal divisions as one faction or another argued that the outdated front structure did not permit true political debate. When still only steps away from underground movements these popular fronts were often criticized as too political; closer to a multi-party system, the fronts were now not political enough.

Solidarity's Citizens' Committee was the first victim of the breakdown of the popular front. The Committee was always a rather improbable institution. On the one hand, it represented the Solidarity trade union, which derived its strength from workers and farmers. On the other hand, the Committee chose a government which launched an economic program impoverishing precisely these constituencies. Succumbing to internal strife, the Citizens' Committee eventually divided prior to the 1990 presidential campaign into a faction advocating Lech Walesa's return to politics and a faction supporting the Mazowiecki government. Some general consensus on economic policy might have been possible between these two groups had not procedural disagreements inherent in a popular front organization—on the distribution of power and political rewards—deepened the divide.

The Czech lands have seen their popular front divide on economic issues. In February 1991, after some internal divisions, Civic Forum disintegrated into pieces. Vaclav Klaus and his more conservative followers formed one group; Jiri Dienstbier and the centrists created the liberal faction. A smaller, left-of-center faction represents the core of a new independent left. (In Slovakia, the Public Against Violence dissolved because of differences over nationalism). Romania has the distinction of possessing several political organizations that aspire to be popular fronts including the National Salvation Front and the Democratic Convention of opposition groups. Bulgaria's Union of Democratic Forces is fragmenting now that it has formed the most recent government. With Slovenia now independent, Demos will continue as a viable coalition only if external threats provide cohesion.

The fragmentation of the popular fronts is an inevitable experience for Eastern Europe in the 1990s. As the threat of the communist parties diminishes, issues surface which tear at the coalitions. In East Germany, unification destroyed any notion of a popular front even before it could consolidate. For the Citizens' Committee and Civic Forum, the controversies were different, but the result was the same. Multi-party systems are taking hold in the region—producing disagreements both healthy and divisive where there was once a unity both suffocating and inspirational.

No experiments

Did Eastern European countries only have a choice between popular fronts and party-run pluralism as practiced in the West? At least initially, other alternatives seemed possible. The East German civic movements called for mechanisms to preserve radical participatory democracy, for instance, through reconstituted roundtables. An editor at Krakow's *Tygodnik Powszechny* had a more Platonic suggestion: a revolving political elite with politicians who are distinguished in other professions serving time as a civic responsibility.[64] Green activists throughout the region hinted at new political categories that would replace the left-right political spectrum.

In virtually no country were political parties held in high regard. As Barbel Bohley explains, "We no longer consider parties capable of solving problems, and that applies not only to parties of the GDR, but to all parties, even Western parties. People see that all parties are very easily corrupted, that within the parties are people who exploit their positions, and that many parties are not credible."[65] In the early days of the Bulgarian opposition, according to activist Deyan Kironov, many members thought that perhaps parties were outmoded—a function of anachronistic modernist thinking—and that political action should be organized around specific issues. Therefore, they considered working for the creation not of a party system but of a hybrid of old and new. People would be elected to parliament not on an ideological basis but according to ability demonstrated in resolving political problems. Neither a technocracy nor a meritocracy, this new system would be based on the old Bulgarian tradition of aldermen, similar to the paternalistic system in Japan. Although he liked this idea, Kironov never believed that it was tenable. "Reality was against us," he concluded.[66]

What was this reality? After the disruption of daily life caused by the revolutions, most East Europeans were not interested in a new political system that would require political participation any greater than that required in the West. Jacek Zakowski, a spokesperson for Solidarity's parliamentary faction, confessed to me: "People are not so much interested in day-by-day participation in politics. What Poles want to do is elect a good parliament, president, and local government and then be free of politics. And live in a happy country. I think Poles are tired of politics and are rather looking for a quiet life."[67] A citizens' movement composed of active citizens, imagined, for instance, by New Forum in the GDR, had disappeared; in its place was, at best, an informed electorate capable of voting responsibly once or twice a year.

Ordinarily, institutions of civil society mediate between the government and the public, enriching democratic life. But civil society in Eastern Europe is weak, incapable of maintaining independence from and improving the government at the same time. Most popular fronts, which saw themselves as the embodiments of civil society, felt the inevitable pull of public office. As their leaders—Vaclav Havel, Tadeusz Mazowiecki, Zheliu Zhelev, Reiner Epplemann—took the giant step from anti-government activities to high office, and as the movements they represented began to lose their movement quality, a new gulf opened up between governors and governed. There were those who participated in the day-to-day compromises of politics and those who, in Zakowski's words, sought the "quiet life."

The political groups that mediate between governors and governed in the West—ecological and peace organizations, lobbyists, consultants—could not be created overnight in Eastern Europe. Because they focused in 1989-90 almost exclusively on toppling and replacing governments, the movements of civil society ironically could not produce civil society. Again, they had succeeded in establishing formal democracy but could not accomplish the more challenging task of establishing democratic cultures. In Hungary, I met with Robert Braun of the Raoul Wallenberg Society, an organization which works on minority issues. Having spent some time in Washington, D.C., Braun knew the art of lobbying. He tried to use that knowledge in Budapest. "We negotiated with the president of the educational subcommittee from the Democratic Forum and she was very aggressive," Braun reports.

> She said, "Why should I debate this issue with you? I'm going to express my opinion in the parliamentary debate." And I told her that it was very important to express her opinion to other parties but that we are not a party. And I told her that even non-governmental organizations try to take part in the parliamentary process. She was upset. She said, "There are the parties and they are good enough to make decisions."[68]

In his 1990 article "Who's Controlling the Controllers," Hungarian sociologist Ferenc Miszlivetz criticizes this exclusive reliance on parties and political experts. Even with new pluralistic institutions in Eastern Europe, power has been concentrated within a relatively small group of people who are not held accountable to the public by watchdog organizations. More disturbing, the new "controllers" have developed a distrust of public activity that bears a suspicious resemblance to the previous communist controllers. Miszlivetz writes that these new controllers

> frequently inform us that independence is suspicious, that there is no more a need for social movements and autonomous initiatives. This country already has a legitimate parliament with many parties and they will arrange everything. Miklos Tomas Gaspar formulates it in the most unambiguous way: "It's enough, he says, if the people become excited politically only once every four years."[69]

Formal democracy—the vote, the parliament—has been established. More participatory mechanisms have taken a back seat to the development of professional politicians. The political future of Eastern Europe then lies not with Cincinnatus figures like Havel and Zhelev, but with a figure like Lech Walesa. Although not an intellectual and prone to the occasional gaffe, Walesa has what is politely referred to in Poland as political "instincts." Having worked as a powerbroker in the opposition for over a decade, he is the closest Eastern Europe has to a professional politician. He relies on expert advice, shifts his positions when necessary, brokers compromises when appropriate, and employs inflammatory rhetoric when all else fails. These qualities produce a high degree of ambivalence among Polish intellectuals who prefer their leaders to be more scholarly. Indeed, most Polish intellectuals prior to the Polish presidential elections in 1990 expressed horror at the prospect of Walesa in the office. An ordinary worker representing Poland to the world—a cruel Polish joke. Of course, the irony is that Walesa more closely resembles Helmut Kohl and Ronald Reagan than does a Catholic intellectual like Tadeusz Mazowiecki. Both Kohl and Reagan often mangled their respective languages and, instead of assuming an air of scholarship, both attempted, like Walesa, to appeal to the common people. The key difference, however, is that the autocratic tendencies of Reagan and Kohl have been tempered (however poorly at times) by other democratic institutions. With a weak civil society, Walesa's dictatorial streak is potentially more dangerous.

The flipside of professional politics is voter apathy. In several countries, the electorate has retreated even further from politics than Zakowski might have imagined. Turnout for local elections in June 1990 in Poland, which produced 52,000 new politicians, attracted only 40 percent of the electorate. The Hungarian local elections, the sixth trip to the polls for Hungarians in ten months, brought out only 30 percent of the eligible voters. After years of non-elections, Eastern Europeans have taken the anti-politics theme to heart, even as the political realm was recaptured by pluralism. Was this emerging political apathy simply the exercise of free choice? As apologists for the low voter turnout in the United States say, voter indifference is a sign of a healthy polis. Much more likely, however, is that Eastern Europeans are discovering that mere voting, while initially exhilarating after decades of non-elections, can be quite hollow in the absence of more widespread democratic institutions.

The cynical attitude to civic political participation stems from the pre-1989 perceptions of democracy. One oppositional stream stressed the moral value of democracy, its ethical superiority to a one-party state that refused to allow its citizens to make real public choices. The realists, on the other hand, saw democracy as the carrot given to the population to ease the pain of economic austerity's stick. In Poland and Hungary, the communist parties had been trying to foist austerity programs—price increases, cuts in social spending—upon their respective populations for the better part of the 1980s. At any hint of a price increase, however, the public would recoil. But maybe, party reformers and some oppositionists argued, the public would accept austerity if imposed by elected parties. "Political reform," as Timothy Garton Ash phrased it, "must sugar the bitter pill of austerity and win popular support."[70] The democratic idealists saw their dreams inscribed in the rhetoric of democracy throughout the region; the cynicism of the realists, meanwhile, has spawned the political twins of apathy and technocracy.

While economic crisis produced this utilitarian notion of political reform, it may also, now that the honeymoon periods for the new non-communist governments have elapsed, reinvigorate civil society. As Eastern Europeans discover new economic interests—whether protecting corporate privilege or demanding greater social protections—political life may become correspondingly more dynamic. Perhaps more radically, citizens in the region may demand increased democracy in the economic sphere—an extension of a principle that communists claimed rhetorically but never put into practice, that many oppositionists originally supported but have seemingly forgotten in the aftermath of the revolutions.

Democracy in the workplace comes in several forms: industrial democracy, worker self-management, trade unionism, co-determination. While the next chapter will look at the economic justifications for such an alternative, it is important here to note a certain political rationale that could prove compelling to Eastern Europeans. Political theorist Robert Dahl puts the matter succinctly: "*If* democracy is justified in governing the state, then it must *also* be justified in governing economic enterprises; and to say that it is *not* justified in governing economic enterprises is to imply that it is not justified in governing the state."[71] The question is not whether private property should exist or whether the state should control the economy or whether the market should be eradicated. Rather, the issue is control of economic institutions: should decisions be made by managers, workers, elected representatives, or a combination of all three? Can workers be transformed into the citizens of their enterprises? Two significant attempts were made in Eastern Europe in the post-war period.

Within the framework of communism, Yugoslavia tried to establish a new economic arrangement that would secure democratic rights in the workplace. Dubbed "self-management," the Yugoslav reforms of the 1950s established workers' councils that at least in theory could participate in the management decisions of the enterprise and share in the subsequent gains and losses. The idea was reminiscent of the *soviets* on workers' councils established after the Russian revolution. But, like its Soviet models, the Yugoslav system eventually concentrated on increased productivity, not democratic organization. A true democratic spirit in the economic realm might have also threatened communist control of the political sphere.

Solidarity in its 1980-81 incarnation also championed self-management. A workers' movement, Solidarity imagined that greater control of the productive enterprises—and therefore the economy—could be devolved to workers participating in newly independent self-management councils (the Polish government had established such councils in 1956 only later to take them over). By the time of Solidarity's reincarnation in 1989-90, the self-management message had softened. This decade-old Solidarity pillar, weakened by economic necessity and political opportunities, finally collapsed in the fall of 1990 when Mazowiecki formed his non-communist cabinet. Self-management was replaced with shock-style capitalism.

Neither Yugoslav nor Polish self-management had a chance to operate under democratic *political* circumstances. With free elections now a matter of public policy in the region, models of economic democracy might become more workable.

West Germany served as the immediate model for East Germany. Its parliament became *the* parliament, its economy became *the* economy. For Eastern Europe more generally, the Western political model served as a lifesaver tossed into still turbulent waters. This model was a particular type of limited democracy, one that emphasized political parties, that encouraged professionalism and technocracy, that narrowly understood public participation as voting, that deliberately uncoupled the political and economic realms. Alternatives based on greater civic activity were drowned out by the oft-heard slogan of "No experiments! We simply want what works." The revolutions had for a short time opened up a world of possibilities. Gradually the field of options narrowed, the revolutionary zeal dissipated in frustration or was channeled into more orthodox activities, and a new model replaced the old.

In excess, the region's technocrats insisted, democracy eroded discipline and compromised efficiency. It interfered with economic functioning. It should be held in check by "liberal authoritarianism." The great rallying cry of the opposition, democracy had suddenly become a problem for the new governments.[72]

* * *

In one year, Germany went from a Cold War-divided, Berlin Wall-split country to a unified entity. This Gordian knot located at the very center of Europe—the "unrealistic aspiration" of Germans, the seemingly insoluble "German question," the specter of revanchism—resolved itself in less than a year. One might say that the fact of unification was not surprising, simply its timing. The two Germanies were, after all, separated unnaturally.

Indeed, in the great scale of European history, the dual Germanies appear to be a mere detour, a 40-year territorial oddity which hardly compares to the 123 years of Polish non-existence or the 500-year Bulgarian term within the Ottoman empire. Viewed against such a backdrop, the revolutionary movements of the GDR—New Forum, Democracy Now, Initiative for Peace and Human Rights, and all the other residents of the House for Democracy—seem even more insignificant than their already modest electoral support indicates.

But is this really true? Will these political movements leave no trace in either the united Germany or Europe in general?

New Forum provided a critique of not only communist but Western-style politics. It envisioned a democracy that was pluralistic but not confined to periodic voting. It imagined a democracy that extended into the economic sphere. It valued public debate and constructed an image of a citizen that was not restricted to consumerism and vague civic spirit. New Forum put forward a radical critique of both communism and capitalism at a time when East Germans did not want radical alternatives.

But the criticisms that New Forum made of technocracy and formalistic democracy will continue in the united Germany, echoing themes already developed by many western German movements. This desire for political alternatives—appearing within Solidarity, Civic Forum, the Union of Democratic Forces, or elsewhere in Eastern Europe—will not disappear with the implantation of the technocratic model. The critical spirit embodied in these movements of civil society will live on, particularly as the debate in Eastern Europe turns increasingly to the economic questions that have remained so intractable in the region for so many years.

Chapter 5

Poland... A shortcut to modernity

One might say that the free market is the latest Central European utopia.[1]

—Timothy Garton Ash

The ugly, box-like building, at the corner of one of Warsaw's busiest intersections, was once the headquarters of the Polish United Workers Party: a symbol of the communist status quo. Today, in post-communist Poland, this unaesthetic structure which Poles refer to as the White House now represents the new order. The Party building has become a business and banking center; on its fifth floor, where *apparatchiks* once roamed, stock brokers and investment analysts scrutinize prices on Poland's new stock market, the second exchange in the region after Budapest's.[2]

Capitalism is in, communism out. On a superficial level, little has changed. The red suspenders of brokers have replaced the red ties of the communist officials. Bankers now address topics that were once the exclusive domain of communist officials: planning and investments, credits and margins, stability and maintenance. Indeed, the two groups of well-dressed professionals had already been growing more alike in the last decade as communists became more interested in capitalism and *vice versa*. International bankers frequently visited the East European governments, checking on loans and Western investments. When communist officials visited the United States, they didn't detour to meet with the chair of the US Communist Party. Even if they had been interested, the schedules of the communist dignitaries from the East were too filled with appointments with economic experts and financial wizards.

Notwithstanding these continuities with the communists of old, the new capitalists occupying Warsaw's White House are the true revolutionaries. More than the new wave of politicians, these capitalists have changed the face of Poland. Where shortages and queues once plagued every city and village, capitalism has exploded, restoring the market in its most literal sense. As the Polish economy experienced a profound transformation in 1990, Warsaw in particular was transformed into an enormous bazaar on the Vistula. Vendors crowded the streets and squares of the city, hawking everything from modest bunches of fresh dill to luxury items: art books, stereo equipment, designer sneakers from the United States, caviar from Russia, watermelons from Georgia, Turkish cigarettes, German baby clothes, South Korean computers. Freelance butchers selling hunks of beef and pork from the backs of trucks were sufficiently legitimate to be listed alongside traditional meatshops in the section on comparative prices in one daily newspaper ("the truck at Defilad Square has the cheapest sirloin in town"). The market hasn't so much arrived in Warsaw. Warsaw has become the market.

This medieval trade fair *cum* urban flea market is not the only result of Polish economic reform. Part of the capitalist revolution has been a growing class divide. Wages have not kept pace with the escalating prices, prompting dozens of large and small strikes. The marginal poor—pensioners, disabled, the chronically unemployable—have been hit the hardest. At bottom is the new class of beggars, some of them AIDS sufferers who can find neither jobs nor health care. The train stations have been filling up with homeless people, and police have discovered new strains of criminality. The existing social structures—whether church or private—are groaning under the new burdens. In 1990, Poland entered its mean season.

At the other end of the spectrum, Warsaw's new Marriott Hotel offers expensive rooms and a casino for tourists and business VIPs. Exchange booths have been set up in every available space—the backs of restaurants, the lobbies of cinemas—to vie for the increased trade in dollar, mark, and pound. For the *nouveau riche* and the *ancien nomenklatura* are new upscale cafes, videotape parlors, and an expensive French wine shop in the center of town. In June 1990, a private Polish auto company announced its new model, the "Gepard," listing its price at 300 million zlotys or $30,000. Since the average yearly wage of a Pole in June was roughly 5 percent of the price tag, the sleek Gepard was instantly out of reach to all but a minority.[3]

Poland 1990 was a very different country from Poland 1989. During the year of the historic roundtable negotiations, an average monthly wage was $25, coupons regulated the sales of meat in the state stores, and key items such as toilet paper, flour, and matches were frequently out of stock. Although 1989 was the year of great political change in Poland, it merely resulted in a change in government. The appearance of an official above-ground Solidarity newspaper in April 1989 was notable, but *samizdat* publications had been readily accessible for several years. Even the expression of political opinions in the open, so much a part of the election campaign, was simply an echo of the Solidarity period of 1980-81. Political change was certainly welcome. It just wasn't extraordinary.

The revolution of 1990, however, aimed to change social relations, and it was ushered in not with a whimper but with the economists' equivalent of the Big Bang. The bang in question was the new Finance Minister Leszek Balcerowicz and his plan for overnight capitalism. This recipe for shock therapy is a modernization plan for the 1990s. A *perestroika* to end all *perestroikas,* it is designed like the Stalinist model to compress transition into a short period of time to allow Poland to catch up to its Western European neighbors.

The story of this modernization plan does not begin with Balcerowicz, however. The communists had in fact anticipated their capitalist successors by more than a decade.

Before shock

Poland in the early 1980s seemed to have turned ideology on its head. The communists were calling for capitalism, and the anti-communists were opposing it. What manner of beast was this Poland that did not know its left from its right, its Karl Marx from its Adam Smith, its reform from its reaction? Examined more carefully, this Polish paradox assumes a certain logic in the crazy context of Eastern Europe in its last decade of so-called communism.

The first half of the 1970s had been a period of remarkable prosperity for the average Pole—well-stocked supermarkets, livable wages, low prices—much of this made possible by foreign loans. By the end of the decade, however, the Polish economy was teetering, burdened by debt and administrative incompetence, and suffering from the global impact of another round of oil price hikes.[4] Instead of being used to modernize the machinery of these industries, foreign capital had been poured into large projects of questionable economic worth and siphoned off to enhance the lifestyles of Party officials. Consequently, the showcase industries of shipbuilding and steelmaking, long the mainstays of the economy, could no longer compete internationally.

The Polish leaders of the 1970s were a new breed: communist-technocrats. Previous leaders were reluctant to challenge the fragile social contract that kept goods cheap, if not always plentiful. The new leaders, taking their cues more readily from the West, were less reluctant to ease food subsidies, increase exports, and introduce modest free market mechanisms. Practically, this program translated into higher prices and fewer imported goods on the shelves. Such an austerity program is never easy to sell. The government's decision to raise food prices precisely when the standard of living was dropping triggered widespread protests and the rise of a mass trade union movement. Austerity produced Solidarity.

As they maneuvered in the new space for opposition activities in 1980-81, Solidarity negotiators considered a trade: a measure of austerity for increased worker control of enterprises. The July 1981 compromise between the government and Solidarity combined the Party's preference for market forces with Solidarity's emphasis on worker participation in decisionmaking. The anti-communist opposition, in other words, still defended the ideal social structures of communism while the communists were arguing for something akin to state capitalism. The compromise was short-lived. In December of the same year, the government imposed Martial Law. One Politburo member justified the move economically: "To recover, the Polish economy needs to reduce the spending power of the population by 40 percent. The Solidarity union under Walesa was unable to achieve this peacefully and the army, therefore, had to step in."[5]

Solidarity was suddenly declared an illegal organization, and its demands for true worker participation were ignored. The Polish government, controlled by military authority, nevertheless implemented the market half of the 1981 compromise, with very mixed results. Prices doubled, and wages increased by only 50 percent (a significant reduction in purchasing power that no doubt satisfied the aforementioned Politburo member).[6] Economic output for the year declined 6 percent, bringing the total decline for 1980-82 to 22 percent.[7] The Polish economy had gone from bad to worse.

After continuing to champion market reforms over the next several years, the government decided in October 1987 to quicken the pace. In its 174 theses "regarding the second state of economic reforms," a government planning commission proposed reforms that would have led to a securities market, a bankruptcy law, a lessening of central planning, price increases, and job losses.[8] Hoping for popular support, the government put its version of austerity capitalism to a referendum vote. Still underground, Solidarity was uncertain whether to hold to a trade union position of defending the Polish standard of living from price increases or give in to its slowly building faith in free market solutions. In the end, Solidarity called for a boycott. Standing by their union, Polish citizens refused to vote in numbers sufficient to ratify the government program. The signal was clear: the promised efficiency of capitalism would not be accepted at the price of political continuity for the Party.

Even though its campaign to bring controlled markets to Poland would eventually undermine its political position, the Party was acting more in its own interests than out of any deep ideological commitment to capitalism. Above all, the Party wanted to make the economy more congenial to foreign investors and international lending agencies (indeed had wanted to do so, off and on, since 1957, when the United States blocked Poland's application to the IMF). With an influx of foreign capital, the Party could theoretically regain political authority by restoring the standard of living to its 1978 level.[9] Furthermore, if the Party could control the economic transition away from planning, the *nomenklatura's* position in society would be secure. Industrial planners under the centralized system would become factory owners and managers under the new capitalism.[10]

A marriage between the interests of Party hierarchy and international lenders would ordinarily have been sufficient to produce an infant capitalism. But the majority of Poles simply annulled the marriage. Politburo member Janusz Reykowski was involved in Party discussions on market reform and confirmed that the Party leadership did indeed want to introduce market reform.

> But first, it was not prepared to introduce market reform in a way that would involve all the social costs. The limited legitimacy of the system meant that if the leadership tried to introduce an unpopular measure, it would create popular discontent, and direct mass resistance: strikes, manifestations, mutiny. In June 1988, at the first public meeting organized by the Sociological Society, I argued that without this public support for the government the implementation of reform would be improbable.[11]

Indeed, in 1956, 1970, 1976, 1980, and 1987, Party-sponsored economic adjustment met with substantial resistance.

But the two sides were gradually approaching one another. While the Party was changing its position on political reform, Solidarity was having second thoughts about its economic philosophy. Responding to strong egalitarian sentiment in Polish society in 1980, Solidarity initially opposed market forces that might dilute the social contract—for instance, the elimination of government food subsidies that would lead to large price increases. Although the trade union's economic position was never fully clarified, an important faction within Solidarity supported independent self-management councils through which workers would have greater input into the day-to-day operations of enterprises. Only after workers gained these decisionmaking powers could countrywide austerity even be considered. The debate on economic policy within Solidarity—between the self-management advocates and the proto-free-market advocates—was cut short by Martial Law. After 1981, Solidarity concentrated on survival first, and rebuilding a movement second. Specific discussions of economic programs were a luxury that an underground movement could ill afford.

In 1981, Solidarity intellectual Bronislaw Geremek could declare: "The system is being challenged not because it is socialist but because it is not socialist enough."[12] Such an open commitment to socialist principles within the opposition would virtually disappear after Martial Law. Under the pressures of economic decline and Martial Law, the egalitarianism so prominent in the early 1980s subsequently dissipated. According to research conducted at the Polish Academy of Sciences, economic egalitarianism peaked in 1980: 89.7 percent of subjects interviewed supported the restriction of income inequalities.[13] In 1980, Solidarity appealed to this egalitarian sentiment by offering an alternative to austerity *and* markets. Workers would gain more control of the industries, and Party officials would lose their privileges. The economy would be democratized, and rendered more equal.

Over the next nine years, however, egalitarian values declined precipitously. By 1988, 91.3 percent of subjects interviewed by Polish sociologists supported major wage differentials: a 180-degree reversal.[14] Market solutions were clearly more popular, and both the Party and Solidarity reflected this dynamic in their programs. For the Party, the fall of egalitarianism merely meant that austerity measures could be inset in a larger, now more popular market-oriented reform. For Solidarity, however, the change was problematic. After all, key elements of its constituency—unskilled workers, the poorly educated, senior citizens, workers in failing enterprises—still feared marketization and austerity. Solidarity could not simultaneously push through reform and please this section of its constituency.

Something had to give. And that something was Solidarity itself. Once a unique blend of working class and *intelligentsia,* Solidarity was by the late 1980s witnessing the domination of one wing. The opposition had been reinvigorated by a series of strikes in 1988 as workers responded to the latest government announcement of price increases with heightened demands for an improvement in the standard of living. But it was the intellectuals who seized the opportunity. In December 1988, with Solidarity still illegal and dialogue slated to begin with the government, Lech Walesa created the Citizens' Committee with many of his chief advisers and activists from 1980-81: the medieval historian Bronislaw Geremek, Catholic intellectual Tadeusz Mazowiecki, KOR alumni Adam Michnik and Jacek Kuron. Not only did this experienced and learned team become the Solidarity negotiators in the ensuing roundtable talks (February 6-April 5, 1989) but they subsequently controlled the selection of Solidarity candidates for the June elections as well.

The Committee emphasized one wing of Solidarity—the pragmatists who, in 1980-81, cautioned about the need for a "self-limited revolution" and grudgingly recognized the Polish Communist Party's strategic concerns and the Soviet Union's geopolitical interests. Solidarity's fundamentalists, meanwhile, placed greater emphasis on certain values that could not be compromised: national independence, democracy, workers' rights. While the pragmatists—particularly Walesa, Geremek, and Mazowiecki—embraced these same values, they preferred different tactics, less uncompromising means to similar ends.[15]

In 1989, through the Citizens' Committee, the pragmatists returned, chastened by the experience of Martial Law but just as committed to compromise. For a trade union-sponsored opposition, the team sent into the roundtable negotiations was short on workers (only 37 of the 232 participants).[16] The nature of the talks, however, encouraged experienced and diplomatic proto-politicians. And the negotiations did come to a resolution, despite the predictions of the opposition's unrepentant fundamentalists. Though vague in spots, the roundtable agreement did nonetheless guarantee a legal Solidarity and mandate semi-free elections.

The greatest of the agreement's ambiguities lay in its economic provisions. On the eve of the negotiations, the vacuum of economic proposals was stunning. The communist government still clung to its unpopular austerity measures. Solidarity maintained the language of worker self-management, but possessed no concrete plan for the larger economic issues of reforming state enterprises, handling the foreign debt, or restructuring wage and price policies. Beyond restricting wage increases, the roundtable agreement did not mandate market reform.[17]

Everyone involved knew, however, that with the political stand-off defused, austerity was just around the corner. Each side was prepared to compromise further. Turning its back on worker self-management, Solidarity resurrected an earlier deal: support for austerity capitalism in exchange for legalization and greater political power. With Solidarity finally backing its austerity package, the Party accepted on principle the privatization of state assets which would disenfranchise it as an institution (though continuing to enrich individual Party associates).

Although exposing themselves dangerously on the economic front, the compromise-oriented intellectuals had won an important victory at the roundtable. They moved quickly to consolidate their gains. With only two months separating the conclusion of the roundtable from the June elections, the Citizens' Committee handpicked the opposition candidates—bowing to key constituencies, accepting input from the regions—but nonetheless circumventing democratic procedures in the interests of unity and speed. Solidarity wanted to enter the elections with a common front—not a loose confederation of interests. That there was such a brief period to launch the campaigns of over 300 candidates made unity all the more important.

Events were to favor the Solidarity intellectuals. With one exception, Solidarity candidates won every seat they contested (according to the roundtable agreement, they could run for any seat in the upper house, but only 35 percent of the seats in the lower house).[18] The Party was frankly astonished at how tenuous its legitimacy had become. Nevertheless the Solidarity intellectuals kept to the principle of self-limitation, allowing Party leader Wojciech to be elected president and the Party to fill parliamentary seats it couldn't muster enough votes for in the first round of balloting. Despite Solidarity's almost self-effacing accommodation, the Party's fortunes continued to decline with the defection of its political allies to the opposition (the Communist Party had ruled in a "coalition" with two major and several small dependent organizations). With the help of the newly independent Peasant and Democratic parties, Solidarity could then muster the power to form its own government.

The intellectuals took charge. The nod for prime minister went, significantly, to an intellectual—Tadeusz Mazowiecki. Active in every key intellectual movement in Poland since 1956, Mazowiecki had been an important link between the *intelligentsia* and the striking workers in 1980, and had gone on to become one of Walesa's most important ministers of compromise. He was active in mediating the 1988 strikes and in helping to inaugurate the roundtable negotiations. After the legalization of Solidarity, he returned to editing the reinstated Solidarity weekly, a job previously cut short by Martial Law. A poor public speaker and a rather weak administrator, Mazowiecki may not have been the most glamorous choice for Poland's first non-communist prime minister. But he was acceptable to Lech Walesa, the Solidarity intellectuals, and the Church. For his cabinet, Mazowiecki gathered ministers of the same stock—a professor, a lawyer, a computer specialist, a theater director, a rector of Warsaw University, a journalist, and an economist. No steelworkers, no coal miners, no electricians. Even the ministry of labor post went to an intellectual—Jacek Kuron.

The Solidarity intellectuals had triumphed and, in their triumph, had demonstrated the difference between 1980 and 1989. Gone was talk of economic alternatives, of workers' rights, of industrial democracy. The intellectuals had begun to assert a new set of interests that more closely reflected their economic station in life. The free market held promise for the white collars. Blue collars would face only austerity, however that pain might be rationalized by intellectuals using sterile Party-speak or glib oppositional rhetoric. Jan Maria Rokita, opposition member of Parliament, remarked after the roundtable negotiations that "reform does not have to be painful. A reform is done to ease the pain."[19] A startlingly similar opinion came from Party-aligned economist Marcin Swiecicki: "The situation is already painful. What is ahead of us has to be less painful. There will be costs, but it will be less than the pain we already have."[20] The sentiment that Poland was at the bottom and could fall no farther was an interesting intellectual conceit, one that would hold little appeal for the victims of austerity and rapidly escalating income differentials.

Solidarity intellectuals were heading for government, and workers remained in increasingly powerless labor unions. The long-awaited austerity was approaching and, as usual, it wouldn't be the politicians—whatever their political stripe—who would be tightening belts.

Shock

At the end of December 1989, the new Solidarity government of Tadeusz Mazowiecki set into motion Poland's "grand experiment."[21] The country had been prepared by its new leaders. The jubilation of the spring had faded, the winter had arrived, and Poles had become long-faced. "We have suffered for most of our history," an elderly Pole told me on a train trip from Warsaw to Krakow in 1990, "we are suffering now under austerity and we will probably suffer in the future as well." A fitting sentiment, perhaps, in a country whose historical experience has been likened to the trials of Christ by its 19th-century poets and 20th-century activists, in a country which now had a prime minister whose face sagged, whose shoulders drooped, and whose entire term of office seemed nothing less than an extended political crucifixion.

Explicitly designed to combat a double-digit monthly inflation, the revolutionary Polish economic program removed government price supports, placed a cap on wages, strictly controlled the money supply, made the Polish zloty internally convertible, triggered a recession, and precipitated a series of social problems.[22] This now infamous recipe for reform was concocted—with much imported Western help—by a Polish economist in his early 40s, Leszek Balcerowicz.

Once a member of the Polish Communist Party, Balcerowicz helped to compose a radical market-based reform plan in the late 1970s which the Party ultimately ignored. Given the posts of deputy prime minister and finance minister in 1989, Balcerowicz eagerly seized this second opportunity to translate theory into practice. He stayed in close touch with the International Monetary Fund, ensuring that when the plan went into effect it had the full support of the international financial community (for its part, the IMF provided a $1.5 billion loan). He drew extensively upon the work of Harvard economist Jeffrey Sachs, a young and persuasive adviser who in the 1980s had devastated the Bolivian economy in the name of monetary stability. Billed as a radical cure for a radical problem, the Balcerowicz-Sachs plan seemed to come directly from the *laissez-faire* school of unregulated capitalism—a la Friedrich von Hayak and Milton Friedman—even though the shapers of "overnight capitalism" more often than not argued in favor of an eventual Swedish or West German outcome.[23]

Social consensus was critical to ensure the plan's success. Balcerowicz announced that he needed six months before his plan could be effectively evaluated: half a year of suspended judgements. During those first months of 1990, while neighboring countries experienced their first taste of electoral politics, Poles waited patiently for Balcerowicz's promises to come true. Minister of Labor and longtime opposition leader Jacek Kuron repeatedly appeared on Polish television to lecture Poles on the art of belt-tightening. Solidarity's leaders promised nearly unconditional support for the plan with a virtual no-strike pledge. Wlodzimierz Kesicki, a Solidarity representative at the Ursus tractor plant in Warsaw, put the matter succinctly: "It is a very necessary plan because it is Draconian. There will be much sacrifice but it will turn the Polish economy into a normal system."[24] Foreign companies seemed to be happy with the approach of "normalcy," and so did the IMF.

Almost immediately the Balcerowicz plan succeeded in its primary objective by reducing monthly inflation to single digits. The cost was heavy, however. By the end of 1990, unemployment had topped one million. A deep recession had sent industry into a tailspin (a 23 percent drop in the first year). The standard of living had declined nearly 35 percent. Although the plan's proponents argued that these figures did not take into account private sector growth, such economic development could sustain only a limited number of people and then, generally, at a rather meager level.[25] A trade surplus was pointed to as a great achievement, but some argued that it was merely a result of starving the population.[26] In any case, by 1991, that surplus had disappeared and inflation had also returned. It is therefore not surprising to discover that although many powerful people in Poland and abroad raved about the Balcerowicz plan, the average Pole found austerity distinctly unpleasant. "Public patience with the belt-tightening government policy has been rather short-lived," deputy chair of the Solidarity National Commission Lech Kaczynski said in an early 1991 interview. "Actually, people had had enough by the end of May 1990."[27] Despite these dispiriting indicators and signs of public discontent, Balcerowicz was enjoying unprecedented support in September 1990. Some even talked of

Balcerowicz as prime minister.[28] Like the trade surplus and the inflation rate, this too would change.

The Balcerowicz plan had taken care of the politically difficult and economically simple tasks first—restructuring the money supply and removing government support for artificially low prices. The more complicated question of the future of state-owned industries remained. Most of Poland's wealth was tied up in its food processing plants, sulfur mines, steel mills, and textile factories. Quite familiar with the Reagan and Thatcher revolutions, Balcerowicz had an answer for this problem as well: privatization.[29]

A decade earlier, a significant element of Solidarity had a different answer to the question of who would administer factories. Workers would gradually take over control of decisionmaking through workers' councils. The system would be based on *samorzad* or self-management. "This was the Solidarity battlecry of 1981," journalist Dawid Warszawski explains.

> Most of Solidarity's economic program was built around the idea of workers' self-management. This is gone, dead, disappeared completely. Essentially because anything which smacks, or seems to smack, of socialism, left-wing or whatever, is a dead political proposal. This does not mean that the social needs addressed by the program of worker self-management have disappeared. They lack a language with which to be expressed.[30]

The term *samorzad* still appears in the Polish political discourse. Deprived of its radical economic meaning, *samorzad* is today used primarily in its other sense of local self-government, the democratically-elected town councils. Workers' councils, some of which have been in place since the 1950s, have lost their viability as alternative decision-making structures. Even Solidarity officials agree. "A third body is not necessary," says Bozena Chojnacka of Solidarity at the Ursus tractor plant. "There is management, and there is the union."[31]

Without the option of either worker control or continued state ownership, the various types of privatization remain, all based on the notion of transforming state enterprises into joint-stock companies. But who will buy these stocks? In 1989, theoreticians of privatization argued that average Poles would buy stocks in the new companies with the excess zlotys they had in bank accounts, under mattresses, or invested in gold. After the massive price increases associated with the Balcerowicz plan, Poles have used all their savings simply to survive, and capital is no longer magically abundant.[32] Only three groups would have money enough to invest: foreign companies, the new rich, and the former privileged elite who had always had access to hard currency. The effect of putting shares on sale, economist Ryszard Bugaj told the daily *Gazeta Wyborcza,* "will be the concentration of most of the wealth in the hands of a narrow group of people."[33]

But even these groups might be reluctant to invest in stocks. Why should foreign investors, for instance, choose Poland instead of safer opportunities in eastern Germany, Czechoslovakia, or Hungary? Poland, after all, has a strong independent trade union movement (sadly enough, even Poles who strenuously supported Solidarity for the last decade are unwilling to invest in privatized enterprises where trade union activity would cut into their stock bonuses). Investment in Poland's infrastructure would perhaps yield long-term profits (after considerable plant restructuring), but the aforementioned groups of investors generally prefer short-term gain.

Furthermore, many state enterprises are simply not profitable enough to privatize and would therefore not attract investors. In June 1990, Krzysztof Lis, the ministry official in charge of privatization, reported that of 100 firms to be privatized, only ten had guaranteed buyers. The government has been very careful not to privatize risky enterprises which, if they failed, would undermine public confidence in the whole process. Although seemingly confused over the various permutations of privatization, Poles have generally supported the most worker-oriented alternative—the Employee Stock Ownership Plan (ESOP).[34] Aside from the *samorzad* faction of Solidarity, however, few political forces have been willing to give ESOP more than token support.[35]

One recent privatization plan sought to solve the problem of scarce capital by giving stocks away for free. But this plan was rejected because it was frankly too egalitarian. The Polish government has decided instead to employ a voucher system in which Poles pay a fee for shares in newly privatized companies.[36] And the workers? They are likely to lose not only their ownership rights but their jobs as well. According to one estimate, privatization will add at least another million Poles to the unemployment rolls.[37]

* * *

As the Polish government prepared to give away its assets to the private sector, many Poles worried that the state might liquidate its other functions as well. Under greatest threat is the social safety net. Poles had never benefited from particularly good health care, but at least it was cheap. Pensions were not generally generous, but at least they were guaranteed. Public transportation, subsidized rents and food, job retraining: what would be the future of these programs under the Balcerowicz plan? The early indications have not been good.

In April 1990, at the second Solidarity trade union conference, Minister of Labor Jacek Kuron stood up to address the audience. "The government has no program of social policy," he announced with surprising candor for a public official. "And I am responsible for this lack."[38] Yet Kuron remained at his post. Oddly enough, many Poles took it for granted that the government simply had no program. "We live in a very pragmatic time," said Tomasz Kazmierczak, one of the advisers responsible for the Mazowiecki government's social policy. "I think it is useless to talk about social justice when there simply is no money. Ten years ago, such wonderful ideas as justice, solidarity, and freedom were what people gathered together around. But now, improving the economy is number one."[39] Pragmatism in this context means: no zlotys. Money may have been flowing in from the West, but it was going into funds to stabilize the currency, into enterprise funds for small business, into balance-of-payments funds. Foreign loans and investments were assiduously avoiding social programs.

Although virtually all Poles suffer from cutbacks in the social sphere, workers have shouldered the greater burden. True, the Polish government designed a makeshift program of benefits and minimal job retraining. But the amount of money provided for unemployment benefits barely covered a couple hundred thousand unemployed workers at subsistence salary. Employment services have frequently consisted of little more than a sparsely filled bulletin board. Prepared neither for the current jobless nor the latest crop of university and secondary school graduates entering the job market, the government has also not made provisions for the flood of disenfranchised farmers whose profession will gradually be made redundant by agricultural reforms. Nor are the cities prepared to handle the eventual exodus from the countryside as the nearly 30 percent of the population working in agriculture is reduced to "modern" proportions.

Once the vanguard of change in Poland and the subjects of glowing profiles in Western newspapers, Polish workers have discovered that they now have few cheerleaders. They are no longer on a winning team. "In many ways," journalist Lawrence Weschler writes, "it was the brute, courageous, historic action of those now being left behind that allowed the breakout by the others."[40] Not only do they have to contend with Solidarity politicans and Party reformers, this group of threatened workers—the chief opponents of drastic market reform—has to face the IMF and Western governments. Ordinarily, a powerful trade union would be expected to protect these interests. But a strong union is not a strong favorite with either the IMF or foreign industries. According to the *laissez-faire* ideology that still holds sway in the US government and among multilateral lending institutions, unions distort market conditions and potentially threaten foreign investments.

True to their history, many workers have struck back, literally. Shipyard and railway workers in May 1990, coal miners in December 1990: these strikes indicated that Solidarity could not guarantee complete worker acquiescence to the Balcerowicz project. The Solidarity government responded with strike restrictions and measures such as the *popiwek.* Instituted at the end of 1990, this limit on wages requires employers to pay five zlotys to a state fund for every zloty given out in salaries over an established maximum. Although tied to cost-of-living increases, the *popiwek* ensures that worker salaries continue to fall in relation to prices. Meanwhile, the new law doesn't apply to private businesses or partially privatized companies. Workers in state enterprises—by far the majority of the Solidarity membership—are thus hit hardest: by the threatened closure of their enterprises as well as by the more immediate erosion of their wages through inflation. Strikes throughout the first half of 1991 focused on repealing the much-hated *popiwek.*

It wasn't only industrial workers who were going on strikes. With the government no longer buying on a regular basis, Polish farmers were feeling the pinch. The drop in sales of potatos to the former Soviet Union, for instance, had created an enormous potato surplus in Poland. Falling prices had made the potato virtually worthless and put the potato farmer at wits' end: two and one-half tons of potatos for a pair of shoes![41] In June 1990, in the small but strategically located town of Mlawa, dairy farmers blockaded the major highway connecting Gdansk and the Baltic Coast to Warsaw and points south. The strike ended only after the *deus ex machina* intervention of Lech Walesa. Indeed, if Walesa hadn't gone directly from Geneva through Warsaw to Mlawa, the police might have intervened in what would have been the first violent altercation of the new Polish democracy (shades of Shays's Rebellion). Walesa managed to play both sides: "Your demands are fully justified," he told the farmers. "But you have chosen a wrong form of protest. You cannot call it a local problem and then block the main road from Warsaw to Gdansk."[42] Scolding the farmers but backing their demands, Walesa was able to defuse the crisis, momentarily. An occupation of the ministry of agriculture and scattered strikes throughout the country nevertheless followed.

How did the organized voice of workers and farmers react to these actions? Compromised by its agreements with the government, Solidarity was at first reluctant to complain too much about the evisceration of the social programs, the squeezing of workers and farmers, and the overall downturn in the economy. It had tacitly agreed to give Balcerowicz a honeymoon period, accepting unemployment as necessary and wage restrictions as pragmatic.[43] With a new leader having succeeded Lech Walesa, Solidarity has made noises more recently that its support of government policy is qualified.[44]

It may be too late. Today Solidarity no longer represents workers in Poland. When it was ten million strong in 1981, Solidarity was truly the embodiment of the Polish working class. Re-legalized in 1989, the trade union focused on electing its slate of candidates to parliament, leaving little time or energy to organize at the enterprise level. Now Solidarity numbers roughly two and one-half million members. The once official trade union OPZZ is roughly twice that size. Since resigning from the once Soviet-controlled trade union federation WFTU in late 1990, OPZZ has ironically become the independent union while Solidarity remains compromised by its links to government.

Solidarity has finally accepted that it can no longer be a force for reshaping society according to its own principles. The Balcerowicz plan should have been the battleground: Solidarity's alternative against the IMF plan. But Solidarity demonstrated that, contrary to 1980-81, it had no alternative beyond anti-communism. Once Poland acquired a non-communist government, Solidarity could only imagine a role for itself comparable to the AFL-CIO. Worse, Solidarity leaders were instrumental in supporting a modernization program that would build the very corporate capitalism that *they knew* would prove to be the trade union's enemy. As Jacek Kuron put it, "I have always said I would like to be a man of the moderate left in a decent capitalist country. Unfortunately we don't have capitalism. So I have to take part in a program of creating capitalism. The program is not left wing."[45] Jan Litynski is more "dialectical" in his approach to the Balcerowicz camp: "We will institute every single one of your reforms, knowing full well that we will spend the rest of our lives fighting their consequences."[46]

The Solidarity revolution of 1989-90 succeeded, at least formally, in establishing political democracy. The more thoroughgoing revolution of Balcerowicz would do little to plant the seeds of economic democracy—the original core of the Solidarity trade union position—in post-communist Poland.

But by 1992, Balcerowicz was on his way out, and Poland was once again at economic crossroads. To understand the fall of Balcerowicz, we have to step back, for a moment, into Polish politics.

Aftershocks

Both the economic problems and successes of the Balcerowicz plan have been closely followed and strenuously debated in Poland and abroad. The political dimension of the scheme, however, has been frequently overlooked. The development of the Balcerowicz plan can be likened to a pyramid. At the bottom, a mass movement demands change. It generates political bodies—Solidarity and the Citizens' Committee—which in turn produce a government. Then, at the pinnacle, a set of experts—both domestic and imported—detail an economic strategy which is implemented without ever having been put to a vote. The chief spokesman of this expert clique, Harvard economist Jeffrey Sachs, suggested the neoliberal remedy of last resort (employed by the Reagan administration in the early 1980s): squeeze inflation out of the system by setting into motion a deep recession. One of the strategy's most salable elements was its political sophistication—put the population through the wringer quickly before voters could throw the rogues out of office via the new medium of democracy. Compared to nothing, which was the Solidarity economic policy at the time, the Sachs proposal was appealing.

But as Sachs's suggestions became the Balcerowicz plan and austerity began to bite, modernization began to lose some of its appeal. The symptoms of deep dissatisfaction could be best measured politically. In the fall of 1990, Poland endured a fractious election for a new president; one year later, a low voter turnout produced a new parliament that was a fragmented mirror of a divided society. The unity of the Solidarity days was a distant memory. Polish politics was now entering an era of factionalism and instability.

The impresario for this political drama was Walesa. The center of Polish politics until the Mazowiecki team took power in 1989, Walesa watched from the sidelines in 1990, the head of a trade union but neither a member of government nor a representative in parliament. Throughout the spring of 1990, he maneuvered for political space. In June, he ousted long-time colleague Henryk Wujec from the leadership of the Citizens' Committee and set about to pack the organization with his own supporters, preparing for the eventual split between himself and the Mazowiecki camp.[47] Attentive to the complaints of average Poles, Walesa was searching for the weak points of a government he ostensibly had created. Stealing a turn from US politicians, he played up his "outsider" status, exploiting the public's perceptions of the Balcerowicz plan as conspiratorial wheeling and dealing (a tactic that combined anti-communism, anti-intellectualism, anti-modernism, and anti-Semitism).

In his quest for the presidency, Walesa had to rise to a significant challenge. Tadeusz Mazowiecki, the prime minister also running for the presidency, was the most respected politician in the country for the better part of 1990. Not only was he more popular than his parliamentary and ministerial colleagues, Mazowiecki also consistently outpolled Walesa.

Walesa also had a handicap: his reputation as a loose cannon. Providing an inestimable government service by resolving labor disputes left and right, Walesa nevertheless was not highly regarded for his statesmanship. Indeed Walesa exhibited some classic authoritarian features—for instance, his predilection for decrees. "Today, decrees are necessary," he told one interviewer. "And they will be necessary for a long time to come. Decrees in the cause of democracy, as an effective response to the gaps Parliament won't fill in on time."[48] Even before assuming the presidency, Walesa attempted to rule by decree, ordering the Solidarity daily *Gazeta Wyborcza* to remove the Solidarity logo from its masthead and trying to oust editor Adam Michnik, a longtime associate but more recent political opponent. The logo went, but Michnik stayed aboard, to conduct a vigorous anti-Walesa campaign in the pages of the newspaper that included photos of the candidate at his most Napoleonic (hand in vest) and long impassioned essays of no confidence. Whatever his virtues, journalist Dawid Warszawski remarks, "Walesa is not and never was a democrat. The Polish democratic opposition sold Walesa to the world as a democrat because that greatly enhanced our status, and God knows we would have been in dire straits without Walesa. But the man is not a democrat and doesn't pretend to be."[49]

But Walesa could certainly play the game of formal democracy quite well. And Mazowiecki, a congenital frowner, could not, despite the edge initial popularity gave him. Poor at public speaking and with virtually no charisma, Mazowiecki placed third in the Polish presidential race in November 1990. Although losing votes through sheer campaign ineptitude, Mazowiecki was really the first political victim of the economic reforms. True, according to most polls, the population supported some form of economic reform. But that didn't mean that Poles wouldn't seek political revenge nonetheless—for the high prices, low wages, unemployment, and homelessness generated by the Balcerowicz shock therapy. Mazowiecki was the messenger of bad news: he was politically executed in December 1990. Balcerowicz was merely an appointee who had promised nothing but hardship. As the late Polish columnist Stefan Kisielewski observed after the elections, "Balcerowicz pulled down the Mazowiecki government only to jump out himself, like a cork out of a bottle."[50] Or, put another way, what had first been a milestone for Mazowiecki ultimately turned out to be a millstone. But even the outcome of this presidential election was mutable. In the quicksilver fluidity of post-communist Polish politics, the next election would reverse the positions of Balcerowicz and Mazowiecki.

The truly disturbing phenomenon of the 1990 presidential elections was neither Walesa's demagoguery nor Mazowiecki's ineptitude. Rather, it was the strong showing of Stanislaw Tyminski, the "man from nowhere," an emigre businessman with a right-wing political bent and a flair for the inaccurate. Returning to his homeland to promise prosperity overnight if elected, Tyminski shocked everyone by coming in second behind Walesa. Compared to Tyminski, Walesa was positively Jeffersonian. Tyminski's libelous smears of Mazowiecki, his hiring of former secret police as campaign personnel, and his use of pornographic movies as fundraisers shocked the Catholic Church out of its neutrality and frightened virtually every Mazowiecki supporter into switching to Walesa in the run-off. The success of Tyminski—among the young, the unemployed, and the rural—was Balcerowicz backlash and an important warning to the modernizers.

The presidential election was not the referendum on the Balcerowicz plan it should have been. Mazowiecki supported the plan, Walesa called for its acceleration, and Tyminski, with typical precision, prattled on about a nation of entrepreneurs. Ironically, Polish voters expressed their dissatisfaction with shock therapy by voting for candidates who promised double shocks. One can attribute this to the naivete of voters who have never experienced the promises of both politicians and capitalists. Or perhaps the voters reasoned, rather logically, that Walesa would bring them through the Balcerowicz ordeal more rapidly.

True to his campaign pledges, President Walesa appointed neoliberal Jan Bielecki as prime minister to replace the departed and discouraged Mazowiecki and kept Balcerowicz on to finish what he had started. The new president reaped early rewards for the move: a 50 percent reduction of Poland's foreign debt.[51] He was granted this concession because he had managed to do the bidding of both the domestic and international business communities, defending "the government against the angry crowd," according to Poland's foremost supporter of corporate interests.[52] But Walesa was also preparing to follow Mazowiecki down the path of diminishing electoral returns.

Meanwhile, with Poland's first entirely free parliamentary elections set for October 1991, the political situation in the country was worsening. As the recession refused to lift, Poles began to lose whatever confidence they once had in their new politicians. The turnout for the October elections was predictably low, around 40 percent. None of the 29 parties that eventually made it into Parliament received more than 13 percent of the vote, with Mazowiecki's coalition, the Democratic Union, only marginally ahead of the post-communist Democratic Left Alliance. The two principal government partners, Walesa's Center Alliance and Prime Minister Jan Bielecki's Liberal Democratic Congress Party, were well back in the pack. Analysts scrambled to interpret the results. Was this a victory for the left, the right, the modernizers, the traditionalists, the Balcerowicz supporters, or the Balcerowicz detractors?

The simple answer is: no one won. Poles declared both their non-interest in party-run democracy and in austerity capitalism. The Balcerowicz plan had not delivered its promised goods: nearly two years after implementation, the Polish economy was still mired in recession, unemployment, and corruption. Industrial production had dropped in the first six months of 1991, nearly 10 percent over the same period the previous year, and 35 percent since 1989. Real wages had again declined.[53] Unemployment stood at two million by the end of 1991 and was rising. The Polish recession would not end shortly as many had predicted, central bank governor-designate Marek Dabrowski admitted to the press, but would last well into 1993.[54] The budget deficit had grown so large that even the IMF decided to suspend credit in the fall of 1991. Walesa had not provided clear leadership, the Solidarity trade union could not be counted on to protect workers' interests, the political parties were absorbed in infighting. If Stan Tyminski's Party X had not been disqualified from participating in the parliamentary elections (because of registration irregularities), Poland might today be governed by a fanatic whose disposition, if not actual policies, qualify him as neofascist.

Why didn't Walesa change policies in 1991, sacrificing Balcerowicz and his plan in order to strengthen the new president's own political position? Several voices from within Walesa's party had urged just such a strategy.[55] According to one government survey in 1991, only 5 percent of respondents wanted to continue with the Balcerowicz plan unaltered.[56] The Polish public had lost its early enthusiasm for capitalism.[57] When asked by a reporter from the French newspaper *Le Monde,* even Walesa himself confessed to being frustrated with the realities of capitalism: "We were naive: we believed all those slogans and were sold down the river."[58] But given an opportunity to change substantially the Balcerowicz approach, Walesa decided to continue with austerity.[59]

Just as Walesa maneuvered for political space in 1990, Mazowiecki executed a flanking maneuver in 1991 that managed to gain him electoral support. By welding together a new political coalition—the Democratic Union—that drew support from both social democrats and modernizing liberals, Mazowiecki was able to translate resentment of the Balcerowicz plan into votes at the polls.[60] Although Mazowiecki's party came in first, the liberal-left was shut out of the new government. A five-party conservative government led by Jan Olszewski started work in December 1991, promising to ease austerity but not making any strong moves in that direction. But there was one important casualty of the transition—Balcerowicz—replaced by the new year.[61] The man was gone; would the plan be sure to follow?

In early 1992, Olszewski offered a new economic blueprint for Poland that softened somewhat the previous monetarism by, for instance, guaranteeing minimum prices for farmers. In other respects, however, the blueprint was Balcerowicz repackaged—wages would still decline, the standard of living would still suffer.[62] But even this tepid mitigation of shock met with IMF disapproval and objections from the *laissez-faire* faction of Parliament. The Polish government and Lech Walesa thus find themselves in a very difficult position, caught between an international community that makes demands but provides little aid and a population that wants rapid economic reform but understandably does not want to suffer the consequences.

With the major parties trying to stake out centrist positions that the international economic community would find acceptable, various ultra-liberal and ultra-conservative forces have taken advantage of the new opportunities. In the market sphere, for instance, where Balcerowicz and company promoted unrestricted private enterprise, there was no greater success story than "Art B." Started by two young entrepreneurs on $300, the company Art B had grown in value to $300 million three years later. Only one catch. Most of this money was made by exploiting the numerous banking loopholes in the new Polish system. When the thievery was discovered, the two owners were already in Israel, leaving several high-ranking officials, including the vice-president of the National Bank of Poland, to take the fall.[63] As a World Bank adviser remarked, with no trace of irony, the Art B scandal "is what the market economy is all about. Other countries wanting to create their own set of dynamic entrepreneurs should look long and hard at Polish mistakes...and then repeat them."[64] In addition to the funds that disappeared in an illegal debt buy-back scheme, Poland has already lost over $1 billion to fraud. And those are only the abuses that are known.[65]

But it wasn't just ruthless entrepreneurs who thrived on the chaos. Having successfully survived the communist years by artfully mixing dissent and collaboration, the Catholic Church was eager to take advantage of the new order to strengthen its own institutional position. The previous primate, Stefan Wyszynski, had kept the Church powerful for nearly four decades, holding together an institution riven by disagreements over its relationship with the government. Jozef Glemp, who succeeded Wyszynski during the height of the Solidarity period in 1981, was a less remarkable man. But Poles had been willing to forgive their primate, even after his ambiguous statements on Martial Law and several questionable comments on Judaism.[66] In 1990, Glemp topped the list of most popular Poles and the Church remained the country's most respected institution.

Capitalizing on this popularity, the Church decided to cash in favors on two critical issues on its agenda: abortion and religion in schools. Victory came quickly and covertly on the second issue. Rather than working through the Parliament, Church officials put direct pressure on the government and succeeded in getting the ministry of education to issue a directive on the matter. Gossip on the street was that neither Mazowiecki nor top officials in the ministry were enthusiastic about the idea. Yet, with his position as prime minister so weak, Mazowiecki pushed the measure through to maintain Church support. Whatever the process of its formulation, the directive was quite explicit. Beginning September 1990, classes in religion were offered at all levels, even kindergarten. Students who did not opt for the classes were offered classes in ethics "wherever possible." Further, *Gazeta Wyborcza* reported, "the hanging of crosses in classrooms and group prayers twice a day will be optional."[67] No other religious denominations participated in the discussions, leading to a Polish Ecumenical Council protest.

Although many Poles were outraged at the Church's extension of its power, demonstrations were limited. One Polish friend told me that in the top grade in her child's school, only 50 percent of the students decided to take the classes while in the lower grades it was not uncommon for the entire class to choose the instruction (not surprising given the peer pressure in the lower grades). Liberal Catholics, such as Mazowiecki, have not been happy with the Church's power play. As an editor at the Catholic weekly *Tygodnik Powszechny* told me, 90 percent of Polish children had already been attending optional religion lessons. The best way of turning Poland into an atheistic country, he argued, was to make these lessons a mandatory school duty to be detested like all other subjects.[68]

Successful in penetrating the educational system, the Church discovered the limits of its support with its attempt to criminalize abortion. Although a Church-supported bill that would have sent patients and doctors involved in abortions to prison passed one chamber of Parliament, it was easily defeated in the other.[69] In repudiating the Church, politicians were simply listening to their constituents. Polls had shown that the majority of the population opposed the abortion bill.[70] Despite the rather minimal consciousness of women's rights in Poland, a newly invigorated independent women's movement organized successfully around the issue.[71] The Church, meanwhile, was slipping in popularity throughout the country.[72] When influential politicians including Walesa began talking of turning Poland into a theocracy, the response was so negative (even from Walesa's own party) that Primate Glemp withdrew the suggestion.[73] In another challenge to Church authority, the courts have begun to address the legality of religious instruction in schools.[74] Although stung by these various repudiations, the Church has certainly not withdrawn from the public arena.

* * *

Poland after shock therapy is by no means pacified: all shock and no therapy has instead made it a crisis-wracked country. Where does Walesa stand in all this? He has registered his support for the Balcerowicz plan but has also spoken out strongly in support of workers and farmers. He has attacked the privileges of entrenched interests—"Give us your FBI," he told one US official, "and we will clean them out tomorrow"—but now on the inside, he has not initiated a witchhunt.[75] He has always supported the Church but may also be in a better position to temper its influence in the worldly sphere. He has talked of decrees and of democracy, of consensus and of kings. He may, like Jaruzelski before him, be little more than a moral figurehead.

Or he may create an imperial presidency. As soon as he took office, Walesa floated the idea of a presidential council. His nemesis Adam Michnik was quick to lead the attack, arguing that "creating artificial, supra-constitutional institutions to replace however slightly, the government or parliament, is dangerous for democracy."[76] Walesa's next dubious proposal to be both president and prime minister met with vociferous disapproval. With the Balcerowicz plan stalled, elements of the religious right wing calling for a theocratic state, and the last round of parliamentary elections inconclusive, Walesa has indicated that the Polish drift requires a strong hand. He likens himself to a bus driver with Poland the wandering bus: "There's no place for democracy when you are driving a bus. Imagine being in a bus where everyone wants to grab the steering wheel. The first tree will finish you off."[77]

Ushering in an era of chaos, shock therapy has only encouraged such undemocratic political responses. But unfortunately for Polish politics, and for the Polish economy, few workable alternatives have been offered in the place of the Balcerowicz plan. The modernization of Poland, if it continues along this trajectory, will continue to claim its political victims as each successive administration shoulders the blame for austerity and stagnation. Yet modernization, as the next section details, continues to be the beacon in the darkness by which all boats navigate.

Modernization and its discontents

Begun in the late Middle Ages when science gradually established independence from religion, modernization came to represent the application of scientific technique to industry by the end of the Enlightenment. In the late 19th century, as industry finally overwhelmed agriculture, the marriage of technology and the economy produced corporate capitalism, the modern vehicle for modernization. This particular model of applied technology—primarily Western, secular, and supported by the middle class—has promised unlimited progress in the modern age through urbanization, industrialization, and centralization. As the carrier of Western cultural values, modernization has, as Theodore Von Laue asserts, recast the world in the image of the West. The modernizers

> foisted their singular qualities on the unwilling and unprepared majority of humanity, dynamically transforming the entire world in their own image and establishing a hierarchy and prestige defined by the success of imitation. In the world revolution of Westernization, Western political ambition and competitiveness became universal—and fiercer because of the fury born of persistent inequality.[78]

The history of Eastern Europe in the latter half of the 20th century can be understood as a painful detour from this main current of modernization.[79] Anti-capitalist, anti-middle class, and anti-Western, Stalinism represented another path to modernity—a fast track—that for all its radical pace and execution, was saturated with the same assumptions of progress and industrial technology as its Western antithesis. Eastern Europe, an area always one step behind in the modernization process, was particularly vulnerable to the quick fix approach. The professed Marxist goals of the Stalinist model—a classless society, equality and prosperity, a dictatorship of the proletariat succeeded by the withering away of the state—were almost incidental. In the emerging geopolitical order, Stalinism was a shortcut to the power and prestige of the West: a method of outmodernizing the modernizers.

Over the course of the Cold War, the ideology of communism gradually faded in Eastern Europe, the result of immediate purges and slow bureaucratic creep. But the desire remained to catch up or even, in Khrushchev's words, to "bury" the West. With only rhetorical adherence to communist precepts, the Eastern European modernizers paid less and less attention to non-Western alternatives and focused exclusively on ends. As economic crisis in the East intensified in the 1970s and 1980s, the communist countries (particularly Poland and Hungary) re-evaluated their commitment to centralized planning and collectivized agriculture, and embarked on the long journey back to Western-style modernity.

The present anti-communist governments in the region, though they might feel uneasy with the continuity, are simply more explicit than their communist predecessors. They want to fit back into the mainstream of modernization as it flows in the West. But it is no longer the late 19th or early 20th century. Eastern Europe is now undertaking its leap forward at a time when the West has begun to rethink the entire modernization project. Unrestricted growth has both social and environmental limits. Industrial production has in part been replaced by the service economy, computer automation, and an information society. Large corporations and government intervention have given the lie to the idealized free market. Fears have permeated Western societies: of the large, of the centralized, of the industrialized, of the overly urban, and of the constantly growing.

Eastern Europe is strangely out of phase. It is caught in the very heart of the modern era, preoccupied with creating a labor market, reshaping industry, making agriculture more efficient, finding a place in the international trade regime. Its definitions of "liberal" and "conservative" are even caught in a time warp. In the 19th and early 20th centuries, "liberal" signified a commitment to the free market, not only as the organizing principle behind the economy, but also as the most democratic and efficient method of organizing political and social space. "Conservatives," on the other hand, recoiled in horror from the market since, after all, capitalism tore apart the family and pulled people away from small communities, from churches, from bedrock values. Only after World War II did "liberal" acquire its Keynesian baggage of government intervention in the economy. Only after the defeat of the Nixon wing of the Republican Party in the wake of Watergate did the neoconservatives rise to power, bringing with them an entirely new brand of conservatism, wedded to a distinctly "liberal" idealization of the market.[80] East European liberals more resemble John Stuart Mill than Michael Dukakis; the region's conservatives are closer to G.K. Chesterton than Ronald Reagan. In other words, East Europeans line up for and against modernization as though the debate were taking place in a 19th century salon.[81]

To complicate matters further, Eastern Europe has also imbibed the "post-modern" aesthetic through popular culture imported via television, movies, and songs. East Europeans, in other words, would also like the clean consumerism of the post-industrial era without the preceding ugly, painful, and dirty industrialization. The cultural contradictions of capitalism—the postponement of pleasure dictated by the Puritan ethic that fuels our investments versus the Dionysian consumerism that keeps our factories running—are not readily exportable.[82] The Puritan ethic is being imposed from above through austerity, whereas consumerism comes all too naturally to populations denied for so long even an uninterrupted supply of fresh eggs, unspoiled meat, and soft toilet paper. Consumer expectations are therefore out of proportion with producer capabilities and investor sensibilities. This inequality was one factor prompting the revolutions of 1989; it may prove explosive in the future as well.

Eastern Europe's awkward position between support for and critique of the modern has made economic discussion there a strange hybrid of old and new. The market is discussed in a 19th-century sense, but the thoroughly post-modern environmental agenda of the Greens is also very popular. Coal miners labor in Victorian conditions, and economists blithely discuss the latest generation of computers. The average Pole has to wait years for a telephone, and the newest joint ventures are not complete without several fax machines. The left and right, liberals and conservatives, are all agreed in Eastern Europe: their pre-modern societies must be taken through the modern era to a post-modern economy as quickly as possible.

Though everyone may agree on the goal (e.g., EC standards), the actual transition is a matter of debate. Take the issue of the market, which Eastern Europe looks to as the engine of modernization. Since Adam Smith immortalized the market in 1776 with *The Wealth of Nations,* the notion of a set of inflexible laws governing the relations between producers and consumers has defined the Western understanding of economics. The purist conceives of the market as a virtually self-contained entity, natural as the moon and tides: political interventions are then dangerous distortions of market relations. More circumspect economists have long realized that a pure market, like a frictionless machine, is only an abstraction.

Denied a close-up view of the reality of today's capitalism, Eastern Europeans tend to see the market as just such an abstraction. In their eyes, the market has truly assumed utopian dimensions, as communism, fascism, and nationalism had in the past. This utopian view of markets is anomalous as far as continental Europe is concerned. The depressions of the 1920s and 1930s had dissuaded most Western European countries from adopting *laissez-faire* strategies that permit unregulated markets to cycle into peaks of frenzied hyper-prosperity and troughs of unspeakable suffering. The state became the tool to control the business cycles of capitalism; planned economies—whether socialist, corporatist, state capitalist, or for a period, fascist—became an integral part of every European country. "In so far as historical endings and beginnings can be precisely dated," British historian E.H. Carr writes, "the unplanned and uncontrolled capitalist system of the nineteenth century everywhere outside the United States was dead in 1933."[83]

The strain of *laissez-faire* was, however, nurtured in the United States—the "European" experiments of the New Deal, the Great Society, and Nixon's wage and price controls notwithstanding. The triumph of Ronald Reagan in 1980 brought a *laissez-faire* revival to the White House and, with the similar perspective of Britain's Margaret Thatcher, into the hearts of East Europeans. Both Reagan and Thatcher proposed the market as the answer to all problems—raising productivity, scaling back government and bureaucracy, reviving production, reinjecting private choice into the public sphere. This utopian project struck several consonant notes in East Europeans at the end of the 1980s. They too wanted to privatize, transform their economies, hobble the apparatus of state. The Reaganite/Thatcherite proposals were admired not so much for their economic exactitude (which is questionable) but for their can-do spirit (which is overabundant).

The sea change of 1989 could not have come at a more opportune moment. The neoconservatives offered an economic theory that championed liberty and dismissed injustice. The economic elite in Eastern Europe—which cut its teeth on underground editions of Hayek and Friedman and later received training at such capitalist training grounds as the International Management Center in Budapest and the Industrial Society in Krakow—needed the *laissez-faire* message to attribute the economic injustice born of austerity to iron economic laws that could be transgressed only at great peril.[84]

There were warning messages coming from the West. John Kenneth Galbraith, the great liberal-minded US economist, did not mince words:

> Those who speak, as so many do so glibly, of a return to the free market of Adam Smith are wrong to the point of a mental vacuity of clinical proportions. It is something we in the West do not have, would not tolerate, could not survive. Ours is a mellow, government-protected life; for Eastern Europeans, pure and rigorous capitalism would be no more welcome than it would be for us.[85]

But Galbraith was not the consultant of choice for Eastern Europe. Poland picked Jeffrey Sachs; Bulgaria turned to the US Chamber of Commerce.[86]

Some Eastern Europeans immediately understood the Galbraith message, especially those who had traveled to the West. "The market will solve all our problems?" Croatian philosopher Zarko Puhovski asked rhetorically.

> You have to be stupid to believe this. I lived in some Western countries so I know that this doesn't work. You have to use some elements of traditional anti-inflation policy which means that you are on some kind of economic defensive. At the same time, you need some kind of planning. Not like socialist planning but some kind of orientation about what you are going to do with the country.[87]

Slovenian political scientist Mitja Zagar offered a similar sentiment:

> If you spoke to ordinary people, they still do expect that democracy and political pluralism will bring them welfare. They do not know that in New York, 500,000 live under the poverty line. They do not know that capitalism doesn't mean being like someone from *Dynasty* or *Dallas,* that real capitalism is something different from what they watch on television. Even the people who were in Western countries who met real poverty there don't realize that in the United States, for example, 5 percent own 25 percent of the wealth, and 30 percent have less than 5 percent of the national wealth. They simply don't think that something like this could happen.[88]

As market utopias fade, what will happen in Eastern Europe economically in the 1990s? After the bright prospects offered by Western economists, the forecasts have dimmed considerably. The salesperson played up the product in the showroom; now that the car is bought, the salesperson can speak more candidly about its defects. The East Germans were the first to discover these problems first hand. Only after monetary union between East and West Germany did Western economists "discover" the impending collapse of the GDR economy. "Even pessimistic economists are alarmed at the economic aftershocks from the July 1 merger of the two German economies," wrote the *Wall Street Journal.*[89] Many people in the GDR prior to monetary union were well aware of what would happen when a protected economy was exposed overnight to rigorous international competitive pressures. Only Western economists with *laissez-faire* blinders could fail to predict the downturn. Only the politicians and Pollyannas who wanted to believe Kohl's promises would be subsequently surprised at the East German economic collapse. Even with massive infusions of western German subsidies ($100 billion in 1991), the new federal states remain mired in recession. The remaining countries of the region will not see aid that even approaches western German largesse.

With the East German experience now recognized (and the market idea already sold), Western economists have begun to spin their gloom and doom messages for the region. Once again, the bait has been taken, the switch is being made.[90] A UN commission reported in late 1991 that Eastern Europe was firmly mired in a depression: the region's output (net material product) declined 1 percent in 1989, 10 percent in 1990, and 15 percent further in 1991. Inflation had also returned; unemployment was skyrocketing, foreign trade collapsing, and budget deficits surging. Warning of an upturn in social unrest, the commission questioned the utility of shock therapy.[91] Even the investment banking firm Morgan-

Stanley joined the chorus of Cassandras, predicting a "calamity" because of the West's insistence on *laissez-faire* reform.[92]

Economic reform in Eastern Europe is not simply the adoption of an idealized market model and the acceptance of the Balcerowicz premise of "overnight" capitalism. In the following areas—industrial planning, ownership, social programs, trade unions, agriculture, foreign aid, foreign investment, and regional economic cooperation—the project of modernization has taken on a different character in each country. Only when the discussion turns to these specific aspects of reform do alternatives to shock therapy begin to emerge.

Industrial planning

The new governments of Eastern Europe are imposing a top-down economic reform, squeezing inflation out of the currency, workers out of the factories, and wages out of the population. Imposing austerity with one hand, these governments are also, with the other hand, removing themselves from the economy. In preparing for capitalism, they are planning paradoxically for the unplanned.

The desire to separate government from the economy, in light of the region's recent history, is understandable. Government intervention—and particularly industrial planning—smacks of communism, of five year plans, of control from the center. The market, it is said by contrast, will solve any problems. Take the issue of unemployment. Many economists in the region explain that the unemployment caused by economic transition will be handled by job-retraining. Workers thrown out of the "sunset" industries will be trained for "sunrise" industries; the market will separate successful ventures of the future from unsuccessful ventures of the past. But how can the government in the meantime train workers for jobs in unknown specialties for businesses not yet chosen by the market as winners? The market functions then not as an answer, but as a substitute for an answer.

The unregulated market as modernization's spur is a myth. The United States erected trade barriers and used government strategies to build its economy throughout the 19th and 20th centuries. Today, in prosperous countries such as Germany and Sweden, the government, labor unions, and business communities have carefully plotted a successful industrial course. Finally, there are the Pacific Rim countries to consider. As economist Alice Amsden explained in a *New York Times* op-ed piece, countries such as South Korea predicated their economic development on government subsidies and deficit spending. "All countries industrializing late need heavy government intervention," she concludes.[93] Without government support, the industrialization is left to corporations with no sense of overall economic policy and no interest in public oversight. Even international economic organizations recognize the role governments and public sectors should play in economic transition in Eastern Europe (for which they are frequently criticized by the United States).[94] The US private sector investment of hundreds of billions of dollars into worthless commercial property in the 1980s should convince all but the most hopeless ideologues that the market does not inherently allocate resources wisely.[95]

Rather than blithely expecting the market to solve this problem, Eastern European governments could in consultation with business and labor choose certain industries or services, allocate resources accordingly, and train workers to do the new jobs. This is not a utopian suggestion by any means. Industrial planning that is democratic and involves all sectors of the population would not only strengthen non-governmental institutions such as unions but ensure that austerity will be democratically negotiated. In Sweden, a "solidaristic wage policy" trades wage restraints for assurances that government subsidies will continue if an enterprise modernizes or creates new jobs by moving into new production. Workers are guaranteed, that should an enterprise fail, they would receive the training necessary to gain comparable positions in other fields.[96]

Where countries held closer to principles of industrial democracy, the recessions have been less intense. Czechoslovakia managed a rough consensus among employers, unions, and the government in late 1990—a Council of Economic and Social Accord—that has forestalled organized protest in the face of a 15 percent drop in real incomes.[97] With its "Pact for Poland" proposal, Mazowiecki's political grouping finally embraced this principle of industrial democracy, though only after Mazowiecki himself had been repudiated in the 1990 presidential elections.[98] When Solidarity decided finally to enter the electoral arena as a party in 1991, it too supported positive state intervention in the economy. But having already squandered its political capital, Solidarity barely managed to squeeze into Parliament.[99] In Hungary, FIDESZ suggested in March 1991 a framework in which the political parties could achieve consensus on economic policy. The most vigorous opposition came from the Alliance's erstwhile political compatriots, the Alliance of Free Democrats, who argued that trade unions should also be included in the arrangement.[100] Only through such structures—the Czechoslovak Social Accord, the Polish Pact, the Hungarian political roundtable—can the countries in the region, in the curious phrasing of one international funding report, gain "strong popular support...to resist pressures to relax adjustment programmes."[101] In return for their support of austerity, however, the public must receive something real, either in terms of power, access, or social services.

More pluralistic economic development need not come simply from above. Building on the recent experiences of roundtables, especially at the regional and local level as in the former GDR, development councils could weave together private enterprise, government support, joint ventures, retraining programs, and worker cooperatives.[102] These economic institutions, in a region with little experience in community development, would help build a political culture of participation and responsibility. Janos David, a Hungarian sociologist active in the independent trade unions, told me of his conception of fitting community development to Hungarian conditions. He envisioned the creation of organizations that would analyze the market potential for a particular region (marketable products, industries, resources, workforce), make the appropriate market connections (between producers and distributors, for instance, or between domestic and foreign capital), and then persuade the government to institute laws necessary to facilitate economic growth in the region (preferential loans, tax abatements for investment). The members of the community would be encouraged to participate in this process of finding solutions to their own problems. Such techniques, if combined with existing institutions devoted to privatization, housing, and workers' rights, might prove useful not only in raising productivity levels and rekindling the work ethic at a local level but in avoiding the populism of resentment as well.[103]

The question is not how to avoid austerity, or how to sweeten it or postpone it or endlessly criticize it. The modernization of Eastern Europe requires sacrifices. But who will sacrifice? How long will sacrifice be required? And in what manner will the decisions be made? The Balcerowicz plans and their exclusive faith in unregulated markets offer painful and undemocratic solutions. The various programs of industrial democracy involving all sectors of society could establish a more participatory framework. Modernization and "structural adjustment" need not be foisted on the population. Democratic principles can indeed be applied to economic reform, not only in the area of government policy, but also on the question of ownership.

Ownership

It is very difficult to identify who exactly owns the majority of factories, supermarkets, and utility companies in Eastern Europe. The previous communist regimes developed the spurious category of "public ownership" to fulfill the ideological rule that the workers should own the means of production. But the vast amount of property was owned *de facto* by either the government or the communist parties (which were until recently identical for all intents and purposes).

The overwhelming consensus of opinion among the new Eastern European governments has been in favor of privatization: the transfer of these "public" assets to the private sector. The conception differs in important ways from the Thatcher and Reagan privatizations of the 1980s. Reagan did not actually sell any state holdings but managed to deregulate large chunks of the private sector. Thatcher unloaded various state properties including Jaguar and British Telecom, but managed to privatize only two dozen or so enterprises in 12 years. If there is any recent analogy it would be Chile in the first years of the Pinochet dictatorship. After seizing power in a coup, the general sold off numerous enterprises, often at ridiculously low prices. The result, large concentrations of wealth and weak firms that required in some cases renationalization, does not provide an auspicious parallel.[104]

Eastern European governments are trying to sell enormous numbers of public properties, from huge steel mills that employ tens of thousands to hotdog stands staffed by only one. In addition to the enormous technical difficulties of such an operation, the privatization process encounters some significant financial roadblocks. Many of the properties are loss-making propositions. Furthermore, there is a palpable lack of domestic capital to purchase all the properties. Foreign investors could and in some cases already have bought many of the properties for a song. As will be discussed below, however, the international business community has demonstrated considerable reticence, and key domestic constituencies have put up patriotic resistance. A final issue is restitution. Many properties were the property of individuals and families prior to nationalization in the 1940s and '50s, and the adjudication of claims is particularly difficult.[105]

Privatization is usually divided into two categories: small and large. The privatization of small-sized enterprises—restaurants, bars, newspaper kiosks—has proceeded first. In Poland, small-scale privatization was accomplished without too many difficulties while in Hungary, surprisingly, less than 100 shops of an estimated 10,000 were sold by mid-1991.[106] In Czechoslovakia, hundreds of thousands of previously state-owned stores went on sale in January 1991. To prevent foreigners from buying properties simply to tear them down and have prime real estate in the middle of Prague, the law excludes all but Czechs and Slovaks from the first round of bidding (unbought properties are open to all in the second round). The new owners are also prohibited from selling the properties to foreigners for two years.

Barring foreigners does not prevent two other sources of "unclean" funds: the red and the black. The *nomenklatura* in Hungary began in the mid-1980s to transform themselves into "red capitalists"; Polish state managers increasingly became private entrepreneurs in 1989.[107] With connections and hard currency, the communist elite could, if ideology didn't intrude (which it rarely did), become managers in the private sectors. Sometimes the managers would covertly transfer state assets into the new private companies; often they would simply use their connections to acquire products at discount which they would in turn sell on the black market. Eastern Europeans have been of two minds in this regard: cautious approval that these red capitalists will ensure a smoother transition to the new economic system, or outrage that the villains of the past should be allowed to profit from their ill-gotten positions.

Treated with the same ambivalence as the red capitalists are the black marketeers, the quasi-criminals of the communist past who made their money on illegal currency and commodity exchange as well as some less savory activities. Responding to the charge that the new class of speculators had generally acquired their money illegally, Czechoslovak minister in charge of privatization Tomaz Jezek replied, "[T]here is dirty money here. But the best method for cleaning the money is to let them invest it."[108] Polish black marketeers have easily rationalized their adjustment to the new economic realities: "All the big family fortunes—the Kennedys', whoever—started out like this: quasilegal, the result of business being done on the margin, in the gray areas. It's the same here."[109] Capitalism did not begin with sparkling IBM offices and robot-run production lines; it has constantly involved the recycling of "bad" money for "good" and the gradual legitimation of what had once been considered beyond the legal pale. As *Business Week* points out, in the Wild West atmosphere in Eastern Europe today, the successful entrepreneur is the dishonest one, the streetsmart operator who bribes and squeezes around tax laws. Honest businesspeople, operating in the new, unregulated arena, are hamstrung by interest rates and heavy taxes.[110]

This leaves the problem of large privatization—the coal mines, shipyards, and steel plants. Most governments in the region will retain between 15 and 30 percent of the so-called "commanding heights." The lower end of this spectrum covers the natural monopolies—waterworks, electricity, roads, railways. The larger the share retained, the more actual productive industries—both extractive (coal, sulfur) and manufacturing (steel)—remained under government control. That still leaves an enormous number of plants—employing an enormous number of workers—whose fate hangs in the balance. Neither the quasi-legals nor the previous *nomenklatura* have the money to buy such symbols of heavy industrialization; even if they have the necessary funds, they would not likely be interested in wasting their capital.

The Poles have decided to give away shares in the state enterprises turned joint stock companies. The Czechs and Slovaks have sold vouchers for a nominal price covering between 40 and 80 percent of state equity.[111] In Romania, the shares of enterprises are to be placed in five mutual funds with 30 percent reserved for citizens and 70 percent for foreign investors.[112] After its first director was assassinated, his successor at the German privatization ministry, the Treuhand, engaged in a mass firesale of former East German state properties, underpricing many of the best properties.[113]

By distributing stocks to as large a portion of the population as possible, Eastern European governments hope to create a middle class, virtually overnight, versed in the complexities of financial transactions and connected to the new capitalist system by a web of investments, production, and consumption. As noted, Eastern Europe has traditionally had a weak middle class.[114] The communist revolutions attempted to collapse the traditional categories—peasant, proletariat, nobility, and *intelligentsia*—and succeeded in creating roughly two "classes": peasants and proletarians in a working class and all non-manual workers in an *intelligentsia*.

The opposition activists who came out of these two classes shared, until the late 1980s, a similar economic perspective. While supporting certain market relations, both workers and intellectuals generally accepted self-management as the most appropriate method of achieving both equity and democracy. Solidarity's statements captured the workers' perspective. Vaclav Havel's comments exemplify the critical intellectual's commitment:

> As far as the economic life of society goes, I believe in the principle of self-management, which is probably the only way of achieving what all the theorists of socialism have dreamed about, that is, the genuine (i.e. informal) participation of workers in economic decision-making, leading to a feeling of genuine responsibility for their collective work.[115]

Class consensus for self-management broke down within the opposition in the 1980s as free-market philosophies captivated first the intellectuals and then to a lesser degree the workers. Still, there was sufficient diversity of opinion in 1989-90 for popular fronts to employ compromise language such as "mixed ownership." According to Garton Ash, Civic Forum used this language in Czechoslovakia for political purposes: "This is a compromise formula, bearing in mind the sensibilities of the revisionists, social democrats and even Trotskyists who are part of the Forum rainbow coalition, and who still believe in various forms of social(ist) ownership. In effect it says: let the best form win! But privately the economists have absolutely no doubt which form will actually win out."[116] It was never a fair contest. With help from powerful interests such as the US government and the IMF, the economists won hands down.

But the issues once expressed in the language of self-management—namely, economic justice and democratic participation in the workplace—have not been answered by privatization. What percentage of property remains under government control and what percentage in private hands does not address the question of the distribution of power *within* economic enterprises. Employee Stock Ownership Plans offer certain voting rights to workers, but management still maintains its dominant position (as a French poster from the 1968 near-revolution characterized this relationship: "I participate, you participate, he participates, we participate, they profit!").[117] The Meidner plan in Sweden, the 1973 program of the Danish Social Democratic Party, the experiences of the Mondragon cooperatives in the Basque region of Spain, the various US worker-owned or -managed cooperatives: these provide some indication of how self-management can work within a social market economy.[118] Even the Japanese system—in which managers serve "as agents of the firm's core employees" and profits are maximized not for stockholders or managerial salaries but for modernization, higher wages, and fringe benefits—offers a more democratic model of ownership and workplace organization.[119] Eastern European countries, if they decide that democratic principles are important, must find their own particular model, however they label it. As Robert Dahl points out, "I would not be greatly distressed if advocates of capitalism were to view it as a new and better form of capitalism, and socialists as a new and better form of socialism."[120]

Does shaping an economy according to precepts of economic justice or political participation impede its efficiency? Economist Robert Kuttner emphatically says no: "A wide range of equality/efficiency bargains exist. Some improve equality at the expense of efficiency; some improve efficiency at the expense of equality; others creatively maximize both; still others make a hash of things and worsen both."[121] There is, in short, a menu of options, and Eastern Europeans have been given only the *plat du jour*.

Why should Eastern European countries, with their recent rediscovery of private property, bother with what might seem to be academic discussions of democracy and the workplace? To begin with, privatization neither answers the previous oppositions' demands for social justice nor does it ease growing class tensions. How will workers react to the new patterns of ownership when they begin to resemble the concentration of wealth characteristic of the great days of the nobility? And how will intellectuals respond to the growth of consumerism and with it the debasement of the *intelligentsia's* values? The US solution—a "middle class" that binds white collar and blue collar workers with the glue of materialism—is one possibility. Outright class warfare is another.

With full-scale privatization still in the future, class conflict is most visible in the battle over economic equity.

Social programs

Communism is an ideology predicated on economic justice: "from each according to his abilities, to each according to his needs." Communist governments in Eastern Europe talked a good deal about their redistributive functions, particularly in the realm of social policy. Universal health care, public education, pensions, free recreational facilities—the communists could point to such public services as the concrete realization of Marx's dictum. Although the quality of these services was often execrable, many people still relied heavily on them and have not been eager to see these programs eliminated. However, through privatization and the contraction of government budgets, social services in the region are now being shaped along class lines: the poor get the impoverished service or nothing at all while the wealthy go to private health clinics, send their children to private schools, and join private clubs.

With growing disparities in income and opportunity, has belief in social justice simply disappeared from Eastern Europe? Polish journalist Dawid Warszawski explains:

> I think that social justice is in for a comeback essentially because there is a great deal of gross social injustice going on. One of the reasons why the communist government was overthrown was that it was a regime of gross social injustice. However, the "refolution," as Garton Ash would say, has not expropriated the expropriators, has not corrected the social evils of communism—and it promises to bring the social evils of capitalism. They say that in the medium run all of this will level out. Well, perhaps. But right now we see people leading pretty desperate lives what with the cost of living going sky high and meanwhile seeing their erstwhile masters living quite nicely.[122]

As Warszawski notes, Poles have not yet experienced the injustices of capitalism. For instance, they know little about unemployment. "Unemployment is two things," Warszawski emphasizes. "First, you lose a job. Second, you can't find another one. Already the first element is rather exotic by Polish standards. The country had full employment for several generations. The second seems next to incredible. People haven't really realized that not only do you lose a job, but you don't get another one."

Austerity knows no political faith. It can be imposed by left-wing as well as right-wing governments. As a Czech journalist told me, "We don't need these Westerners to tell us about macropolicy because everyone knows what has to be done—even me—you can read these tips in every economic paperback. It is simply a question of political will."[123] In Poland, an anti-communist trade-union-supported government following Western advice exhibited the "political will." In Bulgaria, the former Communist Party, before it resigned in late 1990, imposed the belt-tightening measures. Philip Bokov, in charge of "public relations" for the Bulgarian Socialist Party, deflected questions about "socialist" austerity: "This policy of the Socialist government is: we have to work with what we have. Perhaps nobody accuses the Mazowiecki government in Poland that it is introducing the austerity program. I am sure that if the opposition had been in office in this country, the situation would be the same. Because we must operate with the resources that we have."[124]

The resources have been dwindling. The initially promised social benefits such as unemployment compensation and job referral services have either appeared in drastically diminished form or they haven't materialized at all. The private sector and the religious community have been either unable or unwilling to patch up the unraveling safety net. Social protection, I heard over and over again during my travels, can only be provided within the constraints determined by government budgets. Everything else was wishful thinking. Vojko Volk of the Slovenian Socialist Party begged to differ: "We know that we don't have the money for a social state. But that doesn't mean that we must not fight for social rights! The logic would be very beastly then. You can fight for social rights only in rich countries?"[125]

Trade unions often lead the fight for social justice, whether calling for higher wages for workers or working for a more general agenda within social democratic parties. So far, trade unions have played very different roles in Eastern Europe.

Trade unions

Until 1980 and the rise of Solidarity, the only trade unions in Eastern Europe were captive institutions, rhetorically supporting workers' rights yet actively providing a bulwark for the communist governments. Official trade unions, collected in the Soviet-dominated World Federation of Trade Unions, represented one of the most conservative forces in the region.

Despite the presence of these compromised unions, criticisms of working conditions from the point of view of workers occasionally leaked out of Eastern Europe. Workers' revolts in East Germany and later in Poland had focused on low wages and rising prices. Hungarian writer Miklos Haraszti's *A Worker in a Worker's State* brilliantly exposed the worst capitalist excesses that permeated the communist workplace: piece-rates, "looting," and corrupt managers. Working in several machine tool factories, Haraszti told the story from the inside: "We are like natives who, in the early days of colonialism, handed over everything, their treasures, their land, and themselves, for worthless trinkets and who became aware that they had been robbed only when they failed to get the usual junk in return."[126] Intended to stop the robbery of surplus value from workers, Eastern European communism simply extracted it under a different name. Compromised trade unions only facilitated this process.

The growth of independent trade unions in Eastern Europe has followed two models. The first type, closer to Solidarity, involved spontaneous worker response: in Czechoslovakia during the November revolution or Romania after the December revolution. To organize the Czechoslovak general strike so critical to the success of the revolution, workers' committees independent of the old trade unions were established in the factories. Later, after he had already been elected to the Parliament, trade union organizer Ladislav Lis told me, "we didn't destroy the old trade unions. We didn't make parallel trade unions as in Poland. But we went inside the old trade unions to guarantee new elections. And we were successful."[127] In Romania, the workers were so thrilled with the fall of the old order they couldn't wait to take advantage of the situation. Marcu Viorel of the Drivers' Union told me that when the union was first created, the workers wanted to strike immediately. "Why?" asked Viorel. "Why not?" came the response. But, Viorel pointed out, we need funds to support a strike. Don't worry, he was told, we would only strike for a couple days just to see what it is like. "The workers are now more mature," Viorel reported.[128]

The other model involved the creation of a union nucleus around white-collar professionals which then expanded to include blue collars. Hungary's FSZDL, for instance, grew out of a union of research workers. Today, FSZDL engages in traditional trade union activities: collective bargaining, organizing at the enterprise level, negotiations with other trade unions. "Hungary," FSZDL president Pal Forgacs said in July 1990, "is now at the point of crisis. The gap between the small rich part of the population and the poorest is deepening." He estimated that one-third of the population was living beneath subsistence. Unemployment was surging, pensioners and large families were the most adversely affected, education and other public services were deteriorating. Even under such conditions, FSZDL was reluctant to engage in direct politicking. "We want to separate government and trade union," Forgacs said. "We always stressed that we wanted to be only a trade union. We are independent of both government and of employers. Solidarity proves that you can't have a union and a political party in the same organization or you discredit the trade union movement."[129]

Following the pattern of FSZDL, Podkrepa started out in Bulgaria as a handful of intellectuals in the spring of 1989. After the "retirement" of Todor Zhivkov in November 1989, Podkrepa grew rapidly to roughly half a million members by the summer of 1990. Although initially establishing a working relationship with the Social Democratic Party, the union has drifted further to the right under the hard-line leadership of Konstantin Trenchev. Until recently a member of the UDF coalition, Podkrepa also hopes to disentangle itself from politics as soon as it determines that the political situation has become "normal" in Bulgaria.[130]

The reformed "official" unions have also not disappeared. OPZZ in Poland, MSZOSZ in Hungary, NCRFTU in Romania, CITUB in Bulgaria: these newly "independent" unions remain to a greater or lesser extent compromised by their affiliations to the previous regimes. But with the truly independent unions now dependent upon free market fantasies, these "old" unions continue to defend the most threatened and potentially most disenfranchised segment of the working class.

With markets now the rage in Eastern Europe, trade unions, either along the Solidarity, Podkrepa, or "official" models, are not especially popular among economists. In response to a question about restrictions on foreign investment, Laszlo Urban, a Hungarian economist connected to FIDESZ said:

> I would allow foreign investors to exclude trade unions from their plants because the regular practice is that trade unions increase the wage levels. You don't need that type of trade union demand. I prefer employees who are willing to do the work and not be members of a trade union—and this is usually the case. People are much more concerned with wages than trade union membership. But we are a democratic country and it would be difficult to push such [anti-union] legislation through Parliament.[131]

Unions remain the only powerful institution in Eastern Europe that can protect workers' rights from the demands of economists, government officials, and the new class of managers. With a new wave of poverty and unemployment, unions have their work cut out for them.

Agriculture

Eastern European countries also remain heavily agricultural with Poland and Romania at the high end and eastern Germany and Czechoslovakia at the low. Under communism, peasants were transformed not into farmers (i.e., independent producers) but into essentially an agrarian proletariat with the large state and collective farms serving as factories of the field. The exceptions were Poland and Yugoslavia where collectivization never took hold and farmers maintained relatively small plots, selling their wares primarily to the largest single guaranteed buyer—the central governments. Other countries in the region experimented with allowing greater freedom in the agricultural sector, for instance, allowing collective workers to maintain private plots and sell their produce on the free market. In Hungary, 40 percent of the population maintained private plots and kept the private markets flourishing in Budapest in the 1970s and 1980s.[132]

After the political changes of 1989, the various governments faced a decision: what to do with the large state and collective farms? Following the spirit of privatization, the solution would seem simple: divide the farm up among the workers and create a class of independent farmers. On paper, this proposal might appear reasonable. But in practice, it runs up against some significant objections—from the collective workers themselves. Despite its many faults, the collective at least provided security for its workers: guaranteed wages, a pension, and annual vacations. Only the most experienced and fortunate farmers can ever hope for such a safety net. The promise of riches may be attractive, but the very real possibility of poverty drives many collective workers to support a system which elicited only grumbles for years.

One of the factors in the victory of "gradualist" parties such as the National Salvation Front and the Bulgarian Socialist (formerly Communist) Party was precisely the agrarian vote. When capitalism was portrayed as disruptive to the values of the community, the community voted for a more conservative approach. In Bulgaria, the Union of Democratic Forces promised, by breaking up the cooperatives upon reaching office, to reject the communist past decisively. Although winning big in the cities, it had a poor showing in the countryside. Those parties that support "overnight" capitalism have ignored the rural response only at their own electoral peril.

All countries in the region realize that membership in the wider EC will require a major restructuring of the agricultural sector. Countries now reliant on small farmers or envisioning the break-up of the large cooperatives will have to do something about the cheaper food available from the West and South, the former because of greater efficiency, the latter because of cheaper labor costs. The key to reform is making agriculture less labor-intensive and more cost-effective. Western Europe has managed to achieve this, but at great cost. The EC spends the lion's share of its outlays on agricultural subsidies that keep small- and medium-sized farms afloat. Eastern Europe doesn't presently have the capital for such a strategy.

Some economists confidently predict that the problem will solve itself: demographic trends will set the workforce picture straight. After all, some villages in Eastern Europe consist of nothing more than senior citizens, as the young and able go off to the cities for greater opportunities. But demography will not solve everything. The countries in Eastern Europe are encountering the same problem Stalin faced in the 1920s: a large agrarian workforce, an outdated industrial infrastructure, and a deficit of capital for modernization. Germany solved this problem in its eastern lands with a Marshall Plan of its own making. The remainder of Eastern Europe has not been so fortunate.

Foreign aid

When George Bush visited Poland after its national elections in June 1989, Lech Walesa was waiting with a preliminary estimate. The bill for bringing Poland up to Western standards was a modest $10 billion. Surely this was a small price to pay for a stable democracy, a future bulwark of capitalism on the border with the Soviet Union. Bush made a triumphant speech in Warsaw that June. It was heard on television by millions of Poles. In it, he praised Solidarity, capitalism, democracy, US foreign policy, Lech Walesa, and Ronald Reagan. He came, he saw, and he left—only about $100 million.

Eventually Congress would more than double the amount of US funds going to Eastern Europe, from the Bush proposal ($350 million for both Poland and Hungary) to a more significant $738 million. In 1990, Congress would also increase the administration's proposal for the rest of the region, from $300 million to $579 million. Even with the congressional addition, a Marshall Plan it was not.[133] Quite simply, the United States cannot finance this modernization (the "bailing out," as the less charitable call it) of Eastern Europe. A massive Savings and Loan crisis, an economic downturn at the beginning of the 1990s, an ever-expanding budget deficit and government debt: the United States has had its hands full with the consequences of capitalism. There are simply no funds left over to handle the consequences of communism.[134]

The EC has been more helpful. Under the PHARE program, the EC provided large sums of capital for Poland and Hungary.[135] The plan had two chief aims: food aid and the stimulation of agricultural production on the one hand, plant protection, feed supply, and second-hand farm machinery on the other. The EC also organized a stabilization fund of $1 billion for Poland, 160 million in European Currancy Units (ECU) for environmental clean-up, and the TEMPUS program for student exchanges.[136] In July 1990, the Group of 24 decided to expand aid to include

Czechoslovakia, Bulgaria, East Germany, and Yugoslavia. Romania, in the wake of the clashes in Bucharest in June, was deliberately excluded.[137] One significant institution primarily funded by the EC is the new European Bank for Reconstruction and Development (EBRD). Started in 1991, the new Bank will begin with $12 billion in assets, with the EC providing roughly 54 percent, the United States 10 percent, and Japan 8.5 percent.

The strategies adopted by the various funding groups are quite different. The United States has, under Bush, favored seed money and technical assistance for small business—the so-called Enterprise Funds—and has stressed the priority of diluting worker radicalism to ensure that they have no desire for greater state intervention in the economy.[138] The EBRD is mandated to give at least 60 percent of its loans and investments to the private sector;[139] it has also earmarked funds for buying into Western takeovers such as Nestle's bid for Czechoslovakia's largest food producer.[140] The EC has concentrated on agricultural assistance. The multilateral financial institutions have relied on monetary measures—stabilization funds, loans, credits, and debt rescheduling.

In addition to the inadvisability of focusing on monetary measures and the private sector, these strategies share another common flaw: pitting countries within Eastern Europe against one another. After the Socialist Party won the Bulgarian national elections in 1990, the country was immediately accorded second-class status beneath the "Gang of Four" (East Germany, Poland, Czechoslovakia, and Hungary). British Minister for Trade and Industry Nicholas Ridley justified the greater share allocated to the northern countries in clumsy Cold War language. "It is precisely these countries," he intoned, "which have evinced a determination to join the free world."[141] The " free world" in question was defined not by democracy but by *laissez-faire* capitalism. Even among the northern-tier recipients, preferential treatment is given to those who more closely follow the US, UK, or IMF model (depending on who is giving the money). Leaving aside the validity of imposing economic models, the competition engendered among the countries is ultimately destructive. These are countries that have long histories of mutual hatreds; it is not wise to encourage the return of these feelings. Survival of the fittest in Eastern Europe might lead to the war of all against all.[142]

In one respect the countries of the region are unified: they are all in debt. The region is, as a whole, $100 billion in the red.[143] Poland, whose debt had previously been the largest, was forgiven roughly one-third its burden. First in economic reform—first in financial forgiveness. Other countries, which have not been as explicit in accepting outside economic controls, remain more deeply in thrall.

How can increased aid to or preferential debt forgiveness of Eastern Europe be justified when famine, poverty, and disease kill millions throughout the developing world? Funds which the EC made available for the developing world through the Lome Convention required months of heated negotiations. "Six billion for Eastern Europe, meanwhile, was passed with almost no discussion. The contrast was enormous," an EC official told me in Brussels in early 1990.[144] Meanwhile, through trade barriers, the EC is guaranteeing a redirection of capital flows eastward.[145]

One method of justifying preferential treatment for Eastern Europe appeals to cultural distinctions. A Polish cartoon captures this dynamic: an African schoolteacher addresses her students with "Tomorrow, you must each bring a banana for the poor children of far-off Poland."[146] The subtext is disturbing: bad enough that people of the Third World live at "underdeveloped" levels, but that Europeans live in such conditions is truly a disgrace. "Civilized" nations therefore deserve civilized amounts of money (besides which, some Eastern Europeans say, *sotto voce,* the West sold us out at Yalta so we deserve the money, as a sort of repentant Marshall Plan). At the other end of the spectrum, Czechoslovakia's Foreign Minister Jiri Dienstbier has written with compassion about the growing divide between North and South.[147]

Again, the Friedmanites would like to believe that the market will resolve any conflicts as investments pour into the most deserving countries. As Eastern Europe is presently discovering, however, investment doesn't necessarily go to the neediest.

Foreign investment

As soon as you get rid of the communists, the pundits said, capitalism will come rushing in. But after the fall of communism in 1989, capitalists have moved very carefully into Eastern Europe, US capitalists perhaps the most cautiously.

In January 1990, a *Fortune* poll of 500 CEOs revealed that they considered the GDR the most promising investment (not surpising, considering that West Germany had already made that decision). Much further down on the list was the number-two choice, Hungary. Substantially less interest was paid to the rest of the region.[148] US officials have tried a soft sell. Ambassador to Poland John Davis, Jr. summed up the US strategy: "Where else can you sell your goods at world market prices and pay Egyptian wages?" A picture of autoworkers accompanying the article featuring Davis's comment was captioned: "Wages for these workers at the FSO car plant have gone up less than 15 percent while rents have quadrupled." The workers in the picture are smiling.[149]

But even low wages haven't motivated US business to abandon its favored foreign sites in South Korea or the Mexican *maquiladoras*. As one US investor frankly put it to a Hungarian eager for deals—"Look, if I want to lose a few million I can go down the block. I don't have to go thousands of miles away."[150] Added a managing director of a brokerage firm, "A better risk is Latin America where they have the infrastructure of a more recent capitalist tradition."[151]

Western Europe leads in the category of joint ventures, with German companies willing to take the leap most frequently (leading to a revival of significant anti-German sentiment in the region). In December 1990, Volkswagen undertook the largest venture, acquiring over 30 percent of the Czechoslovak car company Skoda. The German automobile manufacturer hopes to corner the new Eastern car market, with huge profits just around the corner. The occasional European business has taken a different tack. Trade unionist Denis MacShane offers the example of a French supermarket chain that opened a branch near Warsaw: "the French company, based on a cooperative near Bresse, has promised not to take out any profits for ten years. No American businessman looks beyond ten weeks, or even ten minutes, in his hunt for instant profit gratification."[152]

Some Euro-deals are just short of scams. An attempt by Swedish and Dutch investors to acquire Hungary's largest hotel chain was canceled by a Hungarian court because of prior manipulation of bids. A similar business spirit animated the push by German media conglomerate Springer into Hungary. *Beszelo* editor Ferenc Koszeg told me: "They simply walked into the editorial offices and said, 'Look, there will be new elections next week and you may lose your jobs because of them. Sign a contract and I'll keep you.' Seven county papers signed. Robert Maxwell and Rupert Murdoch paid something for their shares—perhaps not very much—but something. Springer didn't pay anything."[153]

With its more developed infrastructure and the Viennese atmosphere of its capital, Hungary attracted $1 billion in 1990, one-half of all foreign investment into Eastern Europe. Poland has managed only one-tenth that figure. The laws on joint ventures continue to change, inflation has yet to fall to predictable levels, and large-scale privatization has yet to begin. Until these conditions are met, foreign capital will prefer other regions of the world.

CMEA

Established two months before NATO in 1949, the Council on Mutual Economic Assistance (CMEA or COMECON) was intended to be the next concentric ring of communism. First the Soviet Union, then

Eastern Europe. If communism was to compete effectively against capitalism, it had to do so collectively. The CMEA was to be that mechanism.

The CMEA regulated trade and little more. Joint ventures among member nations—presumably the best example of communist solidarity—never got off the ground. Only 12 CMEA joint ventures involving no more than two countries apiece were ever arranged.[154] As it turned out, the CMEA never rose above a barter system because of the inconvertibility of the various currencies involved. If, for example, Poland sold 200 tons of potatoes to the Soviet Union, it would be paid with rubles. Since Poland could only use those rubles for trade with the Soviet Union, it would then acquire the number of, say, ermine coats equal to 200 tons of potatoes. Since all the Eastern European countries were desperate to attract Western currencies in order to buy needed machinery or consumer goods or pay back debts, they were of course more eager to look outside the CMEA structure if they had any particularly competitive goods to sell. The CMEA became the trade structure of last resort.

It wasn't, of course, simply a paper organization. Roughly put, the Soviet Union sent raw materials, including subsidized oil and natural gas, to Eastern Europe in return for finished products and some agricultural produce. This relationship, reversing the usual colonial equation, remains controversial concerning the amount of energy subsidies the Soviets provided Eastern Europe and how much the USSR relied on Czechoslovakia, particularly, for heavy machinery and armaments.[155] By 1989, Moscow had accumulated a large trade deficit with Eastern Europe, the equivalent of $3.9 billion.[156]

As Eastern European economies turned to markets, the CMEA held little promise. A commission instructed to outline proposals for transforming the CMEA had all of its suggestions rejected as insufficiently radical at the January 1990 meeting in Sofia.[157] In that same month, all CMEA transactions began to be conducted on a hard-currency basis, ending the barter system. The Soviet Union, holder of the essential and precious oil and natural gas reserves, anticipated that it could profit from the change, "to the tune of $10 billion a year if trade continues at its current level."[158] It didn't. The Soviet Union has collapsed along with its economy. All countries thus registered a decline in inter-regional trade in 1990. This collapse of the regional market has deepened the recessions of each of the countries in the region.

Joining the EC would of course obviate the need to reform the CMEA. But the EC will not accept its eastern neighbors before they can stabilize both their political and economic structures. Now, with the CMEA officially dissolved, the region is left in limbo, easy prey to the free-trade palliatives of GATT.[159] A Central European Economic Union, as Jozef van Brabant suggests, would fill an important interim role.[160] At the very least, an Eastern European Payments Union, similar to the one that lasted in Western Europe until 1958, would help the region with its currency reform.[161] As much as they would like to turn to the West, the countries of Eastern Europe still rely heavily on one another. A regional partnership, counteracting the Darwinian strategies of the West, would carry Eastern Europe into the future together, rather than as less than the sum of its feuding parts.

* * *

The Poles were the first to mount a mass challenge to a communist government in 1980-81, the first to enter into roundtable negotations in 1989, the first in the region to have semi-free elections, and the first to bite austerity's bullet. When the Poles unveiled the Balcerowicz plan in 1990, the response from Western governments was overwhelmingly positive. Reaction from Poland's neighbors was not so upbeat. Most announced that, although they shared the goals of the Balcerowicz plan, they preferred a more gradual transition to the market. Civic Forum, Democratic Forum, National Salvation Front, and the Bulgarian Socialist (formerly Communist) Party, in order to preserve fragile coalitional unity, all expressed reservations about "shock." Economists in Hungary and the northern parts of Yugoslavia also argued that because of their already significant market traditions, such a dramatic upheaval was simply not relevant to their situations.

But a political transformation was taking place in the countries of Eastern Europe. The original revolutionaries—the Barbel Bohleys and Vaclav Havels, Lech Walesas and Gyorgy Konrads—were not economists. Their protests focused on political and moral critiques of communism. 1990 ushered in a new group of actors. Suddenly, the economists came to the forefront. In East Germany, New Forum was marginalized by West German bankers and their gold-solid Deutsche mark. In Poland, Leszek Balcerowicz stepped into the limelight to launch a program that in many respects contradicted the principles that had guided Solidarity for many years. In Czechoslovakia, economist Vaclav Klaus—who had not previously been involved in oppositional activities—rose to the position of finance minister and then, in October 1990, to the chairmanship of Civic Forum. In Bulgaria and Romania, leading free marketeers have taken their places in the ministries of economy and finance. If 1989 was the year of the activist, 1990 was certainly the year of the economist.

This transition in authority was reflected in a change from the initially cautious response to the Polish model, to the eventual embrace of most of its critical aspects. The gradualists were, against their better political judgements, bracing to accept shock. An army of powerful

Western economic interests—from businesses to international financial institutions—only hastened the death of gradualism.

In Czechoslovakia, prices shot up in early 1991 with the elimination of government subsidies. In Hungary, the government attempted to raise the price of gasoline and was met with an immediate taxi strike that paralyzed Budapest in October 1990. Prime Minister Petre Roman announced the same month that Romania needed Polish-style shock therapy. Large price increases followed two weeks later. After receiving its reform plan from the US Chamber of Commerce, Bulgaria embarked on its own shock treatment, raising prices in several stages in 1991.

These market reforms will affect more than simply the economy. The Balcerowicz-type plans have elevated a certain crowd to high-ranking positions often sheltered from the vicissitudes of electoral politics. While this group may not intend to benefit from cronyism, it may be establishing a pattern that less noble successors will be more willing to exploit. Furthermore, the reforms are enriching the few and re-establishing a class system which offers little opportunity for advancement to a growing underclass. The elimination of public spending—on schools, health, community affairs—will have disastrous consequences on the most vulnerable: children, elderly, and pregnant women. The enriched section of the population will be able to buy anything it wants; the majority of the population will perhaps muddle along; at the bottom, a permanent underclass is in the making.

The enthusiasm for Balcerowicz-type transformations may only be temporary. Once the semblance of a market is established in Eastern Europe, the governments and the people may shift gears and proceed to fashion an economy that more closely resembles Sweden than Bangladesh. Drawing on models of industrial democracy, regional co-operation, mixed ownership, social safety nets, and strong, democratic unions, the next generation of East European economic reform may proceed both more democratically and more equitably.

Eastern Europe cannot simply adopt foreign models, whether Asian-style industrial planning or more equitable arrangements featuring cooperatives and community development. It must fashion its own particular models for modernizing itself out of its predicament. One additional problem that Eastern Europe must face, however, is timing. The region is attempting modernization at a time when the whole project of modernization has come under renewed scrutiny. And no group has sharpened the critique of modernization more than the environmental movement.

Chapter 6

Hungary... Goulash ecology

We have to somehow find a third way.

—Zoltan Illes

Zoltan Illes was young for a state secretary of the Hungarian Ministry of the Environment. But at 29, he had an impressive resume: stints at the World Bank and Yale University as well as time served in the trenches as an organizer in Hungary's environmental movement. From my ecology movement contacts in Budapest, I had received mixed reports: Illes was either the best environmentalist in the ministry or a rank opportunist. I was prepared for a slick technocrat, Greenish perhaps around the edges, but ministerial to the core. After a meeting in his office in the ministry building below Buda hill, I decided that of all the people I interviewed in government in that particular part of the world, Illes was the most refreshing: lively, articulate, and without the protective pretensions that youth frequently brings to elected office. Of course, Illes had been in office at that point for only one month. Politics had not yet dampened his exuberance.

In that one month, however, Illes had already made enemies. The Soviets were unhappy that he demanded they pay for the cleanup of contaminated areas once used for Warsaw Pact maneuvers. Certain Western corporations had complained when, on Illes' recommendation, the ministry rejected their unsound technology.

Then there was the Foreign Ministry's plan to rent a kindergarten in the verdant Buda hills to a school for the children of French diplomats. Illes was incensed. "You know that 50 percent of Budapest is covered with highly polluted air. So children are going to kindergartens that are polluted (we have analyses of lead content in their blood, for instance). You might ask: why does the ministry want to rent to French children and throw out Hungarian kids?" The answer was predictable: money. "This is not a question of French or Hungarian," Illes continued. "This is not patriotism. I supported the parents who were fighting against the ministry, and I spoke out in public that I'm against selling or renting out. We must bring *all* children, as many as possible, to nice areas. Already the minister of foreign trade has asked the prime minister to fire me."[1]

With so many bureaucratic hassles to untangle, why did Illes leave the non-governmental sphere where he had worked on, among other things, Hungary's Earth Day celebration of 1990? "I call it the Vaclav Havel effect," he said. "It is very nice to be in the opposition and criticize things. Much harder and more difficult is to try to lead, to deal with the questions and try to solve the problems." It certainly was to be more difficult with a forest of ministerial dead wood, a team of green (in both senses of the word) appointees, a toxic stew of problems, and a miniscule budget. Although the West has offered funds for certain projects, the Hungarian budget has been squeezed by the fiscal austerity of the post-communist era. Without adequate finances, the country has often found itself at the mercy of the highest bidder. "A French company would like to sell a very nice nuclear power plant to us," Illes said, complaining that corporations were skirting regulations and Hungary was looking the other way. "It is much better than Chernobyl but not acceptable in the EC. The French government will give the loan, then Hungary will buy the plant."

The conflicts Illes faces are new to a country accustomed to standoffs between opposition and government, cowboy dramas of good and evil battling it out *mano a mano*. Illes represents thousands of activists-turned-politicians throughout Eastern Europe who are now operating in a post-oppositional world. After the elections of 1990, opposition activists were appointed or elected to powerful positions; reforming zeal, in this case Green idealism, was forced to confront the grey areas of compromise.

Environmental activists have a particularly difficult task. After all, ecological threats have not disappeared with the fall of the previous governments. Indeed, it is only now that the full extent of the damage can be assessed.[2] Forty-five years of virtually unregulated development has left the land, water, and air in Eastern Europe in a state reminiscent of England in its days of Satanic mills. Worse, in fact, since the polluters of the industrial revolution didn't have at their disposal the additional chemical nastiness that 20th-century science and industry have invented. The burning of fossil fuels, especially brown coal, has blackened the atmosphere and ravaged the countryside with acid rain. In Katowice, a center of Polish industry, heavy metal residues in the soil have made genetic mutations common among children. A chemical processing complex in Giurgiu, Romania, is an over-the-border polluter of Bulgaria's Rousse, while a Bulgarian nuclear reactor located at another border point pumps back pollution of a different but equally deadly variety. Threading through the entire region, the Danube has become an artery of garbage, a dead river that flows into the increasingly moribund Black Sea (scientists estimate that the Sea will be dead within 30 years if the problem is left unaddressed).

Compared to the so-called environmental basket cases on its borders, Hungary appears to be in relatively good shape, particularly with Greens like Illes in government. Hungarian ecology is notable for another reason. More than any other force, the ecological movement in Hungary galvanized Hungarian civil society in the 1980s, attacked the communist government, elevated ecological issues in the post-Chernobyl era, and tackled political questions at a time when politics could only be broached from an oblique angle. Today, Hungary's approach to the environment—a goulash ecology that can replace the former goulash communism—highlights the problems facing modernizers in post-modern times. At the same time, a new political paradigm can be seen at work shaping the ecological movement. Bolstered by a general public disaffection for the categories of Left and Right, this paradigm may precipitate an unusual configuration of political forces in Hungary and throughout Eastern Europe.

For Hungary it all began with a dam, a poorly conceived, poorly designed, I'll-pad-your-centrally-planned-economy-if-you'll-pad-mine kind of dam.

Nagymaros-Gabcikovo

The Danube is a mythic river, featured in dozens of folk-stories and resonating in countless traditions. It symbolizes the multi-ethnicity of the region through which it snakes: beginning in the mountains of western Germany, skirting Bohemia, passing through Austria, edging along the border of Slovakia and then crossing into Hungary, flowing south to Vojvodina and Serbia, merging with the Sava in Belgrade, then dividing Bulgaria from Romania before angling into Romania proper, cutting north to the Soviet border, and finally emptying into the Black Sea. The Danube is, in the words of Italian writer Claudio Magris, "German-Magyar-Slavic-Romanic-Jewish Central Europe, polemically opposed to the Germanic Reich; it is a 'hinternational' ecumene…it is a hinterworld 'behind the nations.'"[3] Hinterworld or not, the Danube was by the latter part of the 20th century a river less of romance than of garbage: raw sewage dumped by Budapest twice daily combined with oil, cellulose, and chemicals thrown in by Czechoslovakia, Yugoslavia, Romania, and Bulgaria.

Dirty, disparaged, and decidedly not blue, the Danube was valued only for its potential use—as either sewage system or energy source. Energy took priority over sewage in 1977 when Czechoslovakia and Hungary agreed to build a dam on the section of the Danube that separated them.[4] The project's framers had three goals in mind: electric power, navigation, and flood control, with clear emphasis on the first. What sounded like a good scheme—true socialist cooperation—soon became a financial and environmental nightmare.

Environmentally, according to the *Hungarian Observer*, "diversion of most of the river would cause an ecological disaster in the Szigetkoz area of Hungary; since the speed of flow would be slower, there would be massive problems of water pollution and silting; the sub-surface drinking water supplies of two to three million people would be in danger."[5] Diversion of most of the river? Of the Danube? Next to the Volga, the Danube is the largest European river. It has 300 tributaries and drains one-tenth of Europe. This was diversion on a grand scale indeed. What prompted Hungary to undertake this gargantuan project?

"Like everything in Hungary," environmental economist and engineer Tamas Fleischer points out, "it goes back to Trianon."[6] After World War I, the Trianon treaty carved Hungary up like a Thanksgiving turkey, doling out over 70 percent of its territory to neighbors: a drumstick for Czechoslovakia, a wing for Yugoslavia, and the choicest Transylvanian morsel for Romania. Although traumatic for all Hungarians, the loss of mountainous Transylvania particularly affected the country's water management department which had located most of its projects in the region. Deprived of the natural conditions for its projects, this water management department, which Fleischer described in terms usually reserved for the Mafia or the KGB, had continually attempted post-Trianon to expand its power (measured in both political influence and megawattage). Add to the Trianon legacy a Soviet interest in expanding navigational capacity on the Danube and a Slovak desire for more use of the river, and the Gabcikovo-Nagymaros dam project, named for its two main sites, was the perfect pork barrel.

In reality, the dam was a Hungarian Rube Goldberg contraption, a testament to humanity's tragicomic attempts to tame nature.[7] Engineers first had to contend with the project's ludicrous location—at a basin that deprived it of height differential, a dam's greatest natural asset. Construction crews dug a channel parallel to this basin section: in essence a second river 20 kilometers long with the dam at Gabcikovo in Slovakia and an artificially created drop near its end. This solved the height problem. But the power output of a dam also depends on the amount of water flow which, under the initial plan, was simply insufficient to satisfy peak demand. So engineers decided to make a reservoir that could store and release two-and-one-half days worth of Danube flow. Since this reservoir would block water through both the Danube and the parallel "river," a second dam had to be constructed at Nagymaros to regulate flow.

The engineering problems were, given time, manageable. The environmental impact, according to the dictates of communist technocracy, was ignorable. But there was a final problem: money. After initial estimates had been exceeded, Hungary considered withdrawing from the project. Enter the Austrians. After Austrian Greens mobilized public opinion against their equally ill-conceived dam on the Danube at Hainburg in 1984, the idled Austrian companies went looking for new employers. They turned to the stricken Hungarians. In 1986, an Austrian company agreed to build Nagymaros, the Hungarian section of the project, in exchange for electricity for 20 years. The Austrian government provided additional guarantees.

Engineering, environment, and finances—the Hungarian government assumed that it had met all challenges. The one variable upon which the Hungarian government hadn't counted was the public. Some government policies—price increases or job lay-offs—had in the previous 25 years led to sporadic protest but no unified, sustained movement. The democratic opposition had mobilized dissidents throughout the 1970s and 1980s, but involvement was generally confined to the *intelligentsia*. The Nagymaros project changed the complexion of opposition politics in Hungary. And if there was one person responsible for that change it was Janos Vargha and his obsession with the Danube.

In 1980, Janos Vargha was working as a plant geneticist in Szeged. Observing the deleterious effects of waste disposal on the Danube, he began to learn more about environmental issues. The more he discovered, the more he found fault with government policy. Fired from a later position on a journal put out by the water management department, Vargha formed the Danube Circle in 1984 with 30 other environmentally-concerned individuals.[8] It was the beginning of what would be a thriving environmental movement. Originally apolitical, the Danube Circle would eventually attract over 10,000 supporters and publish the first underground environmental journal.[9] Its demonstrations from 1986 on would attract thousands of people and direct not only Hungarian but also world attention to the Nagymaros project.

Participation in the Danube Circle "was not much more than an ordinary Western citizen would do but in this context it was very important," one of the Circle's organizers, Judit Vasarhelyi, said. "You stepped out, took responsibility, and took a risk. You could lose your passport, get detained." She paused, reflecting on Hungary's unique position in the communist world. "For the same kind of oppositional activity in Prague, you could get five years in prison. In Romania, you could have been killed."[10]

Two tendencies faced off in the Circle: the fundamentalists and the pragmatists (a division similar in style though perhaps not content to the split in the West German Greens). The fundamentalists emphasized ecological harm and defined the Circle activities as pro-nature, not anti-government. As the leader of this wing, Vargha always stressed that pollution was produced by no particular political regime. The second tendency, to which Vasarhelyi belonged, was more political, recognizing, for instance, that the dearth of information about the Hungarian environment was intrinsically connected to government policies.

The Circle faced criticisms not only from within but from other environmental groups working on the dam issue. The "Friends of the Danube" movement preferred a compromise in which the Gabcikovo part of the dam operated continuously instead of according to peak energy requirements (continuous flow would have rendered the Nagymaros dam—and therefore Hungarian participation—unnecessary). But the Danube Circle wouldn't compromise. The whole dam project had to be opposed. Meanwhile, the more radical "Blues" found fault with the Circle's moderation, primarily concerning tactics. The Blues instead favored direct action.[11]

The environmental movement served a similar function to the East German Evangelical Lutheran Church, providing a relatively safe forum for criticizing the regime. "The environment question was a substitute for politics," Tamas Fleischer said. "Even people who normally wouldn't care about the environment joined the movement." Both the Lutheran Church and the Danube Circle prepared their members for civic activity by establishing a public arena that may not have consistently been *anti*-governmental but remained nonetheless strictly *non*-governmental. Such institutions prepared the ground for later movements and parties that would take advantage of new circumstances to undertake additional risks.

For Hungary, the ecological issue also functioned, as Solidarity had in Poland, to unite various political persuasions. Ecology did not, for instance, overtly disrupt what Garton Ash has called "the continuum between critical intelligentsia and reformists-in-government" that developed in Hungary in the 1980s.[12] Environmental issues could be supported by both opposition intellectuals not completely estranged from the government and government reformers not entirely isolated from the opposition. More importantly perhaps, the dam protest could paper over the deep division in the opposition between "Central Europeans" and "Populists," as the German writer Hans Magnus Enzensberger has described the two halves of the Hungarian soul. The Central Europeans would eventually form the Alliance of Free Democrats to popularize their more urban, more internationalist, more free-market-oriented platform. The Populists, who would eventually form the Democratic Forum, were a difficult group to pin down. "Only someone who has spoken Hungarian from childhood can grasp the 'Fatherland on high,'" Enzensberger was told during his visit to Budapest, "and with it the Populists' worries about population decline, the swamping of native culture, the decline of folk art, and liberal abortion laws."[13] What better issue than degradation of the environment to promote common cause between those disaffected by communism, modernity, or both.

By 1988, the situation in Hungary was changing. The Danube Circle had been formed before Gorbachev came to power in the Soviet Union. With the tide of *glasnost* rising to the east, purely ecological appeals had become both narrow and ineffectual. A 1988 petition of 120,000 signatures calling for parliamentary reconsideration of the dam project had not appeared to sway Parliament. Consensus within the Danube Circle was breaking apart. "By 1988," sociologist Ferenc Miszlivetz wrote at the time, "activists of splinter groups, the Danube Movements, have changed course, openly accepting political confrontation with the power structure, which is accelerating the pace of construction [of the dam]."[14]

The splintering was not altogether unhealthy. By 1988, Hungarian civil society had generated the greatest variety of movements, quasi-parties, and public associations of any Eastern European country. And virtually every one of these groups incorporated into their programs Green elements such as opposition to the dam project. Meanwhile, at the top echelons of power, the personnel had changed significantly between 1985 and 1988. A new group of reform-minded communists ousted the Party officials clustered around Janos Kadar. These newcomers—Reszo Nyers, Miklos Nemeth, and Kadar's replacement Karoly Grosz—would blur to an even greater extent the line between government reformer and opposition pragmatist.

By the time the Hungarian communists had changed sufficiently to reverse their position on the Nagymaros project, both they and the dam were fast becoming anachronisms. In July 1989, when the Nemeth government officially suspended Hungary's participation in the project, the opposition in Hungary was in full flower. Indeed, its strength could be measured by its diversity: an opposition so varied that it created its own roundtable prior to the talks with the government.[15] The Communist Party reformed into two socialist parties in October 1989, the roundtable provided the framework for free elections, and the opposition had swung 180 degrees: from an anti-political voice in 1984 to a proto-political movement in 1990.[16] No longer a substitute for politics, ecology assumed a more modest position, perhaps even a back seat, in the new Hungarian agenda.

More than a dam

The Hungarian Greens—or Blues, as some groups called themselves—never focused exclusively on the Nagymaros project. But the dam was the easiest issue around which to organize. With the fall of communism, the environmental movement has regained its diversity. At the grassroots, organizations such as Bio Cultura promote organic farming, and the Ecoservice provides advice to the citizens of Budapest. Several universities still maintain well-knit groups of students, scientists, and activists. The international Ecotopia, a summer ecological extravaganza featuring music, an organic restaurant, and even its own currency (the ECO pegged to the Deutsche mark), took place in 1990 at a farm in the Hungarian countryside. There are new institutes, a partially restaffed Ministry of Environment, and, in a refurbished silk mill in the Obuda section of Budapest, the "Bush" center (the "environment president" provided a very modest amount of start-up capital).

The diversity of the Hungarian environmental movement reflects the multitude of problems that Green activists hope to solve. The dam project, for instance, continues to raise problems. Although the Hungarian government plans to begin dismantling the Nagymaros site in the second half of 1992, the Slovak government has indicated that it wants to add the finishing touches to Gabcikovo, prompting several protests by Slovak environmentalists.[17] Meanwhile the Austrian company involved in the construction has demanded $100 million from Hungary. Hungarian activists argue that Austria should absorb the losses. "We petitioned the Austrian parliament not to do this [dam project] in 1986," Janos Vargha says. "They were informed that a movement in Hungary was against it...but they assumed that the police would protect them in Hungary. The Austrian government is responsible."[18] Meanwhile, Tamas Fleischer, together with the Ister Institute (Ister was the old Roman name for the Danube) he founded with Janos Vargha, has developed an alternative use proposal. Ister would like to turn the dam complex into an international ecological park, combining Gabcikovo, Nagymaros, and Hainburg. The three-site stretch along the Danube would integrate environmental protection areas in Austria, Moravia, Slovakia, and Hungary: Magris's "hinternational ecumene." Encouraging appropriate agriculture and industry, Ister would avoid making the people living near the site "prisoners of a national park," according to Fleischer.

A second Ister project concerns Hungary's energy problems. Fleischer showed me a graph of energy consumption per capita measured against gross domestic product. All Western industrialized countries were clustered along a single vector, with energy consumption increasing proportionately with the size of the economy: Japan and the United States at the top right, Ireland and Portugal at the bottom left. All "socialist" countries, meanwhile, were grouped along an arc at the top left: relatively small economies and extremely high energy consumption per capita. The worst of all possible worlds. As Fleischer pointed out, saddled with an enormous amount of energy-intensive production, Eastern European countries could "jump" from one line to the other only with great determination and significant assistance. Fleischer believed that a shift to lower energy consumption, while increasing economic output required a move to an information/service economy. He was not, however, naive on this point, recognizing that the "third industrial revolution" in the West relied on a shift of industrial and agricultural production to the Third World through corporate outsourcing, trade policies, and foreign aid projects. Hungary, he admitted, might also need this Third World—whether in the south of Europe or in the southern hemisphere proper—to propel the country into a post-industrial era. "It is not so clear as we once thought!" he exclaimed, echoing a common realization of Eastern Europeans facing the dilemmas of life after communism.[19]

Vested interests make Hungary's transition more difficult. Coal, nuclear, and natural gas lobbies have sought to protect their privileged position by stressing that Hungary needs to increase its energy supplies to vault into the developed world. Although the necessary power could be imported, the energy lobbies prefer that government funds be directed into their sector to develop domestic energy sources. Yet, with capital allocated to the energy sector, Hungary may have little remaining money to restructure industry: Catch 22. The radical decrease in Soviet oil and gas shipments has only made the Hungarian government more likely to buy the arguments of the energy lobbies. The result may well be continued energy-intensive development instead of more environmentally sound and energy-efficient modernization.

The nuclear lobby has the additional advantage of foreign boosters. At least four foreign firms have offered to build additional reactors at the Paks nuclear plant. The financial terms tempt Hungary to increase the share of nuclear power (which already meets 33 percent of current energy needs). Although Three Mile Island-type disasters cannot be ruled out, the more pressing problem is financial. Neither the waste that the plant generates nor the waste that the plant itself becomes after 30 to 40 years is included in the start-up estimates or the price of the energy.

What seems to be a short cut to modernity might in fact retard economic development in the longer run.

Foreign nuclear power companies are not primarily concerned with Hungary's best interests. The French nuclear industry in particular hopes to build plants close enough to the European market to sell its cheap energy and yet far enough away from French and EC borders to avoid domestic opposition and stricter regulations. In this sense, French nuclear power plants are simply following in the footsteps of Austrian dam builders, turning Hungary into both a cheap source of energy and a potential dumping ground for yesterday's technology. Hungary may indeed realize these facts and perversely solicit the multinationals anyway. Underdevelopment, after all, breeds a certain self-destructive eagerness: the energy-poor cannot be too discriminating. For an economist such as Laszlo Urban from the more laissez-faire school, the trade-offs are a natural product of the market system and should be handled accordingly: "In a poor region where people do not have jobs, they are willing to make certain sacrifices in their environment in order to get the kind of plant which would not be welcomed in a well-to-do neighborhood or region."[20] Imre Szabo, Hungary's undersecretary of state for industry, has turned Urban's assessment into government policy: "The local population did not accept a new chemical-waste burning system, but where we provided new roads, telephones, social services and jobs, they accepted our projects."[21]

The trade-off may not simply involve French nuclear power companies that evade tough regulations in the West by relocating in Hungary. Zoltan Illes provided two more examples:

> A French company decided to set up a company here to recycle the gold and silver parts of computers. Our institute checked the technology and found out that a high percentage of cyanide would go into the air. I also heard a few days ago that an Austrian company wanted to buy hazardous waste from the Soviet Union and use it as material for processing. Standards are stricter in Austria so they can't bring the waste into the country. So they've started to develop joint ventures on the eastern border of Hungary that will bring those hazardous materials into the country.

Given the dangers of these chemical and atomic pollutants, the sacrifices made by impoverished communities desperate for trade-offs will be extremely high.

Nowhere is the energy question more visible than in Budapest. Filled with two million people (in a country of ten million), Budapest boasts an air quality that experts frequently refer to as "catastrophic" and pedestrians more readily identify as poisonous. The previous government was more concerned with providing cars for consumption-hungry Hungarians than with instituting proper regulations. "On air pollution," Zoltan Illes said, "we had strict regulations on exhaust from cars. Only in the footnote could you read: this is not valid for Eastern European cars!" The overwhelming majority of cars in Hungary were made in Eastern Europe, and they virtually never contain catalytic converters. With Hungary's new capitalism has come new consumer tastes—more cars, larger engines, more exhaust.

Another problem is waste. "We produce every year 100 million tons of waste and five to six tons of hazardous waste," Illes reported. "We have only one municipal incinerator and only one for hazardous waste which is being set up now. We have only one precisely developed standardized landfill. Otherwise we know of 2000 illegal landfills. Can you imagine how many there are that we don't know about? The first problem is a waste problem. But people don't see it and therefore air pollution is a priority."[22]

Poisoned by air, Hungary also suffers by land and by water as well. "Water pollution," Illes continued, "is mainly caused by agricultural production because we were using fertilizers such as potassium and nitrates. Plants cannot absorb potassium. Nitrates are also a main problem: we were poisoning our water just to force higher agricultural production. Of course I know that they wanted to sell abroad to get dollars. But it is a circle. Now, our earth and water are contaminated, and we cannot sell this food abroad. In 1992, the EC will not accept our products because they have a high rate of nitrates and other chemicals. It is the same story with pesticides and herbicides."[23]

Many Hungarians have not waited passively for the government to redress the wrongs. "More and more people call me every day," biologist and environmental activist Gyongy Mangel said. "They want to help. They want to do something against the noise, against the industries."[24] Protests in Budapest organized by Green Future had already forced the closing of Metalochemica, a south Budapest factory that had been polluting the neighborhood with lead and copper. A bauxite mine threatening the warm water lake at Hevisz near Lake Balaton was shut down in the summer of 1989 because of community protests.

Hungary must face the ills of communist modernization—financial blunders, unregulated pollution, energy waste—even as it prepares for another round of industrial retooling and expansion. The environmental movement must therefore not only fight the legacy of centralized planning but remain vigilant about the degradation caused by market relations. The fall of communism has not by any means reestablished verdant Eden in Hungary, nor does capitalism promise a future any Greener. The transition does, however, offer certain opportunities. Because it is retooling now, Hungary could conceivably apply state-of-the-art, environmentally sound equipment in its new industries.[25] But state-of-the-art costs money, and businesses will only install scrubbers in the stacks and dump chemicals legally if there is substantial government oversight and, as importantly, sufficient public pressure.

The second wave

Talking with Hungarian activists in 1990, I could see the outlines of a second wave of movements. The first wave—the democratic opposition—toppled the Communist Party. The second wave—Greens, feminists, youth, trade unions, peace activists—grows stronger as people realize that politics is not simply the responsibility of parliamentarians. This second wave of movements understands civil society in a somewhat different fashion than the popular fronts of Chapter 5. Rather than a useful abstraction that could be employed against the communist state, civil society, for the second wave of dissent, is a realm filled with very well-defined and very political groups. Many of these groups existed before, organizing in the shadows of the principal anti-communist movements. Now they are beginning to come into their own. In addition to the environmental groups mentioned above, Hungary's second wave includes a nonviolence group that protests the sale of guns and rifles. A new feminist network recently began in Budapest. Former members of a peace group called 4-6-0 (World War I was four years long, World War II six years long, and World War III...) have been active on military issues. Associations, clubs, movements, discussion groups, networks: not all Hungarians have retreated into apathy and consumerism. Civil society has not simply been a conveyor belt to power; some groups have retained their non-governmental status and are fighting for more than mere leadership change. Watchdogs and gadflys, the proponents of civil society are creating the political culture necessary for democratic institutions not only to thrive, but also to survive in the first place.

In the previous section, the continued work of the environmental movement—from Ecotopia to the closing of Metalochemica—was discussed. But other topics have gained prominence in Hungary's new public space as well: women's issues, for instance.

Before being recently appointed to a foreign service post, Eniko Bollabas was a professor of American studies active in the political party Democratic Forum. At the Attila Joszef University in Szeged, she began the first courses on women's issues within the American studies department. During the 1990 election campaign, she was the informal spokesperson for Democratic Forum on women's issues. "The primary problem," she said, "was that in Hungary we had an official women's organization that lied to Hungarians for 40 years that everything was okay for women, that we were emancipated. We had our jobs, our job security during maternity leaves, we could get abortions: the socialist woman is emancipated. But then people found that the socialist woman is even less emancipated than the capitalist woman. Not that there were no achievements. The ideas were all right, but not the way the ideas were realized. At this point, the word 'feminist' must be cleansed of its bad connotations."[26]

Socialist emancipation had been a mixed blessing. The average Hungarian woman, in addition to holding down a full-time job, had generally been expected to shop, clean house, cook, take care of the children. "A woman's life is all toil," Bollabas said. "A woman works four hours a day on housework. She stands on line. She goes grocery shopping every day because her refrigerator is small and her basket is small, because she must carry everything home herself, because the stores are small and always crowded." The situation has changed little since a 1977 study on Hungarian women described life after work as the "second shift" put in either for husband, for children, or for parents.[27]

When Bollabas began to speak about feminism in public, the response was not particularly gratifying. "In May 1988, I gave one of the first public talks on the situation of women in a series of sort of illegal gatherings organized by the Hungarian Democratic Forum. And I was quite emotional about what was going on. Of course, the response was emotional too. Some people were very positive. Most were very negative." A chief criticism of raising women's issues in the opposition, Bollabas noted, was that "this is not really the issue today. We have more important issues to deal with. This is a luxury problem."

Women's issues did not play a prominent role in the Hungarian elections in 1990. Again, it was deemed a "luxury problem." Bollabas disagreed strongly with this characterization: "I know that we have very important issues to talk about. I just don't accept that women's issues should come later. We cannot build our democracy without solving women's issues." That lack of democracy was demonstrated most visibly during a speech by Anna Petrovits, the leader of the Social Democrats, during March 1990 celebrations. Halfway through her speech, she was interrupted by heckling: "Where's your family?" and "Hey, sexy!" The interruptions were sufficiently loud and persistent to drown her out so she simply returned to her chair.[28] The acceptance of women as public figures on an equal footing with men has not yet become a social fact in Hungary.

A new women's network established in Budapest in 1990 has begun to translate the discussions of feminism and women's rights into concrete actions. One of the major concerns is a proposed anti-abortion law, similar to the Polish legislation. The network is also considering setting up battered women's shelters in Budapest's eigth district—nicknamed "Chicago" because of its poverty and violent reputation. "Since nothing has been done in Hungary," said Agnes Hochberg, one of the network members, "there is so much to do!"[29]

Women's rights in particular have come under attack by Hungary's conservative new government. The populists gathered in the Democratic Forum want abortion criminalized to force a higher birth rate. Their time devoted exclusively to bringing up the new Hungarian babies, women would have to leave the workforce and re-establish the traditional family of pre-war Hungary. By associating women's rights with communism, the nationalists hope to discredit both and push the country not forward into the modern era but backward to some imagined pre-modern (and unreservedly patriarchal) society. As Hungarian anthropologist Laszlo Kurti argues, if the conservative governments in Hungary and elsewhere in the region succeed with their plans for women, "the eastern half of the New European Home will be built of a myriad of creches and kitchens."[30]

Sharing in the fight against the new nationalism has been another sector of Hungary's civil society—the civil rights movement. Because of the Trianon Treaty, Hungary is a relatively homogeneous country. Even so, Budapest has the largest number of Jews of any European city; Gypsies meanwhile represent 8 percent of the overall population. One organization that fights for the rights of these minorities, the Raoul Wallenberg Society, has documented the recent growth of anti-Semitism in Hungary, particularly around the 1990 elections. Some supporters of the populist Democratic Forum used anti-Semitism against the more liberal Alliance of Free Democrats, many of whose members are of Jewish heritage. "They did not use any new methods of attacking Jews," Robert Braun of the Society reported. "They simply recycled the same old traditional anti-Semitic slogans: those who hold mass media in their hands, who only care for money, etc. One of the Democratic Forum leaders who is now in Parliament gave a radio interview one morning in which he spoke of a 'dwarf minority controlling mass media and Hungarian political life.'"[31] Historian Ivan Volgyes writes of signs that appeared during the 1990 campaign such as "Adolph Lives!" and mentions a retired general who publicly stated that Hungary should have fought against the Soviet Union in World War II.[32] The nationalist magazine *Szent Korona* has accused Jews of Trianon, communism, and current political hegemony, recycling charges made by Hungarian fascists in the 1940s.[33]

National minorities living in Hungary who have countries to defend them—Romanians, Germans, and Slovaks—have by contrast been treated well. "Since the 1970s," Braun related, "the Hungarian government adopted a policy which said that the better we treat our minorities, the better the Hungarian minorities will be treated in other countries. So the Hungarian government behaved properly toward ethnic Romanians in order to ask the Romanian government for special collective rights for Hungarians there."[34] A number of Jewish organizations, both in Europe and the United States, have monitored the anti-Semitism in Hungary. But one group for whom there is no state and very limited international solidarity is the Romany people—the Gypsies.

"The worst treated of course were the Gypsies," Braun said. "Our fear at the present is not anti-Semitism because there is no consensus about anti-Semitism and anti-Semites are a minority in the country. But there is a "wonderful" national consensus in Hungary around anti-Gypsy feelings. I read a secret study conducted last year by the Ministry of Construction in which they proposed a kind of reservation in the north for the Gypsies where they could work on their traditional crafts like hut-building and wooden dish-cutting. Very frightening! It is obvious that in a country which is declining economically and in which new elections are not fulfilling the popular requirements of the population, all those aggressive sentiments will be directed against the most-threatened groups—and the group that no one is willing to defend is the Gypsies." The Wallenberg Society is joined by a new wave of Gypsy organizations—cultural associations and parties—in this concern.[35]

Active in both the environmental and women's movements, Zsuzsanna Beres did not view these grassroots movements with any great optimism: "They are very weak and this is inevitable because there hasn't been anything in this vein before. It will take several years to gain momentum." Beres pointed to a disturbing disjunction between the vulnerability of these movements and the needs of the country. Mainstream values are now being shaped by nationalism, fundamentalist Christianity, and, of course, capitalism. "At a time when Hungary is being eaten up by big business," she noted, "there are no other voices to put pressure on the establishment." In her visits with Green activists in Western Europe, Beres repeatedly encountered belief in a third way in the East, if only the countries didn't blindly accept capitalism and install a consumer society. "But the fact is that people voted in a government that wants a market. The Democratic Forum calls it a social market economy, but I don't see where the social is," she said. The type of government mattered little: an official of the World Bank recently told her that it doesn't care what kind of government Hungary has, as long as it institutes the right kind of economic reform. "Grassroots movements are not in a position to put pressure. When they will be in that position, irreparable damage will have been done," she concluded gloomily.[36]

* * *

Though perhaps not as extensive as Hungary's second wave, alternative movements in other Eastern European countries also have their constituencies. In East Berlin, before unification, squatters created a counterculture in abandoned buildings, turning the otherwise gloomy Prenzlauerberg into a colorful neo-Bohemian quarter. A squat cafe with its mix of anarchist politics and 1960s eclecticism would appear in one location for a week before the police closed it down, only to reappear several blocks away for another one-week run. After financial unification brought new investments from the West to Prenzlauerberg, boutiques started to push out the squats.

Tacheles, a squat in East Berlin, was still making a valiant effort to survive in the days immediately before unification in October 1990. In the old Jewish part of the city, 40 artists from both East and West founded Tacheles in a crumbling turn-of-the-century department store in February 1990. When I spoke to them, these artists were struggling to maintain a cooperative and had plans to build a cinema, jazz salon, dance club, cafe, and several ateliers: a multicultural and international center in Berlin. Although not explicitly political, the artists in Tacheles embraced a sort of left anarchism. Skinheads had attacked the cooperative several times, once sending a Tacheles artist to the hospital with severe burns after a Molotov cocktail exploded in his face.[37] This violence from the extreme right was just a taste of things to come, anticipating a major increase in hate crime in the new Germany directed against people of color and the left.

Ljubljana in Slovenia represents a very different context for the second wave of dissidents. Small, old, and quaint, Ljubljana resembles a fairy-tale Austrian city: a picture-book castle on top of a hill, a small river running below, and in between a strip of colorful, well-preserved merchant houses and businesses. By temperament, Ljubljana is almost Scandinavian or, to find a US equivalent, like Burlington, Vermont: an environmentally conscious university town with bike paths and big parks, a peace and nonviolence center, and a thriving alternative scene alive with punk rock and awash in post-modern art. Until civil war disrupted life in the Slovenian capital, you could also play the Yuppie (Yugoslav urban professional) by ordering out for pizza, renting the latest American videos, or eating overpriced banana splits in cafes along the river.

The Center for Peace, Culture, and Nonviolence is located in the very center of Ljubljana, on the second floor of a restored building, above several very fashionable clothing stores. Started in 1990, the group maintains a core of a couple dozen people, each of whom has undertaken a particular project: conscientious objection, conversion of military to nonmilitary production, peace studies. Several members sit on a governmental commission on "peace politics"; others ran on an ultimately unsuccessful alternative list put together for the Slovenian elections in 1990. One intriguing Center-facilitated project calls for the conversion of a former army barracks located in the heart of the city into a space for alternative cultural, political, and social groups. Forty groups, representing over 400 people, developed a proposal for the government.

When I expressed surprise at the number of alternative groups that tiny Ljubljana maintained, Slovenian philosopher and activist Tomaz Mastnak reminded me that the Slovenian democratization "was initiated and carried through by the movements. The political parties, or political organizations, joined much later." Alternative culture, which had retreated into the background during the rise of the political parties in 1989-90, was much stronger than even its recent revival might indicate. "We are living in quite a secular and relatively modern society, in which movements have enjoyed great support and great sympathy," Mastnak said. "Not just in Ljubljana, which is a city, but in the countryside as well. In a way I was happy with the ease in the mid-1980s with which feminist and homosexual ideas were accepted in this country. It was only the conservative politicans which opposed these ideas. But the people accepted these ideas quite tolerantly." The public atmosphere had changed. Mastnak noted. "After the election, political Catholicism re-entered the social and political scene and the Catholic ideologists have the ideological apparatus of the state in their hands. And they have become quite aggressive and intolerant. The first indication was the discussion of abortion earlier this year when Christian Democrats demanded that a relatively liberal law on abortion should be changed."

But there were new voices being added to "civil society." "There is a part of society which is conservative, anti-democratic, intolerant, sexist, homophobic, all of that," Mastnak continued. "And they feel that they can speak their minds now. So they are becoming more loud and aggressive than they used to be. And this might create the impression that they are very strong and represent a considerable segment of society. I don't think so but maybe I'm wrong."

With the outbreak of civil war in Yugoslavia, these voice have become stronger, chiefly at the expense of the alternative movements. True, the barracks conversion movement remains strong, the peace movement has founded an institute for peace research, and the women's movement has managed to wage successful battle against the conservative lawmakers on questions of abortion and domestic violence. But, in general, alternative movements in Slovenia have ceded ground to the politicians, and, since the civil war began, such once-strong sentiments as demilitarization have been widely dismissed as naive.[38]

Slovenia is a relatively prosperous area that has developed a middle class that can support post-materialist values. Even Yugoslavia as a whole has alternative movements—feminist, gay/lesbian, environmental—that have much deeper roots than in any other country in the region. In its Balkan neighbors—Bulgaria and Romania—the second dissidence hasn't consolidated for two reasons: economic despair and the continued vitality (or necessity) of the first dissidence. The political situations in these countries have not clarified to a degree necessary to permit the diversity of a new wave of civil society. The old categories—communists versus anti-communists—still prevail.

* * *

Generating activism in the bi-polar days was chiefly a matter of overcoming fear. In the new parliamentary order, the task of the new movements is overcoming apathy. Many Hungarians, like East Germans before unification, assume that elected officials will simply take movement ideals to the political level. The realization that democratic politics often produces equally misguided and dangerous policies can give way to a paralyzing disillusionment. Green activists, feminists, advocates of nonviolence, and defenders of minority rights are combating that paralysis by continuing to fight for many of the values that motivated the 1989 revolutions. To replace the old opposition movements absorbed in the new government, they are creating a new civil society, a web of movements and independent institutions that will demand accountability from the new political and economic forces of the 1990s.

These new institutions of civil society might content themselves with an organizing space beyond government control according to the tenets of a liberal capitalist democracy. Or the second wave of dissent could spur the development of a different model of society altogether.

Third paths

In strictly economic terms, as the last chapter demonstrated, finding third paths between capitalism and communism lost support during the transformations of 1990. Self-management, ESOP, democratic socialism: these alternatives discussed among the opposition movements in the 1970s and 1980s were quickly replaced, first by the gradual, then by the rapid development of corporate capitalism.

Where economic arguments for third paths failed, however, environmental arguments may succeed.[39] As Zoltan Illes characterized the dilemma:

> We have to somehow find a third way. Western countries have shown that they also pushed aside environmental protection. On the other hand, the communist regime showed that it too could not solve these problems. If we follow your way, we will have to go through the same. But we already have more pollution! We would like to have nice big Western cars, higher living standards, and much more consumption. But if we follow your way, we will face truly vast problems.

Hungary had earlier followed a third path in the economic sphere. In the late 1960s, the Kadar regime, universally reviled for its capitulation to the Soviets in 1956, managed to gain public support with a "goulash communism" directed for the most part toward Hungarian stomachs. By the late 1970s, the Hungarian economy, fueled by this innovative mixture of market mechanisms and centralized planning, began to sputter. Hungary absorbed huge amounts of foreign capital in order to buy the continued allegiance of Hungarian stomachs through artificially high standards of living and well-stocked shop shelves. In the 1980s, Hungary suffered the same problems as its neighbors: growing inflation, stagnant productivity, diminishing output. The removal of Kadar did little to sweep away the malaise. The Grosz and then Nemeth administrations left the economy by 1989 with a $20 billion foreign debt (highest per capita in the region), two-digit inflation, and declining industrial output. The arrival of the market in early 1990 has done little to improve these indicators. Two years into the transition to capitalism, Hungary suffers from 10 percent unemployment, a 35 percent inflation rate, and a deepening recession. Privatization has begun in earnest, and multinational corporations have been wooed with attractive offers. Goulash communism came to an end, and goulash capitalism has begun.

The Greens, however, represent a categorically different third path—a goulash ecology, a model of economic development that seeks to improve the quality of life for the population without causing undue harm to the environment. Such a movement challenges both the technocratic assumptions of restricted notions of democracy as well as the utopian conceptions of the market. It implicitly criticizes the social policies that have already left Hungary with the highest per capita consumption of liquor and the highest suicide rate in the world.[40] Put forward by a movement, this alternative demands that all solutions be democratically approved, not simply rubber-stamped by "experts." Infused with Green values, it recognizes that an unregulated market can, like a bulldozer run amok, lay vast areas to waste.

This third path may very well eschew the traditional categories of Left and Right, and represent what have been called "post-modern" values: a concern for quality of life rather than a "modern" preoccupation with material goods. These post-materialist values, shaped in the crucible of the 1960s, have more recently coincided with "post-industrial" changes—the growth of the service and information sectors of the economy, the spread of automation in factories, and a fundamental change in work habits. Unlimited economic growth promoted by technocrats represents the modern era of both capitalism and communism; the post-modern alternative, meanwhile, conceives of a different relationship between humanity and nature, and, in the workplace, between labor and capital.[41] Taking advantage of the post-modern ethos and the post-industrial conditions, Green parties and movements have brought post-materialism to the political realm, challenging the economic assumptions of both right and left parties.[42]

Qualitative growth, sociologist Fred Block argues, will take the place of the unlimited growth model of capitalism and communism. But, Block cautions, there are two varieties. In the first, growth is determined simply by restructuring the workplace with new technologies. In the second, the qualitative growth is shaped by particular political values such as democracy and equity. It is this second variant which many Hungarian Greens hope to implement in their country.[43]

But how does Hungary skip past messy modernization into a clean economy that relies on high technology, robotics, and services? How do movements such as the Hungarian Greens translate their post-materialist values—such as environmental protection, greater economic security, or more participatory community development—into concrete policy alternatives? Activists in Hungary are presently developing their strategies. The Green alternative may not in the final analysis be chosen in its entirety. But it may find its way subversively into the platforms of all major parties and then into Hungarian policy.

Conversely, the second wave of dissidents may not discover a third path between capitalism and communism so much as a path beyond both economic systems. Ecologism challenges economics as a discipline with particular assumptions—scarcity, utilitarian conceptions of resources and labor, an atomistic philosophy of society—that have been in place for several centuries. Challenging these assumptions, ecologism may dislodge the centrality of economics and, like the Copernican revolution, offer a whole new theory in its place.[44] For Eastern Europe, in deep environmental crisis, such a revolution cannot come a moment too soon.

Regional rot

In the 1970s, as Western Europe went through a minor Green political revolution that, at its peak, propelled Green parties throughout Europe into their respective parliaments, Eastern Europe was wallowing in a mess of its own making.[45] From the ravaged Baltic Coast of Poland to the air pollution of Yugoslavia, the countries in the region competed for the title of ecological disaster area.[46] Here are some examples from too long a list:

- The sulfur dioxide content of the air over Krakow was tested to be higher than London's, a city six times its size.[47] Miraculously preserved through World War II, the medieval architecture of Krakow has turned black from the soot and the sculptures have begun to melt from the acid rain.

- In Sarajevo in Bosnia, Yugoslavia, "air pollution levels were so high...that desperate officials even contemplated installing a giant fan on one of the hills overlooking the city to try to dissipate its atmospheric wastes."[48]

- There are an estimated 30,000 toxic dump sites in the eastern half of Germany. In 1983-84 alone, the Netherlands and West Germany sent 24,000 shipments of hazardous materials to the GDR.[49]

- Half of Polish cities, including Warsaw, do not treat their sewage.[50]

- The Czechoslovak communist government was forced to offer economic incentives to prevent a mass exodus from the worst polluted sections of northern Bohemia. Czechoslovakia also has the highest cancer death rate of all UN member states.[51]

- In Romania's Copsa Mica, 1,400 tons of soot from the surrounding petrochemical plants rain down annually. Eighty percent of river water in Romania is undrinkable.[52]

Communism did not create pollution. But it did intensify the problems. The Soviet model concentrated on heavy industrialization and high growth rates over a short period of time: these two variables compressed the ecological problems of capitalism into several decades of degradation. Worse, centrally planned economies did not have the "alarm systems" of capitalism in which consumers convey their dissatisfaction, however indirectly, back to the producers.[53] US consumers could, for instance, boycott aerosol products; Eastern Europeans rarely had the information or the inclination to engage in such actions.

Following the Soviet lead, Eastern European governments recognized environmental problems as early as 1961 and attempted to craft joint projects accordingly. In 1971, the CMEA established a Joint Council for the Protection of the Environment. The projects the CMEA planned grew out of a realization of the indiscriminate nature of pollution. In 1982, the Polish Academy of Sciences reported that air pollution from Poland had devastated forests in East Germany and Czechoslovakia while, in a spirit of perverse reciprocity, pollution from the latter two countries had contributed to more than half of air pollutants in Poland.[54] This was not the kind of cooperation that the CMEA was intended to foster.

These joint initiatives did not produce any substantial changes in industry, energy, or consumption patterns. Reform at the top was largely formal. "The alarm bells have been rung dozens of times," wrote one Polish source, "for the sake of appearances, to make things look dramatic, to stage a phony pantomime that mimics a real ecological reform movement."[55] A Polish newspaper summed up the real attitude of most Communist governments in the region in 1981: "Environmental pollution is the price that has to be paid for industrial development and the development of civilization. Arresting and eliminating these processes is extremely costly and we do not always have the means at our disposal for the necessary action."[56]

With communist governments substituting rhetoric for real action, the task of improving the environment was left to movements from below. Polish activists formed the Polish Ecology Club in 1981 and, supported by Solidarity, led a highly succcessful campaign to close several plants, including the nation's largest aluminum producer.[57] Chernobyl, and the radioactive fallout that it rained over Eastern Europe, brought the ecological threat closer to home, spurring public protest throughout the region. In Hungary and Bulgaria, the environmental movements would become the most outspoken and daring section of the opposition. In Czechoslovakia, the Anti-Atom group went further than Charter 77 in publicly opposing a new nuclear power station.[58]

In the aftermath of the 1989 revolutions, environmentalism has proven to be a unifying concern second only to anti-communism. Green parties proved more popular than any movement except Solidarity on the eve of local elections in Poland in 1990.[59] In Czechoslovakia, the Green party was, according to some polls prior to national elections, in third place behind Civic Forum and the Christian Democrats. Ecoglasnost in Bulgaria joined with smaller parties and the Podkrepa trade union to form a united opposition. Yet all the public interest and support did not translate into powerful Green parties. In the first national elections in the region, Green and Green-inspired parties and movements managed to obtain seats only in the parliaments of Bulgaria, Romania, Slovakia, and some Yugoslav republics.[60] Most voters preferred, in their first election, to back the most prominent anti-communist party or movement in order to ensure the removal of the communist party from power. Voting Green would have split the opposition.

Creating Green parties in much of Eastern Europe was a uniquely difficult process, in large part because of "melons" and "cucumbers" (melons are green on the outside but red inside; cucumbers are green all the way through). Some Green parties in the region were accused of harboring former communists, indeed sometimes entire communist *apparats*. Three Green parties in Poland traded charges in the 1990 local elections. Similar charges were levelled against the Czechoslovak Green Party. In Hungary, meanwhile, the accusations were often made by people *within* the Green party. Zsuzsanna Beres and others considered creating a Green Alternative to attract the truly Green away from the Green party.

Another problem was with the mechanics of organizing. "Most activists have been quoting party lines, and there haven't been any grassroots movements except for the Danube movement," Beres told me. "It is not easy for people to get involved. They say that they are concerned. Then they join a party, and expect the party will do it for them." She quoted from her experience with the Green party. Several members approached her and asked, "Why isn't the Party doing anything?" She retorted impatiently, "You are the Green Party! So you do something!"[61]

Also divisive for Green politics in Eastern Europe has been the issue of nuclear power. The Green party in Czechoslovakia supported expansion of the nuclear power industry. And while the united Germany was closing down reactors in eastern Germany, Czech Foreign Minister Jiri Dienstbier was announcing that Czechoslovakia should follow the French example of relying on nuclear power for 80 percent of its energy needs. The region's dependence on energy puts many Green parties in a delicate predicament since opposition to cheap fossil fuels *and* nuclear power leaves few readily applicable alternatives. Powerful Western interests—from electric companies to atomic proselytizers such as H-bomb whiz Edward Teller—have swept through the region to pressure governments to choose nukes in order to boost the nuclear industry's flagging fortunes.[62]

Altruism and self-interest converge in the issue of environmental aid to Eastern Europe. On the one hand, Western countries can emphasize their own benevolence by extending assistance to Eastern Europe to clean up rivers, install scrubbers on smokestacks, and improve agricultural techniques. But in the end, this assistance, particularly from Western Europe, is a practical investment into the future. Acid rain is destroying the German Black Forest, pollution is ruining Scandinavian lakes, Yugoslav industry has poisoned the Adriatic.

Since this kind of aid from the West has been limited, capital remains the greatest challenge for the new governments in Eastern Europe.[63] However environmentally conscious they might be, without the necessary funds, the same bad old trends will reappear. After one year of a non-communist government, Poland was still continuing many previous policies: increased extraction of brown coal from the western part of the country, energy-inefficient industry, deforestation. "How can we reshape the entire country's economy and fix the small details as well?" the government officials may cry. But it is in these so-called small details that lives are lost, families ruined, communities destroyed. The Polish ecological movement—now comprised of dozens of new national, regional, and local groups—has broadened to meet the new challenges. A hunger strike by young activists had blocked the construction of the controversial Zarnowiec nuclear power plant in Gdansk. A flyer handed out on Earth Day 1990 in Warsaw indicated how far the environmental movement had to go. On one side was a list of the Polish ecological catastrophes-in-the-making ("In Poland there are 27 areas of ecological danger covering 11 percent of the territory of our country and in which one-third of the population lives"). On the other side was a guide to saving energy put out by the Swedish-Polish Association for Environmental Protection. A diagram showed an apartment roughly twice the size of an ordinary Polish apartment (the subliminal message: if we are environmentally conscious like the Swedes we too can be simultaneously healthy and prosperous).

In Bulgaria, one of the stronger partners in the popular front, Ecoglasnost actively pressed an environmental agenda in Parliament in 1990. Ecoglasnost was a grassroots movement that developed from protests in 1987 in the Bulgarian city of Rousse over air pollution from a chemical complex located over the border in Romania. Responsible in Parliament for economic development and nuclear energy issues for Ecoglasnost, Krasen Stanchev described the situation in Bulgaria as devastating. A country whose economy is so reliant on food exports, Bulgaria must deal with the fact that 41 percent of its soil is polluted.[64] By 1992, the political situation in Bulgaria had yet to develop beyond the two-bloc system. The popular front, Union of Democratic Forces, remains strong in Bulgaria; until greater political differentiation occurs in the country, environmental issues will probably continue to be accorded secondary status.

In Romania, pluralism and the security police are still the major points of controversy while the so-called alternative issues are infrequently discussed. Even in such a polarized political situation, Group for Social Dialogue member Gabriel Andreescu managed to coordinate ecological issues—to save the Danube, to rescue the Black Sea Coast. Yet, the Green Party in the Romanian Parliament has little clout. In Yugoslavia, civil war has not only depressed Green political activity but devastated the environment as well.

* * *

To speak of a post-industrial Eastern Europe—with its clean service economy, new political alignments, and restructured social relations—is to indulge in futurology. The region has too many centuries of economic backwardness for which to compensate. Fragmented and unstable, the political arena is still occupied with the residual problems of the communist era.

Yet while most political and economic actors are simply trying to push the region into modernity, a second wave of dissidents look, consciously or not, past the industrial age. Because they are perhaps most acutely aware of the hazards of modernization, and because they have gathered enormous though still only tacit public support, the eco-activists may be the most successful in changing the terms of debate. As citizens they will constantly challenge new technocratic arrangements. As workers or in conjunction with workers, they will challenge the Balcerowicz models and the over-reliance on corporate capitalism.

The old debate—between communism and anti-communism—is over in the region. Where it still persists—in Romania, in Serbia—the division is anachronistic. A new orthodoxy has replaced the communist order of the past, an orthodoxy that dismisses the issues of the second wave as "luxuries." Feminists who call for women's rights are told to subordinate their concerns to the more important work of political and economic reform. Environmental activists are told that economic restructuring and growth must precede protection. Human rights activists focusing on the rights of endangered minorities are brushed off by talk of general human rights. Gay and lesbian organizers are frequently told to be more discreet (return to the closet). A new power elite, its fortunes tied to the international economic system and its policies sheltered from public debate, has taken its place in government.

Strong Green parties and movements will be important in understanding and challenging the new power elite. After the failure of the Hungarian Green Party to win seats in the national parliament, Zsuzsanna Beres wrote: "It is extremely important to build up a powerful Green Party because at present there is no force to counterbalance the extremely conservative, Christian nationalist, free-market-oriented line that emerged victorious from the elections."[65]

Such activists and organizers and protesters are not, in general, simply carving out part of the public space for themselves. Rather, they are calling for a reexamination of all public policy. Environmentalists are not simply hugging trees—they are calling for a reordering of economic priorities. Feminists are not simply addressing the rights of women—they are criticizing ingrained social patterns validating men and denigrating women that occur in the family, the workplace, and in the highest reaches of government. These are not, in other words, issues that are solved by a particular piece of legislation. Many of the movements are calling for much more radical alternatives: a third way between the new capitalist and the old communist models or a rejection of left-right dichotomies altogether. They have remained the repositories of idealism in Eastern Europe. They have taken the place of the dissidents who came before, who could, in the eyes of most Western observers, never succeed and yet succeeded nonetheless.

This new opposition is likewise fated to lose many fights. After less than a year in office, for instance, environmental official Zoltan Illes was dismissed from his position. His uncompromising stands upset his fellow ministry colleagues and foreign investors alike. But Illes continues to fight for the environment outside of government. The fight, after all, is not simply political—it is moral as well. And morality, as we shall see in the next chapter, plays a notable role in public life in Eastern Europe.

Chapter 7

Czechoslovakia...
A moral foreign policy

The history in our country has ceased to flow against the current of conscience. Let us not allow it—be it under whatever banner—to flow that way again.[1]

—Vaclav Havel

After Czechoslovakia's velvet revolution, Prague swelled with crowds and cheerfulness, like a Disneyland of the East. The tourists pressed in from far and wide—more in the first three wintery months of 1990 than in all of 1989. Chartered buses deposited their charges to stare open-mouthed at the baroque beauty of the medieval city. Czech and Slovak emigres, the children of 1968, returned for unexpected reunions. Political guests paid their respects to the new residents of Prague's famous castle. Everyone wanted to see the historic city, talk to the historic president, take advantage of the historic opportunity. There were even some historic castles and villas that the government offered to interested businesses and international organizations—a compelling architectural reason to open a Prague office.

When the Helsinki Citizens Assembly (HCA) met in the capital in October 1990, it too received a historic venue: the glorious art nouveau municipal building with interiors designed by renowned painter Alfons Mucha. An unusual experiment in grassroots diplomacy, the HCA brought to the *fin-de-siecle* city hall over 800 activists from East and West for a weekend of discussion and debate. It was, needless to say, a historic meeting. New Forum members drank pilsner with Solidarity activists; Hungarian intellectuals mixed with Bulgarian environmentalists; Slovenian peace activists danced with Czech and Slovak student organizers. Interspersed were French anti-racism activists, Welsh nationalists, Dutch church women, Scandinavian Greens, Italian feminists, Canadian professors, Ukrainian politicians, Russian writers, Lithuanian secessionists.

Prague was suffused with autumn color, the beer gardens were still filled with happy tourists, and the conference celebrated the victories of 1989.

More than simply a convenient or beautiful place to hold a meeting, Prague carried symbolic weight as well. Two major supporters of the HCA project had become the president and foreign minister of Czechoslovakia. From their new positions of responsibility, Vaclav Havel and Jiri Dienstbier were vigorously pursuing a major aim of the Assembly: the application of morality to politics and foreign policy. Once principled activists on the fringes of their society, Dienstbier and Havel continued to support civic movements, many of which were as marginal to the new Eastern European order as Charter 77 activists had been to the old.[2]

Valiantly trying not to be marginal, the Assembly brought together an unprecedented geographic mix of participants from virtually every country participating in the Helsinki process, also known as the Conference on Security and Cooperation in Europe (CSCE). But while the CSCE meetings involved high-level diplomats, the Assembly comprised movements from below, movements of civil society, movements which had worked together on peace and human rights issues for the better part of the 1980s. Unified in their opposition to the Soviet bloc system, these groups, East and West, played a key role in ending the Cold War. Designed to carry this activism into the post-Cold War era, the Assembly was to have transformed European politics, encouraging citizens to take a more vigorous role in formulating national policy from economics to international relations. Citizens had, after all, changed the face of Eastern Europe. Why not all of Europe, why not the world?

In its role as a popular front, the Assembly managed a general consensus on a Europe without borders, "unity through diversity," the primacy of ecology, social protection during economic development, and democracy as a first principle. These generalities aside, the Assembly participants discovered that after the revolutions, the Babel syndrome had taken hold. They no longer all spoke the same language. The Assembly lacked what the movements once had: a clearly articulated adversary. In the absence of "totalitarianism," a clear moral vision was no longer as easy to construct or as subject to general agreement. Unity in diversity was clearly more difficult to maintain than unity in adversity. Times had changed.

Thus, the HCA meeting ended inconclusively. Specifics generated argument, particulars spawned controversy, and moral positions of one nature produced equally vehement moral positions of a contrary nature. Havel gave a listless closing address. Dienstbier had to fly off to a distant country and could not participate as scheduled. The Assembly closed with plans for the future but left a lingering dissatisfaction among participants at the tangled process by which a moral viewpoint becomes translated into a tangible reality.

The velvet revolution in Czechoslovakia was a rare moment when a moral vision, cultivated under difficult conditions for several decades, shaped history. Had that moment already passed by 1990? Was the philosophy of Havel and company sufficient to inspire a revolution but limited with respect to post-revolutionary challenges? The Helsinki Citizens Assembly, as a body, was experiencing what Havel and Dienstbier had discovered as individuals: the complicated relationship between morality and politics in the post-communist era.

With the HCA and other innovative international initiatives, Prague was to be the moral center of the world. And indeed, the successes of Czechoslovakia's new foreign policy exemplified the exhilarating alternatives that revolution made possible. But there would be setbacks as well, and whether attributed to human failings, political compromise, or revolutionary betrayal, these accommodations to pragmatism contrasted sadly with the historic achievements and lofty ideals of the velvet revolutionaries.

The pull of the pragmatic

Foreign policy can be terribly dull. Interminable negotiations and official statements, made virtually indigestible by doublespeak, monstrous platitudes, and ubiquitous acronyms, turn an otherwise fascinating subject into an immediate conversation stopper. For the uninitiated, the world of foreign policy is flat and one-dimensional, only compelling at its most life-threatening (war) and life-affirming (peace).

How can a Vaclav Havel survive in such a world? A playwright, a spinner of tales and plots, Havel used his writings to challenge the pronouncements of the Czechoslovak communists, and exceeded with his conscientious objections the limits of officially-sanctioned culture. He is not the stuff of which colorless politicians are made. Indeed, since becoming president of the new Czech and Slovak Federated Republic at the end of 1989, Havel has provided his country with literate (if not always deliberate) leadership. Not content to be a mere functionary, he has aspired to guide not simply through the power of his office but with the strength of his words as well.

In his frequent speeches, Havel has already left his imprint on both idiom and policy. For instance, in addressing the topic of hatred, only a writer could offer this lyrical analogy:

> The Hindus have a legend concerning a mythical bird called Bherunda. The bird has a single body, but two necks, two heads and two separate consciousnesses. After an eternity together, these two heads began to hate each other and decided to do harm to each other. Both of them swallow pebbles and poison and the result is predictable: the whole Bherunda bird goes into spasms and dies with loud cries of pain. It is brought back to life by the infinite mercy of Krishna, to remind people that all hatred harms not only the object of that hatred, but at the same time, and perhaps chiefly, the one who hates.[3]

With this seemingly timeless observation on the reflexivity of hate, Havel managed to describe two very specific conflicts: the multitude of bi-polar hatreds produced by the Cold War and the growing rift between Czechs and Slovaks.

More important than the images and literary language has been Havel's insistence on moral issues. Here too, Havel has gone against the foreign policy grain. With their emphasis on *realpolitik* and the necessary compromises of and with "great powers," practitioners of international relations tend to steer clear of morality, having discovered a realm of rational actors and power calculations that lies far beyond good and evil. By contrast, in his essays from the 1970s and 1980s, Havel created a very different world, one in which people tried to "live in truth," tried to lead meaningful existences even in societies where governments ruled by deception. These were the views of a Socrates, a Nietszche, a gadfly, a critical outsider. Strange, then, that Havel assumed the most powerful position in the country. Leaving aside the attraction of power, Havel fell victim to his own moral standards: living in truth demanded from the individual a high degree of responsibility both to personal values and to fellow citizens. Czechoslovakia was in need of guidance and leadership, and there was really only one logical candidate.[4]

Havel moved quickly to translate his moral vision into reality when he became president at the end of 1989. He elevated Jiri Dienstbier, a journalist and former Charter 77 spokesperson, to the position of foreign minister. He solicited intellectuals such as former student leader Sasa Vondra as advisers. Foreign policy, once a predictable and ignored element of the previous government, was reinvigorated. "Within the President's Office," Vondra told the *East European Reporter*, "the Foreign Affairs department was very much a junior partner: understaffed and performing no more than the most basic service in terms of the previous President's minimal ceremonial functions. The situation is changing of course, and by and large the Foreign Ministry now works very well."[5] The new Havel team took advantage of the post-revolutionary flux to develop and promulgate a distinctive foreign policy.

Havel himself traveled extensively in his first months in office. For the new president, an exchange of visits was no mere formality, no empty ritual. There was history for which to atone, and there were examples upon which to reflect. Meeting with (West) German President Richard von Weizsacher, Havel repeated one of his major moral precepts: do not take on the attributes of your enemy: "We cannot imitate [the Nazis]! If we accepted their lie as our own, we would only be handing on the torch of their destructive errors."[6] The playwright of course had a subtext: Czechs and Slovaks too are recovering from four decades of living a lie—they too must embrace (or at least tolerate) former enemies, not execute them.

Perhaps the most symbolic of Czechoslovakia's foreign policy gestures was toward the spiritual leader of Tibet. Risking a suspension of aid and trade with communist China, Havel invited the Dalai Lama to his country, and in February, the Nobel Peace Prize-winning Tibetan monk arrived in Prague. "I am grateful to President Vaclav Havel for having given me this opportunity to meet him and to visit his beautiful country," the Dalai Lama stated. "I am particularly happy about this because President Havel is in many ways so unlike other political or national leaders. He has been thrust into his present position quite reluctantly and is one of the few national leaders totally dedicated to peace, nonviolence and moral responsibility."[7]

Speeches and the deliberate reinstatement of relations with previously scorned governments and dignitaries were all fine. But a foreign policy is more than protocol. What made the new moral vision distinctive was its attempt to recast East-West relations. No longer would Czechoslovakia be simply a victim of its vulnerable geography. Under its new leaders, the country would propose several bold initiatives to tie together the two halves of Europe—from the Atlantic to the Urals—into a more peaceful and more prosperous whole.

Europe and its institutions are, for most of Eastern Europe, the future; the region's foreign policy can be viewed, at its most basic level, as the means to achieving this end. "With Us to Europe" Civic Forum promised in its election posters: vote for us and we will restore your European heritage. Naturally this was not intended to be the Europe of periodic wars and frequent xenophobia but rather the Europe of economic prosperity and "Western Civilization." Concretely, the slogan translated into membership in the Council of Europe and, as of the end of 1991, an association agreement with the European Community. Under Civic Forum's guidance, Czechoslovakia also joined the IMF and World Bank and signed on to the European Bank for Reconstruction and Development (EBRD). In line with earlier opposition pledges, the new government also called for a new European security system with an accent on demilitarization. It supported the gradual phasing out of the Warsaw Pact and delicately negotiated the withdrawal of Soviet forces stationed on its territory (the 74,000 troops left the country in mid-1991). Initially the Havel government emphasized the CSCE process as the keystone of a new European order, one predicated on conflict resolution rather than conflict.

Moving closer to the EC required powers of persuasion and accommodation but no great sacrifice. Establishing a cooperative relationship with the Soviets, however, posed certain problems, not least of which were historic. After all, the Soviet Union had not lifted a hand to prevent the collapse of Czechoslovakia's First Republic after World War I, had imposed communism there after World War II, had destroyed the delicate Prague Spring in 1968, had soured any lingering pan-Slavism by propping up the Husak regime in the 1970s and 1980s. Yet with no trace of irony, Foreign Minister Dienstbier declared in June 1990 that "we should do everything to pull [the USSR] into Europe. There should be no 'Versailles complex.'"[8] Czechoslovakia was elevating the principle of "love thine past enemy" to the level of diplomacy.

The foreign ministry went one step further. Dienstbier designed a plan that would provide funds for the Soviets earmarked for the purchase of Eastern European goods. Such a policy would simultaneously satisfy consumer demand in the Soviet Union and save Eastern Europe's ailing industries. The Dienstbier plan called for the EBRD to provide $16 billion to the Soviet Union to pay for deliveries of industrial goods from factories in Poland, Czechoslovakia, and Hungary. The Soviet Union would repay the debt by investing rubles in the modernization of Soviet factories; the money collected by the East European governments would likewise go to improving industrial efficiency.[9] In the sense that an economically devastated Soviet Union was a threat to Czechoslovakia, the Dienstbier plan was enlightened self-interest. But the plan's emphasis (help them if you want to help us) and its implicit discrimination between the past wrongs of the Soviet government and the present predicament of the Soviet peoples, demonstrated an elegance and charity frequently found wanting in diplomacy.

With either the Dienstbier plan or the call for a new European security system, Czechoslovakia was still content to make moral appeals, rather than take moral actions. On the question of the arms trade, however, the Havel team adopted a much more radical stance. A major pre-World War II armament producer and supplier, Czechoslovakia became a global center for arms exports in the Cold War era. Both its Soviet-style materiel and its reputation for valuing hard currency over ideology gave the country a competitive edge in the international market. The most famous Czechoslovak product, Semtex, an odorless and hard-to-detect plastic explosive, was the perfect material for terrorist bombs (responsible, for instance, for the 1988 Pan Am airline disaster over Lockerbie, Scotland). With tanks, guns, ammunition, and Semtex, Czechoslovakia outfitted several armies and underground movements through the 1970s and 1980s, the profits flowing primarily through the Slovak military-industrial complex and into the federal government's hard currency accounts. From 1985 to 1989, Czechoslovakia was the seventh largest arms exporter in the world; nearly half of its foreign trade for the past 15 years consisted of arms transfers.[10]

Every country in Eastern Europe has military industries that supplied the Warsaw Pact and provided convertible currency. After the 1989 revolutions, most countries planned to scale back on military production for purely economic reasons: contracts from a crumbling Soviet Union and a Warsaw Pact on its final legs were declining at a rapid rate. But arms continue to be profitable, and the arms industries of Eastern Europe were not going to disappear.

Except in Czechoslovakia. In January 1990, Foreign Minister Dienstbier announced that his country would cease arms exports immediately. "Foreign policy until now was either very pragmatic, or else very ideological," he told the *New York Times*. "It seemed that some things could not be done because they had never been done before, but they can be done if people want to do them. For instance, Czechoslovakia will simply end its trade in arms without taking into account what the pragmatists will say, that it will be a blow to the state coffers, that those people will get arms from somebody else anyway if we don't supply them."[11] It was a breathtaking statement. The cessation of arms exports proved the Dalai Lama's tribute correct and provided an important money-where-our-mouth-is correlative to the poetic statements and visionary diplomatic moves.

There was only one problem. It wasn't going to happen.

Daniel Kumermann is a journalist who covers foreign policy for a Czech daily. The new approach of the Havel-Dienstbier team, he told me, "was a strong reaction to the previous regime which was entirely immoral. Everyone who came from the opposition demanded morality." How long would this adherence to moral standards last? "So far, the world claps its hands and it's very nice. But a conflict will develop between morality and pragmatism and the Czechoslovak leaders will slowly bend their morality."[12]

That bending came quite soon after. The government first qualified its promise by agreeing to honor all outstanding contracts—which could extend for several years. Then it turned out that the government was merely giving up its state *monopoly* on the arms trade. With some minor regulations that could be easily circumvented, newly privatized arms manufacturers could continue, even increase, the Czech and Slovak arms trade.[13] They needed little encouragement, immediately concluding several critical deals: arms to Nigeria in exchange for oil bound for Croatia, a proposed military shipment to the Soviet Union before it collapsed, $200 million in tank sales to Pakistan, and, perhaps the most controversial, $200 million worth of tanks to Syria.[14] After the explosion of domestic and international criticism following this last deal, Finance Minister Vaclav Klaus reportedly "expressed surprise at the fuss over the sale: his country was not doing anything that many other countries did not do."[15]

Why the backpedaling? Journalist Miroslav Zamecnik summed up the situation: "They can't find anything as profitable to produce as a tank."[16] One Slovak worker in the profession echoed Dienstbier's characterization of pragmatism: "If only Czechoslovakia ceases to export arms, then the export markets we have will just be taken by other countries. We are not such a rich country that we can afford this."[17] Nor could Czechoslovakia afford the unemployment—the jobs of thousands of workers, most from Slovakia, were on the line. Although some Slovak firms have shifted to construction, motorcycles, or forest machinery, economic conversion is in its infancy.

In its first real litmus test, morality indeed proved flexible.[18] On other issues, too, the new morality encountered pragmatism's *nyet*. Early statements on the dissolution of the bloc system came up against NATO's determination to maintain itself even as the Warsaw Pact disintegrated. The best alternative, a new demilitarized European security system anchored in the CSCE process, had the support of most East European oppositions-turned-governments. But the CSCE process, bringing together all European nations plus the United States and Canada, was weakened by its lack of institutional structures and its rule by consensus (permitting only the least controversial decisions).

Handicapped by these structural problems, the CSCE process in 1991 failed to solve the Yugoslav crisis and appeared to be equally ineffectual with regard to the disintegrating Soviet Union. Instead of sticking to his original insistence on a new European security order, Dienstbier announced that Czechoslovakia did not rule out eventual NATO membership; Havel called for the fullest cooperation with the North Atlantic alliance.[19] A weak compromise was achieved: a permanent secretariat of the CSCE housed in Prague but possessed of little authority. In the face of strong US resistance to a new European security arrangement, Czechoslovakia's interest in joining NATO is understandable. The chance to create a demilitarized Europe, one free of both the massive US armed presence and its potential European military replacement, had for the moment passed. Thus the change of heart in the Czechoslovak foreign ministry. Morality dictated a stronger CSCE process but pragmatism—and the calculated indifference of the United States—called for aligning with the "safe bet."[20]

So too did the Dienstbier plan of giving targeted aid to the Soviet Union seem noble. But the plan never materialized, derailed by lingering Cold War hostility and the West's misguided prudence. The Soviet Union meanwhile became the "UFFR" (Union of Fewer and Fewer Republics) before its rebirth as the Commonwealth of Independent States. And while the plan remains viable for a newly configured Commonwealth economic community, international capital is satisfied to let the post-Soviet economy twist in the wind (and the peoples of Eastern Europe twist with it). Part of the hesitation lies in lack of funds, part is blind adherence to the supposed creativity of free market principles. In any case, Czechoslovakia certainly doesn't possess the capital to put through its own initiative.[21]

Another commodity in short supply in Czechoslovakia is energy, an issue which has complicated relations with its neighbors. Hungary is infuriated that Slovakia intends to put the Gabcikovo dam into use, thereby threatening the ecological balance on the two countries' border. Austria has likewise objected to a nuclear power plant located near its own ecosystem. It offered free energy supplies if the Czechoslovak government simply closed down the offending reactor. Czechoslovakia refused.[22]

Given this mixed record with its neighbors, it is not surprising that Czechoslovakia has not taken a leadership role in regional cooperation. Although it eagerly joined the "Pentagonal Group" with Hungary, Austria, Italy, and Yugoslavia, Czechoslovakia has not translated its moral diplomacy into greater regional solidarity. An initial meeting in Bratislava in April 1990 among foreign ministers from Poland, Czechoslovakia, and Hungary did not yield any firm regional alliance. When the leaders of the three countries met one year later, Hungarian Prime Minister Jozsef Antall noted: "this cooperation does not create any new organization."[23] Czechoslovakia has been concerned with the economic dislocations of Poland and Hungary, worried that in a closer alliance, these two countries would be a brake on its own development. Poland and Hungary are not immune from this analysis as well, joining Czechoslovakia in rejecting requests from both Bulgaria and Romania to join their triangular talks.

The lines have been drawn in Eastern Europe, separating the most likely to succeed from the intensive-care patients. Instead of working together to promote mutual development, the region has adopted a lifeboat mentality—who can be jettisoned to improve the chances of the others? Havel has unfortunately done little to question these demarcations. Given domestic problems, his reticence is certainly understandable, if frustrating.

* * *

A year after its inception, Czechoslovakia's moral foreign policy had become decidedly low-key. The arms trade was continuing, the region remained disarticulated, the Dienstbier plan had been pushed to one side. At the beginning of 1991, when Vaclav Havel outlined his foreign policy objectives in a New Year's speech, the rhetoric was perfunctory, not poetic, and the goals seemed downright prosaic. There were no Hindu parables, no grand statements. It was just the facts, thank you very much, and diplomacy had lost its grandeur.[24] Perhaps it was the impending war in the Persian Gulf or the economic hardships Czechoslovakia was enduring. Perhaps it was the simmering Czech-Slovak crisis. Perhaps it was the weight of the year's blunders—Havel's meeting with the internationally isolated Kurt Waldheim in Austria, his granting of a general amnesty for prisoners that released petty criminals as well as those jailed for political purposes. Perhaps Havel had simply realized that the strength of ideas and the power of the powerless carried precious little weight in the cold, literal, and one-dimensional world of geopolitics. There is no patience in international relations for poetry.

In 1990, I asked a high-ranking official in the Polish foreign ministry what he thought about Havel. "Diplomacy is the art of the possible," he quoted Bismark. "We must be pragmatic. To be brutal, Havel's view is naive."[25] By 1991, a conservative analyst concluded approvingly that idealistic rhetoric issuing from the Czechoslovak foreign ministry had been replaced by "quiet diplomacy and Realpolitik."[26] If selling tanks to Syria is what passes for maturity in the conduct of international relations, then Prague was better off with its naivete.

A moral universe

Naive or not, Havel's view has a noble lineage: Komensky, Masaryk, Patocka. From these thinkers, Havel has established a unique philosophic underpinning to his moral policies. The 17th-century Bohemian philosopher, Jan Amos Komensky (Comenius), established the modern discipline of education and promoted his ecumenical plan for a reconciliation of the world's churches. A humanist in the best tradition of the Enlightenment, Komensky even proposed a world confederation (an ambitious gesture even though the world to Komensky meant little more than Europe).[27]

When Bohemia next gained its independence, it was fortunate to have on hand another multitalented humanist: the grand statesman of Czechoslovak politics, Tomas Masaryk. A philosopher by training, Masaryk established liberalism in Czechoslovakia at a time when the rest of the region was marching rightward. While authoritarian leaders of various hues glorified the strong and powerful, Masaryk took a different tack: "The modern humanitism recognizes the right of the weak...the protection of the weaker and the weak, the protection of the small, of the individual, of corporations and classes, of nations and states—that is the task of modern times."[28] He fought for the rights of underdogs (defending at one point a Czech Jew accused of ritual murder) and attempted to infuse the moral law into the law of state. "To work means to fight evil consistently: everywhere, always, and especially in its germ," he wrote.[29]

Masaryk's liberalism reappeared in both government and opposition during post-war Czechoslovakia. In the brief Prague Spring, for instance, this liberalism fused with socialism to create a new kind of communist government. Alexander Dubcek, a Slovak communist trained in the Soviet Union, might have seemed an unlikely candidate to carry on the Masaryk tradition. But in 1968, he directed Czechoslovakia down a path of liberalization that, if it hadn't been for Warsaw Pact intervention, might well have restored pluralism and important individual liberties to the country. "In 1968 we tried to bring the revolution through this final phase and among other things to restore human rights and civil freedoms," commented student leader Jan Kavan at the time, revealing the revisionist hybrid of Czech humanism and revolutionary communism.[30] This was a socialism, utopian in intent and Marxist in content, which was profoundly anti-authoritarian—making Czechoslovakia as regionally unique in 1968 as Masaryk's state had been in the inter-war period.[31]

With the promise of reform communism destroyed in Czechoslovakia after 1968, the next vehicle for Masaryk's ideas became Charter 77, founded by Jan Patocka, a philosopher who translated Komensky and wrote essays on history and philosophy criticizing the anti-transcendental tendencies in Western theory and society. To act morally, Patocka argued, was an absolute, one related not to any objective reality or purely subjective whim, but rather to an unconditional obligation. Philosophy was neither useless metaphysics nor a mere tool of ideology. It was, for Patocka, the basis for human action—"living in truth." This truth consisted not merely of facts, but rather of an irreducible human morality.[32] In other words, one "lived in truth" not for purely personal or largely social reasons but because certain transcendental imperatives, which link everyone together, compel one to do so.

Like Masaryk, Patocka avoided the constant intellectual temptation to escape into the haven of words. Shortly before his death in 1977, he appealed to his fellow oppositionists to move beyond protests on paper, a call which subsequent Charter activists would later take up.[33] Influenced by Patocka's moral (rather than political or economic) critique of communism, Charter 77 concentrated on violations of human rights. In the Masaryk tradition, it focused on the weakest link in the system—the individual and the conscience. Attacking collective systems, Charter 77 imagined the individual as the measure of all things. It refused even to conceive of itself as a group—Charter 77 was not a collective, merely a list of individuals with very different points of view.

One of those individuals also happened to be the premier writer of the opposition. As playwright, Vaclav Havel captured the crisis of the intellectual under communism (making deals with the Devil in *Dr. Faustus,* agonizing over political statements in *Largo Desolato).* As essayist, Havel outlined a philosophy of action: how to live as a moral creature under communism. In constructing this philosophy, Havel appropriated Plato through Masaryk and Patocka, substituting communism for the cave, the opposition for the messenger who returns from the world beyond. There is the realm of false appearances (communist propaganda) and the realm of the ideal (moral truth). Unlike the Platonic polis, however, Havel's Republic is governed through democratic values; the conduct of the rulers is always subjected to public scrutiny.[34] Nor do intellectuals possess a privileged capacity to pierce the world of appearances. Available to all, that ability is as likely to reside in the greengrocer and the brewery worker as in the university professor.

Havel's philosophy is syncretic, mixing equal parts Platonism, Christianity, and in its opposition of the Truth to the Lie, Manicheanism. The communist party lives in an anti-matter world of mistruths; the opposition must offer nothing but verity in its defense; there is no compromise between the two worlds, only explosive confrontation. In this black-and-white picture, politics is worthy only of derision since it depends on compromise and collaboration, terms which under different circumstances would denote neutral or even positive activities.

A moral politics, on the other hand, was conceivable. "I favour 'anti-political politics,'" Havel wrote during the days of Charter 77.

> That is, politics not as the technology of power and manipulation, of cybernetic rule over humans or as the art of the useful, but politics as one of the ways of seeking and achieving meaningful lives, of protecting them and serving them. I favour politics as practical morality, as service to the truth, as essentially human and humanly measured care for our fellow humans.[35]

Politics as "practical morality"—this was as clear a rejection of the Machiavellian worldview underlying communist and capitalist politics alike as one could find in Eastern Europe.

Havel was less interested in the formal trappings of a democratic state than, in Martin Luther King's words, a "revolution of values," one that could be neither fully contained within nor fully expressed by "'dry' organizational measures." Still, in the Charter 77 days, he wrote, "I see a renewed focus of politics on real people as something far more profound than merely returning to the everyday mechanisms of Western (or, if you like, bourgeois) democracy...no opposition party in and of itself, just as no new electoral laws in and of themselves, could make society proof against some new form of violence."[36]

Havel critiqued not only arid parliamentarianism but vapid consumerism as well. Color televisions did not inspire Charter 77. Writes Havel: "A person who has been seduced by the consumer value system, whose identity is dissolved in an amalgam of the accoutrements of mass civilization, and who has no roots in the order of being, no sense of responsibility for anything higher than his or her own personal survival, is a *demoralized* person."[37]

Havel's rejection of the sterility of communism, in other words, did not lead to the embrace of equally sterile Western conceptions. "In the end," he writes, "is not the greyness and the emptiness of life in the post-totalitarian system only an inflated caricature of modern life in general? And do we not in fact stand (although in the external measures of civilization, we are far behind) as a kind of warning to the West, revealing to it its own latent tendencies?"[38] A lack of morality, of higher commitment, has robbed *both* systems of legitimacy. It is important to stress these themes in the present period of hyper-enthusiasm for capitalism in Eastern Europe.

In part, skepticism toward the market and "bourgeois" democracy is consistent with the history of the Eastern European *intelligentsia,* which was never absorbed into the middle class, as in the West, and to this day remains uncomfortable with mass culture and the disposability of consumerism.[39] But Havel is not simply another anti-bourgeois aesthete. For him, a belief in transcendental values—inherited from the tradition of Husserl and Patocka—safeguards against both the violence of totalitarianism and the banality of modernity. Neither the market nor the vote by itself produces civic responsibility. According to Havel, truth expressed in a moral system and anchored in invariant principles must precede any political or economic restructuring.

These long quotations are necessary for characterizing fully the intellectual protest in Czechoslovakia, for understanding how the promise of a moral golden age in the post-revolutionary society gradually devolved into less noble metals. In his dissident writings, Havel was clearly calling for a third path, an alternative to both Stalinist and capitalist modernization. He had uncovered a flaw common to both systems—their bracketing off of morality.[40] In pushing economies relentlessly forward, Stalinism had justified tyrannical means with reference to either utopian ends or the iron laws of scientific materialism. Morality did not exist in such a universe. Havel and his philosophical kin identified very different strains of amorality in the Western system. The legalistic drift of politics—and its emphasis on rational-bureaucratic procedure—has left little room in public policy for conscience. According to such a perspective, the state, whether bourgeois, communist, or Kafkaesque, appeals only to the law, not to morality in asserting its authority.[41] In privileging morality over law, Eastern European protesters drew upon a distinguished 20th-century tradition including the civil disobedience of Bertrand Russell, Mahatma Gandhi, and Rosa Parks. Meanwhile, in contrast to slippery deconstructionists, the philosopher-oppositionists maintain that there is clear good and evil: the intellectual task is to speak the truth and live by it, not merely tear down systems and promote unlimited relativism.

Against the orthodoxy of Stalinism and the creeping relativism of some Western theories, Havel and others asserted a new fundamentalism: certain truths exist over and above what Big Brother, big lawyers, or big literary theorists proclaim. This assertion of fundamental truths provided a firm rock on which to cling during the years of repression. But there were some obvious problems. This brand of "living in truth" also encouraged intellectual elitism (the hegemony of the idea), an intoxication with Western Civilization (read: white, male), and a belief that one particular set of values (Christian humanist) is universal, all of which endear the Havel message to certain Western conservatives.[42]

In an article in *The New Republic* in 1985, Leszek Kolakowski characterized this fundamentalism even more bluntly:

> However distasteful our [Western] civilisation might be in some of its vulgar aspects, however enfeebled by hedonistic indifference, greed and the decline of civic virtues, however torn by struggles and teeming with social ills, the most powerful reason for its unconditional defense (and I am ready to emphasize this adjective) is provided by its alternative. It faces the totalitarian civilisation of Sovietism, and what is at stake is not only the destiny of one particular cultural form, but of humanity as we have known it.[43]

Clearly, these fundamental truths were particular, not universal, and were shaped quite explicitly by bi-polarism's magnetic currents.

Some Eastern European intellectuals were less rigidly bi-polar. Miklos Haraszti, in *The Velvet Prison,* portrayed brilliantly the compromises that individuals make daily in order to live in societies. Under communism, artists did not die; rather they accommodated by using the state's strictures as frames upon which to create. Adam Michnik too, in his famous essay on "maggots and angels," discovered in a perusal of Polish history that even the greatest figures—Kollataj, Pilsudski—strayed at one point or another from the angelic path: the pure, virtuous, uncompromised individual can exist only in the imagination.[44] For the worldviews of unconditionalists such as Kolakowski to be successful, for their morality to appear unblemished, they need the unmitigated lie, the maggot with no trace of the angel, the prison with no scrap of velvet. They need totalitarianism that permits no change, no reform, no independent thought, no legitimate opposition. Haraszti and Michnik never understood communist state power in Eastern Europe to be such a totalitarianism. In part, their experiences in the more flexible Polish and Hungarian systems offered more room for sophisticated analyses. The Husak regime, with its clumsy but effective repressions, permitted neither a Solidarity nor a grassroots environmental movement to emerge, much less survive. Havel's worldview, based on the world of Czechoslovakia circa 1968-1989, is understandably more bi-polar. "Manicheanism has been the faith of saints and inquisitors," Michnik writes. "Machineanism has also been the curse of captive peoples."[45] Perhaps Havel was simply more captive than his Polish or Hungarian counterparts.[46]

When the old system fell in Eastern Europe, "living in truth" became quite a different matter. The rule of law became a new priority. A degree of relativism and of pragmatism became suddenly fashionable. Kolakowski's "unconditional defense" was no longer so easily defended. Ambiguities returned and with them a wealth of problems which the Manichean worldview was simply incapable of addressing. Anti-politics merged into politics; collaboration lost its pejorative associations; morality became more than an either-or proposition. Cracks were appearing in the bedrock of fundamentalism.

Havel has tried to adapt to the new rules of the political game. When, for instance, activists organized hunger strikes and large demonstrations calling on Havel to prevent the Communist Party from participating in the national elections, he refused, and justified his position with moral arguments. Adherence to principle—namely free and open elections—prompted Havel to part company with many of his more anticommunist sympathizers. Read another way, Havel, once provoked, chose Danton over Robespierre, recognizing that a certain degree of accommodation with the previous regime was preferable to a witch hunt.[47] Later, reluctantly, he would agree to a law banning the Communist Party and both its current and former members from public office for five years. Personally in favor of letting "sleeping dogs lie," Havel had decided that he would have to act differently in public because of the demands of the populace to "finish" the revolution.[48] This private/public dichotomy, indicative of the new Havel, reveals a degree of flexibility, however unfortunate in this case, injected into the moral fundamentalism.

As Czechoslovakia adjusted to the rhythms of consumerism and Western democracy, whatever hopes the opposition once harbored for a more participatory and less materialistic society retreated to the realm of foreign policy. The political and economic restructuring of Czechoslovakia proceeded along rational-legal grounds; only in foreign policy did ethics continue to play a significant role. This was, for a short time, the last vestige of an alternative public policy that continually measured itself against higher standards rather than utilitarian or populist requirements. A brief exploration of how morality has fared in other aspects of Czech and Slovak reform makes the failure of Czechoslovakia to become the moral center of the world rather more understandable.

Morality in other spheres

The revolution in Czechoslovakia was a remarkably dignified affair—without the Romanian violence, the Bulgarian nationalism, or the East German materialism. As a mass phenomenon, like any event involving millions of people and their heightened emotions, it could have turned ugly. But the Civic Forum leaders, drawn from all walks of life, directed the drama with grace and determination. The term "velvet" applies not only to the virtual absence of bloodletting, but to the gentleness of the entire process—from the candlelight processions to the well-organized general strike.

Many Czechs and Slovaks assumed that if the revolution had been "velvet" then so too must be the transition. Economic reform would be the testing ground. Poland's shock therapy was anything but velvet; if the new Czech and Slovak leaders remained true to their values of civic consensus and democracy, they would surely distance themselves from the Balcerowicz plan. Havel at least initially found himself in this camp, indifferent toward state-directed economies but also leery of "the destructive pressure of technological civilization, with its stupefying dictatorship of consumerism and omnipresent commercialism."[49] True to his philosophical skepticism, Havel did not uncritically embrace the latest regional utopia. He was also loath to unleash the disruptive influences of capitalism on Czechoslovak society. The alternative: capitalism wrapped in velvet or, to play off Civic Forum's symbol of two bright eyes and a grinning mouth, capitalism with a smiley face.

Others in Civic Forum, however, argued that velvet may be a proper fabric for revolutions but not for economic reforms. The chief proponent of this position, Vaclav Klaus, was an economist (or, as the Czechs call him, a "prognostic"). Having never participated in oppositional activities, Klaus joined Civic Forum as soon as it was formed to offer his expertise in financial matters. When the transitional government was announced in January 1990, Klaus was installed as the minister of finance. He was charismatic, a true proto-politician who could translate complicated economic theories into digestable television commentary. But Klaus the economist had a very different perspective from Havel the revolutionary. Without fussing about gradual transitions, Klaus supported a rapid changeover to capitalism, accomplished, since he was the finance minister, by restricting the money supply and removing government subsidies.[50] The Klaus plan bore remarkable similarities to the Polish plan, which was no surprise since the latter had become the preferred model of the region's economic advisers (Jeffrey Sachs, the US Chamber of Commerce, the IMF).

The first sign of conflict over economic philosophy came with the dismissal of Valtr Komarek, the maverick economist who supported a more gradual approach to economic reform. When a new government was announced after the June 1990 elections, Komarek was unambiguously dropped from his interim position in the ministry of finance.[51] Klaus had consolidated control within his ministry and could thus present a unified front against the "gradualists." In the summer of 1990, Havel and Klaus kept their dispute hidden but advisers occasionally leaked tidbits about their growing dispute ("their chemistry simply doesn't match," said one Havel spokesperson).[52] These disagreements, percolating throughout the summer, suddenly appeared in the open the following fall when Civic Forum passed over Havel's hand-picked successor as movement leader, Martin Palous, in favor of Klaus himself.

Whether persuaded or simply bullied, Havel eventually threw his lot in with the free marketeers. The conflict between shock and gradualism then became less a leadership struggle than a division within Civic Forum itself. Klaus the technician had seized control of Civic Forum and begun to remodel it in his own image, much to the dismay of those in the organization who held to the original revolutionary spirit.[53] By December 1990, Foreign Minister Dienstbier and like-minded centrists formed the liberal faction within Civic Forum. The official split between the Klaus and Dienstbier blocs, and a third, smaller, left faction, came several months later.

Civic Forum had not long outlasted the imposition of Klaus's brand of harsh economic reform at the beginning of 1991. Sharp price increases, accelerated privatization, large-scale unemployment just around the corner—a familiar tale of austerity. A comparison between fourth-quarter economic indicators of 1990 and 1991 reveals that real wages declined 27 percent, industrial production dropped 30 percent, and prices had risen 69 percent. Unemployment had jumped from 0.6 percent in 1990 to 5.1 percent in 1991.[54] The reform would sharpen conflict within society as it had first clarified divisions within Civic Forum. The gradualists—who held closer to principles of economic justice and believed for the most part that morality and economics were not estranged partners—lost out to the disciples of trickle-down.

In the political realm too, morality was compromised. During the period of transitional government, for instance, several Civic Forum members criticized the then-Minister of Interior Richard Sacher, a member of the rival People's Party, for stalling investigations into the secret police (and its estimated 140,000 informers). Sacher denied that he was deliberately moving slowly. In what later became known as "Sachergate," Sacher's subordinates then released the police files on the Forum members who had made the criticisms, showing that the Forum members had, decades earlier, collaborated with the police. Civic Forum was outraged—at the tactic, at the implication that its members were compromised, at the feelings of revenge that were stoked. Sacher and his critics reached a private compromise that allowed him to remain in office until the elections.[55]

Civic Forum fought back with a dirty trick of its own. On the eve of the 1990 election it discovered that the chairperson of the People's Party, Joseph Bartoncik, had also collaborated with the secret police. After Havel failed to persuade Bartoncik to resign, a Civic Forum supporter in the interior ministry made the links public two days before the elections. According to Czechoslovak law, the election campaign had officially ended: for the final two days, no parties could appear on television or radio. The image of the People's Party was irreparably harmed. Civic Forum had made an accusation that would *de facto* stick, had retaliated against Sacher's tactic, and had consolidated its own political position. The Bartoncik affair was widely considered to have cost the Christian Democratic coalition, of which the People's Party was a member, substantial support. Expected to challenge Civic Forum (and Public Against Violence) for the top spot, the right-wing coalition managed only third place behind the Communist Party. Although a smart political move, the Bartoncik affair revealed a new, instrumental amorality in Civic Forum.

After political transformation and economic reform, the third divisive issue to test the moral standards of the new leaders has been relations between the country's two primary ethnic groups. Czechoslovakia is composed of three regions, Slovakia and the Czech lands of Bohemia and Moravia. The Czech lands enjoyed occasional independence over the centuries and a privileged economic position since the Enlightenment. Slovakia, on the other hand, was an agricultural dominion of Hungary for nearly a thousand years, a relationship of often brutal inequality.[56] With the break-up of the Habsburg empire after World War I, the Czech and Slovak regions were joined together. The relationship has been far from harmonious. Sensing the chauvinism of the Czechs and well aware of Masaryk's ambivalence toward them, the Slovaks were not as traumatized as their Czech cousins over the demise of the First Republic. During World War II, the country split, Slovakia becoming a semi-autonomous fascist state, the Czech lands absorbed into the Nazi *Lebensraum*.

Rebuilding the reunited country after the war, the communists were well aware that economic disparity between the two regions would provoke resentment. They embarked on a massive industrialization of Slovakia to bring it up to par; responsible for only 13 percent of total industrial output in 1948, Slovakia contributed nearly 28 percent by 1976.[57] Subsidized by the center and reliant on some of the least efficient and most heavily polluting industries, Slovakia has as a rule opposed market liberalizations, whether discussed during the Prague Spring or instituted more recently.[58] Rapid marketization, then as now, would favor the cleaner and more Western-oriented industry of the Czech lands and leave for the Slovaks only unemployment and recession.

Meanwhile, in the political sphere, the federal system was carefully redesigned in 1968 to combine unity and equality. With some amendments, that system has survived into the post-communist era. The federal parliament contains two chambers: the House of Peoples and the House of Nations, each composed of 150 members. The House of Peoples' membership is proportional to population (101 Czechs, 49 Slovaks) while the House of Nations has equal representation (75 and 75). Both the Czech lands and Slovakia also possess separate republican authorities.

Even in the more unified days of opposition, the two ethnic communities did not necessarily see eye to eye, with Slovaks rather distrustful of Charter 77's concentration of Czech intellectuals. Slovak opposition tended to be more church-based and more concerned with environmental questions. The 1989 revolution established a common goal but two separate movements—Civic Forum in the Czech lands and Public Against Violence in Slovakia. Great attempts were made to maintain a democratic balance. When the interim government was formed at the beginning of 1990, the Czech Havel governed with a Slovak prime minister, Marian Calfa, and a Slovak speaker of the federal parliament, the politically resurrected Alexander Dubcek. Czechoslovakia was renamed the Czech and Slovak Federated Republic (or the Slovak and Czech Federated Republic as it is called in Slovakia).

Despite this balance, separatist sentiment inevitably emerged.[59] Grouped into several movements and parties, Slovak nationalists began to demand everything from safeguarded traditions to outright secession from the federation. Although numerous and vocal, these parties received relatively few seats in either the federal or republic parliaments. It seemed, after the 1990 elections, that dissolution of the new democratic federation had been put to the vote and had lost. After all, with federal subsidies and weighted political representation, Slovakia needed the Czech lands more than the other way around.

But separatism didn't go away. While Civic Forum divided along an economic policy fault line, its sister organization, Public Against Violence, split on the question of automony, with federalists going one way and nationalists the other.[60] More recently, the leaders of both factions—Prime Minister Jan Carnogursky and former Prime Minister Vladimir Meciar—have become increasingly separatist in orientation, in part to prove that they haven't sold out to Czech interests.[61] One sign of heightened Slovak nationalism is the republic's policy toward its own minorities—Hungarians, Ukrainians, and Gypsies—who likewise hope to prevent assimilation. Slovak nationalists seem incapable of generalizing from their own condition. Ethnic Hungarian demands for schooling in their national language have not been well received by the same Slovaks who earlier had criticized the hegemony of the Czech language.

But the issue is not simply one of nationalism. One wing of the Slovak movement for autonomy is virulently anti-Semitic, xenophobic, even fascist. Commemorations of Jozef Tiso, the fascist leader of Slovakia during World War II, have become increasingly popular in the republic, with a plaque recently put up in his house of birth.[62] Although organized protest has been minimal in the republic, Havel has strenuously maintained his opposition to Tiso's rehabilitation. The fury of the neo-fascists has subsequently been vented on the president. After an early 1991 visit to Bratislava, Havel was subjected to verbal and even physical abuse from a crowd of nationalists. "Jews out of Hradcany" was one of the chants thrown at Havel (Hradcany is the Prague castle that serves as the seat of the federal government).[63]

Maintaining his commitment to democratic procedure despite these neo-fascist outbursts, Havel promised legislation guaranteeing the right of referendum on Czech and Slovak unity (which the federal parliament eventually enacted). In November 1991, he even set up shop for a week in Bratislava, the capital of Slovakia, to demonstrate that he was president not only of the Czech lands but of Slovakia as well. "Breakup of the state is an alternative," Havel has said. "If the Slovak nation prefers such a solution, it has a legitimate right to get it, but...it must happen in a constitutional manner."[64] Slovak nationalists' greatest opponent is not Havel, but ironically Slovaks themselves. According to one poll, 82 percent of Czechs and 69 percent of Slovaks support the federal system.[65] Because of this overwhelming sentiment, Slovak nationalists fear the proposed referendum will put them out of business.[66]

Of all the domestic issues presently facing Czechoslovakia, none approximates foreign policy more than the Slovak question. Indeed, with appeals for fraternity and good relations, Havel's visits to the Slovak capital of Bratislava resemble diplomatic excursions to a foreign country (Slovakia has even established its own ministry of foreign affairs, the status of which remains unclear). The Havel leadership's handling of the Slovak question has also demonstrated that the values associated with the velvet revolution—democracy, nonviolence, accountability—have not been entirely discarded in the post-revolutionary perod. And predictably, Havel's consistent support for a democratic solution to the federal question has ensured greater support for the federation. Adherence to a principle has proven, in this case at least, to be the most pragmatic option as well.

* * *

Although the once unified Civic Forum behaved as honorably in the political, economic, and national realm as any party in Eastern Europe, the standard that it set for itself was so high that, measured against it, Civic Forum was bound to disappoint. Political manipulations, as in the Bartoncik affair, are "business as usual" in the West. Removal of government subsidies resulted in an unpleasant transition to the market but one a good deal less harsh than in Poland. The handling of Slovak separatism has so far been skilled and diplomatic.

The disappointments have been equally prominent: the rancorous disintegration of the political coalitions, Havel's acceptance of Klaus' austerity plan, Dienstbier's retreat on the arms issue, the failure of any regional plan to emerge with Czechoslovakia's guidance. Civic Forum was forced to compromise on its program of reform, on its privileging of conscience over law, even on its conception of the public. "Maybe someplace in the world we are taken for 'velvet revolutionaries' who are without fear and reproach," Jana Smidova wrote in *Lidova Noviny*. "I cannot get rid of the feeling that our government also sees us this way.

It is much more comfortable to govern a supposedly first-rate, rational, understanding public than to fight unpleasant reality."[67]

These unpleasant realities of the post-communist era—economic austerity, political infighting, social egoism—have forced accommodation. Even the new moral foreign policy, which held out such promise when it debuted, has discovered its own version of unpleasant reality, whether *realpolitik* or the profitability of arms production. Czechoslovakia is a small country. It has neither the world position to enforce its moral attitudes nor the global power that would from the start necessarily corrupt such attitudes. It has set high standards, raised certain expectations, tried to sustain the revolution, and attempted to transmit it to the world through diplomacy. The Helsinki Citizens Assembly was also an expression of these hopes and expectations. These idealistic projects, almost by definition, confront unpleasant realities. But "unpleasant reality" was also an accurate description of the previous years of communism, a reality which many of the present Czech and Slovak leaders refused to accept as dissidents. One can only hope that as these "unpleasant realities" are rejected, the revolutionary legacy of transformation will continue.

Return to Middle Europe?

Eastern Europe is a prisoner of geography. For the northern countries, a central location between Germany and Russia has for centuries determined foreign relations. For the southern countries, inter-Balkan relations and continual irredenta have dominated any foreign policy agenda. For both northern and southern regions, the historical experience has been invasion, subjugation, partition, and, even when a margin of independence has been achieved, second class status to the great powers of the time. Foreign policy under such circumstances is always contingent.

The chief contingent factors shaping the region's external policy today are European unity and Soviet disintegration. The former dictates the adoption of political and economic models that facilitate eventual entry into the European Community. The latter led, even before the collapse of the Union, to a reversal of the anti-Sovietism of the oppositions-turned-governments. An angry Soviet Union—ruled by post-communists, nationalists, or liberal technocrats—would have adversely affected trade and political relations with Eastern Europe. No one wants poverty and disorder on one's border. Worse still is to be positioned as a waystation between chaos and order. The region once served in Soviet thinking as a *cordon sanitaire* to prevent hostile Western encroachment into the Soviet Union proper; now Eastern Europe becomes a corridor to ensure that post-Soviet problems do not disturb Western Europe.

One might expect that the countries of the region, because of their common problems and concerns, might pursue a regional alliance. Such a loose confederation might serve as a temporary substitute for the membership in the EC that each country ultimately desires but will not receive before century's end. Such a regional organization could present a common front in negotiations not only at a foreign policy level with the EC, the post-Soviet Union, and international economic institutions, but could also develop common ground rules for contracts with multinational corporations and the activities of transnational non-governmental organizations. Such a regional grouping, emphasizing cooperation over competition, would be the transnational embodiment of Czechoslovakia's moral foreign policy, an expression on the elite level of precisely what the Helsinki Citizens Assembly has attempted to mobilize at the grassroots.

The history of central European confederations is quite rich, beginning with the Monarchy of the Three Seas in the 16th century, continuing through the Enlightenment (the English Quaker William Penn, for instance, proposed a European imperial federation),[68] and culminating in the 19th century. Competing for attention during the great age of imperial cooperation were the Palacky plan, Popovici's "United States of Greater Austria," Czartoryski's 1848 proposition linking northern and southern Slavs against Austria and Russia, the Balescu and Telki plans for a Danubian United States, the Kossuth, Jaszi, Beck, and Karolyi plans, even a Vatican proposal for a regional confederation of Catholic countries.[69] The German desire for a *Mitteleuropa* with Berlin at its center, itself an expression of the ancient *Drang nach Osten*, gradually merged into Hitler's own conception of the German *Lebensraum*. Soviet Eastern Europe, connected by the Warsaw Pact and the CMEA, was merely the latest in a series of middle European entities under the thumb of an external power.

Several regional groupings have survived into the present day. The Pentagonal Group is a Danubian confederation of sorts, uniting Czechoslovakia, Hungary, Austria, Italy, and Yugoslavia (with the recent addition of Poland, the group became Hexagonal; the splintering of Yugoslavia and the Soviet Union might increase the number of sides of the polygon further still). The Balkan group meets irregularly among the countries of the Balkan peninsula.[70] A brand new Baltic Council that includes Sweden, Russia, and Poland among others began work in March 1992. Perhaps the most interesting of the regional groups is the Alpine-Adriatic Alliance, which counts as members not states but *parts* of states—sixteen provinces from the five countries which include the Alps or border the Adriatic.

Hoping to construct a more inclusive central European space, the socialist parties of the Alpine-Adriatic Alliance have called for a parliament of Middle Europe. Vojko Volk of Slovenia's Socialist Party explains:

> Our idea is to make Middle Europe again a common political and economic space. There are many reasons for this. First, Italians and Austrians and Germans in Bavaria are afraid of the Fourth Reich, as they put it, of the united Germany. They are not afraid in political terms but mainly in economic terms because Germany has the major economic connections with Yugoslavia and Hungary, not Italy. And Italy wants to be our main economic partner. Also, many of the countries of Middle Europe do not have a chance to join the EC for another 10 years. So this would be to prepare politically and economically these Middle European countries for membership.[71]

Regional association would serve as the halfway house for eventual pan-European inclusion and would also diminish Darwinian competition encouraged by history or by the Western powers. With the official death of the Warsaw Pact in 1991 and the paralysis of the CSCE mechanisms, such a regional association becomes a viable alternative to the continuation of the NATO regime.

A thornier foreign policy issue involves minorities and refugees. The aim of European integration is the abolition of borders *within* Europe—not between Europe and the rest of the world. Europe encouraged waves of immigration in the 1960s as growing prosperity created a strong need for unskilled workers. Guest workers, *gastarbeiter* as the Germans call them, flooded in from Turkey, north Africa, and Yugoslavia. Italians, Spaniards, and Portuguese moved northward for better-paid jobs as well. In the early 1970s, however, the need for labor declined, and the European countries adopted harsher regulations on migrants.[72] Those regulations have been made even more stringent under European integration. Although many Eastern Europeans spent summer vacations washing dishes in Sweden or digging graves in West Germany, the freedom to travel back and forth from East to West has recently become dearer. Opportunities for north Africans and Turks to find a space in the common European home will become rarer still.

The border between Hungary and Austria was closed to Romanians in March 1990 but not before several thousand flooded in at the last moment. Thousands from points further east pressed into East Germany before unification in October 1990 suddenly restricted back-door access to the EC. Even Czechoslovakia restricted its border to Poles in the fall of 1990, prompting protests from prominent Poles such as Adam Michnik who defied the restrictions by crossing over the border. Gypsies have been unwelcome throughout the region.[73] Albanians have been turned back from Italy and Greece. Civil war has sent thousands of Croatian refugees into Hungary and Germany.

Western Europeans do not want refugees—escapees not of political repression but economic depression and ethnic strife—to disrupt their integration process.[74] While Eastern Europeans look over their shoulders at crisis and instability in the post-Soviet Union, Western Europeans direct similar glances at their eastern and southern borders. When devising political and economic programs, Eastern European governments must consider the response generated not only by their own citizens but also the governments of Western Europe. As Eastern Europe reasserts its geographic centrality, every domestic issue therefore acquires a foreign policy dimension.

* * *

The decline of alternatives in Eastern Europe has also extended to the foreign policy realm.[75] An enlightened policy on refugees has yet to emerge. A regional structure has not been constructed. The hope for more rapid demilitarization of Europe has stalled over US reluctance to disband NATO and rework the Atlantic relationship, despite the collapse of Soviet communism. Even as NATO planners prepare for a post-Cold War world with troop and materiel redeployment, a bloc mentality lingers on.[76]

The revolutions presented a golden opportunity to retire the bloc system. The Warsaw Pact has indeed disbanded, and NATO has lost much of its European *raison d'etre*. The CSCE process could replace the blocs, but the CSCE too is an elite institution well-insulated from the input of European citizens. Foreign policy is too frequently formulated without the accountability that governs political and economic decision-making domestically. Grassroots diplomacy, along the model of the Helsinki Citizens Assembly, and influenced strongly by the citizens movements East and West of the 1980s, points to a more democratic vision of foreign policy.

These movements from below, to borrow Leszek Kolakowski's helpful insight, are the jesters to the foreign policy priests installed in the new governments.[77] Once Havel too was a jester, a critic of the mainstream values of Czech and Slovak society, resolutely impertinent in the face of orthodoxy. Elevated now to the level of priest, Havel must uphold a new orthodoxy, a role for which he is perhaps ill-suited. The Helsinki Citizens Assembly is the heir to the critical, questioning, jesterly tradition.

It appeals to morality against the Machiavellian grain. It reminds the Havels of the region where they come from, and it points to a future where the principles of the Helsinki Accords are not only inscribed in the foreign policy statements of all countries but guide their real world actions as well. This alternative would be the third way between the *realpolitik* of both the West and of Stalinism.

The velvet revolution carried this idealism into the highest office, promising a radical break with the past. When Havel invited the Dalai Lama to visit Czechoslovakia, it appeared that a new era of foreign policy had dawned in Eastern Europe. But not long after the Tibetan monk's visit, another East European leader arrived in Beijing to meet with the communist leaders responsible for crackdown in the Himalayas. The first European to visit China since the Tiananmen Square tragedy, Romanian president Ion Iliescu served notice that the past had not been completely transcended. Power still took precedence over principle.

As we shall see in the next chapter, the Romanian situation is a powerful reminder that the previous structures and ways of thinking cannot be so easily swept away, by either the most velvet or the most violent revolution.

Chapter 8

Romania... Amoral domestic policy

In any group of three Romanians one was Securitate.

—Romanian saying

While other Eastern European countries have made government files public, promoted press freedom, and, in general, opened up what were previously closed societies, Romania remains shrouded in mystery. When I visited the country in 1990, rumor was still the primary source of Romanian information, especially the information that people trusted. Too many times I would ask where someone had acquired his or her information and the response would be "from a very reliable source." "A newspaper?" I would press. "Oh no, a very reliable friend." Some Romanians had friends in the political parties who fed them inside tips; journalists could refer to colleagues and off-the-record asides; the head of Bucharest's drivers' union told me about the trustworthy information that the rank-and-file picked up on the street. Everyone had a personal source for news as they once had informal connections to get meat or foreign magazines.

Not only is the informational infrastructure lacking—a reliable press agency, credible non-governmental organizations, accepted statistics—but the very approach that most Romanians have toward the "news" is distinctly non-informational. The people I interviewed frequently editorialized without substantiation, spoke in the abstract, or simply avoided reference to historical detail and stubborn facts altogether. Faced with this informational tangle, a journalist must construct a "truth" out of a multiplicity of subjective accounts.[1] Romania truly is "a plotless detective novel," as literary critic Nicolae Manolescu once observed.[2]

The contemporary Romanian situation is therefore best expressed not by a series of propositions, but by a set of questions that can only be half-answered. What exactly is the National Salvation Front and why did it win the national elections in May 1990? Where do its leaders, President Ion Iliescu and Front leader Petre Roman, stand politically? What happened in March 1990 in Tirgu Mures? Who were the real organizers of the seven-week demonstration in University Square? Who burned down the police station in June 1990? Why did the miners return to Bucharest in 1991, this time to confront rather than defend the government?[3]

But the most mysterious element of Romanian life by far is the Securitate. It is, as Churchill once described the Soviet Union, a riddle wrapped in a mystery inside an enigma. An almost mythic secret police, the Securitate played a pivotal role in maintaining the position of communist leader Nicolae Ceausescu. Its size, function, and current status are all shadowy topics. East Germany's Stasi, the Securitate's closest rival, left behind 100 miles of files—and now Germany must handle the burden of overdocumentation. For Romania, the problem is the reverse—an almost complete absence of information. During the December 1989 revolution and several later episodes, the Securitate succeeded in obliterating its own trail, protecting the reputations of many operatives and the government officials with whom they dealt.

For the long and often brutal years of communist control in Romania, the Securitate functioned in place of an information matrix. It was ironically the only institution that connected people in this atomized society. Either one was an informer, the person informed upon, or the as-yet-unimplicated innocent worried about encountering the organization. Architect and activist Mariana Celac told me that Romanians could be described as having "intrauterine" personalities—withdrawn, fearful, suspicious of the outside world.[4] The Securitate, more than any other institution, kept the intrauterine Romanians in the dark. Although it has retreated into the post-revolutionary shadows, the Securitate still holds sway—if not over access to information then at least over the imaginations of the country's people.

The Securitate

An exciting cultural center of Eastern Europe earlier in this century, Romania gave to the world the absurdities of Eugene Ionescu, the elegant sculptures of Constantin Brancusi, the theological musings of Mircea Eliade. Unfortunately for Romania, its tyrants have more readily captured the popular imagination—Vlad the Impaler (the historical Dracula), the strongarm dictator Ion Antonescu, the leader of the fascist Iron Guard, Corneliu Codreanu. And, of course, no one will soon forget the latest heir to this illiberal tradition—the tyrannical communist, Nicolae Ceausescu.

Ceausescu began his career a little recognized political organizer whose greatest fortune was to spend the bulk of World War II in jail with the leading figures of the Romanian Communist Party. Twenty years after the war ended, when Party leader Gheorghe Gheorghiu-Dej died, Ceausescu assumed the top position, at 47 the youngest communist leader in the region. Why the relative novice when other more experienced Party functionaries were available? Most reformists had been purged or executed; the Stalinists were no longer acceptable. "The ousted leaders who remained alive," Romania specialist Mary Ellen Fischer writes, "were perceived to have been as close or closer to Stalin than Gheorghiu-Dej himself. After his death, there were no prominent non-Stalinist alternatives like Nagy, Kadar or Gomulka."[5] A close confidante of Gheorghiu-Dej and without any damaging quirks in his background, Ceausescu was the logical choice despite his age.

At first suspected to be a Stalinist himself, Ceausescu quickly acquired a liberal reputation, loosening domestic controls and steering Romania toward an independent foreign policy that won praise in the West for its anti-Sovietism. Better late than never, Romania enjoyed its post-Stalinist thaw, albeit a controlled one. Ironically, as soon as he acquired this reformist label, Ceausescu moved in the opposite direction, once again confounding expectations. Romania specialist Trond Gilberg wrote at the end of the 1980s that "since the early 1970s, the Romanian leader's tolerance for *any* kind of autonomy in society has diminished (and in this decade it has vanished altogether)."[6] Striving for a totalitarian control hitherto deemed either unachievable or undesirable by neighboring communist leaders, Ceausescu attempted to establish, in Gilberg's words, "a society of mass atomization and also mass alienation on a scale unknown elsewhere in the region."[7]

Established in 1947 within the ministry of internal affairs, the Securitate played a pivotal role in Ceausescu's transition from reformer to reactionary. In keeping with his first persona, Ceausescu initially "promised Romanians a new era free from abuses of police power."[8] He provided proof of this assertion by ousting Alexandru Draghici, the interior minister in charge of security forces, and linking in the public mind the sins of Stalinism with the excesses of the secret police under its former chief.[9] But the police power so integral to the communist seizure of power proved critical as well to the maintenance of Ceausescu's new political position.[10] For a leader about to embark on several unpopular domestic programs, the Securitate was an ideal instrument of social control: a secret police *cum* paramilitary corps of elite troops *cum* foreign intelligence gathering outfit. Ion Pacepa, once the head of the CIA's equivalent within the Securitate, describes the military aspect of the Securitate:

> Copied after the Soviet model, the Romania Securitate Troops have since 1950 been a special service branch beyond the traditional army, navy and air force, with its own uniform and regulations and subordinate only to the general secretary of the Communist Party, through the minister of interior. The troops constitute an elite Communist military force, strongly indoctrinated—the ratio of political commissars is five times that of the Ministry of Defense—with substantially better equipment and standard of living, and more severe discipline than any other Romanian military unit.[11]

In the Ceausescu era, the Securitate served its master faithfully, discouraging assassination attempts and palace coups. Expanding its intelligence operations, the Securitate maintained extensive files on an extraordinary number of Romanians and regularly tapped the phones of suspected dissidents. Handwriting samples of 60 percent of the population were kept on file, and all typewriters had to be registered.[12] When the short-lived underground movement Romanian Democratic Action issued a manifesto, it was neither typed nor duplicated. Rather, in order to escape detection, a handwriting expert prepared the document in an "antiquated script."[13] Some of the stories floated about the Securitate's omnipotence were surely exaggerated—with help from the Securitate itself. Far more cost-effective to have the population believe every letter and phone call monitored than to actually administer such an enormous project.[14]

Ceausescu used the Securitate to defeat any potential domestic rivals, to compromise diplomats and foreign leaders, and, predictably, to control the Romanian population. The number of informants the Securitate employed domestically is a point of controversy. Conservative estimates are in the tens of thousands while the top figure is in the millions. Trond Gilberg writes: "All groups either have agents of the police as members, or the membership suspects that one or more of the group is an informer, thereby producing an atmosphere of insecurity and effective self-censorship. The Ceausescu era is the era of mass supervision and the expanded use of informers in all walks of life."[15]

The Securitate may not have had the external capabilities of a CIA or the fearful reputation of a KGB or even the firepower of Romania's own army. But it was able to control the entire Romanian society through intimidation. When Ceausescu implemented such draconian measures as a ludicrous export-intensive strategy to pay back Romania's foreign debt, the population meekly complied with the cutbacks in food and energy that left even the major cities dark and cold. When he destroyed a historic part of Bucharest forcing the evacuation of 40,000 people in order to construct an entirely new city center with grandiose boulevards and neo-fascist architecture, most Romanians protested silently.[16] Many international institutions condemned Ceausescu's plan to raze villages and relocate peasants in immense agro-communities, but Romanians were afraid of expressing their opinions. With good reason. Those who had opposed any of these policies were immediately isolated and subjected to internal exile.[17]

No leader since Stalin had attempted such grandiose schemes with such little public support. The little Stalins who ruled Eastern Europe in the post-war era took advantage of the general confusion in the battle-torn region to kill opponents and establish state security systems. But these leaders were readily deposed as thaws of one degree of liberalism or another came to the region. Ceausescu did not depend on Moscow for his authority. Indeed, after his tactical support of the Eurocommunism movement, relations with the Kremlin deteriorated. Instead, Ceausescu and his wife Elena built their own patronage system held together by fear of the Securitate.

Anyone wanting to rid Romania of the Ceausescus had to wrestle with the Securitate. Many assumed that this highly-trained and indoctrinated elite would defend the imperial family at all costs, thus ruling out all but the bloodiest of revolutions. When that revolution came and went rather quickly in December 1989, it left virtually all observers, and even the participants, scratching their heads. From where did the revolution come? Why was it so comparatively easy to destroy the tyrant? Three major competing scenarios have emerged:

1. The Hungarians

The revolution began in Timisoara, a western city with a sizable Hungarian population near the border with Yugoslavia. In December 1989, Romanian authorities had tried to remove ethnic Hungarian pastor Laszlo Tokes from his parish because of his impassioned defenses of human rights. The move provoked an immediate response from a community primed by the anti-Hungarian policies of Bucharest. When Romanian protesters took to Timisoara's streets on December 17, the security forces opened fire, killing hundreds.

Was this simply an uninstigated revolt? Or, as some Romanians maintain, did the Hungarian intelligence services play a role? Throughout the 1980s, even under communist leaders, Hungary had expressed great displeasure at Ceausescu's plans to raze peasant villages, many in the predominantly Hungarian regions of the country. Hungary's first legal protest in 1988 was an anti-Ceausescu rally, an unprecedented opportunity for citizens of one Soviet ally in the region to legally criticize the government of another. Hungary had made diplomatic protests, had extended political asylum to Romanian dissidents, had maintained contacts with ethnic Hungarians in Transylvania and the Banat region.

Ceausescu was an embarassment to communism, the worst kind of negative advertising. But if he was a problem for the Kadarist regime in Hungary, he was even more irksome for the Hungarian Party reformers that came to the fore in 1988-89. To be placed in the same category as the Romanian autocrat discredited the reformers' attempts at changing the system from above.

Of course, Ceausescu most irritated Hungary's democratically elected government. The populist Democratic Forum promoted Hungarian national culture, the triumphant achievements of Hungarian history, the reinstilling of Magyar pride into the population, and, naturally, the rights and freedoms of their brothers and sisters in Romania. Ceausescu's injection of nationalism into the dying carcass of communist ideology may have won him a certain degree of support from ethnic Romanians, but it only antagonized minorities within his own country and the governments of his increasingly independent neighbors.

Hungarians clearly wanted Ceausescu out. Hungarian intelligence probably had contacts in Romania. How these two elements combined to produce a revolutionary spark, however, no one knows.

2. The coup

The December revolution seemed spontaneous. Angry Romanians filled the streets and persuaded the army to join them, several communist leaders switched sides, and Ceausescu was suddenly isolated. All within several days.

In June 1990, however, the French newspaper *Le Monde* reported that elements of the Romanian Communist Party had been planning a coup since the fall of 1989. Top leaders in the National Salvation Front, including Ion Iliescu and Silviu Brucan, had, in other words, prepared for the revolution months in advance. It was not the first rumor of a coup. According to journalist Edward Behr, top army officers had considered a coup on three separate occasions: 1970-71, 1975-76 and 1983-84.[18] In 1983, Ceausescu removed a cohort of middle-level army officials, a sign of concern over a potential palace revolution. Having always played a secondary role to the Securitate, the military was a powerful and disgruntled constituency.[19] Top level Party officials might have taken advantage of this resentment in the late 1980s to further their own program.

One might think that such a plot would enhance the reputation of the NSF. After all, it would show that, in high places, anti-Ceausescuism had some precedents, however limited. Political scientist Vladimir Tismaneanu disagrees: "If [NSF leaders] admit that a Party plot existed, then their sudden appearance at the balcony of the well-guarded Central Committee building in Bucharest's Palace Square on December 22, 1989, might begin to look more like a pre-emptive Party coup against the people's revolution than the fulfillment of that revolution."[20] By August 1990, several key NSF members had admitted to participating in a coup, although the full story has yet to emerge.

For Romanian-born poet and radio commentator Andrei Codrescu, a Party coup not only toppled Ceausescu but stage-managed the entire revolution. "If I were in charge of the Emmys, I'd give one to the Romanian directors of December 1989," he writes. Contrary to earlier reports, there were no mass killings, no poisoned water in Sibiu, no terrorists—only the manufacturing of a revolutionary smokescreen to conceal pre-planned machinations that resulted in the creation of the National Salvation Front.[21]

If indeed such a split emerged in those early hours—between the people's revolution and a Party coup—what would the people's revolution have produced in Romania as an alternative to the National Salvation Front? Or perhaps a more important question—would the people's revolution have succeeded unless a coup had been in the works? Without the coup, would the December revolution have simply degenerated into the bloodbath many had expected?

3. The Arabs

When the Ceausescus fled the Communist Party headquarters in their helicopter, the revolution seemed to have succeeded. The army appeared to have joined the side of the protesters; the National Salvation Front had proclaimed itself the new interim government. Yet Bucharest suffered the majority of its casualties only after this point. Who was still opposing the revolution? The Securitate? As we shall see below, probably not. Then who?

After the Ceausescus were executed and sniperfire had ended, the National Salvation Front released photographs of the "terrorists" who had formed an elite guard surrounding the ruling family. In addition to orphans trained from birth to blindly obey the Ceausescus, the squad included Arab and North Korean sharpshooters. The photos revealed several somewhat dark-skinned individuals labeled "terrorists." As suddenly as the fingers were pointed, however, they were withdrawn. Talk of the Arab terrorists stopped. Privately, government officials mentioned that the NSF was worried about strained relations with the Arab countries concerned and possible "terrorist" retribution. A couple of photos. A lot of rumors. Very little proof.[22]

* * *

Conspicuously absent from the above discussion has been the Securitate. Although saddled with the responsibility for most of the deaths resulting from the revolution, the Securitate was not necessarily the guiltiest party. Most Romanian observers told me that it was simply convenient to blame the Securitate, a much-hated organization from the start. But the revolution would never have gotten off the ground if the Securitate had not supported it or at the very least remained indifferent. The most dramatic example of counter-revolution was the sniperfire from the Securitate building on crowds gathered to hear the new provisional government. But as one Romanian journalist told me, the Securitate members from that office had already surrendered their arms and handed themselves over to the interior ministry.[23] The army, meanwhile, could be praised as heroic for its rapid switch to the opposition without disrupting the deep-seated respect many Romanians still maintain toward the military. Careful scrutiny, however, reveals that it was probably the army that caused most deaths in Timisoara and Cluj, probably acting under the assumption that the uprising was indeed engineered by the Hungarian secret service. The National Salvation Front implicated the Securitate as the cause of deaths after December 22, and that has remained the commonly accepted explanation in the West.[24]

* * *

If determining the precise activities of the Securitate during the revolution is difficult, then pinpointing its role today is an even more frustrating task. Within a month of the revolution, many activists were accusing the NSF of harboring Securitate elements, even of using former Securitate agents against opposition parties and movements. The NSF responded that it had disbanded the Securitate. That story began to disintegrate, however, as dissidents emerged from the ranks of the NSF. Dumitru Mazilu, the first deputy chairman of the NSF who had once served as the head of the secret police school at Baneasa, resigned his new office in January 1990, accusing the Front of being the Communist Party reincarnated.[25] Ion Caramitru, the famous actor and member of the NSF Provisional Council, left the Front that May, before the national elections. He told *Expres* newspaper that destruction of the Securitate was "cross my heart" never discussed at the top levels of the Front.[26]

Eventually the NSF revealed that elements of the Securitate had indeed been retained. Although NSF press spokesman Velicu Radina initially insisted in a July 1990 interview with me that the Securitate had been destroyed and its members could not work for the government, he switched his position several breaths later. Confirming what Gabriel Andreescu of the opposition Group for Social Dialog had already told me, Radina revealed that Securitate files on "external operations" would be used by the new Romanian Intelligence Service, that this was normal, that the information could not simply be ignored.[27]

Then Radina completely broke with the official line. The people who had worked for external operations—espionage, counter-espionage—also had stayed on. Though previously involved with the Securitate, they had not been involved in Ceausescu's repression. Yes, members of the Securitate had cooperated in the revolutionary events, but they understood at the time that their organization would be destroyed and their leaders put on trial. Some operatives had been pensioned off, others retained in the Intelligence Service, and the bulk had returned to the "private" sector as engineers, architects, and so on. Iliescu would confirm these details formally several months later: "There are a few thousand professionals who did not have any political responsibilities, mainly technicians who are now used in the army and in counterintelligence, after being scrutinized."[28]

Others have argued that the Securitate has greater influence. Silviu Brucan, former member of the NSF, reported that elements of the 2000-member Securitate Military Academy in Baneasa, an "anti-terrorist" group, and Ceausescu's security detail have gone unpunished. Some have escaped to Hungary and Turkey but many have remained in Romania.[29] Virgil Magureanu, head of the new Intelligence Service and allegedly a former Securitate official, told the Romanian Parliament that the new service was indeed conducting wire-tapping and domestic surveillance as the opposition had long maintained.[30] Another analyst placed the overlap between the Securitate and the Intelligence Service, now under ministry of defense jurisdiction, at 60 percent. After Romanian journalists discovered several tons of Securitate files in a forest, the Intelligence Service finally admitted that it had expended considerable efforts to destroy such documents.[31]

The Securitate was not simply an academic issue—a couple thousand security bureaucrats retained to keep their mouths shut and their pensions safe. The political situation in Romania in 1990 was extremely volatile, and nothing emphasized the central importance of the former secret police more than the events of June 1990 in Bucharest.

Turmoil continues

On June 13, government forces clashed with demonstrators in University Square in Bucharest. After a still disputed series of events, the newly elected president Ion Iliescu appeared on television to declare a state of emergency and to call upon the citizens of Romania to defend the new government from "hooligans." The next day, thousands of miners poured into Bucharest, chased demonstrators from the Square, killed six people, threatened members of the opposition, ransacked several newspaper offices, and tarnished Romania's international reputation. Protest telegrams from around the world flowed into Bucharest and Western lending institutions immediately suspended economic aid.

It was not the first incident of instability in the post-Ceausescu era. In early 1990, two months after the revolution, several hundred demonstrators broke into the provisional government's headquarters, trashed the offices, and assaulted the deputy prime minister.[32] Miners had come to Bucharest on that occasion as well to "restore order" and left only after extracting concessions from Iliescu in exchange. The following March, a coalition of groups in Timisoara issued a proclamation calling for a change in the electoral law forbidding former members of the top communist leadership and high-level Securitate agents from running for office in the first three legislative elections. A new confrontation was shaping up between the NSF and a diverse opposition movement. To add to the confusion, violent clashes broke out between ethnic Hungarians and Romanians in the Transylvanian town of Tirgu Mures around the same time, killing six people.

But it was the June incident in Bucharest that captured world attention. When I visited Romania in August 1990, I received several versions of what had happened during the time between the first demonstrations in University Square in April and the miners' intercession in June. Some in the opposition insisted that the group protesting in the Square over the two-month period was firmly in the Civic Forum tradition, pressing for a velvet revolution to accomplish what the first violent revolution did not—the removal of overnight democrats whose political histories were dubious at best. A computer scientist friend, working at the University throughout the the strikes, was substantially less enamored of the group's composition. While students and intellectuals filled out the crowds during the day, the people who stayed overnight were quite different. "American gangsters are babies compared to these dealers, hustlers, and prostitutes," my friend told me.

Idealistic revolutionaries or gangsters? Confused, I turned to Petru Clej, an editor at the independent *Romania Libera*. A former computer analyst who turned to journalism only after the revolution, Clej provided me during my stay with the most balanced accounts of Romanian life. He also gave me what seemed the most plausible version of the events of June (which bears up quite well against Helsinki Watch's version).

The University Square demonstration was started in April by a small group led by a former NSF provisional council member, Dumitru Dinca ("a professional revolutionary who likes power and adventure," Clej told me). When police tried to dislodge this group, student and intellectual sympathizers flocked to the square, despite Iliescu's branding of the demonstrators *golan* or hooligans. One of these subsequent participants was the president of the League of Students, Marian Munteanu. Although only 100 to 200 people were present on the square during the day, tens of thousands gathered by evening including a large number of intellectuals who had come to hear speeches by Dinca, Munteanu, and others. The so-called "lumpen"—black marketeers, adventure-seekers, petty criminals, prostitutes—operated on the margins. Television coverage, Clej told me, distorted the demonstration by emphasizing these marginal people. Since many people in the countryside could only know of the demonstration by way of television, these "half truths" were especially influential. Some of the speakers from the balcony, Clej admitted, were not the "cleanest" politically speaking, but the majority were very honest.

Television coverage was not a marginal issue. Throughout the region, television played a critical role in disseminating or preventing the dissemination of information during the reforms and revolutions of 1989-90. Television spots, more than radio or newspaper advertisements, guaranteed Solidarity's success in the 1989 national elections. Czech students poured out of Prague during the velvet revolution to carry to outlying industrial and agricultural areas the news that state-controlled television at first refused to broadcast. Protesters in Bulgaria in the spring of 1990 and in Serbia in the spring of 1991 put at the top of their demands the replacement of the directors of state television. As the revolution was just breaking out, the sight of Ceausescu panicking on a television broadcast before the station abruptly left the air indicated the sudden vulnerability of the regime. Television speeded the transformations in the region; control of television determined the outcome of elections. State-controlled television was making the demonstrators in University Square look bad. They in turn placed one demand over all others: an independent television station. Elections were approaching that May, and the opposition wanted to convey its message to the country at large.[33]

In part because of its control over the airwaves, the NSF trimphed in the May 20 elections, winning over 65 percent of the vote. The Front's leader Ion Iliescu, a former high-ranking communist dissident who had fallen from favor with Ceausescu in 1984, captured 85 percent in a separate ballot for president.[34] Even a sophisticated television campaign probably could not have rescued the opposition. Led by the reconstituted Liberal and Peasant parties, the opposition had failed to persuade the Romanian population that it represented a clear alternative to the Front. Workers worried that the Liberal Party's economic program would subject Romania to shock therapy; farmers fretted over the Peasant Party's talk of dismantling the cooperative system. Especially in the latter days of the election campaign, the attempts by the opposition parties to use the University Square demonstration backfired. Because of the provocative behavior of some demonstrators, many Romanians shifted their support away at the last moment from the opposition parties. In fact, neither the Liberals nor the Peasants would capture second place after the NSF. That distinction would go to the Democratic Hungarian Union in Romania, the ransacking of whose offices by Romanian nationalists had set off the riots in Tirgu Mures.

In the wake of the Front's victory, the League of Students and the Group for Social Dialog called for a retreat from the Square. The elections were over, the citizens had decided, and the international observers had declared the elections reasonably free and fair.[35] Despite the withdrawal of the more important opposition groups, hardcore demonstrators remained in the Square: predominantly young, generally unemployed, some of them extremists, some of them infiltrators from the police.[36] Backed by an overwhelming mandate from the electorate, the government wouldn't give in to the demand for an independent television station. The stand-off lasted for three weeks.

Then, on the night of June 12, the state prosecutor called for the police to dispel the demonstrators. On the morning of June 13, over 1,500 police and soldiers began to clear the Square, using violent techniques and encountering violent reactions. Police arrested 263 people.[37] That same afternoon, another group of demonstrators returned to the Square, confronted the police and, after a brief struggle, forced them to retreat to the police headquarters under a hail of stones and Molotov cocktails. The police station was subsequently set on fire, by whom it is still unclear. An attack on the state TV complex, which provided an excuse for suspending the evening broadcast and for Iliescu's appeal that brought the miners to Bucharest, is still being debated: authentic, staged, or a mixture of the two?

Those who responded to Iliescu's appeal, contrary to early reports, were indeed miners (though there may have been a handful of provocateurs sprinkled among them). Interviewed after the events, most miners said that they had simply believed the Front's labeling of the demonstrators as "hooligans" and had truly expected to find drugs, weapons, and evidence of a conspiracy to overthrow the government.[38] But, as Helsinki Watch correctly notes, "it is irrelevant whether the vigilante mobs that attacked innocent citizens and terrorized Bucharest were composed only of miners or of a representative sample of the Romanian population. What is important is that extra-legal forces were used, instead of the police and army who have the responsibility to maintain order."[39] Like the Mississippi police who stood by and watched while white racist mobs attacked civil rights activists in the early 1960s, the Romanian police allowed the miners to do what they themselves could not by law attempt.

As a result of the June events, over 1,000 Romanians were arrested and incarcerated for various periods of time in uniformly dreadful conditions. Many were beaten by police, some severely. A parliamentary commission investigating the events produced two reports, one by the opposition, another by the government. Although the investigation failed to receive full cooperation from several important government offices (for instance, the Intelligence Service), the reports did result in dismissals for the minister of internal affairs and the chief of police.

And the Securitate? Opposition leaders have argued that, whether sanctioned by the NSF or not, former Securitate agents infiltrated the crowd in University Square, monitoring opposition activities, furtively recording names, even escalating the violence to discredit the gathering. Securitate agents had also, the opposition charged, infiltrated the ranks of miners.[40] The independent weekly *Expres* printed an article on the work of the agents during the events, charging that these operatives, now working for the Intelligence Service, took photographs of protesters. The newspaper relied in part on information from previous Securitate informants who wouldn't give their names for fear of being killed.[41] In another suspicious event of the June 13-15 period, the group December 21, which had been trying to document post-revolutionary events and the legacy of the Securitate, had their offices sacked by miners and their materials burned.

The Romanian government had lost important international credibility in the wake of the June incidents. Both the NSF and the opposition parties came out of the affair with tarnished images. The Securitate, in its new incarnations, had simultaneously exposed itself as a present force and destroyed its past. If there was a winner that emerged from the June incidents, it was the Securitate. The loser, in any case, was Romania.

* * *

The Allied powers after World War II found it useful to recycle fascists through their respective systems. Nazi rocket scientists who presided over slave labor and extermination camps were welcomed into both the US and Soviet scientific communities after their pasts were carefully cleansed. Nazi security officers were pumped for information and even employed on additional assignments because of their considerable experience and expertise (however immorally obtained). Nazi police, judges, and bureaucrats merged into the new German civil services.[42] Although de-Nazification figured prominently in the rhetoric of the Allied powers, the recruitment of former Nazis practically advanced security interests during the Cold War. Post-war Romania was no exception, despite the routine vilification of fascism. Under secret police chief Teohari Georgescu, the Romanian Communist Party relied on fascist collaborators to build a new power base. This pragmatic lesson would not be lost on later regimes.[43]

The Securitate, too, possessed a wealth of information and a well-developed network of informers. It was both too useful—and potentially too embarassing—to be ignored by the new power elite. Entering the realm of conjecture, a deal was probably negotiated in Romania in 1989-90. To facilitate its takeover and prevent even greater bloodshed, the emerging National Salvation Front was forced to deal with the Securitate, trading future immunity for cooperation. The top echelons were targeted as scapegoats, the most useful operatives were absorbed into the new establishment, the dross was pensioned off. Even given the best of motives, what could the NSF have done otherwise? A disgruntled Securitate would have been its greatest threat, perhaps not single-handedly orchestrating a coup but influencing through sly blackmail or selling its knowledge and firepower to a competing force (the military? Romanian nationalists?). After negotiating this compromise, the NSF learned soon enough (if it hadn't known already) how useful the newly tamed Securitate was for spying on the opposition. The Securitate had become harnessed to the new order, and this could not be attributed solely to the legacy of communism or of Ceausescu. This was also in part the politics of revolution (as demonstrated, for example, in the disturbing continuities characterizing the German unification process discussed earlier).

Does the Securitate still pose a threat to either stability or democracy in Romania? In minor ways, yes. But as long as the present government doesn't threaten the existence of the larger mass of former members, they won't band together for survival. Scattered throughout the system, they will probably serve their new masters faithfully, as Virgil Magureanu has, for instance, as head of the Intelligence Service. But such continued allegiance, as the events of 1990-91 in Bucharest bear out, should not put anyone's fears to rest.[44]

Other problems

The Securitate is distressing not only for its activities but also for its ability to detract attention from other pressing problems in post-communist Romania. The newly independent newspapers in Romania are understandably obsessed with stories of hidden intrigues, shadow communists, and lurking agents. The Securitate makes for good stories and larger sales. And this often unsubstantiated reportage can pass for investigative journalism in a country only now establishing such a tradition.

But framing issues simply in terms of the Securitate distorts the debate. One can, for instance, discuss the National Salvation Front in terms of its dealings with the Securitate and its successor institutions. But such a tack would obscure other features of the Front, namely the evolution of its programs and the degree of its popular support. Like several other oppositional coalitions in the region, the Front promised a gradual economic reform for Romania, endearing it to the more conservative population in the countryside (the opposition parties attracted significant support only in the cities where the largest demonstrations took place). A perception in the countryside—fostered by the NSF—that do-nothing intellectuals and their unsavory supporters among the urban proletariat were indulging in mere hooliganism only furthered this city/country divide. Miners against students, blue-collar against white-collar, provincials against metropolitans: the NSF exploited these conflicts while the opposition parties were undone by them.

Put another way, the NSF didn't win the elections in Romania: the opposition parties lost them. Led by elderly politicians with famous names, the Peasant and Liberal parties failed to offer a contemporary alternative to the NSF. Anti-communism was insufficient as a platform. In overthrowing the communists, the NSF had established its revolutionary credentials and taken that ground away from the opposition. So the opposition turned to history for legitimacy. Vote for a return to the 1930s, they suggested: a restoration rather than a reform. The countryside didn't buy the message. "The problem with the opposition in Romania right now is that they would like to forget the last 45 years. It didn't happen, it was a bad dream," a young financial reporter Sorin Mitran told me.

> To my ears, the great names mean something, but out of a history book, not in a political sense. And if you read any history book you get the distinct impression that politics was not all that it was supposed to be between the wars. There was a lot of violence used by everyone, there were a lot of lies and old boy arrangements. And I think that the old people who have jumped up to the key positions in these parties right now are using the same tactics, and this has turned off a lot of people of my generation even though we feel inclined to go with these ideas.

Without a serious opposition, the NSF discovered that its worst enemy was itself. The foreign press, fond of exposing closet communists, indulged in numerous allegations that the NSF was simply a collection of crypto-Stalinists, a secret engine of the Securitate, the last Moscow-controlled government in the region. Even supposedly objective news reporting often indulged in simplistic formulations such as the NSF "consists almost entirely of Communists."[45] Whatever the ultimate intentions of the NSF, this brand of labeling is quite inaccurate. First of all, communism as a formal political force barely exists in Romania so NSF members, if indeed they had belonged to the Party, should be referred to as "former communists." Second, communism as an ideology ceased to function in Romania a decade or more ago, as it did throughout the Eastern bloc. Leaders could be placed along a spectrum from *realpolitik* to Stalin-like paranoia, but communism as an ideological force had long since dropped out of the equation.[46] Former communists still operate within the NSF, but as politicians long disabused of Marxism-Leninism. Rather than monolithic, the politics of the NSF are sufficiently flexible to encompass radical free marketeers, centrists, liberal reformists, and unreconstructed authoritarians.[47] Third, the Party played such a dominant role in organizing political life in Romania that it would be difficult to put together a government without including former communists, however morally repugnant some might find this compromise. Mainstream parties throughout Eastern Europe—from former East Germany's Christian Democratic Union to Czechoslovakia's Civic Forum to Poland's Solidarity—are comprised in no small part by former communists. But this fact was rarely included in the glowing reports these parties received in Western press. As for the final Cold War atavism, the Kremlin hardliners could barely control a rebellious Moscow City Council, much less Ukraine, much less the Baltics, and much, much less the government of Romania. Their failure in the August 1991 *putsch* revealed most dramatically their weakness.

Dominated by former communists or not, the NSF committed many errors in its first year of office, some of them disastrous. It adopted many of the unfortunate characteristics of the past regime, in part because 45 years of communism, including 25 years of Ceausescuism, have left indelible imprints on Romanian society. An execution and an election cannot undo these influences so readily.

Why has the West been so hostile to the National Salvation Front? Some Romanians wonder aloud why the United States granted most-favored-nation status to Ceausescu, withdrawing it only in 1987 after the human rights abuses became impossible to ignore. In the same breath, they wonder why the international community was so quick to suspend aid in the aftermath of the Bucharest battles in June 1990. Even members of the opposition questioned the logic of withdrawing money from a country so desperately in financial need.[48]

The NSF soon discovered that the path back to the good graces of the international economic community was paved with austerity. A self-described center-left party that used the rose of democratic socialism as its emblem, the NSF had consciously distanced itself from the Balcerowicz model. This strategy worked well electorally with peasants and many industrial workers (though not with urban dwellers and intellectuals). Cast beyond the IMF pale after June, the NSF began to reexamine its commitment to the tenets of democratic socialism. By the summer of 1990, the government of Petre Roman had announced more sweeping market changes including more rapid privatization. In the fall, Roman announced large-scale price increases. By the end of the year, he was calling for Polish "shock" therapy as the only cure for the sickly Romanian economy. The opponents of gradualism were accepted into the government in April 1991. Liberal party members took over the ministries of labor and public works; the Agrarian Democratic Party head became agriculture minister. Romania's Balcerowicz—Eugen Dijmanescu—assumed control at this time of a combined finance and economy ministry.

It was therefore no surprise that the international economic community welcomed Romania back into its fold in 1991.[49] The government had not fully explained the events of June and had punished only two of those responsible.[50] Adherence to market values—like Ceausescu's earlier maverick criticisms of the Soviets—sufficed for Western leaders. The issue was never communism; after all, the former communists in other countries such as the GDR had been forgiven—but only after they had embraced the IMF economic model.

Regaining international credibility through austerity, the NSF badly damaged its domestic base. The miners returned to Bucharest in the fall of 1991, but this time they were attacking, not defending, the government. Angered at the rapid pace of economic change, the miners besieged the Presidential Palace demanding the resignation of Prime Minister Roman. Again the rumors flew. The NSF was working with hardliners from the Soviet Union; the Intelligence Service was again fomenting dissatisfaction among the miners in order to force the technocrats out of government.[51] The miners had indeed changed their position, but for perfectly understandable reasons. Supportive of the NSF because of its commitment to gradual economic change, they switched their loyalties when the Roman government began to implement rapid austerity.

Because of the Bucharest protests, Roman resigned to devote his energies to party activities. His replacement Theodor Stolojan pledged to continue transition to the market but with greater social protection.[52] This message served the Front well with its rural constituency. In local elections in February 1992, the NSF still did better than the Democratic Convention, a coalition of the major opposition parties. But the opposition swept the cities and key regions. Two years after the revolution, Romania remains both politically and economically unstable. With instability, the rumors of a continued Securitate will continue to be persuasive. In troubled times, conspiracies provide an explanation in lieu of an understanding, a consolation that there is at least an organization responsible for the suffering.

If Romania is not torn apart by the class conflicts brought on by economic reform, then perhaps ethnic strife will lead to civil war. Ethnic Hungarians, ethnic Germans, and ethnic Romanians barely tolerated one another in the post-war era. Most Jews were allowed or encouraged to emigrate when Ceausescu discovered that Israel would pay hard currency per capita. Several million Gypsies have been routinely discriminated against, kept out of well-paid jobs, and locked into a cycle of poverty. Ceausescu and the Securitate deliberately kept these communities in a competitive balance; but fear and hatred of the government also provided these communities with a fragile unity. After the revolution, ethnic tensions have increased precipitously. Germans have emigrated by the hundred-thousand-fold, Gypsies have been scapegoated for various conflicts, and Hungarians have increasingly demanded their rights in Transylvania.[53]

More disturbing has been a resurgence among ethnic Romanians of an extreme nationalism reminiscent of the inter-war period. Rehabilitation of the wartime leader, Ion Antonescu, is currently popular, particularly with members of the National Salvation Front.[54] One Romanian historian told me of Antonescu's brilliant maneuvering for space within the Romanian political scene as well as within the international context of the early 1940s. He deliberately overlooked Antonescu's role in the destruction of Romanian Jewry.[55] Meanwhile, nationalist Romanians have created the organization Vatra Romaneasca (Romanian hearth) to campaign for majority rights. In a particularly galling continuity, the editors of the nationalist mouthpiece, *Romania Mare* (Greater Romania), had previously been two of Ceausescu's most obsequious eulogists. More recently, believers in Greater Romania have created a political party to fight against "threats" from ethnic Hungarians, Gypsies, Jews, and other groups imagined to be tearing the country asunder and "poisoning" the culture.[56]

Economic austerity, political intrigues, ethnic hostility—the unpleasantness sowed by Ceausescu and the Securitate has taken different forms in the new era. One unusual location where I discovered a particularly offensive indifference—a coldness that contrasted with the warmth of so many Romanians that I met—was in the health care system. The Western press devoted much space after the revolution to the AIDS babies, the orphanages, the appalling conditions of the hospitals. These stories did not prepare me, however, for the experience of the "irrecuperables."

I had been told by the French organization Medecins du Monde of the "irrecuperables," children deemed by the Romanian medical profession to be lost causes. One sunny Saturday morning, I took a taxi to Gradinari, the nearest camp, 20 miles outside Bucharest. After traversing some seemingly untraversible roads, we found Gradinari's only street and followed it to the gates of the camp. A large, institutional-looking building stood several hundred meters from the road. Wearing an old Los Angeles Rams T-shirt, the supervisor warily came out of his office to meet us, not at all pleased at our arrival. Yes, many foreigners come here, he said through my interpretor. They all come, express their outrage, promise all sorts of aid and assistance, and then leave, probably to paint a negative picture of his country. Nothing more is heard from them. He was not particularly impressed with my business card or with my profession. But, well, since we had traveled all the way out to this place, we might as well have a look around.

Because of the pleasant weather, the children were all outside in the back yard, malnourished, crowded onto two long picnic tables, standing idly off to one side, or rolling around in a group of pens set up beneath a tent. All the children were filthy, some with cuts, some only half-clothed. The mixture of disabilities was staggering: Downs syndrome, autism, and physical birth defects. Many of the children were dark-skinned, probably Gypsies. The supervisor explained the ratio: 120 children to only two nurses. I gave one of the nurses the box of chewing gum that I had brought with me. As she began distributing the pieces, the supervisor remarked that virtually none of the children had ever chewed gum before. Some might choke to death. This didn't seem to bother him particularly. The high mortality rate had hardened his heart.

Lack of staff was the major problem, the supervisor explained. Fights over food could not be prevented. The children were lucky if they got one bath a week. There was often no heat in the winter. Perhaps the most depressing statistic that the supervisor quoted was this: the Gradinari institution is not unique. Each district in Romania has two or three. Romania has nearly 40 districts.[57]

Although deemed "irrecuperable," a large proportion of the children could indeed be helped, the Medecins du Monde people told me. Many were physically handicapped and only needed rehabilitation. Some were simply malnourished and would shed their symptomatic behavior after several weeks of care. The largest problem was not funds. Most Romanian doctors simply assumed that the children could not be helped, and if money was provided they would use it for other purposes.[58]

The Ceausescu years have left behind a deep-seated callousness, a rejection of the weak, of the outcasts, and of the unorthodox. Fostering an overall atmosphere of fear and mistrust, the Securitate substituted rumor for fact, made information into a dirty word, turned honest people into informers, transformed altruism into mean-spirited selfishness. But the Securitate does not need to exist as an institution for these qualities to have their lasting effects.

The comparison to Czechoslovakia is telling. Havel and Ceausescu seem to be polar opposites, one promoting peace and understanding, the other encouraging ill will and discord. With his infusion of morality into public policy, Havel concentrated on the weakest links in society; with his bottomless arrogance, Ceausescu cast out the weak and glorified the powerful. Havel exemplifies the promise of a new model for the region; Ceausescu and the legacy of the Securitate represent the residual influence of the old.

It is of course tempting to put Havel on a pedestal and consign Ceausescu to the deepest circle of Hell. But this dichotomy ironically allows Havel to be dismissed as idealistic and the evil of Ceausescu to be understood as an individual aberration. What lies in between, we are told, is politics, neither good nor evil, simply bureaucratic and utilitarian. But there is a different relationship between morality and politics in Eastern Europe, and the current debates around the question of the secret police make that clear.

Maintaining the peace

Every social system creates laws and the institutions to enforce those laws. Anarchic states, to indulge in an oxymoron, have yet to come into existence. Even the most radical libertarians—who claim that the best government is the government that governs least—have imagined some police force to keep order. How the constabulary function is structured, who regulates it, the nature of its foreign policy component—these are points of contention in democratic societies. The Securitate was one particularly vicious guardian of order. Its horror lay not in its function—for all countries have their equivalents—but in its aspiration toward and perceived ability for total control.

Communism's founders did not anticipate a need for a police force. The "new man and woman"—the ultimate creations of communism—would always have the community's interests at heart, and the community would thus be self-regulating. The problem communist ideologists had to face, however, was transition: how to achieve this new human being. The simplest answer, though not one in keeping with the original theory, was coercion. In Eastern Europe, this coercion consisted of an imposed model: one-party state instead of democracy, centralized planning instead of the market, Soviet domination instead of an independent foreign policy. A well-developed security police facilitated this imposition of Stalinism. After its initial revolutionary function, the police fulfilled its more traditional role of upholding the status quo, becoming a Praetorian guard for increasingly conservative regimes.

The conventional picture of 45 years of communism in Eastern Europe is bi-polar. On one side were the forces of coercion (the government, the security police) and on the other, the coerced (the opposition). According to this view, a relatively small clique held the innocent majority in mortal fear for four decades. But in reality, after the Stalinist interlude, the communist governments maintained power by methods more sophisticated than naked coercion. A system was created that demanded innumerable daily compromises by millions of people: from party membership to small bribes for fresh bread to communist slogans placed in store windows. However much people may have resisted communism consciously, they had internalized a range of values and adjusted to particular behaviors, some positive (egalitarianism), others negative (rigid conformity). Collaboration did not consist principally of deliberate spying for the secret services; collaboration lay in the mere act of living in the society (though a minority chose prison and exile to this compromise).[59] Nor was this system characterized by unmitigated evil, a totalitarian interregnum of 45 years. Certain undeniable improvements were made—for certain people, classes, or regions.

These observations should be kept in mind when assessing guilt and responsibility for the last decades. Who should be considered "collaborators," who should be punished, who should be barred from holding public office? Eastern Europeans did not at first indulge in a witchhunt. Only two people—the Ceausescus—have been executed. Several top leaders (Honecker, Zhivkov) were brought up on criminal charges. Ceausescu's son and some other top officials including the head of the Securitate went on trial in Romania. In May 1991, the former prime minister of the GDR, the former defense minister, and two former national defense council ministers were arrested for the notorious shoot-to-kill policy at the Berlin Wall. But for the thousands, possibly millions of operatives and informants within the various secret police organizations—and the piles of evidence incriminating them—no one has yet implemented mass trials or mass pardons. But as disappointments multiply throughout the 1990s, the desire for revenge will intensify.[60]

East Germany's secret police, the Stasi, has dominated the headlines in this regard, with news of its connections to revolutionary movements in the West and its miles of incriminating files. A number of high-ranking CDU-East politicians have been felled by revelations of their past connections. Information so far released has not only proven embarassing to politicians but to the unmaskers themselves. A senior aide responsible for overseeing the dismantling of the Stasi resigned after his own damaging connections were uncovered.[61]

Now in charge of this weighty task, Hans Joachim Gauck does not agree with those who argue that the past should not be raked over. Nor does Pastor Gauck agree that western German counter-intelligence experts should have his job. "People in eastern Germany don't want to see this investigation taken over by people from the west," he told the *New York Times*. "They are hungry for freedom and for justice. Who in the west can understand what that really means?"[62] In November 1991, the German government finally announced that it would allow citizens access to their Stasi files, at the same time cautioning the public in a television address that the information would in many cases be tremendously upsetting.

Still recovering from the abuses of the previous system, Eastern Europeans are now discovering that the new order too requires its agents of coercion. Bulgaria's National Security Service, Poland's Office for Defense of the State, the Czechoslovak Federal Security and Information Service—these "new" secret services have taken over where the previous structures left off, fighting "terrorism," protecting state information, no doubt spying on new sources of government irritation.[63]

Hungary did not have a security force to inspire the feelings of revenge found in the GDR or Romania. Ferenc Koszeg, appointed to the parliamentary commission on security issues, explains:

> Average people didn't meet the police very much. Mostly the police acted aggressively toward younger people. There was an acceptance of the police, even police violence, because many people said it was good against criminals, against the Gypsies and other minorities, and against the poor. There was no division between the political and the non-political police. The state security police was quite invisible for most people although they knew that it existed. Some people were reported, some harassed because of their political activities. But there were limits and the limits were more or less acceptable.[64]

Many members of the Hungarian security police, created to deal specifically with political demonstrations, were still active in 1990, according to Koszeg. Indeed, the government was considering an increase in such emergency police, in part to counter strikes that might paralyze the economy. The new order also requires its agents of coercion.

In virtually every country, major political figures have been brought low by research into their connections with security police. Perhaps because of the size of the Stasi and the preservation of its files, East Germany has witnessed the greatest number of casualties, including the former prime minister Lothar de Maiziere. The leader of the opposition coalition in Bulgaria, Petar Beron, was also forced to resign his seat in Parliament when allegations of his previous role as an informant were made. In addition to the Bartoncik affair mentioned in the previous chapter, Czechoslovakia saw the resignations of the Czech minister of environment and the Czech deputy prime minster after charges of collaboration.[65] Most countries have adopted a procedure by which parliamentary candidates are screened for their past connections. Hungary's court system struck down an attempt to put on Nuremberg-style trials that would have judged former and current communists on the basis of their past conduct.

Revelations of collaboration must also be understood in a political context. Accusations leveled against Jan Kavan, a well-known Czech oppositionist, can be construed as an attempt by more conservative political forces to discredit what remains of a democratic left of which Kavan is part.[66] The new law banning the Communist Party in Czechoslovakia is also such an attempt to muzzle dissent. The Party, after all, is still a significant political force which, if austerity and recession continue, could potentially unseat the present government in the next elections. In the absence of agreed-upon definitions of collaboration and legal norms, the process of assessing guilt for the past remains a highly charged political affair, subject to manipulation and distortion.

It is precisely this issue of democratic control that should distinguish the secret police of the old regime from the constabulary function of the new. Oversight and accountability—these should be the new watchwords. In the meantime, the still damaging information collected by previous institutions should, like unexploded bombs, be handled with extreme care. Nonpartisan commissions should assess the evidence and, bearing in mind the pressures that most people were under, release their findings to the judiciary.

As with economic reform, Eastern European governments are now engaged in the two-fold task of destroying the old security structures while simultaneously constructing the new. Information gathered by the previous apparatuses is being used to discredit political opponents; new security police are being used to contain destabilizing threats. In this process of transition, the new governments are discovering that secrecy and force are not merely attributes of communist states but have their functions under capitalism as well. Although perhaps not as domestically brutal as the Securitate, Western intelligence agencies have a long history of public surveillance, censorship, and particularly in foreign operations, violence. These agencies have served both narrow political interests and more general national security purposes. The more idealistic of the Eastern Europeans—who envision a meshing of morality and politics—may talk of limiting all secret instruments of coercion. The previous structures are not so easily neutralized; because of their knowledge and expertise, the Stasis and Securitates are also useful to the new ruling elites. Revolutionary idealism—and the promise of an open and accountable police force—must do battle against both the sins of leaders past and the opportunism of leaders present.

* * *

The Romanian revolution is still incomplete. The issue of political control—who will guide the country through transition—has not been adequately resolved. Therefore, the political problems endemic to the region as a whole—mistrust of new political institutions, the shallow accountability of new politicians, and the fragility of civic initiatives—are especially visible in Romania. Nevertheless, the modernization continues, and while the pace of change might not be as brisk as the Balcerowicz plan mandates, the effects are similar—recession, falling standard of living, political instability, heightened ethnic conflict. In its attempts to bring Romania into Europe *via* shock therapy, the National Salvation Front has managed only to push the country into the moral hinterlands. Morbid symptoms are proliferating. Motivated by poverty and manipulated by the political priests of the old order, some Romanians have even reestablished a cult of Ceausescu, praising the discipline of the old regime much as some old Russians and Georgians still sing the praises of Stalin.[67]

Under such conditions, an organization deriving its legitimacy from fear and coercion might be expected to thrive. If the Securitate hasn't survived in a form that would allow it to take advantage of the current chaos in Romania, then new forces can be expected to take its place, with policies equally amoral and effects comparably insidious.

Chapter 9

Bulgaria... The wrath of nations

It can mean emancipation, and it can mean oppression: nationalism, it seems, is a repository of dangers and opportunites.[1]

—Peter Alter

When the newly elected Bulgarian Parliament arrived for its first meeting of 1990 in the historic town of Veliko Tarnovo, the demonstrators were waiting. The several hundred chanting, aggressive protesters who filled the streets outside the Parliament building that hosted Bulgaria's first constitutional convention in 1879 did not identify themselves as communist or anti-communist. They were simply Bulgarian patriots who had traveled to this ancient city by the Yantra River to prevent the 23 representatives of the Movement for Rights and Freedoms from taking their rightful seats. Composed primarily of ethnic Turks, the Movement was the worst nightmare of Bulgarian nationalists—a threat to ethnic purity, national autonomy, even historical pride. And there they were, only steps away from entering Parliament. In the end, democracy fortunately prevailed over nationalism. Military police kept the protesters at bay, and the Movement politicians took their seats next to their ethnic Bulgarian compatriots.[2]

The Veliko Tarnovo protesters were no mere fringe activists whose extreme racism propelled them to the furthest reaches of the country to demonstrate for majority rights. They unfortunately represented more widespread prejudice. During the roundtables negotiations in the spring of 1990, for instance, both the former communists and the united anti-communist opposition agreed that Bulgaria should not allow political parties based on ethnic or religious affiliation. When these two forces came in first and second respectively in the national elections that June, they argued that the third-place Movement violated this pre-election agreement and should not be allowed into Parliament. Yet, no attempts were made to apply the new rule to the various Christian parties in the country. The sheer opportunism of the demand, its questionable application, and the sharp response from the ethnic Turkish population forced an eventual retraction.

When communists and anti-communists agree in Bulgaria, there must be a deep consensus that lies beneath the political differences. In this case, the blood of nationalism indeed proves thicker than the water of ideology.

From persecuted to persecutors

Western Europe ignores Eastern Europe. Eastern Europe ignores the Balkans. Balkan countries ignore Bulgaria. Bulgaria ignores its ethnic Turks (who constitute 10 percent of the population). In the great chain of European indifference, the predominantly agrarian ethnic Turks occupy nearly the lowest link (another group, as we will see later, holds that dubious distinction). Many books on Eastern Europe indeed neglect Bulgaria altogether, concentrating instead on the northern tier, the countries frequently referred to as "central" Europe. In major newspapers and magazines, Bulgaria is accorded the fewest column inches.[3] The discrimination arises not simply because Bulgaria is Balkan. Its neighbors on the peninsula, after all, occupy their niches in the European grand narrative: Yugoslavia has its proximity to Mediterranean culture, and until recently its popular vacation spots; Greece its EC membership; Romania its Latin roots. Even little Albania, with its unique proto-Illyrian language, odd political history, and desperate asylum-seekers, receives a decent share of media coverage.

Bulgaria, on the other hand, suffers from being too "Eastern," a Slavic mystery hidden behind a Cyrillic alphabet and an Orthodox religion. The country was sufficiently reviled in past centuries to inspire the term "bugger"—derived from "Bulgarian" and meaning heretic or sodomite.[4] Within this "Eastern" society, associated linguistically with heresies both religious and sexual, the "Oriental" Turkish minority, even further from the "Occidental" European standard, has merited that much less attention and respect.

Bulgaria is, like much of the region, imprisoned by its geography. Located at the crossroads of East and West, the country has been subject to the whims of both Western Christianity and the Moslem Ottomans. Breaking away from the Byzantine empire at the end of the last millenium, the Slavicized Bulgar tribes converted to Christianity, acquired the Cyrillic alphabet, and developed a unique Bulgarian culture. By the 14th century, however, the country had fallen into Turkish hands, a colonial position it would endure for 500 years. Only in 1878 was Bulgaria formed from the territory of the receding Ottoman empire.

The memory of the Turkish yoke has stubbornly lived on in the collective Bulgarian consciousness. Italian journalist Claudio Magris captures the quality:

> Every people remembers the violences to which it has been subjected by others, and if the Turks committed atrocities in Bulgaria, such as the Batak massacre in 1876, it is to be presumed that they were no more tender-hearted in the other territories of their dominions. Why, as soon as we cross this frontier, does rancour seem to be more long-lasting?[5]

It is not, as Magris points out, a general animus. Indeed, I found Bulgarians to be one of the warmest and most welcoming of the various peoples that I visited in the region. But neither I nor Magris is an ethnic Turk. And therein lies the rub.

Tender-hearted or not, the Ottoman empire has few admirers among European historians. While one can always find praise for the Habsburgs or even the Romanovs, the Turks rarely get a kind word. Oscar Halecki writes, for instance, that "the Ottoman Empire, completely alien to its European subjects in origin, tradition and religion, far from integrating them in a new type of culture, brought them nothing but a degrading foreign domination which interrupted for approximately four hundred years their participation in European history."[6] More temperate historians have a different perspective. Not only did the Turks bring paprika, tobacco, cotton, coffee houses, and thermal baths but, as historian George Logio points out, "the Turkish conquest put a stop to a state of anarchy and oppression and its rapid spread is to be explained by the preference the local populations showed for the foreign invader."[7] Peasants generally suffered less under Ottoman rule than elsewhere in Eastern Europe. The 17th-century conversions of Bulgarians (as well as Albanians and Montenegrins) were not forced, but rather undertaken for professional advancement in the Ottoman civil bureaucracy. The Islamic rulers' tolerance certainly compares favorably to the widespread persecution of religious minorities under the Habsburgs and many other European empires.[8]

While the northern Normans and the Magyar tribes from central Asia succeeded in creating a home on the new continent, the Arabs, Mongols, Tartars, and Turks were viewed as the so-called uncivilized trying to muscle in on the civilized by sheer force. While the former invaders adopted Christianity and the dominant culture of the Europeans, the latter stubbornly asserted their own cultures. In addition to being Moslem, the Ottomans committed the cardinal sin of seizing Constantinople in 1453, bringing an end to the Byzantine empire. Two centuries later, the Turks tried to breach Vienna for the second time but were beaten back, with Polish cavalry providing the critical edge. After the humiliation of the 1699 Treaty of Karlowitz, the Ottoman empire gradually ceded more territory over the centuries until, by the mid-19th century, their only European possessions were Bulgaria, Albania, Constantinople-Istanbul, and parts of what became Yugoslavia. As the empire shrunk territorially, its population swelled with Moslem immigrants forced out by the advances of the Russians in central Asia and combined imperial assaults in the Balkans.

Having already granted independence to Greece and Serbia and having lost Georgia, Moldavia, and Wallachia to the Russians, the Ottomans stubbornly held on to Bulgaria, their last Christian possession. In 1876, a failed Bulgarian uprising precipitated a series of horrifying Turkish massacres. In 1877, Russia intervened on the side of its Slavic kin and, within a year, concluded a treaty guaranteeing the new country's independence. As new leaders replaced old, Turkish atrocities against Bulgarians (as in Batak in 1876) quickly became Bulgarian atrocities against Turks and Pomaks (Bulgarian converts to Islam). According to the Bulgarian side of the controversy, Turks willingly emigrated. Constituting 25 percent of the Bulgarian population in 1881, they had dwindled to only 11 percent by 1910.[9] As one historian sympathetic to Bulgaria puts it: "The principal cause of Turkish emigration was the unwillingness of the former dominant element to adapt to the *mores* of the new, Christian state."[10]

Turkish historians have a different view. According to Bilal Simsir, one million Turks were forced to emigrate after the Turko-Russian war. An additional half million died in massacres, cold, hunger, and epidemics. *Mores* were less a factor in determining emigration than legislation which took land away from Turks and distributed it to Bulgarians. Turks were also locked out of the more prosperous middle-class professions.[11] Over 100,000 of the Turks who remained behind were Christianized, given Bulgarian names, and forcibly assimilated.[12] Whether Bulgarians believed this to be just punishment or not, their histories generally conceal these abuses.[13] In the first Balkan War (1912-13), when Bulgaria captured more territory from the Ottomans, the abuses didn't end. Simsir estimates that 60,000 Albanians, 40,000 Turks, and 100,000 Moslems were killed by occupying Bulgarian troops.[14] In 1934, another round of Bulgarization eliminated the Turkish names of towns and villages.[15]

Until 1945, ethnic Turks and Bulgarians lived in one country but two separate worlds. Although massacres had long since become history, relations between the two groups were far from harmonious. When the communists came to power, their rhetoric of equal rights so much appealed to the ethnic Turks that many initially supported the new Fatherland Front. When the new government took power, one Turkish paper editorialized that "it gave equal rights to all citizens and repealed all illegal laws. Then we Turks heaved a sigh of relief and embraced the Fatherland Front...because it permitted us to use our mother tongue and reopened our schools so that we could again study Turkish."[16] Active Communist Party recruitment of minorities continued until 1947.[17] As in other Eastern European countries, minorities were attracted to the new government's championing of the underdog as well as its stated intention to dismantle the old patronage systems that so much favored the major ethnic groups.

The ethnic Turkish honeymoon with the new administration did not last long. Communism meant equality, but it also demanded a new homogeneity as well. New Bulgarian citizens, whatever their ethnic background, were required under communism to become members of a larger community: the farm collective, the factory council, the Party committee. People with different backgrounds would then transcend their particular cultures in building a common history by eating, working, and living together. The new Bulgarian would leave ethnicity to the past and become simply a communist, the equality of communism paid for by sublimating ethnic identity. The divide that had separated Bulgar from Turk, perpetuated by both the Ottomans and the successive Bulgarian governments, was being bridged. Ethnic Turks were given the choice: join or leave. Many left.

Nor did the Communist government mourn the departing ethnic Turks: as after 1877, the land reform of collectivization redistributed the land of the emigrating peasants. In the immediate post-war period, roughly 150,000 ethnic Turks—including many of the most educated—left the country. The once-independent institutions catering to the remaining Turkish population were gradually brought under state control or were eliminated. As conservative religious institutions were yoked to the now conservative state apparatus, the Grand Mufti became a quasi-governmental figure.[18] By 1960, the separate Turkish schools so praised when the Fatherland Front took power were assimilated into the Bulgarian school system. Turkish language instruction for children had virtually disappeared by 1966 and was prohibited in the early 1970s. In 1968, after another wave of nationalism sponsored by the Bulgarian government, a plan to send a large percentage of ethnic Turks to Turkey foundered on technical details, and fewer than 30,000 managed to leave. In the 1970s, the campaign to Bulgarize the country's largest minority intensified. The campaigns of the summer of 1972 resulted in the government's use of infantry troops in small villages and an unknown number of dead.[19] In 1974, at Sofia University, the Turkish department was replaced by the department of Arabic Studies. The last Turkish-language newspaper was closed in 1985.[20] For many ethnic Turks, emigration continued to be a substitute for protest.

Bulgarian nationalism had clearly not been eliminated by communist internationalism. On the contrary, in one of the contradictions that Marx did not anticipate, communist governments throughout Eastern Europe resorted to nationalism to regain the legitimation lost when economic reform faltered, political respectability evaporated, and raw force was discredited by de-Stalinization. Instead of creating an entirely new society from the ashes of World War II, the Communist government very quickly learned that the Bulgarian revolution would be better safeguarded by certain important continuities (even its name, the "Fatherland Front," explicitly drew on a millenium of powerful associations). At the level of international rhetoric, the Bulgarian Communist Party reached out in solidarity to both communist and developing countries; for domestic consumption, however, appeals to things Bulgarian became commonplace. By 1974, "knowledge of the Fatherland" had become a mandatory school subject. When the 1,300th anniversary of the founding of the Bulgarian nation came in 1981, it was much celebrated by the ordinarily forward-looking communists. The 1,000th anniversary in 1985 of the death of St. Methodius, who brought Christianity and an alphabet to the Slavs, was also treated with fanfare by the supposedly godless revolutionaries. The "reactionary" history had been pulled from the dustbin, recycled, and shaped to new purposes.

The celebrations of the millenium of St. Methodius's death meanwhile coincided with the most severe campaign of assimilation since the communists came to power. During the 1985 campaign, an estimated 300 to 1,500 ethnic Turks were killed when they refused to change their names, repudiate historic customs (such as circumcision), and adopt Christianity.[21] Methodius and his brother Cyril had brought both a script and Western culture to Bulgaria. One thousand years later, the Bulgarian authorities similarly cast themselves in the role of civilization bearers, their supposed communist tolerance notwithstanding.

Opposition mounts

Just as communism was beginning to crumble in Poland and Hungary in 1989, communist leader Todor Zhivkov revived the anti-Turkish campaigns in Bulgaria.[22] But this time, ethnic Turks had had enough. The policy of forced assimilation had stretched them to their breaking point, prompting them to do what no organized group had done for the entire 45 years of Bulgarian communism. They revolted—

peacefully but *en masse*. "Anywhere from several hundred to tens of thousands of ethnic Turks participated in each demonstration," Helsinki Watch reports. "According to eyewitness accounts, a demonstration would begin in one village and the protesters would then march through adjoining villages, where more ethnic Turks joined in. Whole villages participated. Support was frequently spontaneous."[23]

The Zhivkov regime responded quickly. Fearing that discontent might spread beyond the ethnic Turkish community, which is concentrated in certain areas of the country, the government pursued a dual policy. Bringing in the troops, it broke up the demonstrations, killing anywhere from 30 to 60 people in the process.[24] Then came the expulsions. The first round targeted the political leaders of the demonstrations. As the summer of 1989 wore on, the campaign of expulsions widened to include nearly 300,000 ethnic Turks. Some were forced to leave, others left "voluntarily" (the anti-Turkish atmosphere created by the Zhivkov government added an element of covert coercion to the decisionmaking). Reaction from the West was negative, but it was both slow in coming and muted. "The West gets excited over human rights in Turkey when Europeans are involved," Turkish Prime Minister Turgut Ozal groused to a reporter, "but doesn't give a damn when Turks are the victims."[25]

Zhivkov did not, however, count on the reaction of the emerging opposition movement in Bulgaria. As in Hungary, Bulgaria's opposition had coalesced initially around ecological issues, first in the border town Rousse then in the national organization Ecoglasnost. Using Gorbachev's policies for legitimation, the Discussion Club for the Support of *Perestroika* and *Glasnost* collected reform-minded intellectuals together in 1988. The more radical Independent Society for Human Rights formed the same year. The independent trade union Podkrepa joined the fray in the spring of 1989.

The mass demonstrations by ethnic Turks were the perfect opportunity for the emerging opposition to expose the weakness of the Zhivkov government. The fate of Eastern Europe hung in the balance that summer. Poland and Hungary had staged their roundtabless. But the Berlin Wall had not yet fallen, and the velvet revolution was yet to sweep through Czechoslovakia. The intellectuals in the Discussion Club, Ecoglasnost, and Podkrepa were determined to push Bulgaria closer to the reform camp. A Discussion Club statement in July 1989 insisted that the ethnic Turkish question was not merely one of human rights, but encompassed the entire political and economic crisis in which Bulgaria was then embroiled. Opposition intellectuals, some of whom had leaked information to the West about the assimilation campaigns of 1984-85, began to work on behalf of jailed Turkish dissidents.

Then there was the problem of the returnees. After discovering a disheartening state of affairs in Turkey, thousands of ethnic Turks came back to Bulgaria only to find their apartments gone and their employers unwilling to rehire them. The Bulgarian opposition immediately offered legal advice. In September and October 1989, an immense opposition spontaneously appeared in East Germany. Bulgarian activists were emboldened; through the ethnic Turkish question, they increased pressure on the Zhivkov government.

This pressure eventually worked. On November 10, Zhivkov was forced out of his position as leader of the Party. With an opposition about to explode onto the streets, the Bulgarian reformers within the Communist Party had decided to forestall an East German scenario with prompt action against Zhivkov and carefully chosen words about pluralism. "A state without the means of some change is without the means of its conservation," wrote Edmund Burke, and Bulgarian reformers took this philosophy to heart. But it would be a later theorist, Alexis de Tocqueville, who would better anticipate the Bulgarian circumstances with his observation that liberalization frequently indicates the fatal weakening of tyranny. Although reform prevented immediate revolution, the Bulgarian demonstrations came anyway: the anti-Zhivkov opposition simply widened to become more generally anti-communist. The communists would not be able to hold on to absolute power for long.

By late December, with revolution in Romania drawing to a close and the Bulgarian opposition drawing into a coalition, the new head of government Petar Mladenov came to a decision. Combining principle and pragmatism, he officially ended the assimilation campaign against the Turks, declaring that "everybody in Bulgaria will be able to choose his name, religion and language freely."[26] The principle was clear: the Communist Party had reverted to its initial wartime coalition promises. The pragmatism was designed to give the Party more space within which to maneuver. Quite apart from Mladenov's shrewd (or, if one prefers, desperate) politicking, the reversal of the Zhivkov policy reshaped political discourse in Bulgaria, driving a wedge through the opposition and isolating the reactionary elements of the Party. No longer could the Bulgarian situation simply be read as communist versus anti-communist.

Within a week of Mladenov's announcement, thousands of nationalists crowded the streets of Sofia, reviving anti-Turkish chants and appealing to their fellow ethnic Bulgarians with patriotic songs. Superficially, the demonstrations seemed to attract Stalinists-in-nationalist clothing, bused into Sofia by regional bosses whose power bases in Turkish communities were threatened by the new government position. At least this was the picture that the opposition at first presented.

But the opposition was forced to take another look. Many of the demonstrators were equal parts anti-communist and anti-Turkish. According to longtime opposition activist Deyan Kironov, this was the opposition's first test: to distinguish between outright provocations sponsored by the Party and genuine but manipulated movements. Prior to the nationalist demonstrations, Kironov laments, "we had a rare, precious, beautiful human rights movement here."[27] Afterward, however, the opposition failed to identify within itself the same intolerance that it had exclusively associated with the so-called Stalinists.

That the coalition between the anti-communist opposition and the ethnic Turks fell apart early on was therefore not surprising. The opposition as a whole had ousted Zhivkov and set reform in motion; the ethnic Turks had halted the Bulgarization campaign. Although both had registered successes, the time when anti-communism and Turkish rights could coexist had passed. By the end of December 1989, with elections in the offing and new political ground rules being set, the opposition bifurcated, ethnic Turks forming the Movement for Rights and Freedoms, and the remaining dissidents gathering together in the coalition of parties and movements called the Union of Democratic Forces (UDF). The founder of the Movement, academic and dissident Ahmed Dogan, had objected that the UDF was no longer concerned with ethnic Turkish issues. The UDF, meanwhile, reasoned that it could ill afford to alienate the majority of the population over a principle about which it was ambivalent in the first place—namely, affirmative action to offset historic injustice toward ethnic Turks.

"The opposition here was not so certain that it was popular within the nation," Vikhr Kristev of the opposition newspaper *Vek 21* told me. "It felt unsafe. At the beginning of 1990, the opposition was actually bound together. But the nation responded and said that the opposition was a traitor to the nation. And some people in the opposition did not feel certain enough that they could persuade the nation. We did not have any one opposition leader so popular that he or she could come out in front of the nation and the nation would forget its hatred of the Turks because of their love of this person."[28] So eager was the UDF to convince the Bulgarian population of its patriotism that it worked with the former communists on an agreement banning parties based on religion or ethnicity, breaking with the convention for the region.

The nationalists were not "out there," a handful of noisy extremists, pushy Stalinists, or cranky xenophobes. Rather, like one of Thomas Kuhn's scientific paradigms, nationalism was so well internalized that few Bulgarians recognized its existence, was so much part of the culture that it even appeared in opposition statements specifically designed to be anti-racist.[29] For instance, the Discussion Club's 1989 statement reads in part:

> For an entire century after their liberation, the Bulgarians displayed tolerance and magnanimity toward minorities. They sympathized profoundly with the tragedy of the Armenian nation at the beginning of this century. They saved the Bulgarian Jews from Hitler's gas chambers. Now, when we are keeping silent about the real causes of the endless outflow of refugees, who are said to be "vacationers," our national dignity is dying.[30]

The ugly side of Bulgarian nationalism—displayed vividly toward the Turks and Greeks after independence, toward Greeks and Moslems after the first Balkan War (and again during World War II), toward Jews during World War II, and toward Gypsies throughout—had been deliberately denied by the opposition, in part to highlight its own commitment to human rights, in part to reach out to a larger community that might be put off by statements devoid of national pride.[31] Certainly there were oppositionists such as Deyan Kironov who gave nationalism a wide berth ("I don't believe in blood and sperm arguments," he told me). But these were the exceptions.[32]

More common was the sort of inflexibility of Social Democratic Party and UDF member Piotr Diertliev when he complained that the Movement thought "that separately they can solve their problems. That is not reasonable. They are a minority."[33] Other oppositionists hinted darkly of Turkish infiltration, for instance interpreting an earlier Dogan statement about Islam coming into Europe through Bulgaria as a threat to Bulgarian autonomy. "I don't agree with Islamic fundamentalism trying to find its way into Europe through Bulgaria," Bojko Nikolov of the UDF newspaper *Demokracja* told me. "And this possibility really exists."[34] Suddenly a minority's struggle for rights became transformed rhetorically into an attempt to dominate the majority.

The renamed Bulgarian Socialist Party (BSP) was no better. Petar Mladenov's reversal of the anti-Turkish campaign had by no means flushed nationalism out of the former Communist Party. Even after winning the national elections in 1990, the BSP continued to play the nationalist card, attacking, for instance, "the constant pressure coming from our South-Eastern neighbor as well as from its perpetual pretentions to represent and to 'defend' our Moslem population." Criticizing "the role of the Turkish intelligence and mass-media inciting people to move out of the country," the editors of the BSP newspaper made little mention of the role that the Party itself played in inciting, nay forcing, ethnic Turks to leave Bulgaria.[35] The implication further that the Movement for Rights and Freedoms worked as a fifth column in the pay of the

Turkish government was a common smear tactic, employed by the Party openly and the opposition more discreetly.

Although victorious in the 1990 elections, the BSP was desperate to find a replacement for the communist ideology that served so long as its *raison d'etre* and motive force. Conservatism and jingoism were compelling alternatives, though the BSP frequently tried to dress these sentiments in different clothing. Party-supported editorials began to appeal to the same blood and soil rationales (or, in this case, irrationales) as right-wing ideologies: "Foreign powers manipulate a part of our compatriots. Some want to persuade us that the best weapon against that is to close our eyes and wad our ears. They discover jingoism and conservatism where one should only find extreme love for the Motherland."[36] Having established itself as the proper vehicle for "pure" Bulgarian nationhood, the BSP had unabashedly become a party of reaction.

More sophisticated members of the Party were a trifle embarassed with the ham-handed rhetoric. But their responses were equally alarmist, if more politely put. Philip Bokov was the head of ideology, or "public relations" as he preferred to call it, for the BSP when I talked with him in August 1990. "Among many politicans, including the opposition side, there is a suspicion that the organization that elected members of Parliament from the Turkish areas has very clear Turkish nationalist connotations," he told me.

> They claim that they are not a movement based on ethnic origin but rather that they work for the freedom and human rights of all. But if one looks at where they campaign and hears their speeches, it is doubtless that they are a movement based on ethnic origin of its members. So this movement causes another reaction on the Bulgarian side which also starts to organize on an ethnic, nationalistic basis. This movement cannot be viewed outside the context of Bulgarian-Turkish relations, what Turkey does to encourage this movement. There is also the fear that this movement might put up the question of autonomy in this country which might be encouraged by Turkey. We are very aware of Turkish policies in the last 20-25 years in Cyprus.[37]

* * *

After the June 1990 elections, the victorious Bulgarian Socialist Party attempted at various points to bring members of the opposition (but not members of the Movement) into a coalition government. Student strikes in July forced socialist Prime Minister Petar Mladenov to resign and prompted the removal of communist hero Georgi Dimitrov from his mausoleum in the center of Sofia. Continued public pressure brought in Zheliu Zhelev, a leader of the UDF quite sympathetic to the plight of ethnic Turks, as President in August. Yet, the opposition consistently refused to enter into a coalition government with the Socialists for fear of being compromised.

A suspicious fire at the Socialist building in late August, continued street protests throughout the fall, and a country-wide strike supported by all major trade unions eventually caused the Socialist government to fall in November 1990. In December, a coalition government was announced, led by a lawyer without party affiliation, Dimitar Popov. The 18-member government included eight Socialists, five independents, three members of the UDF, and two from the Agrarian Union (and no one, predictably, from the Movement).

By September 1991, the Movement had won a victory in the courts when the Bulgarian Supreme Court ruled that it could participate in the ensuing parliamentary elections. Although coverage remained minimal, when the Movement came in third place once again behind the former communists and the UDF, newspapers were forced to acknowledge the political importance of the ethnic Turks. With 24 seats in Parliament, the Movement held the critical balance between the almost evenly matched blocs. But neither side was eager to work too closely with the Movement, and the UDF decided to form a cabinet by itself in the fall of 1991.[38]

The Movement

A movement for all Bulgarians? A fifth column in the pay of Turkish intelligence? What exactly is the Movement for Rights and Freedoms? I spoke with Miroslav Darmov in Sofia about the Movement's goals.

One of the Movement parliamentarians known as a "freethinker," Darmov often presented the Movement's views to members of the press. "The movement strives to unite Bulgarian people and resolve the problems remaining from totalitarianism," according to Darmov.

> The main task is to bring the rights and freedoms of different communities up to international standards. The Movement has a central council with Ahmed Dogan as president as well as a regional council structure. Membership stands at 120,000. We are a universal organization defending the rights of Bulgarian citizens. Now, we are accentuating the rights of Islamic groups in Bulgaria because their rights are in the most desperate condition. We want their rights to be at the same level as other Bulgarian citizens...We had a separate list in the [1990] elections because both parties, UDF and BSP, did not accentuate the rights and freedoms of various Bulgarian groups. We emphasize the social orientation of the market economy. Because our electorate are people of middle position, they are concerned with the social plan of the government. We also

> differ with the UDF on land policy. Because the Turkish population is mostly agrarian, they are not interested in having the land go to the previous owners. At the moment, the Movement doesn't work on international questions. We are oriented to Bulgaria. My personal opinion, however, is that it is impossible to talk of defending rights in Bulgaria if we do not pay attention to the situation in Turkey—not simply the political rights but, for instance, the rights of Kurds. The same applies to the 2 million Hungarians living in Romania.[39]

Concentrating on domestic reform, the Movement wants to reopen schools for religious education but does not support the reinstitution of separate schools that once conducted instruction solely in Turkish. "Ethnic Turks live in Bulgaria," Darmov said. "In order to work in this country they have to speak Bulgarian. It is the official language of the country. But their right is also to know well their own language. Therefore, four hours a week of Turkish instruction will be available." In conjunction with a presidential commission established on the nationalities question, the Movement is still working on behalf of ethnic Turks who returned to Bulgaria and the 50,000 or so who had already sold their apartments and left jobs only to find the border closed. "The situation is improving," the presidential counselor on the national issue told me in 1991. "But this process is too slow."[40]

The Movement has not been an easy phenomenon to study under the traditional communist/anti-communist lens through which most observers view the Bulgarian situation. It is an opposition party but not part of the opposition coalition. It criticized the communists but did not cloak itself in "Bulgaria first" rhetoric. It spoke the language of human rights but concentrated on the rights of a particular group. Led by an atheist who had never been to Turkey, the Movement nevertheless stressed the importance of religion and ties with the Turkish government. Ahmed Dogan has predictably emphasized ethnic Turkish culture but has also said publicly that "Bulgaria is our fatherland and our national self-consciousness is a Bulgarian one."[41]

Not even attempting to understand these ambiguities, the Bulgarian press generally ignored the Movement during the 1990 election campaign. Relying on a grassroots approach, Dogan traveled to two or three villages a day to talk with people personally. With no headquarters and almost no television coverage, the Movement was truly a dark horse. Subsequently entering Parliament, it still was not given an office in Sofia proper but instead had to cobble together a bureau from several apartments on the outskirts of the city.[42] Adding insult to indifference, the parliament approved both a new constitution and a new election law during summer 1991 that banned parties composed along "ethnic, racial, or religious 'hues.' "[43]

Refusing to accept its allotted marginal status, the Movement held fast to its initial demands throughout 1991. But the government equivocated. With the four hours of weekly Turkish instruction to have begun in February of that year, President Zhelev compromised with irate nationalists, postponing the reforms to the fall. Twenty thousand ethnic Turkish school children went on strike to protest the government's reneging on its promise.[44] Organizations such as the Christian Patriotic Youth Union, whose sole purpose was to prevent the introduction of Turkish into the classroom, sprang into existence throughout the country.[45] The prime minister in 1991, Dimitar Popov, only strengthened the nationalist hand with remarks such as, "Moslem aggression is starting now, and in some way it must be blocked so that it does not invade Europe."[46] Neo-Nazis reappeared for the first time since World War II, calling for a "Bulgaria for Bulgarians" even as they sang "Deutschland, Deutschland uber Alles" at their meetings.[47] In October 1991, the National Assembly, still controlled by the BSP, banned the teaching of minority languages in school, rejecting even optional instruction.[48]

While the conflict heated up publicly, a behind-the-scenes rapprochement was slowly emerging. Helped by the court system, the Movement managed to skirt the new laws banning parties of religious or ethnic orientation. On other fronts too, the Movement quietly won some victories—an Islam Institute in Sofia, a bi-lingual newspaper, a Moslem high school in Shumen, compensation for returning ethnic Turks who lost apartments and jobs after the 1989 exodus. Even in an apparent political failure, the Movement may only have been taking steps backward in order to better jump forward. Although holding the key parliamentary votes after the November 1991 elections, the Movement simply declared its support for the UDF, content to hold no ministerial posts in the new government. Its reward for this acquiescence: an announcement that Turkish language lessons would finally be an option in the school system.[49] If the government once more rescinds this promise, however, the Movement will be left two steps back with no opportunity to jump ahead. The UDF has meanwhile made very clear its primary allegiances. At the first governmental meeting, a priest offered the blessing and all the new ministers kissed the cross, declaring to the public their religious commitment in general (*contra* communism) and in specific (*contra* Islam).

This movement of ethnic Turks fit uncomfortably into the usual framework for understanding post-communist developments in Eastern Europe. According to the regional hierarchy of nations—which privileges those peoples closest to Western European culture—this grassroots movement of Moslems was not a world-historical movement. Predictably, the Movement was almost invisible as far as the Western world was concerned.[50] Only after the repeat third-place finish in the 1991 parliamentary elections did the Western press devote much attention to the Movement, even then neglecting to mention its strong showing at the municipal level.[51] Meanwhile, from the Bulgarian point of view, the Movement was an unwelcome detour in a centuries-long process of nation-building.

Construction of a nation

Since 1878, a powerful force has propelled Bulgaria toward a more homogenous, more *Bulgarian* Bulgaria. Having spent half the millenium under foreign control, an independent Bulgaria was eager to expand its borders and establish firm majority control domestically. Immediately after World War II, the communists challenged the expansionism (giving Macedonia back to Yugoslavia) and opposed the domestic racism (throwing the Party open to all comers regardless of ethnicity). But the nation-building impulse returned with a vengeance in the Bulgarization campaigns against the Turks.

Communism is gone, but nationalism remains in Bulgaria. In addition to the chauvinistic facets of the UDF and the BSP, more explicitly nationalist parties appeared after the collapse of communism, including the Fatherland Party of Labor, and the Radical Nationalists. Although small, these groups nonetheless express opinions publicly that many hold privately. "In the future," a member of one of these groups told Helsinki Watch, "we should pay special attention to the patriotic upbringing of the Bulgarian nation because in the past 45 years the Bulgarian nation lost much of its patriotism. In 50-60 years, it is possible that the Bulgarian nation will not exist. If at this historical moment we do not unite, I fear we will be doomed."[52] Nationalism is best measured by its pronouns, the "we" that proves comfortably inclusive if one is an ethnic Bulgarian but distinctly cold if one is not.

Many peoples have been excluded from the patriotic upbringing, from the collective sense of nation-building, from the embrace of that "we." Although the Turks have been the major casualties in this march toward a monoculture, other groups have also felt distinctly unwelcome. Jews suffered with the rise of the right wing prior to and during World War II and were not encouraged to stay in Bulgaria by the communist authorities. By 1956, nearly 90 percent of the Jewish population had emigrated, most to Israel.[53] For the purpose of internationalist solidarity and because of the more compelling need for cheap labor, Bulgaria's communist regime invited guestworkers from the Third World, particularly Vietnam. By 1990, the 25,000 Vietnamese had replaced the Turks in the minds of many as the "devils" inhabiting Sofia. No longer able to get jobs in the tumbling Bulgarian economy, many Vietnamese had turned to illegal work such as black market dealing and money changing. One Bulgarian student, a self-styled social democrat, confessed his illiberal thoughts to the *New York Times:* "I hate them because they are really people doing dirty things to us. They kill people."[54] In 1991, the government unceremoniously flew thousands of Vietnamese back home, citing crime and the expiration of work contracts as the reason.[55]

Occupying final place in the hierarchy of the hated have been the Gypsies. Demonized in virtually every country in Eastern and Western Europe, the Gypsies are so routinely vilified that they are often not even mentioned as victims of prejudice.[56] A dark-skinned people whose language is related to Sanskrit, Gypsies are scattered throughout Eastern Europe and the former Soviet Union with particularly large populations in Hungary (800,000), Yugoslavia (1,000,000), Bulgaria (1,000,000), and Romania (2,000,000). Generally poor and often illiterate, Gypsies are discriminated against in all countries: sometimes sterilized under the old regimes, frequently refused jobs, and, with some exceptions, kept in a permanent underclass.

Like ethnic Turks, Gypsies in Bulgaria were not allowed to form a political party based on their ethnic identity and were thus prevented from participating in the 1991 elections. When a roundtables was convened on ethnic problems in December 1991, Gypsies were not even invited.[57] Even the Bulgarian Turks, themselves victims, discriminate against the Gypsies—as though to assert a meager status in the pecking order. In 1929, the ethnic Turks launched a characteristic complaint: "Moslem Gypsies were also included in the council elections, as a result of which the pious foundations of Turks...were being entrusted to irresponsible Gypsies."[58] The situation did not change in the communist era. In 1950, Turkey closed its borders to Bulgaria because it deemed the inclusion of Moslem Gypsies to be unacceptable.[59] In 1989, Turkish authorities turned back hundreds of Gypsies who had joined the mass Turkish exodus from Bulgaria despite their Moslem religion and ability to speak Turkish.[60] Nevertheless, Bulgarian Gypsies have organized in the face of adversity, forming many new political and cultural organizations.

A final issue shaping Bulgaria's national image is Macedonia. Once the mighty empire of Alexander the Great, Macedonia had over the centuries become divided among neighboring powers. Macedonian nationalists founded the underground Internal Macedonian Revolutionary Organization (IMRO) at the end of the 19th century as a vehicle for demands for nationhood. But as other nations such as Serbia and Bulgaria reconstituted themselves from the remnants of the Ottoman empire, Macedonia continued to be an adjunct to other powers. In the course of the struggle for national self-determination, Macedonians brought down a Bulgarian government in a 1923 coup and managed to achieve republic status within Yugoslavia after World War II. Today, Macedonians live primarily in the Pirin region in the southwest of Bulgaria.

Bulgaria considers Macedonians to be Bulgarians.[61] Although their language and culture are similar to Bulgaria's, Macedonians have generally stressed their unique ethnicity. Yugoslavia, meanwhile, has generally supported Macedonian claims. Indeed, Bulgaria has accused Yugoslavia of harboring hopes of incorporating a greater Macedonia within its own borders. As Stevan Pavlowitch points out, Bulgaria and Yugoslavia have used Macedonia as the ball in their geopolitical soccer game. "The Bulgarian authorities did more than put an end to Yugoslav interference in their portion of Macedonia. They reversed the process by beaming propaganda from Sofia towards Yugoslav Macedonia. This incited the Yugoslav government to a new campaign for "Macedonification" of language and history, which won over many more people to the idea of a Macedonian nation with the Yugoslav federation."[62] The most popular political party today in Macedonia is none other than a reconstituted IMRO; needless to say, it doesn't agree that Macedonians are really only Bulgarians.[63]

Like the question of ethnic Turks, the Macedonian issue unites both communists and non-communists, with the national "idea" serving as the backbone of this improbable alliance. Bulgaria is a country whose national boundaries have shifted several times in the 20th century, and with the resurgence of nationalism, maximalist claims can be heard, particularly around the Macedonia issue. As Yugoslavia falls apart, Bulgaria might take advantage of the confusion to advance its own territorial interests, creating a Greater Bulgaria to protect itself from either a Greater Serbia or a Greater Romania.

Ethnicity does not merely determine relations between groups within Bulgaria. As the previous example of Macedonia illustrates, ethnicity directly affects foreign policy as well. Bulgarian-Turkish relations, for instance, will hinge on the Bulgarian government's treatment of the ethnic Turkish population. Ethnicity even shapes the foreign aid question. Bulgarians have correctly perceived that they have been accorded a priority lower than the northern and central countries of the region. Many Bulgarians have turned that inferiority around, arguing that "they deserve better especially as they consider themselves in the front line of Christendom."[64] In other words, Bulgaria may be Eastern, but it should receive even more aid to prevent the rest of Europe from becoming more Eastern still.

That logic dictates a strong tie to NATO as well. "In the course of many centuries, Bulgaria has been an inseparable part of the history, civilization and culture of Christian Europe," Foreign Minister Viktor Valkov writes. "We have always suffered when attempts to forcefully separate us from this natural environment have been made."[65] Christian Europe? Natural environment? These desperate efforts to join the West—and to christen that association with NATO membership—would be merely ridiculous if they weren't also so permeated with dangerous ethnocentric assumptions.

Ethnicity and economy also have their ties. In October, a group of neo-liberal US economists announced their "Action Plan for Bulgaria," calling for rapid privatization and elimination of wage and price controls.[66] Protests have already accompanied price increases on basic food items. The Popov government announced in January 1991 several contradictory aims: ending both recession and inflation simultaneously, and curbing price increases while eliminating price controls. In the past, economic reform has inequitably affected ethnic Turks. Land reform after Bulgarian independence left many Turks landless. Collectivization under communism also disenfranchised Turks, providing additional lands as a lure to attract a greater number of Bulgarian "volunteers." The opposition's support for immediate de-collectivization and the return of land to its previous owners would, for the third time, adversely affect ethnic Turkish peasants. The Movement has so far taken a more gradualist position toward marketization than the current Bulgarian government.

It would, of course, be absurd to understand the Bulgarian situation solely from the point of view of ethnic conflict. The traditional template for understanding Bulgaria used by most Western observers—communists versus anti-communists, post-communists versus post-oppositionists—is useful because it does explain a good deal of the political and economic situation. But a sizable portion of the Bulgarian population does not employ this template for understanding its reality. Although nationalists might object, it is important to see at least one country in the region from the perspective of a harassed minority.

The exercise could have been fruitfully conducted in virtually any country in the region. A Gypsy could describe what German unification meant for her as she awaited citizenship in an overcrowded train station in Dresden. An ethnic German from Wroclaw (formerly German Breslau) could discuss the fixing of borders between Poland and Germany. An ethnic Pole in Bratislava could address the topic of rising Slovak nationalism. An ethnic Slovak in Budapest has a very different view of the

Democratic Forum than does the majority of Hungarians. Romania viewed from Cluj (in Transylvania) rather than Bucharest (in Wallachia) becomes an entirely different country. An ethnic Romanian living in Vojvodina would have a unique perspective on the collapse of Yugoslavia. This kaleidoscope of perspectives complicates Eastern Europe, splintering the region into a network of overlapping enclaves that continually challenges simple majoritarian solutions. There is no one reform for Eastern Europe, nor even one reform for any of the particular countries. Ethnic diversity demands a range of reforms. The various minority populations in the region will accept nothing less in their quest for self-determination.

In Bulgaria, ethnic Turks in particular have not passively accepted that minority status means second-class citizenship. Victimized for 45 years by both communism and Bulgarian nationalism, they were the first to attack Zhivkov's government openly and in large numbers. Their refusal to accept assimilation into a Bulgarian communist nation challenged all three terms: Bulgaria, communism, and nation. The middle term has subsequently dropped out, but ethnic Turks still confront a strong and imposing majority. Their refusal to accept assimilation into a united Bulgarian opposition also produced a begrudging pluralism, one that neither the communists nor the anti-communists really wanted.

Since ethnic Turks have not called for secession, Bulgaria is not looking at a Yugoslav, Soviet, or even Cypriot situation. Nor are Turks, like Slovaks, demanding autonomy within a confederation. Nor are they demanding separate schools and separate communities: an apartheid of choice. Yet even their mild demands for political representation and weekly language lessons are deemed provocative and dangerous by the majority of Bulgarians. The Movement is not of course without its flaws. It has, for instance, focused exclusively on the rights of Turks, ignoring the rights of Gypsies; it has made some injudicious comments that have only made political compromise more difficult; Ahmed Dogan has publicly called for the banning of the BSP. Still, the Movement represents the kind of social self-organization that must take place in the post-communist era: a grassroots pluralism that will not only challenge the reform process, but enrich it as well.

Centrisms

Nation-states do not exist outside time. Contrary to much nationalist propaganda, they are not graced by a particular God/dess or established within "natural" boundaries. Nations have emerged through bloody struggles with neighbors and violent campaigns for domestic homogeneity. The apparent (and not altogether unmitigated) national harmony of many of today's Western European countries conceals centuries of war and repression. As Hungarian historian Oscar Jaszi notes, "The truth is that England and France in the earlier Middle Ages were also states of an extreme racial and national complication and there, too, an assimilating and unifying process of several hundred years was necessary in order to create a national solidarity."[67] As the English are part Angle, part Saxon, part Jute, and part Dane, so too are the Hungarians, Poles, Romanians, Czechs, and Bulgarians composite peoples, the products of inter-tribal subjugation and exogamous marriage. As a result of this process, certain peoples simply disappeared (Pomeranians, Avars, Prussians) while the victors formed Eastern Europe's proto-nations during the late Middle Ages.

But in both East and West, this emergent nation-building was accomplished without ideological nationalism. After all, the modern concept of nationalism was only developed in the 18th century. As the old aristocratic order eroded around the time of the French revolution, new abstractions—political frontiers, cultural distinctness, linguistic purity—began to hold sway over *national* populations.[68] In the West, movements with this recently acquired consciousness overthrew or restricted the power of the royalty and established modern states. In the East, however, the Habsburg absolutism prevented the creation of such entities. Many of the great turmoils of the 19th and 20th centuries can be attributed to this arrested national development in Eastern Europe.

When the Austro-Hungarian reign ended with World War I, the proto-nations of Eastern Europe leapfrogged into official nationhood. Boundaries determined by rapid diplomacy struck many as arbitrary (though why any more arbitrary than boundaries determined by war and occupation is hard to say). Yugoslavia and Czechoslovakia were chimerical creatures, the body of one nation, the head of another. Hungary, by contrast, was dismembered, portions distributed around. Poland, Romania, and Bulgaria were carved out of the former empires. Nation-states were created on paper, legislated, conjured into existence by the diplomats. Ethnic conflicts which in Western Europe had filled centuries with blood and terror and which had in the East been held in delicate balance by the divide-and-conquer policies of the Habsburgs, were not to be dissipated by the mere redrawing of lines. Nationalism was fated to erupt with cataclysmic results prior to and during World War II, inspired by but not exclusive to the Nazis and their brutal racism.

Nationalism did not recently come to Eastern Europe nor did it hibernate for the last 45 years. The roots of intolerance run deep, and the communists were merely the latest usurpers to have exploited the tensions. In 1968, one faction of the Polish Communist Party used anti-Semitism to discredit student activists protesting in Warsaw and to appeal over their heads to the population at large. The subsequent forced emigration of 20,000 Polish Jews—supported by a good number of Catholic Poles—sent a powerful message to the growing Polish opposition that anti-Semitism was part of the problem, not part of the solution. Gustav Husak cleverly used Slovak nationalism to consolidate power in Czechoslovakia after 1968. Ceausescu styled himself a Roman emperor, part of the great pageant of Romanian history. Zhivkov placed communism at the head of Bulgaria's millenial consolidation of nationality. Even the profoundly anti-religious Erich Honecker, in an improbable historical juxtaposition from 1983, called Martin Luther "one of the greatest sons of the GDR."[69]

The revolutions of 1989 have, like the aborted "spring of nations" in 1848, rekindled the national aspirations of countries and ethnic groups in Eastern Europe. The spring of *nations* does not necessarily entail the spring of *nationalism,* Garton Ash maintains.[70] The renaissance of nations in the region could indeed lead to little more than the establishment of territorial boundaries and the promotion of ethnic consciousness—a plurality, that is, of different cultures.[71] Or, when it appears among minority groups, this resurgent nationalism could spur the noble fight for self-determination.

If only nationalism could be so neatly circumscribed. Unfortunately, the nationalist appetite, when conjoined with political, economic, or military power, becomes voracious, ever-expanding, and increasingly intolerant of competing perspectives. Nationalism cannot be so readily identified as emancipatory or oppressive. Nor can nationalism simply be dismissed as either a chimera or the mere result of economic inequality. This "chimera" has sent more people—rich and poor—to "glorious deaths" than any other ideology.

Nationalism—or the construction of what Benedict Anderson calls "imagined communities"—has taken many forms in Eastern Europe:[72]

- Movements for the autonomy of minority groups often expressed in the language of self-determination.

- Chauvinism of the majority ethnic group turned against domestic minority groups.

- Aspirations of submerged nations such as Slovakia, Slovenia, and Macedonia, which have either never or but briefly enjoyed independence and which are using the new regional order to advance their centuries-old demands for full national autonomy and the right to build a state.

- Irredentisms in which one already constituted nation-state lays claim to the territory of another. Albania covets regions of Yugoslavia, Hungary waxes nostalgically about Transylvania, Romania contemplates Bessarabia (part of the former Soviet republic of Moldavia).

- National arrogance that asserts the superiority of one nation over another, for instance Bulgaria over Romania.

- Eurocentrism that draws a line between those nations and peoples of "European" lineage and the heritages of those considered non-Europeans.

These six categories proceed from the smallest communities to the largest, and form an overlapping pattern of identifications. An ethnic Czech can therefore express "nationalist" opinions about: the rich Bohemian culture, Gyspies in her republic, Slovaks in a neighboring republic, German territory considered historically Bohemian, Poles considered biologically or socially inferior, or non-Europeans who threaten to mongrelize Czech "purity." These attitudes all fall into the nationalist category, for they are not based on class or race but on Czech-ness, a quality that can be defined positively in terms of cultural continuities or negatively as not Gyspy, not Slovak, not Polish, not German, not Asian, not African. The claim is a particularistic one, based on the "true" Czech, but it is also established according to a universal type—the Slav or the European archetypes, for instance.[73] Thus, the micro-nationalism of a tribe can co-exist with the supra-nationalism of pan-Slavism or Eurocentrism.

The nationalisms of Eastern Europe are frequently grouped together as a regional negative—a splintering, a refraction, a Balkanization—that is perversely juxtaposed to Western European integration. But the two processes are not as contradictory as they first seem. They are, after all, linked by the concept of "European," and both developments reflect an urge to establish a European identity that supplements and even improves each national character. As soon as they freed themselves from Soviet influence, the new democratic governments of Eastern Europe moved quickly to establish European pedigrees. East Germans merely appealed to their brothers and sisters on the other side of the fallen Berlin Wall; Poles pointed to their Catholicism; Czechs rolled out the map to show that Prague is farther west than Vienna; Hungarians talked of running a Habsburg as a presidential candidate; Romanians emphasized their lingusitic and cultural relationship with Latin culture; Croats and Slovenes referred to their previous positions within the Austro-Hungarian empire. Each country recalled its role in saving Europe from the marauding Turks in centuries past. Not surprisingly, common Slavic heritage between Poles, Slovaks, Czechs, Serbs, Croats, Bulgars, Ukrainians, and Russians was rarely mentioned.

This rush to establish pedigree, however much it might sound like the East European equivalent of tracking down an ancestor from the Mayflower, is nonetheless understandable. For the past 45 years, the countries of Eastern Europe had been denied their historic place in Europe. Through a mixture of Soviet manipulation and Western indifference, they had been dragged eastward, into what the Soviets had initially hoped would be a pan-Slavic confederation. Such a cultural and then military alliance of Slavic peoples was intended to serve as the defensive perimeter against Western intervention and to evolve into a relationship based less on shared history and more on common ideology. The Soviets expected that those peoples who didn't fit by ethnicity—Hungarians, Romanians, Germans, Turks, Jews—would stand by as comrades-in-arms until that time when internationalism triumphed over nationalism.

A pan-Slavic confederation never happened. However strong Slavic nationalism might have been in Poland, Slovakia, Bulgaria, and so on, it was rendered quickly unpopular through association with pro-Sovietism. The notion of *ex oriente lux* ("the light from the East") was accepted on a propaganda level and, depending on the country, on a social level for several years after World War II. But ultimately the "captive" hearts and minds of these western and southern Slavs belonged to Europe.

Many studies of the region focus on this particular dynamic—the domination of the East from above, the pull of the West from below. Historian Jacques Rupnik, for instance, explores the notion of "Central Europe," its hold over European intellectuals and the overvaluation of Europe that Soviet influence caused. Addressing Milan Kundera's thesis that Eastern Europe was the "kidnapped West," Rupnik writes:

> As soon as you start drawing cultural boundaries you run the risk of being accused either of cultural determinism or of "excluding" whole nations from Europe. Everyone is always someone else's "Eastern barbarian." After all, the Russians too feel that they have been the rampart of the Christian world against the Asian hordes, while in the Balkans, Orthodox Serbs see themselves (even now, in the conflict with the Albanians in the Kosovo) as defenders of Christian Europe against the onslaught of Islam.[74]

In their eagerness to embrace the once forbidden fruits of European identity, Eastern Europeans have indeed spent a good deal of time drawing cultural boundaries. In order to anchor themselves in the West, they have had to distance themselves as much as possible from the East.

The Polish novelist Tadeusz Konwicki illustrates this tendency by depicting Russia an Asian power, the successor to the barbaric hordes of Tartars. One character in his novel, *A Minor Apocalypse,* exclaims, "Oh, why are there always quarrels between Russians and Poles! Aren't we all Slavs?" To which the main character responds, "But, you know, there are no Russians left...Lenin murdered the last of the Slavs, the upper classes. Now it's strictly Asia from the Bug to Khabarovsk."[75] In *Moonrise, Moonset,* Konwicki again addresses his Slavic neighbors to the east, this time directly: "Nicest of brothers, it's time, it's high time, it's last call. You must become European, meaning human."[76]

This identification of Russia (and previously the Soviet Union) as an Asian (therefore "alien" and non-European) culture is not peculiar to Russophobe Poles. The program of the liberal Hungarian Young Democrats (FIDESZ) talks of the post-war "subjection of Eastern Europe, including Hungary, to Asian despotism."[77] Regional specialists in the West frequently refer to the intrusion of "Oriental" despotism into the governance of Eastern European communists as a legacy either of the Russians or of the Ottomans.[78]

The cultural boundary is not simply drawn along the Eastern border; it gerrymanders within the countries as well. "Eastern" populations such as Gypsies, Turks, and Albanians are singled out: for not being civilized, for producing too many children, for being too dirty, too poor, too rich, for engaging in crime, for polluting the Fatherland, for stubbornly resisting assimilation into the dominant culture. For those with long memories, epithets applied to these populations call to mind characterizations of Jews in this part of the world in the inter-war period. One example will suffice, from a 1922 guide to Warsaw, describing the Jewish ghetto: "This quarter of the city has the appearance of something completely other. There is very little that is European in its character. Here one meets Semitic types with long gabardines and characteristic round caps, reminiscent of an Eastern city."[79]

The Asian, the Oriental, the Turkish, the Islamic—these are the threats that come from the east, from the south, and from within. Imagined and distorted and magnified, they are too often characterized as obstacles placed on the path to Europe. Yet ironically, these non-European threats also serve their purpose: to unify an ideologically heterogenous population, to turn attention away from serious economic and political problems, and finally to give greater legitimacy through contrast to the populations which consider themselves unalterably European.

The dichotomy Europe/non-Europe is a mere step away from Europe/Third World: the connections between the alien within and the alien hemisphere without are variously justified by race, religion, standard of living, birthrate, proximity to Hellenized culture, and so on. For

45 years, the communist governments in Eastern Europe papered over these connections with a thin internationalism. The Third World was, as a concept, an anti-colonial and anti-capitalist force, a friendly group of socialist allies. Even when a particular government employed racism and nationalism domestically to maintain power, relations with Third World countries generally did not suffer.

Trade between Eastern Europe and the Third World has never amounted to much percentage-wise, compared with sales to and purchases from the Soviet Union or the two Germanies. Military exports, especially from Czechoslovakia, were important for key Third World countries. But for the average East European, it was the cultural exchanges which brought the Third World closer to home. Students from Angola, Libya, and North Korea studied at Eastern European universities; workers from Mozambique, Cuba, and Vietnam labored in East European factories. Because the Third World communities remained relatively isolated from the population at large (partly through choice, partly through government policy), solidarity with the Third World remained largely abstract, just one more element of communist propaganda. Not surprisingly, when the Eastern European governments fell, the majority populations held to the dictum "the friends of my enemy are my enemies as well."

In Romania, for instance, the "terrorists" in Ceausescu's private army (non-Romanians, worse, non-Europeans) were blamed for the immediate post-revolutionary violence. Skinheads and nationalists attacked Cuban and Vietnamese guestworkers in post-revolutionary eastern Germany and Czechoslovakia; while by no means supported by the respective governments, the anti-*gastarbeiter* sentiment has received a degree of support from the populations, which will likely increase proportional to unemployment. Polish attitudes toward visiting Arab or Black African students are generally negative (Poles often describe Arabs as dirty, dishonest moneychangers, the exact words once used to describe Jews in the region). Croatians and Slovenians routinely complain of Tito's infatuation with the Non-Aligned Movement and his eagerness to include Yugoslavia in an alliance with African and Asian countries "with whom we do not belong."

The countries of Eastern Europe have thus "de-ideologized" their foreign relations, searching for reliable trade partners in the Third World, severing ties with countries such as Cuba, and trying to guarantee repayment of debts incurred under previous regimes. East European governments now put the issue in cash terms: they no longer have the money to support "charity" for and "solidarity" with the Third World.

* * *

The European idea discussed at the beginning of this book has returned as a factor shaping the emerging consciousness of Eastern Europeans. The pedigrees have been established, and the external and internal threats have been identified. The struggle between ethnic Turks and ethnic Bulgarians is just a small skirmish in a much larger battle that has been going on for several millenia. Europeans still occasionally fight one another—Irish against British, Corsicans against French. But these intra-European disagreements pale to insignificance when measured against the protracted conflict of European versus non-European. The founding documents of Western Civilization have glorified this struggle—the Greeks against the Persians, the Romans against the Carthaginians, the knights of the Crusades against the Moslems, Europeans against the Huns, Saracens, and Turks. A battle of Biblical proportions, this tug-of-war pits the chosen people of history against the infidels denied a place in history.[80] The former, in conquering, write the histories that reinforce their chosenness; the latter are remembered by the dominant culture only as scourges to be eradicated or subjects to be assimilated.

When two world wars laid inter-European fratricide to rest in Western Europe, the European idea could finally be realized through European integration. The unifying pressures of the Cold War contributed considerably to this process—reconciling historic enemies and smoothing over stubborn particularism. Eastern Europe is approaching the unifying idea of Europe without benefit of the Cold War's centripedal forces and without the regional associations to channel and contain these forces. With the West reluctant to treat the region regionally, East European countries are forced to compete to be first through the European door—the first to become part of the EC or NATO, the first in trade or in aid. This competition then becomes translated into the various domestic idioms—Yugoslav civil war, Czech and Slovak antagonism, Polish ethnocentrism. Ironically, by drawing lines through the region and through the countries themselves, the European idea only threatens to balkanize the region further.

One method put forward to achieve a European consensus in the East has been through homogenization: the creation of a quilt of small, "pure" nation-states from the present overlapping ethnic map. This solution by partition has a bloody history (India, Ireland). There is no reason to believe that, for instance, separating Bulgarians from Turks would achieve any greater harmony. Such partitions merely shift domestic problems to the foreign policy realm. The only other answer is the resolution of conflict through political negotiations and the acceptance of compromises which all sides consider unsatisfactory—but equally so.[81]

The vision of a region of homogenous states in Eastern Europe is a dangerous one, involving mass population transfers, confusing subdivisions, rekindled ethnic hatreds. When politicians can no longer agree on structures that preserve "unity through diversity," as we shall see in the case of Yugoslavia, the results can be disastrous.

Chapter 10

Yugoslavia... Things fall apart

> *...as horses absurdly harnessed together, they will scatter in all directions as soon as the advancing spirit of the times will weaken and break the bonds.*[1]
>
> —Franz Grillparzer

In the late summer of 1990, a group of ethnic Serbs within Croatia began campaigning for their own brand of independence. They blockaded some roads and demanded a plebiscite. They had guns. Some said they were in the pay of the Serbian government.[2]

In the increasingly independent republics of Slovenia and Croatia, life nevertheless went on. Occasionally, people would talk of the horrific possibility of civil war—Serb against Croat, Macedonian against Albanian, Christian against Moslem. But the specter of revived blood feuds had been raised so frequently in Yugoslavia during the 1980s that it had become an observation more banal than harrowing. Civil war was certainly possible, but no one was ready to sell the house, quit the job, and move to Austria. Calmer heads would surely prevail. Negotiations were taking place. Stubbornness would eventually dissolve into compromise. Europeans would resolve their differences in a "civilized" manner.

These Europeans wouldn't. War did indeed come in 1991 and with a ferocity that even the most pessimistic prophets found shocking. The former Yugoslavs, now referred to by their particular ethnic identities, seemed determined to prove that even as the 20th century neared its end, Europeans could still commit atrocities.

What a brave new Europe this was. Western European leaders gathered in banquet halls in Brussels and Luxembourg to toast their new consensus on economic and political integration. In the ancient port of Dubrovnik and the Danubian towns of Vukovar and Osijek, Yugoslavs slaughtered one another. The Cold War was over, the Berlin Wall was no more, the Soviet Union had disappeared. But in 1992, a new iron curtain in Europe threatened to separate not capitalism from communism, but order from chaos.

To single out nationalism as the factor distinguishing Eastern from Western Europe would be imprecise. The French are arguably as racist and ethnocentric as the Hungarians; Gypsies are attacked in both Czechoslovakia and Great Britain; Bulgarians treat ethnic Turks no worse than Italians treat ethnic Albanians. Divergent methods of organizing state power rather than the degree of nationalism characterizes Europe's new iron curtain. For its part, the East is in varying stages of disintegration. The former Soviet Union is passing fitfully from federation to confederation to confusion. Yugoslavia, meanwhile, has suffered statestroke, its central nervous system irrevocably damaged. The country has slipped back into a Europe of a previous era.

Western Europe is moving in the opposite direction, ceding greater authority to central authorities, positioning itself for a 21st century of competitive trade blocs. The EC has, in other words, finally reconciled the conflicts that tore apart the continent in the 20th century, while the peoples of the former Yugoslavia are preparing to replay both world wars—if they must, all by themselves.

How has Yugoslavia come to epitomize the chaos of the post-communist era? The country was once the darling of the West, in an Eastern European category all its own. Benefiting from most-favored-nation status, technology transfers, and cultural exchanges, Yugoslavia was first in line for membership in pan-European institutions. Today, the first has become last. Yugoslavia has, like the Soviet Union, become an uncountry, a crisis-wracked region which European leaders would prefer to keep at arm's length from their integration process. After all, this fragmenting entity challenges the consensus on territorial integrity that has kept the European order more or less intact since the end of World War II. Many European leaders worry that if Yugoslavia's borders suddenly become mutable, then not only will the Balkans become an irredentist free-for-all, but movements closer to home—Corsicans, Carinthians, Basques, Bavarians, Flemish—might challenge existing territorial divisions and state structures. Europe once balkanized Yugoslavia; today Yugoslavia threatens to balkanize Europe in return.

For Eastern Europe, Yugoslavia has replaced Tiananmen Square as the worst-case scenario. While Eastern Europeans braced for possible government crackdown during the revolutions of 1989, their greatest fear is now the breakdown of government, a chaos precipitated by ethnic hatreds, a disorder hastened by both the austerity capitalism and political indifference now sweeping the region. The result will not necessarily be a Yugoslav-style civil war. Instead the deterioration of state structure may usher in a new brand of Eastern European authoritarianism already prefigured in Walesa's decrees and Iliescu's reliance on mob violence. Undemocratic order or uncontrollable disorder—these are the choices offered by Yugoslavia's recent history.

Yugoslavia is therefore more than simply a problem for Yugoslavs and more than merely an unpleasant anachronism located uncomfortably close to the new EC. The civil war is challenging reform in the East, disrupting a comfortable consensus on territorial integrity in the West, and threatening to tear down a common European home whose foundations have not even been properly surveyed, much less established.

Six republics in search of a structure

In the years leading up to the civil war, when the demons still jostled within Pandora's box and the evil genie had yet to be conjured from its bottle, the debate on the structure of the Yugoslav state was often conducted on a dizzyingly abstract plane. Was Yugoslavia a federation, a cooperative federation, a confederation, a quasi-confederation? The state structure's very complexity made categorization difficult. Political scientist Zvi Gitelman writes:

> The Yugoslavs seem to have made a national hobby of designing intricate, complicated and seemingly incomprehensible structures for just about everything, and especially for their government. One can stare at an organization chart of the Yugoslav government for five minutes and still not be able to determine the division of jurisdiction.[3]

There was one very good reason for the complexity of the Yugoslav state: the ethnic diversity of the country. Multicultural by both geographic inevitability and deliberate design, the country consisted of six republics: Macedonia, Montenegro, Bosnia-Herzogovina, Slovenia, Croatia, and Serbia (which also contains the once autonomous regions of Vojvodina and Kosovo). The ethnic groups do not neatly conform to the republic divisions. Serbs spill over into Croatia and Bosnia. Albanians live not only in Kosovo but in large numbers in Macedonia and Montenegro as well. The most ethnically homogeneous republic, Slovenia, maintains a non-Slovene minority population of roughly 10 percent; the most diverse republic Bosnia is split among three Slavic communities—Croatian, Serbian, and Moslem. Further complicating matters, the regions possess very different histories. Slovenia endured over five centuries under the Habsburgs. Croatia enjoyed some independence during the Middle Ages and then spent seven centuries under the Hungarian crown.

Having at one time controlled much of the Balkans, Serbia was absorbed into the Ottoman empire where it remained with Macedonia and Montenegro until independence in 1878.

These diverse regions and peoples formed Yugoslavia in 1918. The country's conception, however, can be traced back to earlier calls for a modern-day Illyria, a dream that had a brief reality after Napoleon's surge into southeastern Europe in the early 19th century.[4] This Illyrian memory spurred the southern Slavs to rebel against both the Austro-Hungarian and Ottoman empires. As independence became more likely in the 19th century, the Habsburgs tried their best to drive a wedge between the two largest groups, the Croats and Serbs.[5] But the hapless Habsburgs only managed to push the southern Slavs together, in German historian Hermann Wendel's memorable words, "by the unity of the gallows, of the court-martial, of the internment camps, and of the jail-cells."[6] With the Habsburg empire collapsing as a result of World War I, the Kingdom of Serbs, Croats, and Slovenes (renamed Yugoslavia in 1929) managed to consolidate itself despite critical constitutional and territorial disagreements.[7] The Illyrian dream would shortly merge into a cacophonous Yugoslav reality as tensions among the three dominant ethnic groups made consensual rule virtually impossible. The national question, historian Ivo Banac writes of this period, "was solved by day and unsolved by night. Some days were particularly bright for building, some nights particularly dark for destroying."[8] With the outbreak of World War II, Yugoslavia descended into what seemed to be permanent night. The Serbian-Croatian conflict in particular claimed untold thousands of lives even as Yugoslavs of very different political perspectives and ethnic backgrounds battled the forces of Hitler and Mussolini.

Although World War II visited immense suffering upon the country, Yugoslavia nevertheless emerged from the carnage as the preeminent Balkan power, united by the underground communist leader Tito and enlarged by lands taken from the losing powers. With the savage nationalism of World War II a sobering memory, economic development and the deteriorating relationship with the Soviet Union preoccupied the new communist Yugoslavia. On the ethnic issue, the propaganda of the new regime emphasized that the internationalist spirit of communism began at home with the harmonious cohabitation of the southern Slavs and their Albanian, Moslem, Hungarian, and Italian brothers and sisters. Tito's slogan, "brotherhood and unity," repeated *ad nauseum* down through the decades, both romanticized the otherwise fratricidal partisan struggle of World War II and glossed over the simmering ethnic tensions of the communist era.

Compared with previous arrangements, the imagined communist brotherhood was no mere facade. As analyst Dennison Rusinow writes,

"Once upon a time, in the 1950s and early 1960s, few Western observers of the Yugoslav scene disagreed with the regime's claim that the Yugoslav 'national question' was at least on its way to a peaceful and happy solution, if indeed it had not already been solved."[9] But the ghost of the Austro-Hungarian empire—and the perils of multinationalism—would ensure that Yugoslavia was still far from a "peaceful and happy solution."

In 1963, after having achieved a detente with the Soviets, Yugoslav leaders began to experiment with the structure of their state by decentralizing federal authority and according greater powers to the republics. The new constitution that year expressed the same ambivalence toward tight control that Tito had translated into self-management in the economic sphere and into ideological distance from Moscow in international affairs. Nearly two decades had passed since the end of the partisan struggle, and Tito needed new justifications for communist control and national unity. Regional autonomy seemed to be a reasonable answer. "Was Yugoslavia still a federation of nations," one Yugoslav specialist asked, reflecting on the 1963 constitution. "Or was it already on the way to becoming a confederation of territories?"[10]

This trend was hastened by developments later in the decade—liberalization from above, greater geographic division of wealth, and reinvigorated nationalism. A turning point came with the forced resignation in 1966 of Alexander Rankovic, the hardliner in charge of the State Security Service. A major center of Serbian conservatism had been rooted out. Gradually, the valves on internal dissent were loosened, particularly in Kosovo.[11] Protests such as the 300,000-strong demonstration in Belgrade against the Soviet invasion of Czechoslovakia suggested a renaissance in civic activity. Criticism would soon turn from relatively safe external targets to issues that challenged government policy more directly.

One of those issues was economics. By the late 1960s, the developmental differences among the regions of Yugoslavia had still to be eliminated by the industrial growth of communism. The northern republics—Slovenia, Croatia—were still benefiting from their pre-war economic achievements, their location near the EC market, their membership in the Alpine-Adriatic group. Montenegro, Macedonia, Bosnia, and sections of Serbia, on the other hand, remained predominantly agricultural and locked in a dependent relationship with northern trade and industry. The late 1960s saw these challenges of under- and over-development pull at Yugoslavia's federal structure, a process fueled by the country's nemesis of nationalism.

The first revolt, in 1968, came from the poorest. Kosovo is a region of Serbia, the historic source of Serbian culture, and the scene of the celebrated military loss to the Turks in 1389 which spelled the end of

Serbian autonomy for 500 years. As the Serbian Orthodox Church has explained, Kosovo is "our memory, our hearth, the focus of our being."[12] With the highest birthrate in Europe, however, ethnic Albanians soon achieved an overwhelming majority in the region. In 1968, filling the streets of the capital Pristina, they called for Kosovo to be raised to republic level. Other nationalities in Yugoslavia possessed republics, so why not the Albanians? The federal authorities had three reasons to deny the request. Some demonstrators in 1968 made a tactical error by calling for union with Albania. Elevation of Kosovo to a republic could be then seen—particularly by Albania—as the first step in redrawing the Balkan map. Second, because of the large number of Albanians in Macedonia, the leadership there feared a Kosovo republic that included Macedonian land. With a consistent Macedonian veto, the federal authorities could not change Kosovo's status. Finally, Kosovo was the poorest region of the country and unlikely to achieve self-sufficiency as a republic.[13]

A compromise was reached. Having been named "autonomous" regions by the first post-war constitution, Kosovo and the Vojvodina enclave in the north of Serbia with its large ethnic Hungarian minority were accorded higher status. No longer subservient directly to Serbia, both regions answered to federal authorities and, represented in federal institutions, could block legislation just like their republic cousins.[14] But politics was only one part of the deal, particularly for Kosovo. "If the other regions in Yugoslavia walk," a popular saying in the country goes, "then Kosovo must run." Capital poured into the region to bring it up to speed.[15] But money and greater political autonomy did not solve the tensions. Feeling like second-class citizens within Kosovo, Serbians moved out. Sensing that they remained second-class citizens in Yugoslavia as a whole, Albanians continued to clamor for more rights.[16] The Kosovo compromise, like many of its ilk, left all parties involved dissatisfied.

The nationalist bug was also infecting the more prosperous region of Croatia. In 1970-71, a student strike at Zagreb University showcased the republic's new spirit of independence that had percolated up through the Croatian Communist Party. Croatian intellectuals agitated for greater republic autonomy that included control over all revenues collected within the republic, an independent republic bank, a territorial army, and the right to secede from the union.[17] The heresy was soon extinguished as the federal government jailed hundreds of nationalists, and the Communist Party purged its Croatian chapter.

Although Belgrade is the seat of federal power, the quashing of Croatian nationalism in the early 1970s was not simply another chapter in a Serbian-Croatian conflict. Indeed, in 1972, the federal government also turned to stem the tide of rising nationalism within the Serbian

Communist Party. As one writer comments, "from the time of the Chetniks, Serbia has consistently been the regime's principal problem."[18] The redistricting of Kosovo and Vojvodina, for instance, was designed to pare Serbia down to a more modest size—"strong Yugoslavia, weak Serbia," according to the Yugoslav saying. Before 1980, the Yugoslav structure was not simply a vehicle for Serbian domination. Federal policy was designed to safeguard communist control from nationalist challenges, whether Serbian, Albanian, or Croatian. In 1973, it was the Slovenian Party's turn for purges as Tito systematically weeded his opponents from the various Party apparatuses.

By 1974, however, Tito felt sufficiently secure to substitute carrot for stick. His 1974 constitution fulfilled the decentralizing promise of 1963 and weakened the Yugoslav federation considerably. The nationalists may have been sitting in jail cells but many of their demands were inscribed in public policy by the 1974 constitution. The federal government retained the chief attributes of a nation-state—defense, overall monetary and fiscal control—but devolved virtually all other functions to the republic level. Republics were even conducting their own foreign policies.[19] More importantly, all federal decisions had to be achieved by the consensus of republic representatives in the federal council. As in a confederation, federal decisions concerning republic policy could not be implemented without that republic's consent (in the United States, by contrast, states must abide by all national legislation). With the republic representatives once again his allies, Tito could, for a time, control the new structure as easily as the old. But with the 1974 constitution, the federal government had essentially signed its own death warrant.

The 1974 solution only half-satisfied the demands of the republic nationalists. Serbians felt that they had been robbed of land and authority in Vojvodina and Kosovo. The large influxes of capital that Macedonia, Bosnia, and Kosovo received to raise their standards of living were never considered sufficient. Croatia and Slovenia, meanwhile, resented the federal redistribution of funds away from their more productive regions. The greater liberalization of the 1963 constitution fueled the nationalism of the latter half of that decade. The confederalism of the 1974 constitution was going to lead to even greater disarray.

Then, in 1980, came the death of the only leader communist Yugoslavia had ever known. Tito's passing created a profound political vacuum that coincided dangerously with a region-wide economic slump. More importantly, Tito had been able to strike a balance, however brutal, among the republics. After 1980, the tensions of decades past returned, and, as before, Kosovo led the way.

Whatever his faults, Tito had been a staunch defender of ethnic Albanian rights in Kosovo. He had pushed for the changes in the 1974 constitution over the strenuous objections of Serbian nationalists. "Kosovo should become the concern of Yugoslavia as a whole," he declared not long before he died.[20] Demonstrations in Kosovo in 1981—which spread to Montenegro and Macedonia as well—were a vote of no confidence for Tito's successor, an indication that ethnic Albanians were simply not satisfied with the status of autonomous region. After federal police killed 11 and injured 257 in the riots of '81, the federal government followed up with its usual good-cop/bad-cop routine.[21] It arrested the instigators and stepped up the propaganda war with Albania, restricting the latter's access to the Kosovo region.[22] But the federal government also pumped money into the region to satisfy demands for faster development. Not only were funds being directed in large part toward the underdeveloped regions of Yugoslavia, they were disproportionately going to Kosovo.[23]

Money did not buy ethnic Albanian support, however. As the 1980s advanced, the situation in Kosovo simply worsened. Serbians were leaving, economic development had failed to bridge the gap with wealthier republics, and demands for greater autonomy within the Yugoslav structure were intensifying. Without Tito to keep them in check, Serbian communists were calling for a reversal of the 1974 agreements and the reimposition of Serbian control over the region. In March 1989, Serbia made good on its threat and rescinded the 1974 constitutional provisions guaranteeing Kosovo's special status.[24] Ethnic Albanians fought back—against both their indifferent and corrupt political representatives and their Serbian "protectors." When demonstrations broke out in Pristina in late March 1989, riot police killed 24 protesters.[25] The federal government responded as earlier with widespread arrests and human rights violations. By 1990, Kosovo was in open revolt, the population engaged in an ethnic Albanian *intifada*.

The imposition of direct rule both resulted from and encouraged growing Serbian nationalism. Responsibility for the Serbian hybrid of nationalist-communism, a close cousin to the Bulgarian communist-nationalism, must go to Slobodan Milosevic, who built his reputation in the Party by purging liberals and reformers at every step. Milosevic first proposed direct rule for Kosovo in 1988 in order to "rescue" Serbs victimized in Kosovo (foreshadowing his position on ethnic Serbs in Croatia).[26] While some ethnic Albanians indeed envisioned a homogeneous Kosovo free of Serbs and Montenegrins, that threat did not justify home rule. Milosevic even urged Serbs to fight in Kosovo—a call to arms which naturally led to an intensification of ethnic hatred in the region.

The cause of Kosovo fired the imaginations of human rights groups within Yugoslavia, in much the same way that the situation of ethnic Turks initially consolidated the opposition in Bulgaria. "There is quite a lot of support for the people in Kosovo," Croatian philosopher Zarko Puhovski told me, "The problem is you can't be sure whether they are doing it for the cause or because it's anti-Serbian."[27] In 1968, movements for autonomy in other republics took their cue from ethnic Albanians. Twenty years later, Kosovo would again be the bellwether, but this time the revolt against federal authority would take a much more serious turn. The Serbian government, with some effort, could clamp down in Kosovo. Its attempt, through the federal army, to impose control in Slovenia and Croatia in 1991 would meet more serious resistance and lead to much greater consequences.

* * *

As Eastern Europe began to unravel in 1989, so too did Yugoslavia. Its economy was laboring under hyper-inflation (2,500 percent annually) and experiencing a crisis in self-management. The European Community offered a large assistance package with several strings attached, democratic elections being perhaps the foremost. In the beginning of 1990, with a Euro-infusion near at hand, the federal authorities finally and belatedly acceded to the new pluralist standard in the region by permitting legal opposition parties. The 1974 constitution, with its insistence on consensus among all republics for rule changes, made agreement on democratic federal elections virtually impossible.[28] Yugoslavia therefore permitted republic elections *before* federal elections. The result: a lost opportunity to create a democratic Yugoslav alternative. By extending democracy to the republics first, the federal Communist Party undermined the legitimacy of federal institutions.

Slovenia and Croatia immediately called free elections to coincide with the spring of elections that their Eastern European neighbors were celebrating. Bosnia-Herzogovina and Macedonia followed suit in the fall, along with Serbia and Montenegro. New nationalist governments took over in Croatia and Slovenia while Serbia and Montenegro retained formerly Communist leadership and Bosnia and Macedonia elected coalition governments.

By 1990, Yugoslavia both did and did not exist. Intermarriage had created a generation whose nationality, to avoid confusion if nothing else, was Yugoslav. At the level of culture and intellectual achievement there was a Yugoslavia that consisted of the inter-republic collaboration of actors, professors, dancers, and writers. But these were frail social bonds compared to the only other functioning Yugoslav institution—the army. With an officer corps comprised disproportionately of Serbs and soldiers drawn from every republic, the military had the greatest stake in the continuity of federal structures.[29]

Previously, the Yugoslav Communist Party would have been the clearest sign of the country's existence. By 1990, however, the brinkmanship of Serbia's Milosevic had led to the fragmentation of Yugoslav communism into its republic components. With the weakening of the federal Party, a confrontation was shaping up between the forces of Yugoslavia (the army) and the forces of non-Yugoslavia (the republics). The decentralization begun several decades earlier was leading to disintegration. The horses had begun to gallop, and they were certainly not heading in the same direction.

Mechanics of breakdown

Locating someone in Slovenia in 1990 who supported Yugoslavia was like trying to find a flat-worlder, an alchemist, or a Shaker. For most of the inhabitants of this northwestern republic, Yugoslavia was a construct which had outlived its historical usefulness. When polled, nearly 90 percent of Slovenians wanted to create an independent country.

In Ljubljana, the attractive capital of Slovenia, Marko Hren made his living as a computer specialist and peace activist. As far as Slovenians were concerned, Hren told me over lunch during the summer of 1990, Belgrade and Serbia fell under the category of "international relations" or, more precisely, "international problems." Slovenians rarely visited Belgrade and were more likely to take trips abroad to Vienna, Rome, or Munich. Serbia was clearly beyond the pale—the villain, the alien aggressor, the less-developed power that controlled its dominions much as Moscow once dictated to the Baltics. This control was not direct but rather mediated through federal institutions. Federal meant Yugoslav so, as the Slovenian syllogism went, achieving independence from Serbian control meant bringing Yugoslavia to an end. The Slovenian alternative was confederation.

Confederation? But, I asked Marko Hren, wasn't Yugoslavia already a confederation? Didn't the 1974 constitution decentralize the country sufficiently to become a confederation? Two different notions altogether, Hren replied. The confederation he and many Slovenians envisioned would be composed of six or more independent units tied together by contracts. But what would be the difference between such contracts and agreements signed between sovereign nations? Certain things would still be in common, Hren answered. Such as telecommunications? He shook his head. The military? He shook his head. The postal system? He shook his head. So what would remain in common, I pressed. Nothing really, Hren finally admitted. Confederation, it turned out, was a negotiating term. Slovenia preferred outright secession but Serbia, still arguing for federation, would not permit the unilateral dissolution of Yugoslavia. Confederation was therefore a linguistic compromise that allowed the two republics to continue discussions.[30]

Federalism, it was constantly repeated in antebellum Slovenia, concealed a plan for Serbian domination. Confederation, on the other hand, represented autonomy and democracy. But, it could be countered, federalism also could reflect the egalitarian principle of diverse peoples living together in a political arrangement that distributes capital from richer to poorer regions. And confederation could also legitimize desires for greater territory, greater ethnic homogeneity, or simply greater distance from the problems of and conflicts inherent in diversity.

Then why not a democratic federation? Indeed, as Tomas Masaryk wrote at the beginning of this century, "federalism without freedom is impossible."[31] Leery of the nationalism that lay just beneath the surface of Croatian and Slovenian demands for confederation, a small group of Yugoslavs from various republics banded together to form the Yugoslav Democratic Initiative and resurrect Masaryk's idea of a democratic federation. Early in the democratization process, this "Yugoslav" option appeared to be the most logical strategy, attracting the support of newly reconstituted Social Democratic parties and even two explicit federal parties.

By the end of 1990, the Yugoslav option had lost whatever momentum it might once have possessed. Republic elections had given democratic legitimacy to essentially nationalist parties and coalitions. The Democratic Initiative, as a movement, could not survive in the world of party politics. "We have all the time feared that we would have to decide if we were for Yugoslavia or for democracy," early Initiative supporter Zarko Puhovski told me. "Of course, my option would be for democracy. But I still hope that there will be some kind of possibility to preserve Yugoslavia as a democratic state."

Another problem with the federal option was its association with austerity capitalism. An economic reform, led by federal Prime Minister Ante Markovic, arrested Yugoslavia's galloping inflation and transformed the country from one of Europe's cheapest to one of its most expensive. Markovic earned high marks for his fiscal stringency from international economic institutions, and even grudging respect from various republic leaders.[32] "Markovic offered the best program at the time," Croatian sociologist Dushitsa Sefaragic told me. "No one, not in Slovenia and not in Croatia, had a better one."[33] As with the Balcerowicz program in Poland, however, improved financial indicators came at the expense of industrial and agricultural production. When Yugoslavs felt the pain, they blamed Yugoslavia, not the individual republic governments.

Federalism was discredited, the economy was in shambles, the republics were increasingly independent. Still, perhaps the debate on state structure—federation versus confederation—could have remained on a political level had it not been for a century-old dispute between Serbia and Croatia. This tension revived in the 1980s as internationalism and communism could no longer be enforced from above.

Serbians are predominantly Orthodox and generally use the Cyrillic script. Croatians are predominantly Catholic and use the Roman script. The language they speak is Serbo-Croatian—a hyphenated fiction, according to many Croats. The greater the Croatian nationalist, the more he or she will emphasize the distinctiveness of the two languages. "The language has changed in the newspapers," Croatian sociologist Mira Oklobdzija told me. "They are using all these Croatian words to differentiate as much as possible between Croatian and Serbian. There are regional dialects within Croatia and people within the republic sometimes can hardly understand one another. People from Belgrade and Zagreb, on the other hand, have no difficulty whatsoever. The difference between the two languages is probably similar to American and English."[34] During the Tito era, the differences were standardized in favor of the dominant Serbian dialect; today the differences are accentuated to buttress spurious claims of purity.

If only the controversy remained on a linguistic plane. The hatreds, however, run deep. During World War II, Chetniks (Serbian royalists) killed Croats and Moslems, though without the thoroughness that a state apparatus can provide; the Ustasha regime in Croatia orchestrated the slaughter of untold thousands of Serbs (with a large number of Jews and Communists as well). "The Ustasha policy toward the Serbs," writes Aleksa Djilas, "which clearly stated that there was no place for them inside the NDH [independent fascist Croatia], planned to kill about half the Serbian population and to expel the rest to Serbia or force them to convert to Catholicism, which the Ustashas believed, would eventually transform them into Croats."[35] At war's end, the partisans took their revenge on Croatian supporters of the Ustasha, the casualties reaching up to 100,000 when Slovenian and Serbian Axis supporters are included (long rumored mass graves of those killed by the partisans began to show up in 1990).[36] These wartime holocausts have continued to obsess both Serbs and Croats, permeating the inflammatory rhetoric of nationalists and even breaking out with violent results beyond Yugoslav borders.[37]

Despite the many pronouncements of the Milosevic government in Serbia, the present Croatian leadership is not fascist. Nationalist yes, but not Ustasha. The Croatian president, Franjo Tudjman, was jailed two decades ago for his part in the nationalist turn within the Croatian Communist Party. The Croatian Democratic Community (HDZ), Tudjman's latest political vehicle, captured the majority of seats in parliament (though not the majority of votes) in the 1990 elections. Heavily financed by Croatian emigres, HDZ trounced its more liberal rivals, including the

Coalition for National Agreement, despite the latter's impeccable opposition credentials.[38] Although consisting of different factions, HDZ is generally ultra-patriotic, Catholic, and right-wing in perspective. Translated into the contemporary political vernacular of the region, HDZ is anti-Serbian, anti-federal, anti-Yugoslav. Its victory in the Croatian elections could be declared only a partial victory for pluralism. "In Croatia," Belgrade activist Sonja Licht explains, "it is very difficult to talk about the beginning of a genuine democracy because this Croatian Democratic Union is so much stronger than anyone else. One can even talk about one-party rule which is no longer communist in essence, but nationalist. They don't really have a strong economic program at all. They have a strong national program and this is a very unsophisticated one: the sovereignty of Croatian people over everything else."

In 1972, the question was simply autonomy for the republic. In the 1990s, the stakes have been raised. Independence for Croatia necessarily resurrects the competing visions of "greater" Serbia and Croatia. The "bio-geographic" plan for a greater Croatia incorporates pieces of Bosnia where a large number of Croats live. At the same time, however, there are sections of Croatia and Bosnia where large concentrations of Serbs live and which Serbian leaders would like to make part of their "greater" homeland.

Tudjman and HDZ have been dangerously ambiguous on the Serb question. "There is a wing which would really be happy to get rid of Serbs," Croatian philosopher Puhovski told me. "No one would say to kill them. But you can hear some Croats say that there is no place for Serbs in Croatia. Or they say that they will put them a thousand meters under the ground if the Serbs say anything against the Croat state. President Tudjman, for instance, said in an interview—'I have heard rumors that my wife is of Serbian-Jewish origin but thank God that is not the truth.' That was his exact formulation."[39] In his book on the Nazi holocaust, Tudjman asserts that the figures for both Serbian and Jewish deaths during World War II have been inflated.[40] But even Tudjman is moderate compared to Croatia's revived fascist movement, the Party of Rights, a coalition of Ustasha followers, skinheads, national socialists, and extreme nationalists.[41] Again, contrary to Serbian government claims, the Croatian leadership has as much difficulty with the Party of Rights as the Serbians do.

Fearful of being deprived of their rights within a new Croatia, ethnic Serbs began in 1990 to call for an autonomous state of their own. The separatist shoe was suddenly on the other foot. The new Croatian government reacted quickly, refusing to honor a proposed referendum on the issue and calling the movement a direct provocation by the Serbian government. In an increasingly polarized environment, the referendum went ahead over the objections of the Croatian government. Of those who voted, 99 percent supported Serbian autonomy.[42] Whether assisted materially by Belgrade or not, the aspirations of the Serbs in Croatia were certainly supported morally by the Serbian government. One government-controlled Serbian newspaper declared that all two million Serbs would be willing to go to Croatia to fight over the issue of Serbian self-rule.

Since Serbs constitute the largest group of dispersed peoples in Yugoslavia, Serbian nationalism has been predicated on protecting the rights of the diaspora. The comparison is deliberate. Like European Jews, Serbs suffered greatly at the hands of fascists during World War II. In recent years, however, Serbia has, like Israel, taken on an aggressor role in protecting its population. The Serbian government has treated the southern region of Kosovo like an occupied territory, ruling this predominantly Albanian region directly from Belgrade. All indigenous political structures have been dissolved in Kosovo, and even a program for resettling the region with Serbs has been attempted.[43] Militant Serbs have also, like Israeli hawks, developed a particularly virulent siege mentality which holds that all surrounding powers—from Croatia to Germany to the CIA—are bent on destroying the Serbian homeland. When the federal army shelled the Croatian presidential palace in Zagreb, Belgrade announced without a hint of irony that Croatian president Tudjman had in fact ordered the bombing on his own headquarters to gain world sympathy.[44]

The appeal of federalism to Serbs is clear. Under federal guarantees, the Serbian diaspora maintains equal rights; should Yugoslavia fall apart, these guarantees would disappear and Serbs would become instant minorities (and vulnerable to the abuses that Albanians presently suffer). As long as Belgrade remains the federal center of Yugoslavia, communist nationalists reason, Serbia will remain first among equals.[45] A primary vehicle for serving this function has been the Yugoslav federal army, in part because of the concentration of Serbs in the officer corps. Serbia has managed to intervene in Croatia using "federal" justifications much as the United States invaded Korea and Iraq using the United Nations as a cover for its own interests.

If federation becomes untenable, Serbian nationalists resort to the Greater Serbia option.[46] Anti-communist nationalists—and most Serbs are anti-communist—simply favor an expanding homeland.[47] Led by the charismatic Vuk Draskovic, these Serbianists perceive communism as an obstacle rather than the vehicle for the realization of Serbian values. Although Draskovic shares many of Milosevic's chauvinisms, he has called for peace, one that would divide up Bosnia, permit independence for Croatia and Slovenia, and leave the remaining lands in a federal structure.[48]

The Serbian elections at the end of 1990 offered a choice between two nationalisms, one post-communist, the other pre-communist. Serbia's democratic opposition, small and harried, could do little to overcome Serbocentrism. With Draskovic still a wild card, the Socialists under Milosevic easily won the contest (Albanians boycotted the elections, only increasing Milosevic's lead). But all of Serbia was not behind Milosevic despite his 65 percent win in the presidential vote. His crude attempts to control Serbian media have been particularly galling. In March 1991, opposition parties held a demonstration in Belgrade to protest state control of television. Police attacked the immense crowd (roughly 100,000), killing two, injuring 203, and arresting 213 (including Vuk Draskovic).[49] Subsequent student demonstrations led to the release of Draskovic and the solidifying of Milosevic's siege mentality.

* * *

By the beginning of 1991, the trajectory for Yugoslavia was all too clear. Both Serbia and Croatia were under nationalist rule. The federalists and confederalists could find no grounds for compromise. Slovenia was leaving Yugoslavia's orbit, ethnic Serbs within Croatia were clamoring for their own independence, and the remaining republics were being forced to line up on one side of the question or the other: did they support the concept of Yugoslavia or not? Political negotiations yielded no answers.

Instead of reforming the state structure, both sides moved to destroy it. The fiction of possible consensus was replaced by the friction of civil war. "I used to say quite often that Yugoslavia is not a problem only for itself," Serbian sociologist Sonja Licht pointed out in 1990. "Yugoslavia can really become a very huge problem for a good part of Eastern and Central Europe: Bulgaria, Greece, Romania, Hungary, Albania, and even Italy and Austria. The dissolution of Yugoslavia will not happen without a civil war."[50]

This would be the great irony for Yugoslav foreign policy. Tito steered the country along the path of non-alignment, successfully negotiating respect from both the Soviets and United States by playing one off the other. Yugoslavia also led the Non-Aligned Movement, a grouping of countries of differing political dispositions almost exclusively from the Third World. Now Yugoslavia faces a non-alignment problem of a very different kind—the division of the country itself.

"Everyone in Yugoslavia fears Yugoslavia," said Slovenian political scientist Mitja Zagar. "It is very strange. It is needed by everyone and everyone fears it. I still believe that the Yugoslav option, before a civil war, is the best possible solution. All other solutions are worse." But Zagar believes cooperation inevitable, even if it comes after a period of intense conflict. "I think that ideas of confederation will change quite soon into something else. The first idea would be to establish a completely independent state. Political ideas would be fulfilled—there would be an independence day which everyone would celebrate—then people would think about what would happen in the future. Then they would find out, for instance, that transport in Yugoslavia is very closely connected, something they didn't expect."[51] The citizens of the new states would discover that Yugoslavia had not simply been a slogan or a substanceless fiction, but rather, a real set of relationships. Tearing such relationships asunder instead of reforming them democratically would then be seen, perhaps too late, as the product of nationalist illusions.

War

The Yugoslav civil war has so far been nasty, brutish, and short. By 1992, a fragile ceasefire (and what ceasefire has not been "fragile?") was holding, as the warring factions awaited the introduction of UN peace-keeping troops. Considerable damage had already been done. The federal army had laid waste to Vukovar in the east and laid seige to the ancient coastal town of Dubrovnik in the west. There were thousands dead and hundreds of thousands left homeless. Both Serbs and Croats had brutalized each other and, eyeing Bosnia-Herzogovina, were still keen to expand their territory. The federal government had effectively ceased to exist. Yugoslvia had been reduced to its component parts.

How did a debate on federation versus confederation degenerate so quickly into civil war? The Habsburgs too considered restructuring their empire into a democratic federation, but at a time when centrifugal forces had become insuperable.[52] Yugoslavia's centrifugal forces were equally strong—the structural decentralization, the constitutional impasse, the erosion of communism, the residual ethnic tensions, the power vacuum created by Tito's death, the association of federation with economic austerity and military service. In both cases, war needed only a spark: for the Habsburgs, the assassination of the crown prince in Sarajevo; for Yugoslavia, the June 25, 1991 declarations of Croatian and Slovenian independence.

The June declarations spelled an immediate end to playacting: confederation was finally replaced by what it meant all along—secession. The most prosperous regions of the country, Slovenia and Croatia declared that their future was in Europe proper, not the Balkan backwaters. Economically, Croatia and Slovenia were tired of subsidizing a federal center located in Belgrade and equally unwilling to subsidize the development of poorer regions of the country (Kosovo, Macedonia, Montenegro, and Bosnia). Culturally, both republics wanted to dissociate themselves from the so-called "eastern" Serbs, their Orthodox Christianity, and their Cyrillic alphabet.

With a relatively homogenêous population and few territorial disputes with other republics, Slovenia managed to leave the Yugoslav federation with comparatively little travail or loss of life.[53] The only republic in the 1980s to undergo a successful process of democratization from below, this northernmost part of the country felt it had no choice but to leave what it considered an undemocratic structure. When Slovenians moved to take control of the republic's border posts after the declaration of independence, the Yugoslav federal army attacked. Fighting back, the breakaway republic battled to a stalemate. According to the subsequent three-month truce signed in July 1991, Slovenia temporarily suspended its declaration of independence and federal troops returned to their barracks.

The truce did nothing, however, to defuse tensions between the Serbs and Croats. Incidents between armed Serb insurgents and Croatian police multiplied during the summer of 1991. Using the pretext of separating the combatants, the Yugoslav army turned its attention from Slovenia to Croatia. It was a lopsided contest. Possessing greater firepower, the federal army moved to secure nearly one-third of Croatian territory.[54] One-time dentist Milan Babic established himself as the Serbian president of Krajina, an enclave in eastern Croatia. The Milosevic government developed a plan to resettle the occupied area with Serbs. The Croatian army, together with mercenaries and paramilitaries, tried to check the federal army's advance but could do little against the more advanced airpower. Both sides committed egregious human rights abuses, but it is generally accepted that Serbia and the federal army are responsible for the lion's share.[55]

The conflict was not confined to Croatia and Slovenia. The war has also threatened the territorial integrity of Bosnia-Herzogovina. The center of the country and also the center of any possible territorial restructuring, Bosnia has perhaps the most to lose. Once forced to identify as either Serbian or Croatian in the early part of the 20th century, the Bosnian Moslems were able to achieve "ethnic" status in the early 1960s and have pushed for "nation" status ever since. In the 1990 elections, a Bosnian Islamic party narrowly edged out Serbian and Croatian parties but was obliged by its slim majority to form a coalition government.[56] But external factors were not in favor of such consensus. During the summer of 1991, Milosevic and Tudjman met secretly to divide Bosnia-Herzogovina between them, a meeting which produced no conclusive outcome.[57] When Bosnia declared its independence from Yugoslavia in October 1991, the ethnic Serbs in the republic balked, eliminating perhaps the last positive sign of cooperation from the region.[58] On the eve of the introduction of UN troops, Serbia and Croatia set about once again to divide the Bosnian spoils.[59]

The remaining two republics have different stakes in the conflict. The smallest republic and traditionally a loyal Serbian standby, Montenegro has more recently made independent noises. Montenegrin leader Momir Bulatovic has moved closer to accepting a European-brokered peace treaty.[60] In the past, too, Macedonia has sided with Serbia in inter-republic matters. After all, it is only in Yugoslavia, *federal* Yugoslavia, that Macedonians are a recognized national group (neither Bulgaria nor Greece considers them so).[61] At the same time, clashes between Serbs and Macedonians have recently increased, and some Macedonians fear that the country will simply be added (or "returned" as the Serbian nationalists put it) to greater Serbia.[62] Although the single largest political group to emerge from the Macedonian election is nationalist, a left coalition actually won the majority of seats. If there is one republic that might have supported a true democratic federation, it was Macedonia. Forced to choose sides, the republic opted for independence, encountering strong resistance from Greece but garnering recognition from a Bulgaria eager to see Serbia's power balanced.

When Germany recognized Croatia and Slovenia in early 1992, the old Yugoslavia was laid to rest. The debate over recognition—with the French, British, United States, and United Nations initially opposing the German decision—revealed the divisions over Western policy toward the region. After managing to secure a fragile ceasefire, the United Nations proposed a peace-keeping force of 13,000, its largest since the Congo operation of the early 1960s. Having achieved newfound recognition for Croatia, Tudjman immediately began to flex new muscle, disrupting the UN accord with claims on Bosnia-Herzogovina, insisting on retaking the disputed enclaves, and contracting for new military hardware.[63]

Another disruptive factor was Babic, the leader of Krajina. Having established his position by virtue of the war, the dentist-who-would-be-king was reluctant to jeopardize his presidency in peacetime by agreeing to UN supervision. Eager to broker an agreement if only to salvage its own ravaged economy, Serbia worked to persuade the Krajina Serbs to change their minds. They eventually did, over Babic's objections.

Peace-keeping troops will not, by themselves, solve Yugoslavia's problems. The troops can separate warring factions, but they cannot turn back the clock. The war has destroyed lives and stirred up old hatreds.

It has also shaken the social fabric of the region, extinguishing much that was progressive about Yugoslav society. The country once had, for instance, a flourishing civil society—peace groups, women's networks, environmental movements, human rights organizations. In Slovenia, where the alternative groups were the chief promoters of democratic culture, the atmosphere has now changed. Whereas the majority of the population supported disarmament in 1989, such a proposal is deemed utopian today. The war has also squeezed pluralism out of the political sphere—civil strife demands national unity. Those who opposed the war in Serbia were branded traitors. Dissent has become difficult in Croatia. The struggle of Kosovo Albanians for self-determination has been completely overshadowed.

There has been some opposition to the war. A peace caravan, carrying 400 people from Europe and North America, made its final stop in Bosnia at the end of September 1991. Although it did not generate very much support in Serbia or Croatia, the caravan met with enthusiastic response from Bosnians—10,000 at the final rally in Sarajevo. During the war, the large number of Serbian deserters indicated further the antipathy among young people toward the Milosevic policy. Aside from these encouraging responses, however, voices from the peace, human rights, and women's movements have been drowned out by nationalism and militarism.

The debate on state structures has not been canceled by war, merely shifted to the realm of interstate relations. The problems of resolving regional and ethnic differences in a state structure, reminiscent of the Moslem and Hindu standoff in post-colonial India, still remain for Yugoslavia's replacement, whatever it will be called. And what holds true for Yugoslavia, applies to the region as a whole: the balance of unity and diversity in politics is not so easily achieved, claims to European heritage notwithstanding.

Federation is elsewhere

The crisis in Yugoslavia has challenged two pillars of recent European consensus—territorial integrity and state structure. On the first issue, Europe has for the past 45 years been quite explicit—there shall be no redrawing of borders by force.[64] To dissolve borders through economic integration is one thing; to redraw borders through the creation of new nation-states is quite another. Through integration, the countries of Western Europe cede a measure of sovereignty to supranational institutions such as a European bank, a European parliament, and a European court. Indeed, much of what has traditionally defined the nation-state—a separate currency, distinct tariffs, a unique set of laws—will disappear in Western Europe by the end of the 20th century, replaced by Euro-this and Euro-that. In Eastern Europe and the post-Soviet Union, on the other hand, borders are being re-established to separate currencies and cultures.

Western Europe was certainly willing to bid farewell to Comecon and the Warsaw Pact, thus accepting the collapse of transnational mechanisms in Eastern Europe. It has shown far greater reluctance to recognize any new borders in the East. Contested borders have bloodied European history, particularly in the first part of the 20th century. To suddenly call into question these borders today may reawaken old conflicts or intensify current ones (Corsica, Jena, Flanders, the Basque area, not to mention throughout the former Soviet Union). By recognizing the independence of Croatia and Slovenia in early 1992, the EC has acceded to the inevitable: remaining inflexible on the border issue would have produced the same violence and chaos that the original consensus was designed to avoid.

On state structure, the consensus has often been overlooked. The development of federal structures has been one of the truly underappreciated revolutions of the modern era. Federations have traditionally been the democratic solution to balancing the demands of multiethnicity: a federal government and a set of republics, cantons, lander, or states divide up political responsibilities, ensuring a measure of both central stability and regional autonomy.[65] The United States, Switzerland, Australia, Canada, the former Soviet Union: these are all examples of multi-ethnic nations that have, with varying degrees of success, struck a balance between unity and diversity.

The age of nation-states offered two principal options for government structure: the federation or the unitary state.[66] An arrangement in which the center is not sovereign, confederations by contrast have existed only fitfully in Europe—the Netherlands from the 16th to 18th century, Germany for part of the 19th century, Switzerland roughly until 1948. Even outside Europe, confederations have been unsuccessful—as in the United States—and have not survived into the 20th century.[67]

Despite the historical record, Czechoslovakia, the post-Soviet Union, and Yugoslavia have all considered confederal structures. Federations, after all, have been linked with communist control in these countries. But establishing an effective substitute has been difficult. The world simply is not prepared to deal with a confederation. Such structures cannot join international organizations or sign human rights conventions because they would not be considered states according to the informal international consensus.[68]

More critically, such confederations would have grave internal pressures to resist. Take, for example, the new Commonwealth of Independent States which has brought together 11 of the former Soviet republics. Like the *matryoshka* dolls that conceal smaller and smaller dolls within, each new Commonwealth state contains minority regions and then minority regions within these as well. Poles in Lithuania, Azerbaijanis in Armenia, Tadzhiks in Uzbekistan, Gagauz in Moldava, Russians in Kazakhstan, Chechen-Ingush in Russia—these and hundreds of other cases demonstrate that the devolution of power from federation to confederation may not be the final one. Why do Russians have a right to a republic and we don't, ask the Tartars. (And then won't we be discriminated against in turn, asks the Russian minority within the Tartar autonomous zone.)

Federations, which are democratic in both structure *and* process, protect minority rights. Without federal government intervention, the South would never have accepted integration in the 1960s, and the Civil Rights Movement would have been considerably weakened. The comparison can be drawn out further. The rhetoric of "states' rights," whether during the 1960s or under Reagan, had its racist, exclusionary dimension. The logical endpoint of such a reading of states' rights—partition and the forced homogenization of populations—has a dubious track record.[69] Autonomy without constitutional guarantees for minorities and the democratic and legal procedures to enforce such guarantees is simply unacceptable. In an imperfect world, federations offer a democratic framework for a healthy multiculturalism.

In Yugoslavia, the federal system broke down in 1990, and the European Community, because it had never developed mechanisms for handling such situations, was helpless. Its insistence on democratic elections may have been fine in theory; given the Yugoslav constitutional barriers preventing an agreement on free, federal elections, however, the ensuing republic elections only exacerbated the problems. The EC should have instead made its financial aid contingent on free elections at the federal level.

War didn't sharpen the EC's thinking. In its attempts to forge a lasting compromise between Milosevic and Tudjman, the EC managed to act, in the words of EC Commission president Jacques Delors, like "an adolescent taking on an adult problem."[70] Yugoslavia was the second major foreign policy challenge for Europe after German unification, and in this, Europe failed dismally. The United States wasn't any better. With characteristic aplomb, the Bush administration distanced itself as much as possible from the conflict. "After all, it's not our problem," one US official commented early on in the war. "It's a European problem."[71]

Having missed earlier opportunities, the international community can only fall back on tools of damage control such as peace-keepers.

More critically, the West is repeating the same mistakes with the rest of the region. The economic austerity packages foisted on the governments of Eastern Europe and the new Commonwealth of Independent States only aggravate ethnic disputes and erode the legitimacy of newly democratic political institutions. Nationalism provides the satisfaction of scapegoating and the imagined community of interests that fragile pluralism has yet to produce. Outside observers might point out that the Yugoslav scenario proves the ultimate irrationality of nationalist pretensions. It might be difficult to expect, however, that any group of people suffering from economic deprivation and political malaise will act rationally. Decrying the stupidity of the Yugoslav civil war, other groups in the region may nonetheless rush headlong into similarly bloody conflicts.

* * *

At the periphery of Europe, the convulsions of a new era are beginning. For a time, the Cold War subordinated the interests of nation-states to the requirements of the bloc system. Western Europe ceded autonomy on foreign policy questions to the United States and NATO while economic decisions were increasingly being made within the European Community; Eastern European countries coordinated with (or had their policies coordinated by) the Soviet Union. With the end of the Cold War came the end of the bloc system. Europe has yet to define its new independent foreign policy, and Yugoslavia must suffer for this lag in development. But at least the West can maintain certain cooperative institutions (EC, CSCE) that temper the excesses of the nation-state. Eastern Europe and the Soviet Union have not been so fortunate. With no transnational institutions carrying over from the bloc era, Eastern Europe is forced back into the world of 19th-century nation-building, and this recapitulation of history is not surprisingly accompanied by an upsurge in nationalism.

Rather than absorbing the East into NATO or expanding the EC immediately, the West should encourage Eastern Europe and the former Soviet Union to establish collective security arrangements and cooperative economic policies. In this fashion, the issues of borders and state structure become less explosive. If Slovakia or Macedonia or Armenia is represented in a regional body, there will be less emphasis on autonomy within the recently revived but already anachronistic nation-states. Without such regional solutions, Yugoslavia will convulse the Balkans, the

Balkans will destabilize Eastern Europe and the Soviet Union, and the East will threaten to spread the chaos westward.

Shortly after World War I, Karl Polanyi has observed, 19th-century civilization finally collapsed.[72] The 19th-century Concert of Vienna's balance of power, the gold standard, the self-regulating market, and the liberal state had all been whisked away by communism, fascism, and the welfare state. With the emergence of the League of Nations and then the United Nations, it seemed as though the last element of 19th-century civilization, the nation-state, would also leave the world's stage. It was not to be. Indeed, the nation-state would enjoy a renaissance in the post-colonial era of the 1950s and 1960s.

With the collapse of bi-polarism, the integration of Europe, and the increasing internationalization of culture, capital, and communications, the nation-state may have finally met its match, however. National powers are increasingly being delegated upward to supranational organizations and downward to regions and localities. Soon the nation-state may be nothing more than a formality—a flag, an anthem—the institutional equivalent of the royal family. Localities will be self-governing; international organizations will monitor political, economic, and human rights abuses, and enforce internationally agreed upon charters. The nation-state will have joined the transitory structures of the past, and Polanyi's description of the collapse of 19th-century civilization will have been realized.

What is presently happening in Eastern Europe seems to throw a monkey wrench into this rosy scenario. The 19th century has returned with a vengeance, despite the acuity of Polanyi's insights. They might only be temporary, these outbreaks of nationalist violence. Or they may be more permanent. A great deal depends on how the European Community handles the situation. Let us then, in the conclusion, return to the beginning and re-examine afresh the European idea.

Conclusion

Things come together

If it is anachronous, as advocates of the idea of European union often tell us, to think of ourselves any longer as Germans or British or French, it may also be no less anachronous to think of ourselves as Europeans.[1]

—Geoffrey Barraclough

If Yugoslavia is Eastern Europe's worst nightmare, then Brussels constitutes its radiant future. As provisional seat of the European Community, Brussels will both directly and indirectly influence the development of Eastern Europe. A powerful magnetic force, the process of political and economic integration in the West is already changing life from Warsaw to Sofia perhaps more radically than did the events of 1989. The revolutions were, after all, sudden ruptures; the inexorable pull of the West has a longer history, and will consequently cast a longer shadow upon the future.

Attempts to integrate Western Europe go back to Charlemagne's unification of the Frankish tribes. European integration was viewed as a necessary bulwark against an enemy with a thousand faces (Turkish, Norman, Saracen, Magyar, and so on). European integration in the 20th century has also had its useful enemies. Establishing a coal and steel community that linked historic adversaries, the 1951 Treaty of Paris directly countered the consolidation of communism in the Soviet bloc and the creation two years earlier of the CMEA. This resurrection of the Concert of Vienna proved to be an invaluable accompaniment to NATO in rounding out a united Cold War front.

What began as a rudimentary arrangement governing access to coal and steel became, with the Treaty of Rome in 1957, a trade zone free from internal tariffs—the European Common Market.[2] But those pushing for a more federal Europe had greater aspirations, including closer economic coordination and even more integrated political and social policymaking. The breakthrough came with the 1986 Single European Act.[3] Accelerating what had only several years earlier appeared to be a moribund process, the assembled ministers of the 12-member European Community (Belgium, Germany, France, Italy, Luxembourg, Netherlands, Denmark, Ireland, United Kingdom, Greece, Spain, and Portugal) set 1992 as the magic year for a Europe without internal frontiers.

Another threat, more amorphous than any given regional hegemon, was conjured up to justify this further integration. Europe had to come together simply to survive in the increasingly competitive world of international trade.[4] Economically more than the sum of its parts, Western Europe exports three times as much as the United States or Japan.[5] Integration is expected to improve this position, adding 5 percent to the Community's gross domestic product and creating two to five million new jobs.[6]

Besides a response to various threats, what does European integration mean? In 1951, Ernest Bevin, Britain's foreign secretary described it as the ability "to take a ticket at Victoria Station and go anywhere I damn well please." Since that time, integration has developed into much more than unrestricted travel. Europe '92 has its free market side (a single market "free of the physical, technical and tax frontiers that still hinder the movement of people, capital, goods and service")[7] as well as its regulatory virtues (a uniform set of laws, social policies, and democratic procedures). At their meeting in the Netherlands at the end of 1991, the assembled ministers also agreed to go ahead with European Monetary Union (EMU). Before the end of the 20th century, Western Europeans will buy and sell with one currency—the European Currency Unit.[8]

A prosperous market, a well-developed social policy, a stable currency, unrestricted permission to travel, work, and live anywhere on the continent—unified Europe presents quite a compelling vision for the post-communist countries of the East. No wonder that virtually every political movement of any significance in Eastern Europe has placed integration with the EC as a top priority. The great East-West divide—in wealth, in stability, in expectations—has not diminished the enthusiasm. These substantial differences are only temporary if the stated intentions of every European leader are to be believed. Integration will put everything right, harmonizing all that is disharmonious. East Europeans must simply wait their turn, patiently and without complaint.

The East is not taking any chances. To guarantee eventual entry into the EC and to prove their innate European-ness, the new Eastern European governments have attempted to act politically, function economically, and think culturally as in the West. Radical alternatives more in keeping with the revolutionary principles of the opposition movements have been discouraged.

The preceding chapters described what these indigenous alternatives might have produced. East Germany might have still existed today, perhaps not as an autonomous country, but at least as a political structure within a united Germany distinguished by its grassroots political structures. With a well-organized workforce, Poland might have been a social democracy with workers playing an important *political* role in determining the country's future path. Led by a powerful Green party, Hungary might have been the ecological trendsetter in the region, translating international funds into a model Green economy: productive, efficient, and clean.

Drawing upon their pre-revolutionary philosophies, Vaclav Havel and Jiri Dienstbier might have made Czech and Slovak foreign policy a moral exemplar and Europe a bloc-free and nuclear-free space. Secret services connected to the previous regimes—such as Ceausescu's Securitate—could have been abolished and replaced by a police force well-scrutinized by the public. Members of different ethnic groups could have worked together as fellow citizens after the revolutions instead of engaging in power struggles that subjected the small and the weak to the will of the large and the strong, as happened in Bulgaria. Yugoslavia might have been a democratic federation, with problems addressed in a political framework, rather than in a military confrontation.

Instead, today's Eastern Europeans hear the rhetoric and promises of European-style prosperity but experience the angry, alienating chaos of everyday life. Western Europe, of course, does not want a region of impoverished and irate xenophobes on its border. But European policies have unfortunately pushed the East in that direction. For instance, at the end of 1991, the EC signed "association agreements" with Poland, Hungary, and Czechoslovakia. Concluded after strenuous negotiations, these agreements on trade and assistance prepared the ground for eventual inclusion in an integrated Europe.

The agreements fail on two levels, however. Instead of treating the region as a whole, the EC has selected out the most promising candidates, drawing a familiar line that separates the "more" European from their lessers. Moreover, the agreements substitute for a more substantial financial commitment. Eastern Germany remains an economic backwater despite the considerable capital pumped in to it by Bonn. The rest of Eastern Europe will not receive resources comparable to the intra-German largesse. Not even opening EC markets to key Eastern exports, the association agreements are a sop thrown to the increasingly disappointed post-communist governments.[9]

Western business has been, as one might expect, even less charitable. The Organization of Economic Cooperation and Development (24 of the richest countries of the world) puts the matter daintily: "Given the extremely imperfect asset markets in the region there is a risk that private investment will in part be characterised by predatory maneuvers rather than longer term developmental considerations."[10] Translated, this means exploitation. The countries of Eastern Europe need foreign investment and are willing to accept social strain in the short term to get the products on the shelves that will alleviate social strain in the long term. Various deals have already been made: Italian firms acquiring huge profit margins in Poland; West German media magnates buying up newspapers in Hungary; Greek firms establishing over-the-border operations in Bulgaria to escape stringent environmental laws. The new Eastern European governments spend more time encouraging this activity than regulating it; without coordinated and massive Western assistance, the post-communist governments are desperate for capital in whatever form it arrives.

A particular type of modernization, in other words, is being imposed in Eastern Europe—by businesses from below, by Western governments and multilateral institutions from above. The IMF and World Bank have made loans contingent on "structural adjustment": reduced government spending, less public moneys, imposed austerity, undemocratic economic reform. This form of Westernization has been exported to other regions of the world with grave consequences. "If Eastern Europe copies the mistakes of its Western models," George Brockway writes in *The New Leader,* "the best it can hope for is that the suffering imposed on the present generation will be followed by a better life for the next generation. This, you will recall, was the promise of communism, too. Such promises are rarely fulfilled."[11] Spurred on by these promises, Eastern Europe is being turned into an exploitation zone, a waystation for escapees from post-Soviet problems, a dumping ground for Western waste and old technology. When the ecological sins of capitalism are added to the already considerable problems left by communism, this zone will be anything but Green. "Though the countries of the region have a unique chance to avoid some of the West's mistakes," writes Hilary French, "powerful forces pull them toward repeating the errors."[12]

For all its grand statements, the West has done little to help Eastern Europe. The Western model has so far translated into little more than economic austerity and political instability. The cultural impact of "Europe," to return to a theme from the very beginning of this book, may have an even more problematic influence on the East.

The consolidation of European identity culminating in a new European union is part of a centuries-old process that required the identification and often the fabrication of enemies, both at home and abroad. Opposition to various perceived threats—the "marauding" Turk, the "traitorous" Jew—helped to forge a unified European identity from a collection of often very different national characters. Fears of the Soviet Union—in part manipulated by the United States—pushed Europe together again after the seemingly irreconcilable animosities of World War II. By the mid-1980s Italian journalist Luigi Barzini could write that "the West is in danger, as everybody knows. Europe is where Western ideas and hopes were born. It is their home. We want to defend them simply because we know that life without them is not livable."[13] The threat of communism had replaced the threats of previous eras: of other European countries, of other classes, of other non-Christian peoples, of Others in general. With the disappearance of communism as a formal threat, the European idea is in need of a new unholy contrast. A resurgent Russia? An isolationist United States? A economically expanding Japan? The debt-laden Third World?

Some might object that the consolidation of European identity will be a more humane process. With turmoil in the post-Cold War world still convulsing dozens of countries, Europe seems a veritable island of tranquility and progress (Yugoslavia being the unappetizing exception). The unpleasant byproducts of European identity-building are often dismissed as temporary manifestations in an otherwise enlightened space (the implication, to recall Konwicki, is that "European" simply means human while inhumanity is only imposed from the outside—Stalin—or arises from a singular mutation—Hitler). Hugh Seton-Watson declares with a "civilized" air: "Europe remains the heart of the human race."[14] That heart, diseased for so long from internal strain, now aspires to revitalize world civilization.

But beware: the new Europe also has its unpleasant facets including racism, austerity capitalism, intolerance, and greed. Fascism and xenophobia are by no means restricted to the eastern parts of Europe. Jean-Marie Le Pen capitalizes on widespread French intolerance (25 percent of French citizens in a recent poll thought France has too many Jews; 94 percent of those polled believed racism, mostly toward Arabs, was rampant in their country).[15] French fascist groups, designed to "defend Christian Western civilization" cast themselves as modern-day crusaders saving a holy Europe from the infidels.[16] There is also anti-Pakistani violence in Britain, anti-immigrant sentiment in ostensibly tolerant Sweden and Denmark, and a racist skinhead network throughout the region.[17] After a rash of bias crimes against minorities, 75 percent of Italians in a major opinion poll declared that they prefered to close the borders to all immigration.[18] This sentiment infects more than simply Italians. So tight have the new EC immigration laws become that even the generally conservative *Economist* editorialized against the policy slant toward the "mainly white and rich."[19]

Nor is austerity capitalism to convulse only Eastern Europe. Although the EC is carefully larding its documents and statements with references to social provisions, the full impact of European unification on workers and farmers is by no means clear.[20] And the new economic divide in Europe has sent thousands of Eastern workers West, only to find, in the words of *Business Week*, "long days, low pay, and a moldy cot."[21] Worse still, the post-Soviet Union has already begun to copy the mistakes of the Balcerowicz model, urged on by the same Western economists who first developed Polish "shock therapy."[22]

Then there is the military question. As the era of bi-polarism comes to a welcome end—with the Soviet Union no more and the United States drifting into a peculiar superpower provincialism—the European Community appears well positioned to fill the new geopolitical void. Not by the sword: expensive arms races and military interventions do not figure as largely in the new European identity as they have in the identities of the two declining titans. With greater emphasis on the social and less on the military, Europe seems well on the way toward becoming—to borrow a Bushism—a kinder, gentler superpower.

Still, superpowers tend to act in their own interests according to often ruthless domestic and international calculations, regardless of the longevity of democratic institutions (as in the United States) or the richness of culture (as in the former Soviet Union). Although still functioning beneath the NATO umbrella, the EC will in the 1990s gradually establish a more independent military line. As the aftershocks of the Cold War's demise continue to abate, unified Europe will see that its interests are no longer completely compatible with the United States.

While the EC has yet to put forward an alternative to NATO, it has nonetheless emphasized various complementary structures, including the military grouping of EC nations known as the Western European Union. France and Germany serve as the pivotal members of this Union and have caused some speculation that the Union could serve as the eventual replacement of NATO and become the military arm that will safeguard and perhaps even extend the EC's economic power. The French have possessed an independent military since withdrawing from NATO in 1966, while the Germans have an extensive weapons-producing capability.[23] Together with the British military, the new Euro-army would more than make up for the current US and Canadian forces in NATO. An independent military makes the superpower potentially aggressive, regardless of benign pronouncements to the contrary.

Despite the economic manipulations, the cultural chauvinisms, and the potential militarism, the idea of Europe also provides some real hope for Eastern Europeans. Western Europe offers a more equitable economy and a more participatory democracy than what either the

United States or Soviet Union has brought into the world. The Helsinki Accords—whose principles of human rights permeated the philosophies of the oppositions—can still provide inspiration for the region. "I would like to read the Helsinki Final Act," Timothy Garton Ash writes, "and what has followed it, as...a charter that Europe has given itself, for itself, but also against itself—not against American values, not even primarily against Soviet values, but against the perverted values of European nationalism and European barbarism."[24]

It would be truly breathtaking if one day we could agree with Geoffrey Barraclough's statement at the beginning of this chapter. It would be fitting if European identity lost its exclusive meaning just as it began to establish itself in the post-Cold War era. It would be fitting if the Eastern European dream of becoming full partners with Western Europe occurred just as Europe itself opened up more fully to the world at large. The principle by which the EC subsidizes a Portugal until it reaches the same level as a Germany should be applied to Eastern Europe, should be applied to the world at large. This transformation of Europe would require, of course, that the fledgling alternatives represented by the revolutionary civic movements of 1989 are not extinguished, but nurtured and ultimately adopted throughout Europe.

Utopian?

Perhaps. But, in important respects, so were Solidarity, Charter 77, New Forum, the environmental movement in Hungary, the alternative groups in Slovenia, the human rights activists in Bulgaria, the brave, isolated dissidents in Romania. The revolutions of 1989 were their victories: unbelievable, thrilling, fragile. Such utopianism, when applied to the concrete problems of a post-Cold War world, will prove invaluable as we struggle together to create more democratic and more equitable societies.

Background statistics

The seven countries of Eastern Europe discussed in this book have a combined population of 136.4 million people. In 1989, the economies of the region declined (in terms of net material output) by 1 percent. In 1990, the output fell another 10 percent. By 1991, the net regional output had declined another 15 percent. Here is a snapshot view of each country.

Population and per capita GNP figures are from the CIA's 1990 report. Since per capita GNP figures can be computed in various ways, those presented are meant only for comparison purposes. Other statistics are from the Economic Commission for Europe's *Economic Bulletin for Europe,* Volume 43, November 1991. The figures for percentage decline in industrial output 1990-1991 are only estimates, as no firm figures are available.

(East) Germany

Population: 16.5 million

Religion: Protestant majority with Catholic minority

Per capita GNP: $9,679

Decline in industrial output from 1989 to 1990: 28 percent

Decline in industrial output from 1990 to 1991: 50 percent

Unemployment rate (December 1990): 7.3 percent

Unemployment rate (September 1991): 11.7 percent

Poland

Population: 37.8 million

Religion: over 90 percent Catholic

Per capita GNP: $4,565

Hard-currency debt (1991): $40.2 billion

Decline in industrial output from 1989 to 1990: 23 percent

Decline in industrial output from 1990 to 1991: 15 percent

Unemployment rate (December 1990): 6.1 percent

Unemployment rate (September 1991): 10.4 percent

Hungary

Population: 10.6 million

Religion: 65 percent Catholic, 30 percent Protestant

Per capita GNP: $6,108

Hard-currency debt (1991): $18.2 billion

Decline in industrial output from 1989 to 1990: 5 percent

Decline in industrial output from 1990 to 1991: 12 percent

Unemployment rate (December 1990): 1.7 percent

Unemployment rate (September 1991): 6.1 percent

Czechoslovakia

Population: 15.6 million

Religion: Catholic majority with Protestant minority

Per capita GNP: $7,878

Hard-currency debt (1991): $7.2 billion

Decline in industrial output from 1989 to 1990: 3.7 percent

Decline in industrial output from 1990 to 1991: 23 percent

Unemployment rate (December 1990): 1 percent

Unemployment rate (September 1991): 5.6 percent

Romania

Population: 23.2 million

Religion: Orthodox majority with Catholic minority

Per capita GNP: $3,445

Hard-currency debt (1991): $2 billion

Decline in industrial output from 1989 to 1990: 19.8 percent

Decline in industrial output from 1990 to 1991: 18 percent

Unemployment rate (August 1991): 2.2 percent

Bulgaria

Population: 9 million

Religion: Orthodox majority with Moslem minority

Per capita GNP: $5,710

Hard-currency debt (1991): $10.4 billion

Decline in industrial output from 1989 to 1990: 14 percent

Decline in industrial output from 1990 to 1991: 32 percent

Unemployment rate (December 1990): 1.5 percent

Unemployment rate (September 1991): 7.8 percent

Yugoslavia

Population: 23.7 million

Religion: 40 percent Orthodox, 30 percent Catholic, 12 percent Moslem

Per capita GNP: $5,464

Hard-currency debt (1991): $10.5 billion

Decline in industrial output from 1989 to 1990: 10.3 percent

Decline in industrial output from 1990 to 1991: 20 percent

Unemployment rate (June 1991): 14.7 percent

References

All interviews that are not marked otherwise were conducted by the author. *Report on Eastern Europe* (changed to *RFE/RL Research Report* in January 1992) is published by Radio Free Europe and Radio Liberty. This report is, despite the reputation of the parent organizations, a valuable source of information on the region. *East European Reporter* is a more left-leaning quarterly; *Eastern European Reporter* is published by a financial clearinghouse; *Across Frontiers* is, sadly, no more. *Warsaw Voice, Voice Business,* and *The Insider* are all English-language papers published in Poland. Any translations from Polish that occur in the text were made by the author.

Preface

1. Malcolm Bradbury, *Rates of Exchange* (New York: Knopf, 1983).

2. Timothy Garton Ash, *The Uses of Adversity* (New York: Vintage, 1990), p. 299.

3. See, e.g., Timothy Garton Ash, *The Magic Lantern* (New York: Random House, 1990); the compilation of *New York Times* articles in Bernard Gwertzman and Michael Kaufman, eds., *The Collapse of Communism* (New York: Random House, 1990); Charles Gati, *The Bloc That Failed* (Bloomington: Indiana University Press, 1990); Elie Abel, *The Shattered Bloc* (Boston: Houghton Mifflin, 1990); William Echikson, *Lighting the Night* (New York: William Morrow, 1990); Gwyn Prins, ed., *Spring in Winter: The 1989 Revolutions* (Manchester: Manchester University Press, 1990; Misha Glenny, *The Rebirth of History* (New York: Penguin, 1990); J.F. Brown, *Surge to Freedom* (Durham, NC: Duke University Press, 1991); Ivo Banac, ed., *Eastern Europe in Revolution* (Ithaca: Cornell University Press, 1992). For a Marxist analysis, see Alex Callinicos, *The Revenge of History* (University Park: The Pennsylvania State University Press, 1991).

Introduction

1. Stanislaw Baranczak, *Breathing Under Water* (Cambridge: Harvard University Press, 1990).

2. The Spring 1989 issue of *Telos* devoted entirely to Eastern Europe offers a window onto the emerging diversity of the region, with articles on Hungarian entrepreneurialism, Albanian *glasnost,* and the lack of reform in Czechoslovakia.

3. Laszlo Bruszt and David Stark, "Remaking the Political Field in Hungary: From the Politics of Confrontation to the Politics of Competition," in Banac, ed.

4. See, e.g., the *New York Times* editorial, 3/12/85, on Gorbachev's succession, which reads, in part, "Continuity, caution and consensus are the hallmarks of a system revolutionary in doctrine but deeply conservative in practice. Whatever his ambitions, Mr. Gorbachev is unlikely soon to make waves."

5. For a partial list of sources, see John Feffer, *Beyond Detente* (New York: Hill and Wang, 1990), p. 162 (footnote #4).

6. See Karen Dawisha, *Eastern Europe, Gorbachev and Reform: The Great Challenge* (Cambridge: Cambridge University Press, 1990), p. 207. For Gorbachev's more developed statement at the 70th anniversary of the October revolution in 1987, see p. 87.

7. Francis Clines, "Gorbachev Calls, Then Polish Party Drops Its Demands," *New York Times,* 9/22/89.

8. Gwertzman and Kaufman, eds., *The Collapse of Communism,* p. 163.

9. *Ibid.,* p. 204.

10. Peter Gowan, "Old Medicine, New Bottles," *World Policy Journal,* Winter 1991-92.

11. Carl Bernstein, "The Holy Alliance," *Time,* 2/24/92.

Chapter 1

1. Milan Kundera, "The Tragedy of Central Europe," *New York Review of Books,* 4/26/84, p. 36.

2. There is some controversy over the meaning of "Europe." Though most agree that the word has Semitic origin, Denys Hay maintains that the Greek derivation in fact means "broad-faced." Denys Hay, *Europe: The Emergence of an Idea* (Edinburgh: Edinburgh University Press, 1957), p. 1.

3. Kundera, "The Tragedy of Central Europe."

4. At 1.27 million square kilometers, Eastern Europe is one-seventh the size of the United States, one-sixteenth the size of the Soviet Union, but four times the size of Great Britain. These figures come from David Turnock, *Eastern Europe: An Economic and Political Geography* (New York: Routledge, 1989), p. 4.

5. For the influence of this opposition between Greek and Persian on the development of the later dichotomy of "Oriental" and "Occidental," see Edward Said, *Orientalism* (New York: Vintage, 1979), pp. 56-7. As Samir Amin points out, the conceptualization of Greece as Western and Persia as Eastern came much later. See his *Eurocentrism* (New York: Monthly Review, 1989), p. 26. Also see Bernard Lewis, *The Muslim Discovery of Europe* (New York: Norton, 1982), p. 59.

6. Some locate Europe's origins in the fusion of Gallic and Roman under Julius Caesar's celebrated conquests. Denis de Rougemont, *The Idea of Europe* (New York: Meridian, 1968), p. 6.

7. Hay, p. 14.

8. Oscar Halecki, *The Limits and Divisions of European History* (New York: Sheed and Ward, 1950), p. 28. Later, in the 16th century, the Turks would limit European expansion to the East, thus encouraging the exploration/exploitation of the New World. Paul Coles, *The Ottoman Impact on Europe* (New York: Harcourt, Brace and World, 1968), p. 108.

9. Bernard Lewis cites the example of the Islamic writer Said ibn Ahmad who, in 1068, discriminated between those peoples possessed of a science and those not. Indians, Arabs, Greeks, and Jews fell into the civilized category; the Chinese and Turks received honorable mentions; the Europeans did not even merit consideration. Lewis, p. 68.

10. Hay, p. 25. De Rougemont elaborates: "There is the fact that in the eighth century those who defended this continent found it natural to be described not as the defenders of a Romania which had become mythical, or of the West in general, or of the papacy, or of their particular 'nation' or homeland, but as members of the same family of nations." De Rougemont, p. 45.

11. Philippe Wolff, *The Awakening of Europe* (Middlesex: Penguin, 1985), p. 19.

12. On the importance of Christian consensus, see, e.g., David Herlihy, *Medieval Culture and Society* (New York: Harpers, 1968), p. xiv.

13. Eugene Rice, Jr., *The Foundations of Modern Europe, 1460-1559* (New York: Norton, 1970), p. 1. Put another way, Europeans created a capitalist world-system after 1500. Immanuel Wallerstein, *The Modern World-System I* (London: Academic Press, 1980).

14. Rice, p. 38.

15. *Ibid.*, p. 32.

16. Martin Bernal, *Black Athena* (New Brunswick, NJ: Rutgers University Press, 1987).

17. Amin, p. 73.

18. The association between the new worlds of the Americas and the Ancients was sufficiently novel in the early 19th century to inspire John Keats's comparison between a translation of Homer and Cortez's conquering of the Aztecs. "On First Looking into Chapman's Homer" (1816).

19. Rice, pp. 119-20.

20. Coles, p. 148.

21. Geoffrey Barraclough in Edward Stettner, ed., *Perspectives on Europe* (Cambridge: Schenkman, 1970), p. 7.

22. Paul Kennedy, *The Rise and Fall of Great Powers* (New York: Random House, 1987), p. 30.

23. E.L. Jones, *The European Miracle* (Cambridge: Cambridge University Press, 1981).

24. Peter Gunst, "Agrarian Systems of Central and Eastern Europe," in Daniel Chirot, ed., *The Origins of Backwardness in Eastern Europe* (Berkeley: University of California Press, 1989), pp. 53-4.

25. Eric Wolf, *Europe and the People Without History* (Berkeley: University of California Press, 1982); Eduardo Galleano, *Open Veins of Latin America* (New York: Monthly Review, 1973).

26. A handful of contemporary sources, for instance Frank Tipton and Robert Aldrich, *An Economic and Social History of Europe* (Baltimore: Johns Hopkins Press, 1987), have gone to some lengths to redress this wrong.

27. In a celebrated passage, Oscar Halecki attempts to locate the geographic boundaries between East and West, and although learned, the discussion serves chiefly to reveal the author's own prejudices as to who is and is not truly European. See Halecki, pp. 105-24.

28. Historian Geoffrey Bruun writes: "Their basic aim was to restore not the injustices of the old regime but its remembered virtues, above all the benefits of stable government and the security of a state system in reasonable equilibrium." Bruun, *Nineteenth Century European Civilization, 1815-1914* (London: Oxford University Press, 1969), p. 9.

29. Karl Marx, *The Eighteenth Brumaire of Louis Bonaparte* (New York: International Publishers, 1963), p. 15.

30. Norman Cantor and Samuel Berner, *The Modern Era, 1815 to the Present* (New York: Crowell, 1971), p. 62.

31. As historian Priscilla Robertson notes: "Most of what the men of 1848 fought for was brought about within a quarter of a century, and the men who accomplished it were most of them specific enemies of the 1848 movement. Thiers ushered in a third French Republic, Bismarck united Germany, and Cavour, Italy. Deak won autonomy for Hungary within a dual monarchy; a Russian czar freed the serfs; and the British manufacturing classes moved toward the freedoms of the People's Charter." Priscilla Robertson, *Revolutions of 1848: A Social History* (Princeton: Princeton University Press, 1952), p. 412.

32. Karl Polanyi, *The Great Transformation* (Boston: Beacon, 1957), p. 76.

33. *Ibid.*, p. 139.

34. Bruun, p. 172.

35. For more background on Eastern and Central European history, see the especially useful early chapters of Leslie Tihany, *A History of Middle Europe* (New Brunswick, NJ: Rutgers University Press, 1976). As Tihany points out, even the unity of the Jagiellonian monarchy bred "not only contempt but hatred as well" (p. 62).

36. Ivan Berend, *The Crisis Zone of Europe* (Cambridge: Cambridge University Press, 1986), p. 3. Also see Daniel Chirot, "Causes and Consequences of Backwardness," and Robert Brenner "Economic Backwardness in Eastern Europe in Light of Development in the West," in Chirot, ed., *The Origins of Backwardness in Eastern Europe.*

37. Rice, p. 42.

38. The German Fuggers' activities in Hungary—as copper barons and bankers—are one such example. *Ibid.*, p. 46.

39. Immanuel Wallerstein, *The Modern World-System II* (London: Academic Press, 1980), pp. 131-141.

40. Berend, p. 13. Also John Lampe, "Imperial Borderlands or Capitalist Periphery? Redefining Balkan Backwardness, 1520-1914," in Chirot, ed., *The Origins of Backwardness in Eastern Europe.*

41. Aleksander Gella, *Development of Class Structure in Eastern Europe* (Albany: State University of New York Press, 1989), pp. 97-8.

42. See Perry Anderson, *Lineages of the Absolutist State* (London: NLB, 1974).

43. Bruun, p. 23.

44. Berend, pp. 14-5.

45. Max Weber, *The Protestant Ethic and the Spirit of Capitalism* (New York: Scribner's, 1958).

46. Berend, p. 22.

47. Galleano, p. 11.

48. Thomas Friedman, *From Beirut to Jerusalem* (New York: Farrar, Straus and Giroux, 1989), p. 12.

49. Rice, p. 108.

50. "Admiration for the splendid culture of Austria-Hungary, and regret for its destruction, have become a cliche among historians, journalists, and politicians," writes Hugh Seton-Watson in *The "Sick Heart" of Modern Europe* (Seattle: University of Washington Press, 1975), p. 5; Franjo Tudjman prefers to stress the Habsburgs' foreign policy strengths: "The Habsburg empire played an important role in European history: It was a bulwark against the Ottoman onslaught on Europe and shielded numerous small nations both from Russian tsarist imperialism and the pan-German imperialism of the German Reich." *Nationalism in Contemporary Europe* (New York: Columbia University Press, 1981), p. 14.

51. Jacques Rupnik, *The Other Europe* (New York: Pantheon, 1989), p. 5.

52. Oscar Jaszi, *The Dissolution of the Habsburg Monarchy* (Chicago: University of Chicago Press, 1966), pp. 68-9.

53. *Ibid.*, p. 15. Robert Kann provides a very different picture in his *History of the Habsburg Empire, 1526-1918* (Berkeley: University of California Press, 1974). In Kann's generally dispassionate analysis, the excesses of the early years of empire are tempered by gradual reforms that, by the end of the 19th century, yielded major cultural advances.

54. Jaszi, pp. 116, 436.

55. The pressures of revolution and the aspirations of both liberal intellectuals and patriotic nationalists led to a period after 1849 of "neo-absolutism" before constitional absolutism took over in the 1860s. See Kann, pp. 210-16.

56. See, e.g., Kennedy, *The Rise and Fall of Great Powers*, pp. 151-58.

57. Tony Judt, "The Rediscovery of Central Europe," *Daedalus*, Winter 1990, vol. 119, no. 1, p. 48.

58. For more detailed discussion of these irredenta and pseudo-irredenta, see Jaszi, pp. 379-433.

59. *Ibid.*, p. 41.

60. Joseph Rothschild provides a thorough list of irredenta on the eve of World War I in *Return to Diversity* (New York: Oxford University Press, 1989), p. 8.

61. As two social historians point out: "The willingness of Czechs, Poles, Rumanians, South Slavs and Italians to submerge their interests in the struggle to maintain an empire dominated by Germans and Magyars disappeared rather rapidly." Tipton and Aldrich, p. 149.

62. Norman Cantor and Michael Werthman, eds., *The Twentieth Century: 1914 to the Present* (New York: Crowell, 1967), p. 9.

63. Rupnik, *The Other Europe*, p. 17.

64. Tipton and Aldrich, p. 251.

65. Norman Davies, *Heart of Europe: A Short History of Poland* (Oxford: Oxford University Press, 1987), p. 303.

66. See Krystyna Olszer, ed., *For Your Freedom and Ours* (New York: Unger, 1981), pp. 26-53, for excerpts of the 1791 Polish constitution and background on Polish humanists Andrzej Frycz Modrzewski (1503-1572), Stanislaw Staszic (1780-1820), and Hugo Kollataj (1750-1812).

67. For a look at Eastern European fascism, see Bela Vago, "Fascism in Eastern Europe," in Walter Laqueur, ed., *Fascism: A Reader's Guide* (Berkeley: University of California Press, 1976).

68. Charles Gati, *Hungary and the Soviet Bloc* (Durham: Duke University Press, 1986), p. 49.

69. Barbara Jelavich, *History of the Balkans, Twentieth Century*, vol. 2 (Cambridge: Cambridge University Press, 1983), p. 163.

70. Stevan Pavlowitch, *The Improbable Survivor: Yugoslavia and Its Problems, 1918-1988* (Columbus: Ohio State University Press, 1988), p. 37.

71. Stephen Borsody goes so far as to claim that if only Czechoslovakia and Hungary could have put aside their mutual antagonisms, the "national independence of the Danube Valley" could have been preserved. Borsody, *The Tragedy of Central Europe* (New Haven: Yale Concilium on International Area Studies, 1980), p. 48.

72. Davies, p. 65.

Chapter 2

1. John Acton, *Essays on Freedom and Power* (Gloucester, MA: Peter Smith, 1972), p. 335. Following this passage is the famous line: "Power tends to corrupt and absolute power corrupts absolutely."

2. See, e.g., V.I. Lenin, "Six Theses on the Immediate Tasks of the Soviet Government," in *Selected Works*, vol. 2 (Moscow: Progress Publishers, 1977), p. 622, and, in the same volume, "'Left-Wing' Childishness and Petty-Bourgeois Mentality," p. 631.

3. Moshe Lewin, *Russian Peasants and Soviet Power* (New York: Norton, 1975), p. 21.

4. For a more detailed discussion of this political struggle, see Stephen F. Cohen, *Bukharin and the Bolshevik Revolution* (New York: Vintage, 1975).

5. While Lenin was fascinated with US-style capitalism, Stalin seemed more interested in borrowing from the Prussian school of modernization, a process facilitated by military power. Stalin also drew from Russian history, particularly the reforms of Count Witte, who saw turn-of-the-century Russian agriculture as the source of funds for the modernization of his country.

6. For a short overview of the Stalinist model, see Paul Gregory, "The Stalinist Command Economy," in Jan Prybyla, ed., *Privatizing and Marketizing Socialism, The Annals of the American Academy of Political and Social Science* (Newbury Park, CA: Sage Publications, 1990).

7. For pros and cons, see Jan Adam, *Economic Reforms in the Soviet Union and Eastern Europe Since the 1960s* (New York: St. Martins, 1989), p. 16. For an in-depth critique of centralized

planning, see Janos Kornai's elaborations of his notions of disequilibrium, shortage, and "hard" and "soft" budget constraints in *Contradictions and Dilemmas* (Cambridge: MIT Press, 1986), and *Vision and Reality, Market and State* (New York: Routledge, 1990).

8. See Leszek Kolakowski's defense of Kant in *Modernity on Endless Trial* (Chicago: University of Chicago Press, 1990), pp. 44-54.

9. Hitler also sweetened the Axis deal, for instance, by promising Transylvania to the ally—Romania or Hungary—whichever offered most to the war effort against Russia. Rothschild, *Return to Diversity*, p. 41.

10. Soviet influence percentage-wise for the region was to be: Hungary (80 percent), Bulgaria (80 percent), Romania (80 percent), Yugoslavia (50 percent), Greece (10 percent). Charles Gati, *Hungary and the Soviet Bloc* (Durham: Duke University Press, 1986), p. 31.

11. In February 1946, Stalin made a speech predicting an "inevitable" war. George Kennan, in his famous "long telegram," pointed out something the US government mysteriously ignored: Stalin had not been referring to an inevitable war between the USSR and the West but to an unavoidable conflict between England and the United States. See Albert Resis, *Stalin, the Politburo, and the Onset of the Cold War, 1945-6*, The Carl Beck Papers in Russian and East European Studies, no. 701 (Pittsburgh: University of Pittsburgh Center for Russian and East European Studies, 1988). Anglo-American conflict over the zoning of post-war Germany may have influenced Stalin's scenario-making as well as remarks such as Truman's "[I]t is not Soviet communism I fear, but rather British imperialism." Quoted in John Ranelagh, *The Agency: The Rise and Decline of the CIA* (New York: Touchstone, 1987). A poll in February 1945 revealed that more Americans worried about conflicts with the British than with the Soviets. By May the situation had reversed, but Stalin was notoriously slow in adjusting to changes in the international situation. See Walter Isaacson and Evan Thomas, *The Wise Men* (New York: Simon and Schuster, 1988), p. 270.

12. For this argument in detail, see Robert Schaeffer, *Warpaths* (New York: Hill and Wang, 1990), pp. 46-59.

13. In 1938, Germany, Britain, France, and Italy accounted for 29.8 percent of world manufacturing output. The United States and Soviet Union produced 28.7 percent and 17.6 percent respectively. Kennedy, p. 330.

14. Isaacson and Thomas, pp. 339-62; Martin Sherwin, *A World Destroyed: The Atomic Bomb and the Grand Alliance* (New York: Vintage Books, 1977), pp. 143ff.

15. See Christopher Simpson, *Blowback* (New York: Weidenfeld and Nicolson, 1988), pp. 96, 123, 173-4. On the "Red Sox/Red Cap" programs see Ranelagh, p. 287. For information on the Office of Policy Coordination, the Labor Service Organization, and Operation Focus, see Bennett Kovrig, *Of Walls and Bridges* (New York: New York University Press, 1991), pp. 39, 45, 64, 71-9. For information on Greece, see Isaacson and Thomas, p. 401.

16. John Lewis Gaddis, *Strategies of Containment* (Oxford: Oxford University Press, 1982), p. 71.

17. For an elaboration of the "inclusionary" versus "exclusionary" strategy, see Gati, *Hungary and the Soviet Bloc*, p. 42. For Stalin's appeals to communist parties, see Lionel Kochan and Richard Abraham, *The Making of Modern Russia* (New York: Penguin, 1983), p. 482.

18. "The essential feature of this [bogus coalition] stage is that peasant parties, and any bourgeois parties who may have been tolerated at the beginning, are driven into opposition." Hugh Seton-Watson, *The East European Revolutions* (Boulder: Westview, 1985), p. 170.

19. Quoted in Davies, p. 3.

20. Some scholars prefer to see in this retreat on collectivization a deliberate Soviet design for better achieving control over Poland. "Deferment was permitted by Moscow during the formative years of the bloc as a temporary means toward the desirable end of solidifying communist control." Richard Staar, *Communist Regimes in Eastern Europe* (Stanford: Hoover

Institute Press, 1984), p. 176. But this argument gives too much credence to the idea that Moscow completely and totally controlled activities in Eastern Europe, and doesn't recognize the domestic pressures influencing regimes in the region.

21. Charles Gati quotes Paul Marer's estimate that the Soviet gain for the region as a whole in the immediate post-war era was $14 billion. Gati, *The Bloc That Failed*, p. 24.

22. Martin McCauley, "Legitimization in the German Democratic Republic," in Paul Lewis, ed., *Eastern Europe: Political Crisis and Legitimization* (New York: St. Martins, 1984), p. 49.

23. Stephen Fischer-Galati, *Twentieth Century Rumania* (New York: Columbia University Press, 1970), p. 111.

24. Jelavich, p. 292.

25. Rupnik, *The Other Europe*, p. 119.

26. Jelavich, pp. 288-94.

27. Garton Ash, *The Uses of Adversity*, p. 256. Throughout post-war Europe, communism and socialism gained popularity, not only as the antithesis of fascism but also as a refreshing alternative to conservative wartime governments. In the first post-war election in Britain, for instance, the Labor Party trounced the charismatic Churchill and his political allies.

28. Richard Rhodes, *The Making of the Atomic Bomb* (New York: Simon and Schuster, 1988), p. 312.

29. Davies, p. 67.

30. Jaszi, p. 89.

31. Borsody, pp. 128, 160.

32. Thomas Masaryk, *The New Europe: The Slav Standpoint* (Lewisburg: Bucknell University Press, 1972), p. 143.

33. Quoted in Staar, p. 44. Zhivkov even appealed to Khrushchev to incorporate Bulgaria as the Soviet Union's sixteenth republic.

34. Tipton and Aldrich, p. 31.

35. Poland is an instructive example of how a series of non-fascist authoritarian governments pursued statist policies. Its cycles of state control peaked during the Polish-Russian war and the depression years of the 1930s. See Zbigniew Landau and Jerzy Tomaszewski, *The Polish Economy in the Twentieth Century* (London: Croom Helm, 1985), pp. 33-5, 111.

36. Quoted in Jaszi, p. 102.

Chapter 3

1. Quoted in Jaszi, p. 47.

2. See Paul Lewis, "Legitimation and Political Crisis: East European Developments in the Post-Stalin Period," in *Eastern Europe: Political Crisis and Legimitation.*

3. Gati, *The Bloc That Failed*, p. 17. It is important to note that the Yugoslavs were also the first to attack "national communism" in 1947; they are thus ironically responsible for their own later ostracism. See Norman Naimark, "Revolution and Counterrevolution in Eastern Europe," in Christiane Lemke and Gary Marks, *The Crisis of Socialism in Europe* (Durham: Duke University Press, 1992), pp. 73-5.

4. See Jelavich, pp. 321-31.

5. Allen Dulles, then head of the CIA, has asserted that the Titoist purges in Eastern Europe were the product of a deliberate disinformation campaign, indeed the CIA's most successful. Kovrig, p. 42.

6. Pavlowitch, p. 18.

7. Quoted in Kovrig, p. 51.

8. *Ibid.*, p. 53.

9. Rothschild, p. 161.

10. Paul Lendvai, *Hungary: The Art of Survival* (London: I.B. Tauris, 1988), p. 69; also Elemer Hankiss, "In Search of a Paradigm," and Janos Matyas Kovacs, "Reform Economics: The Classification Gap," *Daedalus*, Winter 1990.

11. See Imre Tarafas, "Hungary's Reforms: Past and Present," *Finance and Development*, March 1991.

12. Ivan Szelenyi, *Socialist Entrepreneurs* (Madison: University of Wisconsin Press, 1991).

13. Adam, pp. 93-4.

14. *Ibid.*, p. 155.

15. Bruce Allen, *Germany East* (Montreal: Black Rose Books, 1989), pp. 24-5.

16. R.J. Crampton, *A Short History of Modern Bulgaria* (Cambridge: Cambridge University Press, 1987), p. 178.

17. Kiro Gligorov, "The Economic System of Yugoslavia," in George Macesich, ed., *Essays on the Yugoslav Economic Model* (New York: Praeger, 1989), p. 3. Also see Howard Wachtel, *Workers' Management and Workers' Wages in Yugoslavia* (Ithaca: Cornell University Press, 1973).

18. Sharon Zukin, "Self-Management and Socialization," in Pedro Ramet, ed., *Yugoslavia in the 1980s* (Boulder: Westview, 1985), p. 79.

19. See, e.g., Bogdan Denitch, *Limits and Possibilities* (Minneapolis: University of Minnesota Press, 1990), p. 35; Pat Devine, *Democracy and Economic Planning* (Cambridge: Polity, 1988), pp. 99-100. Devine also argues that market forces have substantially undermined worker self-management in Yugoslavia.

20. Originally confined to Yugoslavia and Italy, the phenomenon spread to Spain, France, and Romania. Pierre Hassner, "Postwar Western Europe: The Cradle of Eurocommunism?" in Rudolf Tokes, ed., *Eurocommunism and Detente* (New York: New York University Press, 1978). The Soviet intervention in Czechoslovakia in 1968 only furthered disenchantment with Moscow and culminated in a 17-country boycott of the 1969 Third World Communist Conference in Moscow. Wolfgang Leonhard, *Eurocommunism: Challenge for East and West* (New York: Holt, Rinehart and Winston, 1978), p. 124.

21. Quoted in William Griffith, "The Diplomacy of Eurocommunism," in Tokes, ed., *Eurocommunism and Detente*, p. 419.

22. Rudolf Tokes, "Eastern Europe in the 1970s: Detente, Dissent and Eurocommunism," in *ibid.*, pp. 480-1.

23. The phrase comes from Janusz Bugajski and Maxine Pollack, *East European Fault Lines: Dissent, Opposition and Social Activism* (Boulder: Westview, 1989), p. 51.

24. Garton Ash, *The Uses of Adversity*, p. 247.

25. The Home Army was able to engage 500,000 German troops and prevented one out of every eight Nazi transports from reaching the Eastern Front (Rothschild, p. 28). Conflict between Home Army units and Soviet forces is the context of Jerzy Andrzejewski's famous novel *Ashes and Diamonds* (London: Wiedenfeld and Nicolson, 1962).

26. Davies, p. 80.

27. Tobacco workers in Plovdiv, Bulgaria and worker riots in Plzen, Czechoslovakia, both in 1953, were earlier, but did not spark more widespread protest.

28. Allen, pp. 24-9.

29. Davies, p. 9.

30. Ivan Volgyes, *Hungary: A Nation of Contradictions* (Boulder: Westview, 1982), p. 17.

31. The story of KOR is well worth retelling if only space constraints allowed such an undertaking. For an extensive treatment by an insider, see Jan Josef Lipski, *KOR: Workers' Defense Committee in Poland, 1976-1981* (Berkeley: University of California Press, 1985). For a more critical perspective, see Lawrence Goodwyn, *Breaking the Barrier: The Rise of Solidarity in Poland* (New York: Oxford University Press, 1991).

32. For background see Timothy Garton Ash, *The Polish Revolution: Solidarity* (New York: Vintage, 1985), pp. 50-1.

33. Goodwyn, *passim.*

34. Gella, p. 130.

35. Miklos Haraszti, *The Velvet Prison: Artists Under State Socialism* (New York: Basic Books, 1987), p. 9.

36. Kolakowski, *Modernity on Endless Trial,* p. 38.

37. See Paul Zinner, *Revolution in Hungary* (New York: Columbia University Press, 1962), pp. 187-202.

38. Adam Michnik, *Letters From Prison and Other Essays* (Berkeley: University of California Press, 1987), pp. 135-49.

39. Gyorgy Konrad makes this analogy in *Antipolitics* (New York: Harcourt, Brace, and Jovanovich, 1984), p. 75.

40. Quoted in Hans-Peter Riese, ed., *Since the Prague Spring* (New York: Vintage, 1979), p. 14.

41. I have only treated intellectuals as dissidents in this section. As Gyorgy Konrad and Ivan Szelenyi argue persuasively in *The Intellectuals on the Road to Class Power* (New York: Harcourt Brace Jovanovich, 1979), intellectuals from the opposition and from party circles could also be seen as one class, with a common set of values and a common enemy—the ruling elite. In *Socialist Entrepreneurs,* Szelenyi writes that intellectuals from party and opposition did not cooperate as much as he had expected; rather the Party technocrats in Hungary forged a relationship with rural entrepreneurs. I believe Szelenyi spoke too soon in amending his original thoughts. The 1989 transition in Hungary required unprecedented communication between intellectuals in both camps; rural entrepreneurs played a relatively insignificant role in this process.

42. Quoted in Paul Mojzes, *Christian-Marxist Dialogue in Eastern Europe* (Minneapolis: Augsburg, 1981), p. 96.

43. *Ibid.,* pp. 77ff.

44. *Ibid.,* pp. 51-2.

45. Quoted in Allen, p. 93.

46. "In many churches it is not unheard of for more than 1,500 young people to attend to listen to the sermon and often also to a concert. Pastor Theo Lehmann in Karl-Marx-Stadt has a rock group playing pop songs, and the congregation sings Lehmann's Christian lyrics to the Beatles tune of 'Yellow Submarine.'" Werner Volkmer, "East Germany: Dissenting Views During the Last Decade," in Rudolf Tokes, ed., *Opposition in Eastern Europe* (Baltimore: Johns Hopkins University Press, 1979), p. 123.

47. "The Berlin Appeal," in *From Below: Independent Peace and Environmental Movements in Eastern Europe & the USSR* (Helsinki Watch, 1987), p. 213.

48. Allen, pp. 96ff.

49. Interview with Peter Zimmermann in Leipzig, week of April 2, 1990. Also see Sabrina Ramet, "Priests and Rebels: The Contributions of the Christian Churches to the Revolutions in Eastern Europe," *Mediterranean Quarterly,* Fall 1991. For a critical view of the "Volkskirche" see William Downey, "A 'People's Church' Out of Touch with the People," *The Christian Century,* 4/24/91.

50. Bill Lomax, "Pacifist Movement Within the Hungarian Catholic Church," *Across Frontiers*, Spring/Summer 1988; "Catholic Conscientious Objectors," *East European Reporter*, Summer 1988.

51. Some elements of the East German peace movement wished to remain separate from the Evangelical Lutheran Church because of the latter's conciliatory style. See "Roland Jahn Interview," *Across Frontiers*, Summer 1984.

52. See "Hidden Opposition of the GDR," *East European Reporter*, vol. 3, no. 3; Helsinki Watch, *From Below*, p. 30; Vladimir Tismaneanu, "Unofficial Peace Activism in the Soviet Union and East-Central Europe," in Vladimir Tismaneanu, ed., *In Search of Civil Society* (New York: Routledge, 1990).

53. See Miklos Haraszti, "Dialogue: Two Years of Hungary's Independent Peace Movement," *Across Frontiers*, Winter-Spring 1985; Miklos Haraszti, "The Beginnings of Civil Society: The Independent Peace Movement and the Danube Movement in Hungary," in Tismaneanu, *In Search of Civil Society*.

54. For information on other unofficial peace groups in Czechoslovakia at this time see Milan Hauner, "Anti-militarism and the Independent Peace Movement in Czechoslovakia," in Tismaneanu, *In Search of Civil Society*.

55. See Joanne Landy and Brian Morton, "East European Activists Test Glasnost," *Bulletin of Atomic Scientists*, May 1988; Mary Kaldor, ed., *Europe From Below* (London: Verso, 1991).

56. "Chernobyl is Everywhere," "Chernobyl in Poland," and "Punk and Protest in Slovenia," *Across Frontiers*, Fall 1986.

57. Noticeably absent from the region have been military *putschs*. The armies were subsumed under national communist and Warsaw Pact control, and military challenges were therefore rare. In Bulgaria, a military plot to oust Zhivkov in 1965 was unsuccessful. See Vladimir Kostov, *The Bulgarian Umbrella* (New York: St. Martins Press, 1988), p. 94. Jaruzelski's seizure of power in Poland also doesn't quite qualify as a *putsch* since it was sponsored by the Communist Party.

58. "Charter 77 Calls for Solidarity With Romanian People," *Across Frontiers*, Winter 1988.

59. For one particularly unsophisticated version see Fred Barnes, "Communism's Incredible Collapse...How It Happened," *Reader's Digest*, March 1990.

60. Dawisha, p. 196.

61. Peter Gowan, "Old Medicine, New Bottles," *World Policy Journal*, Winter 1991/92.

Chapter 4

1. One of the more palatable examples is Serge Schmemann, "The New Politics: East German Baptism in Democracy Embitters the 'Citizens' Movement," *New York Times*, 1/30/90.

2. Interviews with Thomas Klein, Reinhard Weisshuhn, and Petra Wunderlich in East Berlin, week of March 26, 1990.

3. Ronald Asmus, "An Obituary Without Tears," *Report on Eastern Europe*, 1/14/91.

4. Quoted in *The Independent*, 3/14/90. Many in the West German left expressed similar ambivalence over the Wall's collapse. See Andrei Markovits, "The West German Left in a Changing Europe," in Lemke and Marks, eds.

5. See interview with Reich, "From Submission to Revolution," *Time*, 3/19/90, p. 12. Also Jens Reich, "Reflections on Becoming an East German Dissident, on Losing the Wall and a Country," in Prins, ed., *Spring in Winter*.

6. "Interview with Barbel Bohley," *East European Reporter*, Winter 1989/90, p. 16.

7. "New Forum 'Founding Appeal,'" *Across Frontiers*, Fall/Winter 1989, p. 3. The "Theses for a Democratic Transformation in the GDR" of Democracy Now (in the same issue) offered a more

programmatic approach, though still sketchy in the details. Compared to Civic Forum's proposals, however, New Forum's program doesn't seem all that much less specific. See Civic Forum's "What We Want," *East European Reporter,* Winter 1989/90.

8. Quoted in Gwertzman and Kaufman, eds., *The Collapse of Communism,* p. 169.

9. You didn't need the September emigration figures to prove East German desires for emigration. In 1975, after the signing of the Helsinki Accords, between 100,000 and 200,000 GDR citizens applied for exit visas. In all, 4.6 million East Germans went west and 1.1 million Westerners (and returning Easterners) moved east. Norman Naimark, "'Ich will hier raus': Emigration and the Collapse of the German Democratic Republic," in Banac, ed., pp. 78, 80.

10. Hubertus Knabe, "Bonn Occupies the GDR—The Sudden End of the East German Spring," *East European Reporter,* Spring/Summer 1990, p. 46.

11. Garton Ash, *The Magic Lantern,* p. 72.

12. Representatives of the women's association managed to squeeze in late.

13. For an analysis of this period of time, see Peter Rossman, "Dashed Hopes for a New Socialism," *Nation,* 5/7/90.

14. The East-SPD began on the left, moved to the center to attract more support, neglected to cultivate a labor vote, and ended up practically giving the election to the CDU. For a pre-election profile, see Amity Shlaes, "Where Socialism Binds the Germanys," *Wall Street Journal,* 1/23/90.

15. Judy Batt, "The Political Context," in J.M.C. Rollo, *The New Eastern Europe: Western Responses* (New York: Council on Foreign Relations Press, 1990), p. 36.

16. Katie Hafner, "Eastern German Buyers Learning the Hard Way," *New York Times,* 2/24/91.

17. Marxist revisionists in Eastern Europe did not disappear completely after 1968. An organized socialist opposition lingered in Czechoslovakia until finally extinguished by political trials in 1972. Marxist intellectuals around the journal *Praxis* in Yugoslavia maintained a degree of cohesion despite government harassment.

18. Bahro, Rudolf, *The Alternative in Eastern Europe (London: New Left Books, 1975),* pp. 11, 453.

19. Susan Buckingham, "Freedom to Think Differently," *East European Reporter,* vol. 3, no. 2.

20. Allen, p. 143.

21. Joachim Fest has argued that Germany for the first time was having "a revolution that has not been preceded by its theorists." He is correct in terms of the second revolution but not the New Forum-led first revolution. Joachim Fest, "The Silence of the Clerks," *National Review,* 4/16/90, p. 34.

22. Interview with Hans Mislivitz in East Berlin, week of March 26, 1990.

23. Quoted in Tim Whipple, ed., *After the Velvet Revolution* (New York: Freedom House, 1991), p. 97.

24. Interview with Helmut Domke in Potsdam, week of March 19, 1990.

25. Echikson, p. 156.

26. For more scholarly definitions, see Reinhard Bendix, "State, Legitimation and 'Civil Society,'" *Telos,* Winter 1990/91; George Schopflin, "Post-communism: Constructing New Democracies in Central Europe," *International Affairs,* August 1991. For an excellent discussion of civil society in Poland, as well as the various corporatist and neo-corporatist scenarios of the 1980s, see David Ost, *Solidarity and the Politics of Anti-politics* (Philadelphia: Temple University Press, 1990). Also see Goodwyn, pp. 257-9; Jan Gross, "Poland: From Civil Society to Political Nation," in Banac, ed.

27. For more background on the conventional characteristics of the *nomenklatura,* see Michael Voslensky, *Nomenklatura: The Soviet Ruling Class* (New York: Doubleday, 1984). Konrad and Szelenyi distinguish between a ruling class and a group of technocrats. "The stability of the post-Stalin era," they write, "is founded on an alliance between the technocracy and the ruling

elite." Konrad and Szelenyi, p. 207. For a revealing fictional depiction of the conflict between Stalin and an emerging technocratic elite, see Anatoly Rybakov, *Children of the Arbat* (Boston: Little Brown, 1988), pp. 371-73.

28. For discussions of technocracy, see Anthony Giddens, *The Class Structure of the Advanced Societies* (New York: Harper & Row, 1973), p. 282ff; also Devine, pp. 44, 181.

29. Interview with William Beittel, former American Friends Service Committee representative in Germany, in West Berlin, week of March 19, 1990.

30. Interview with Wolfgang Ullmann in East Berlin, week of March 26, 1990.

31. See Stephen Kinzer, "Germany's New Custodian of Stasi Secrets Insists on Justice," *New York Times*, 1/20/91. Guy Martin ("Old Nazis, New Nazis," *Esquire*, January 1991) estimates 86,000 agents and two million informants.

32. Says one German observer: "The government wants to sweep all this under the rug so everything will stay calm. I am convinced that the basic reason is that they're afraid of what is in the Stasi files about politicians from West Germany." Quoted in Stephen Kinzer, "Bonn is Said to Keep Report on East German Secret Police a Secret," *New York Times*, 3/9/91. Martin ("Old Nazis, New Nazis") points out that under the last interior minister of the GDR, Peter-Michael Diestel, 3,700 former Stasi were left on payroll and were thus able to cover even more of their tracks.

33. "Pro-East," *Economist*, 11/30/91.

34. Bahro, *The Alternative in Eastern Europe*, p. 281. The average East European intellectual possessed a similar disdain for market impulses, at least prior to the 1980s. See Konrad and Szelenyi, p. 70. Compare also Branko Horvat's desire to replace "accumulation of things by personal development, having by being." Horvat, p. 503.

35. Other options—such as universal stock ownership plans—were simply variants on the capitalism that unification promised. When I interviewed Wolfgang Ullmann, he interrupted our discussion at one point to retrieve a book from another room. He came back clutching *Mainstreet Capitalism*, a relatively little known book in the United States on something known as the "universal stock option plan" or USOP. According to the various versions of USOP, corporate shares are distributed to as great a percentage of the population as possible. But this alternative, presently being pursued by several Eastern European countries, also presupposes corporate capitalism. Stuart Speiser, ed., *Mainstreet Capitalism* (New York: New Horizons, 1988).

36. See, e.g., Gail Schares, "Dealmakers are Pouring Through the Brandenburg Gate," *Business Week*, 2/12/90.

37. The effect of the GDR's entry into the European Community not only had East Germans worried about the stiffer competition. The EC countries also worried that funds earmarked for underdeveloped regions of the Community would be absorbed by its newest region. See Alan Riding, "Europe Struggles to Admit Germans," *New York Times*, 5/27/90.

38. Interview with Bernd Beier in East Berlin, week of March 26, 1990.

39. What was projected to cost 115 billion Deutsche marks for five years turned out to cost 120-150 billion Deutsche marks per year over the same period. *East Germany, Economist Intelligence Unit, Fourth Quarter 1990*, p. 6.

40. "Eastern Europe: Long Road Ahead to Economic Well-Being," paper by the Central Intelligence Agency presented to the Subcommittee on Technology and National Security of the Joint Economic Committee, Figure 1.

41. Interview with Bernd Beier in East Berlin, week of March 26, 1990.

42. Eugen Weber, "Revolution? Counterrevolution? What Revolution?" in Laqueur, ed., p. 462.

43. *East Germany, Economist Intelligence Unit*, Fourth Quarter 1990, p. 5.

44. See Frederick Zilian, Jr., "A Year After Reunification," *Christian Science Monitor*, 11/4/91.

45. Demonstrations continued through 1991. See, e.g., John Tagliabue, "Strikes Sweep Eastern Germany Reflecting Increasing Discomfort," *New York Times*, 3/1/91.

46. Quoted in Stephen Greenhouse, "East German Unions Trying to be Eastern Europe's Strongest," *New York Times*, 7/7/90.

47. John Tagliabue, "Young Germans Still Flocking From East to West," *New York Times*, 3/11/91.

48. Quoted in *The European*, 7/6-8/90.

49. Quoted in an interview reprinted in *World Press Review*, February 1991, p. 62. The quote resembles a passage from an early Wolf work: "Make a wry face if you like, but all the same one must, once in a lifetime, when the time was right, have believed in the impossible." *The Quest for Christa T.* (New York: Dell, 1972), p. 52.

50. *Economist*, 10/20/90.

51. Indeed, many eastern Germans have finally realized that the promises of instant wealth and security were illusionary. See, e.g., Stephen Kinzer, "Kohl, Visiting Reunited East, Finds No More Cheers," *New York Times*, 4/8/91. East German grumbles have not prevented the *Economist* and other magazines determined to emphasize any silver linings they can locate from sugarcoating the coverage. See, e.g., "Cheer Up, It's Working," *Economist*, 8/10/91. For the real story of German stagnation, see Quentin Peel, "Germany is given grim warning on economy," *Financial Times*, 10/22/91; Marc Fisher, "On German Birthday, Easterners Await Happy Returns," *Washington Post*, 9/19/91; Marc Fisher, "Economy Migrates in Germany," *Washington Post*, 2/27/92.

52. Quoted in Brunhild de la Motte, "Come Back, East Germany, All is Forgiven," *New Statesman and Society*, 10/4/91.

53. Anna Tomforde, "East Germans Quit Kohl in Disgust," *Manchester Guardian Weekly*, week of 9/1/91.

54. For a good description of the "popular front," see Judy Batt, *East Central Europe from Reform to Transformation* (New York: Council on Foreign Relations Press, 1991), pp. 55ff.

55. The Party had on earlier occasions recruited nationalists who would later join the Forum. The Forum's support of the Party's proposal to hold direct presidential elections (as opposed to allowing parliament choose the president) only underscored these suspicions. See Glenny, p. 79.

56. The reformist Socialist party came in fourth place with 11 percent of the vote; the Socialist Workers came in seventh with only 4 percent.

57. The United States allotted $1.3 million for advising the UDF. Bulgaria's moratorium on debt payments in the spring of 1990 added to US concerns over a possible Socialist Party victory at the polls. Glenny, p. 176.

58. Interview with Deyan Kironov in Sofia, week of August 20, 1990.

59. Czechoslovak Information Agency, daily summaries in English of Czech newspapers, June 1990.

60. Interview with Paule Gantor in Ljubljana, week of September 10, 1990.

61. Interview with Tomaz Mastnak in Ljubljana, week of September 10, 1990.

62. Rudolf Tokes, "Hungary's New Political Elites: Adaptation and Change, 1989-90," *Problems of Communism*, November/December 1990, p. 61.

63. Interview with Kazimierz Duchowski in Warsaw, week of April 6, 1990. Editor of the Polish journal *Res Publica* Marcin Krol remarks, "Mazowiecki chose not to put the fear of God into one million *nomenklatura* of the old regime, but to incorporate them into his government. By doing this, he won their loyalty and kept the government from paralysis, but he never explained to the public what he was doing." Quoted in Goodwyn, p. 353. As new parties took political control in Poland, change at the top echelons would occur more rapidly.

64. Interview with Maciej Kozlowsky in Krakow, week of April 30, 1990.

65. Interview with Barbel Bohley, "Germany After the Wall," *World Policy Journal,* Winter 1989/90, p. 196.

66. Interview with Deyan Kironov in Sofia, week of August 20, 1990.

67. Interview with Jacek Zakowski in Warsaw, week of April 23, 1990. Zakowski echoes many Western attitudes on the "quiet life." Compare John Updike: "I had voted for Lyndon Johnson, and thus earned my American right not to make a political decision for another four years." *Self-consciousness* (New York: Ballantine, 1989), p. 124.

68. Interview with Robert Braun in Budapest, week of July 16, 1990.

69. Ferenc Miszlivetz, "Who's Controlling the Controllers," mimeo, May 1990, p. 2.

70. Garton Ash, *The Uses of Adversity,* p. 295.

71. Robert Dahl, *A Preface to Economic Democracy* (Berkeley: University of California Press, 1985), p. 110.

72. For a defense of liberal authoritarianism, see Ken Jowitt, "The Leninist Legacy," in Banac, ed. Also see Timothy Garton Ash on "excessive democracy" in "Eastern Europe: Apres Le Deluge, Nous," *New York Review of Books,* 8/16/90. Also Walter Lippman's arguments with Randolph Bourne on this issue are illuminating. See Edward Abrahams, *The Lyrical Left* (Charlottesville: University Press of Virginia, 1988), p. 17.

Chapter 5

1. Garton Ash, *The Magic Lantern,* p. 152.

2. *Warsaw Voice,* 4/28/91; *The Insider,* 4/26/91.

3. For more on Poland's new upper crust, see Christopher Bobinski, "Too busy for fun," *Financial Times,* 5/2/91.

4. See Wlodzimierz Brus, "Economics and Politics: The Fatal Link," in Abraham Brumberg, ed., *Poland: Genesis of a Revolution* (New York: Vintage, 1983).

5. Quoted in Jacques Rupnik, "The Military and Normalisation in Poland," in Paul Lewis, ed., *Eastern Europe: Political Crisis and Legitimation* (New York: St. Martins, 1984), p. 169.

6. World Bank, *Poland: Reform, Adjustment and Growth,* vol. 1 (Washington, DC: The World Bank, 1987), p. 5.

7. *Ibid.*

8. See, e.g., Martin Myant, "Poland: The Permanent Crisis?" in Roger Clarke, ed., *Poland: the Economy in the 1980s* (London: St. James, 1989), p. 13. Also Bartlomiej Kaminski, *The Collapse of State Socialism: The Case of Poland* (Princeton: Princeton University Press, 1991).

9. The standard of living peaked in 1978 and had not, by 1987, recovered. *Rocznik Statystyczyny* (Warszawa: GUS, 1988), pp. xxxii-iii.

10. During the last great economic transformation in the aftermath of World War II, economic planners under the old military/etatist regime also transferred their planning skills to the new communist regime. Zbigniew Landau and Jerzy Tomaszewski, *The Polish Economy in the Twentieth Century* (London: Croom Helm, 1985), p. 196.

11. Interview with Janusz Reykowski in Warsaw, week of April 16, 1990.

12. Quoted in Gary Fields, "The Road to Gdansk," *Monthly Review,* July/August 1991, p. 96.

13. Krystyna Skarzynska, "Egalitarian and Hierarchical Orientations in Polish Society," *Polish Academy of Sciences,* mimeo, 1989, p. 2.

14. *Ibid.,* p. 3. These results are also borne out by other research, notably Lena Kolarska-Bobinska, "Poland Under Crisis: Unreformable Society or Establishment?" in Clarke, ed., *Poland: the Economy in the 1980s.*

15. Timothy Garton Ash, *The Polish Revolution: Solidarity* (New York: Vintage, 1985), p. 192.

16. Goodwyn, p. 342.

17. Discussion of the economic aspects of the roundtable agreement is drawn from "Stanowisko w sprawie polityki spolecznej i gospodarczej oraz reform systemowych," *Porozumenia Okraglego Stolu* (Warszawa: NSZZ Solidarnosc, 1989).

18. The one exception, a wealthy businessman, used his riches to beat his Solidarity opponent for a Senate seat.

19. Interview with Jan Maria Rokita in Krakow, April 1989.

20. Interview with Marcin Swiecicki in Warsaw, June 1989.

21. From Lawrence Weschler, "A Grand Experiment," *The New Yorker*, 11/13/89.

22. The best outline of this program, written by Jeffrey Sachs and David Lipton, can be found in "Creating a Market Economy in Eastern Europe: The Case of Poland," *Brookings Papers on Economic Activity*, vol. 1, 1990 (Washington, DC: The Brookings Institution, 1990). For an update on Sachs's views, see Jeffrey Sachs, "The State of the East European Economies," in Dick Clark, ed., *United States-Soviet and East European Relations: Building a Congressional Cadre* (Queenstown, MD: The Aspen Institute, 1991). For a breezier treatment, see interview with Sachs in *Omni*, June 1991.

23. Jeffrey Sachs says that "in United States terms, I'd be identified as a liberal Democrat and the country I admire the most is Sweden." Quoted in Lawrence Weschler, "A Grand Experiment," p. 88. On Sachs's "Keynesian" impulses, see Robert Norton, "The American Out to Save Poland," *Fortune*, 1/29/90, p. 133. Even Balcerowicz rejects the label of "doctrinaire liberal." Interview with Leszek Balcerowicz, *Warsaw Voice*, 3/3/91.

24. Interview with Wlodzimierz Kesicki in Warsaw, week of April 16, 1990.

25. Sachs updated his defense in "Crossing the Valley of Tears in East European Reform," *Challenge*, September/October 1991 and "Building a Market Economy in Poland," *Scientific American*, March 1992. For a less coherent and more ideological defense of the Sachs plan, see the interview with Alan Walters, "Poland, Another Argentina?" *Forbes*, 2/5/90. For one of the best critiques of the plan see Tadeusz Kowalik, "The Costs of 'Shock Therapy,'" *Dissent*, Fall 1991.

26. Ryszard Bugaj in Weschler, "Shock," *The New Yorker*, 12/10/90, p. 90.

27. Quoted in *The Insider*, 2/28/91.

28. Balcerowicz's approval rating had risen to 35 percent (compared to 26 percent in July) and 37 percent of those polled wanted to see his political influence increased. In the same poll, 54 percent said that "he was well serving society" (compared to 45 percent in July). *Gazeta International*, 10/25/90.

29. For the Sachs approach to privatization, see his paper with David Lipton, "Privatization in Eastern Europe: The Case of Poland," *Brookings Papers on Economic Activity*, vol. 2 (Washington, DC: The Brookings Institution, 1990). Sachs and Lipton are particularly scornful of ESOP, whose effects they consider "pernicious." Still, Sachs and Lipton are cautious concerning the pace of privatization. Compare their caution to a Thatcherite like Anne Applebaum, "Who Owns Central Europe," *American Spectator*, February 1991.

30. Interview with Dawid Warszawski in Warsaw, week of April 16, 1990.

31. Interview with Bozena Chojnacka in Warsaw, week of April 16, 1990. While it is true that workers' councils have exercised their recently granted right to dismiss enterprise managers, this was only an interim solution. Under privatization, workers' councils will probably lose this right among others. See Stephen Engelberg, "Polish Workers Wield New Power," *New York Times*, 12/28/90.

32. Even before austerity struck, in November 1989, economist Adam Gwiazda estimated that the money resources of the population could cover only 10 percent of the stocks; now estimates

run as low as 2 percent. *Warsaw Voice,* 11/19/89. For the 2 percent figure, see Katarzyna Wandycz's interview with Andrzej Machalski in "Lech Walesa, Meet Alexander Hamilton," *Forbes,* 11/26/90, p. 120.

33. *Gazeta Wyborcza,* 5/6/90.

34. One poll in *Gazeta Wyborcza* revealed that most Poles supported privatization, but only if foreigners were kept out and shares went predominantly to workers in enterprises. *Gazeta Wyborcza,* 4/20/90. But several months later, another poll revealed that fully 76 percent supported the promotion of foreign capital in Poland. *Konfrontacje,* June 1990. And then, to complicate matters even more, a *Polityka* poll discovered that only 13.2 percent of workers favored privatization. Weschler, "Shock," p. 35.

35. For the program of the *samorzad* faction of Solidarity, see, e.g., Karol Modzelewski, "Solidarity of Labor," *New Politics,* vol. III, no. 3.

36. "Sharing in Future Profits," *Voice Business,* 8/4/91; Christopher Bobinski, "Poland Outlines Mass Privatisation Scheme, *Financial Times,* 6/28/91; Anthony Robinson, "Poles Reject Idea of Shares Gift from State," *Financial Times,* 2/28/92.

37. Estimate from Ian Hume, director of the World Bank's Warsaw office. Quoted in Francine Kiefer, "Political Standoff in Poland Puts Reform at Risk," *Christian Science Monitor,* 11/4/91.

38. Quoted in *Gazeta Wyborcza,* 4/23/90. For earlier statements by Kuron, see interview with him in *Across Frontiers,* Fall/Winter 1989. From a ministry of labor document: "We are not psychologically or organizationally prepared for unemployment." *Gazeta Wyborcza,* 5/6/90.

39. Interview with Tomasz Kazmierczak in Warsaw, week of April 16, 1990.

40. Weschler, "Shock," p. 93.

41. Stephen Engelberg, "Glut of Potatoes in Poland is Showing the Price of Change to Free Market," *New York Times,* 5/15/90.

42. Quoted in *Gazeta International,* 6/28/90. Dairy protests continued into 1991. *The Insider,* 4/26/91.

43. In 1990, the Solidarity weekly published this statement from Jerzy Eysymontt: "Every economist is positive that without some degree of unemployment, the restructuring of the Polish economy after forty-odd years of communism is not possible...above all such very deep and possibly rapid structural changes are inevitable, without which our economy will never become competitive." *Tygodnik Solidarnosc,* 4/27/90.

44. Evidence of early dissatisfaction can be found in Stephen Engelberg, "Polish Free Market Planner Comes Under Solidarity Fire," *New York Times,* 4/24/90; response can be found in Stephen Engelberg, "Poland Agrees to IMF Aid and Asks Solidarity's Help," *New York Times,* 2/25/91.

45. Quoted in Stephen Engelberg, "Anti-Walesa Faction in Solidarity Meets in Warsaw to Draft Strategy," *New York Times,* 7/29/90.

46. Quoted in Weschler, "Shock," pp. 122-3.

47. See Voytek Zubek, "Walesa's Leadership and Poland's Transition," *Problems of Communism,* January/April 1991.

48. Quoted in *Warsaw Voice,* 9/23/90.

49. Interview with Dawid Warszawski in Warsaw, week of April 16, 1990.

50. *Warsaw Voice,* 3/3/91.

51. This is Poland's $33 billion debt to foreign governments. See Stephen Greenhouse, "Poland is Granted Large Cut in Debt," *New York Times,* 3/16/91.

52. Andrzej Machalski in Wandycz, *Forbes,* p. 120.

53. "Sliding into 1992," *Voice Business,* 8/25/91.

54. *Financial Times*, 9/11/91.

55. With fall elections utmost in his mind, Center Alliance leader Jaroslaw Kaczynski called for the replacement of Balcerowicz and the easing of monetary policies. See Christopher Bobinski, "Polish Call to Loosen the Reins," *Financial Times*, 6/11/91.

56. *Eastern European Reporter*, 11/11/91, p. 67.

57. This trend has only become more pronounced in 1992. See Blaine Harden, "Poles Sour on Capitalism," *Washington Post*, 2/5/92; Stephen Engelberg, "Gloom and Economic Anxiety Overtake the Poles," *New York Times*, 2/6/92.

58. Sylvie Kauffmann and Jean-Pierre Langellier, "Walesa says the West has got it wrong," *Le Monde*, reprinted in the *Manchester Guardian Weekly*, week of 9/22/91. In the same article, Walesa insisted, however, that he was still a capitalist. "But I want to be an intelligent capitalist," he said, "who has his eye on the long term."

59. "Three Approaches to the Economy," *The Insider*, 5/30/91. For the clearest pro-Balcerowicz position, see Marek Dabrowski, "Inflationary Fever," *The Insider*, 2/21/91.

60. "Marriage without Romance," *The Insider*, 5/2/91. It should be noted that not everyone in the Democratic Union favored a change in the Balcerowicz plan.

61. Blaine Harden and Mary Battiata, "Walesa to Replace Finance Minister, Ease Austerity Plan," *Washington Post*, 11/1/91.

62. Stephen Engelberg, "Polish Fiscal Plan Inspires Criticism," *New York Times*, 2/21/92.

63. "Fall of an Empire," *Voice Business*, 8/18/91.

64. Quoted in David McQuaid, "Art-B and the Pathology of Transition," *Report on Eastern Europe*, 9/20/91. Also see Stephen Engelberg, "Poland's New Climate Yields Bumper Crop of Corruption," *New York Times*, 11/12/91.

65. Figure from Blaine Harden, "In Poland, Gains Mixed With Pains," *Washington Post*, 1/2/92.

66. Garton Ash, *Solidarity*, p. 269.

67. *Gazeta International*, 8/16/90.

68. Interview with Maciej Kozlowski in Krakow, week of April 30, 1990.

69. At the same time, the government did end subsidies for birth control pills. For more background, see Gabrielle Glaser, "New Poland, Same Old Story," *Village Voice*, 4/2/91.

70. A February 1991 poll revealed that 58 percent opposed the law compared to 30 percent who supported its passage. *The Insider*, 3/14/91.

71. As one writer characterized the situation of women in post-communist Poland: "Women formed the basis of resistance against communists; they organized assistance for those who were persecuted after Martial Law was declared in December 1981. In spite of their skills, very few women hold important state or political positions in today's society." She went on to note that women are underrepresented in the government, in parliament, in Solidarity, and in local councils. *Gazeta International*, 7/19/90.

72. One poll placed the army first, the police second, and the Church third in the minds of Poles as the most respected institution. "Polish Church and Press Criticize Each Other," *New York Times*, 9/15/91.

73. Stephen Engelberg, "Poland May Meld Church and State," *New York Times*, 4/28/91.

74. *Warsaw Voice*, 2/10/91.

75. Quoted in *Eastern Europe Reporter*, 10/28/91, p. 12.

76. Quoted in *Warsaw Voice*, 4/14/91.

77. Blaine Harden and Mary Battiata, "Walesa to Replace Finance Minister, Ease Austerity Plan," *Washington Post*, 11/1/91.

78. Theodore Von Laue, *The World Revolution of Westernization* (New York: Oxford University Press, 1987), p. 4.

79. For helpful background, see Charles Gati, ed., *The Politics of Modernization in Eastern Europe* (New York: Praeger, 1976), particularly chapters by Vernon Aspaturian, Gyorgy Ranki, and Ivan Volgyes.

80. See Garry Wills, *Confessions of a Conservative* (New York: Penguin, 1979), pp. 213-15.

81. The Polish opposition even had a label for itself that defied these categories. As philosopher Leszek Kolakowski defined himself as a "liberal-conservative-socialist," so did the opposition define itself. Capitalism is for production, government for moderate redistribution, family and church for everything else. This vision is an artful amalgam of modernity and traditional values. For the famous essay on being a liberal-conservative-socialist, see Kolakowski, *Modernity on Endless Trial,* pp. 225-27. For his early criticism of categories of left and right, see Leszek Kolakowski, *Toward a Marxist Humanism: Essays on the Left Today* (New York: Grove, 1968), pp. 78-83.

82. Daniel Bell, *The Cultural Contradictions of Capitalism* (New York: Basic, 1976).

83. E.H. Carr, *The New Society* (Boston: Beacon, 1957), p. 30.

84. For this bracketing off of morality, the shock therapists owe more to Malthus and Ricardo than Smith. As Robert Heilbroner points out, both Ricardo and Malthus established iron laws that described what is, not what should be. See Heilbroner, *The Worldly Philosophers* (New York: Simon and Schuster), pp. 93-5.

85. John Kenneth Galbraith, "Which Capitalism for Eastern Europe," *Harpers,* April 1990, p. 20. In another piece, Galbraith criticizes the Sachs-type plan as "an ideological construct that exists all but entirely in the minds and notably in the hopes of the donor." See also Galbraith's "The Rush to Capitalism," *New York Review of Books,* 10/25/90, p. 51. Twenty years ago, Robert Heilbroner made similar arguments which, convincing then, seem to have been all but forgotten now. See *Between Capitalism and Socialism* (New York: Vintage, 1970).

86. David Binder, "Bulgarian Strategy is Made in US," *New York Times,* 10/9/90.

87. Interview with Zarko Puhovski in Zagreb, week of September 3, 1990.

88. Interview with Mitya Zagar in Ljubljana, week of September 10, 1990.

89. *Wall Street Journal,* 7/23/90.

90. A glance at the titles of a *New York Times* series on the region is revealing: "For Eastern Europe Now, a New Disillusion" and "Long, Painful Road Ahead to Free Markets for East." An eight-part series in the *New York Times,* 11/9/90 to 11/16/90. The more ideologically conservative attempted to counter the gloomy messages. The *Economist,* for instance, titled its 1/26/91 article on the Eastern European economic prospects "Look on the Bright Side." *Fortune* pitched in with a 12/3/90 article entitled "The New Germany's Glowing Future." Also see David Buchan, "E. Europeans pessimistic about effects of reform," *Financial Times,* 1/29/92.

91. UN Economic Commission for Europe, "Economic Bulletin for Europe," vol. 43, November 1991, pp. 1-6.

92. Anthony Robinson, "Eastern Europe 'faces second economic shock,'" *Financial Times,* 12/23/91.

93. Alice Amsden, "An Asian Plan for Eastern Europe," *New York Times,* 4/6/90. Also Silviu Brucan, "An Austro-Korean Model for Eastern Europe," *New Perspectives Quarterly,* Fall 1990.

94. From an OECD report on Hungary: "The state (whether at the national, regional, or local level) has to assume some important functions, not only to assure genuine, fair and effective competition and, thereby, the proper working of markets, but also to assure social justice (which is not an attempt to create equality or an egalitarian society) and to help correct distortions that may result from competition and from market functioning." Otto Hieronymi, *Economic Policies For the New Hungary* (Columbus, OH: Battelle Press, 1990), p. 13.

95. For this point see Robert Kuttner, "Is There a Democratic Economics?" *The American Prospect,* Winter 1992, p. 30.

96. See Michael Harrington, "Eurosocialism," in Nancy Lieber, ed., *Eurosocialism and America* (Philadelphia: Temple University Press, 1982). In the same volume, see also Brian Turner, "Plant Closings and Economic Dislocations," and Rudolf Meidner, "A Swedish Union Proposal for Collective Capital Sharing." The 1991 electoral loss of the Social Democrats indicates new economic trends in Sweden. Although the shift to the center and the heightened interest in EC membership will probably accelerate partial privatization of some industries, the key elements of industrial policy appear to remain untouched. See Robert Taylor, "Sweden comes in from the cold," *Financial Times,* 6/14/91.

97. Jan Obrman, "Czechoslovakia: Organized Labor—A New Beginning," *Report on Eastern Europe,* 3/39/91; Anthony Robinson, "Czechs Hand 'For Sale' Sign on 50 of Republic's Key Companies," *Financial Times,* 6/14/91.

98. *The Insider,* 4/4/91.

99. David McQuaid, "The Political Landscape Before the Elections," *Report on Eastern Europe,* 10/18/91.

100. Batt, *East-Central Europe,* p. 94; "A Hungarian Pact," *The Insider,* 5/9/91.

101. "Perspectives for Coordinated Assistance From the G-24 to the Countries of Central and Eastern Europe," p. 6.

102. For an alternative that eschews the market and relies entirely on democratic planning, see Michael Albert and Robin Hahnel, *Looking Forward: Participatory Economics for the 21st Century* (Boston: South End Press, 1991).

103. Interview with Janos David in Budapest, week of July 23, 1990. For a theoretical treatment of this "local corporatism," see Gudmund Hevres and Arne Selrik, "Local Corporatism" in Suzanne Berger, ed., *Organizing Interests in Western Europe* (Cambridge: Cambridge University Press, 1981).

104. In "Privatization in Eastern Europe: The Case of Poland," Sachs and Lipton quote this example to caution against too rapid privatization.

105. Czechoslovakia has enacted two laws, one returning small shops taken since 1955, the other covering larger properties seized after the war. Hungary has provided vouchers equal to the value of properties seized after 1949 but has discovered that some properties have changed hands so frequently that it is difficult to decide who gets what. See Celestine Bohlen, "Hungarians Debate How Far Back to Go to Right Wrongs," *New York Times,* 4/15/91. The newly unified Germany has decided to return to its former owners' property located in the former GDR that had been seized by the Nazis. John Tagliabue, "Bonn Will Return Property in East," *New York Times,* 2/3/91.

106. "Hungary's Sell-off Hits Hard Times," *Financial Times,* 5/21/91.

107. For information on Poland, see *The Insider,* 3/21/91. Roughly 3,500 companies were established in Poland in 1989 with shares of state-run enterprises. For an analysis of "red capitalism" see Elemer Hankiss, *East European Alternatives* (Oxford: Clarendon, 1990), pp. 254-57; Douglas Rediker, "Revolving Boors," *New Republic,* 5/20/91; Erzsebet Szallai, "The New Elite," *Across Frontiers,* Fall/Winter 1990.

108. "Czechoslovakia Auctions Stores to Private Buyers," *New York Times,* 1/27/91.

109. Weschler, "Shock," p. 94.

110. "Reawakening: A Market Economy Takes Root in Eastern Europe," *Business Week,* 4/15/91.

111. Peter Martin, "Privatization Stirs Controversy," *Report on Eastern Europe,* 10/4/91; "Czechs by Millions Invest $35 in Big State Sale," *New York Times,* 12/21/92.

112. Judy Dempsey, "Romanians Set Stage for Ambitious Privatisation," *Financial Times,* 8/10/91.

113. Leslie Lolitt, "Treuhand Director Suspended Over Sale," *Financial Times*, 10/2/91.

114. Gella, pp. 57-167.

115. Vaclav Havel, *Living in Truth*, edited by Jan Vladislav (London: Faber and Faber, 1987), p. 119.

116. Garton Ash, *The Magic Lantern*, p. 105.

117. Quoted by Clive Jenkins in Lieber, ed., p. 146.

118. There are numerous economic drawbacks to self-management, as there are for every economic model. For a somewhat sympathetic critique see Alec Nove, *The Economics of Feasible Socialism* (London: Allen and Unwin, 1983), pp. 133-141. The Yugoslav experience led Howard Wachtel to conclude: "Formal membership in workers' management bodies tends to increase general work satisfaction in nonautomated plants, as well as satisfaction with working conditions, wages, and job control. However, paradoxically, it also increases alienation, probably owing to the gap between the workers' expectations about workers' management and the reality of this institution." Howard Wachtel, *Workers' Management and Workers' Wages in Yugoslavia* (Ithaca: Cornell University Press, 1973), p. 92.

119. Alan Blinder, "More Like Them?" *The American Prospect*, Winter 1992.

120. Dahl, p. 152.

121. Robert Kuttner, *The Economic Illusion* (Boston: Houghton Mifflin, 1984), p. 3.

122. Interview with Dawid Warszawski in Warsaw, week of April 16, 1990.

123. Interview of Miroslav Zamecnik in Prague, week of June 25, 1990.

124. Interview with Philip Bokov in Sofia, week of August 20, 1990.

125. Interview with Vojko Volk in Ljubljana, week of September 10, 1990.

126. Miklos Haraszti, *A Worker in a Worker's State* (New York: Universe, 1978), p. 114.

127. Interview with Ladislav Lis in Prague, week of July 2, 1990.

128. Interview with Marcu Viorel in Bucharest, week of August 6, 1990.

129. Interview with Pal Forgacs in Budapest, week of July 9, 1990.

130. Interview with Oleg Choulev of Podkrepa in Sofia, week of August 20, 1990.

131. Interview with Laszlo Urban in Budapest, week of July 23, 1990.

132. David Turnock, *Eastern Europe: An Economic and Political Geography* (New York: Routledge, 1989), p. 236. See also Szelenyi, *Socialist Entrepreneurs*.

133. The Marshall Plan provided $12.4 billion to 16 countries between 1948 and 1952. Were the United States to extend similar aid to Eastern Europe over four years, it would amount, in 1989 dollars, to $65.4 billion. Jozef van Brabant, *Remaking Eastern Europe: On the Political Economy of Transition* (Dordrecht: Kluwer, 1990), pp. 107-8.

134. Some US politicians covered up the lack of US financial assistance with bewildering free trade rhetoric. See Phil Gramm, "For Eastern Europe, Free Trade, Not Aid," *New York Times*, 3/30/90.

135. PHARE (Poland and Hungary Assistance and Economic Restructuring) is a program that includes US, Japanese, and World Bank funding as well.

136. *The Courier*, May/June 1990, no. 121.

137. The IMF and World Bank have allocated $8 billion and $3.7 billion, respectively, compared to $19.3 billion from the Group of 24. "The IMF and World Bank Survey," *Economist*, 10/12/91, p. 43. Total aid goes disproportionately to Poland and Hungary.

138. See, e.g., Robert Bednarzik, "Helping Poland Cope with Unemployment," *Monthly Labor Review*, December 1990, pp. 27-30.

139. Samantha Sparks, "The European Bank for Reconstruction and Development," Overseas Development Council, 1990, no. 3.

140. Ariane Genillard and Ian Rodger, "Nestle, BSN Plan Joint Czech Bid," *Financial Times,* 1/9/92.

141. Glenny, p. 198.

142. For an elaboration of this argument, see Jan Urban, "Eastern Europe—Divided It Falls," *New York Times,* 11/21/90.

143. The debt breakdown is: Poland ($43 billion), Hungary ($20 billion), Yugoslavia ($16 billion), Bulgaria ($10 billion), Czechoslovakia ($7 billion), Romania ($1 billion). John Pinder, *The European Community and Eastern Europe* (New York: Council on Foreign Relations Press, 1991), p. 93.

144. Interview with Brian Kendall in Brussels, week of March 12, 1990.

145. Michael Davenport, *Europe: 1992 and the Developing World* (London: Overseas Development Institute, 1991).

146. *Czas!,* 4/28/90.

147. Jiri Dienstbier, "Central and Eastern Europe and a New European Order," in Whipple, ed., p. 117.

148. "Wary Hope on Eastern Europe," *Fortune,* 1/29/90, p. 125. There were the prominent exceptions. General Electric, in a celebrated move, bought a Hungarian lightbulb manufacturer declaring that they were there to penetrate the Western European market. "GE Carves Out a Road East," *Business Week,* 7/30/90, p. 32.

149. "Poland's Gamble Begins to Pay Off," *Fortune,* 8/27/90, p. 92.

150. Quoted in Phyllis Berman, "An impolite question: Were you a Communist?" *Forbes,* 10/15/91, p. 133.

151. Quoted in Nicholas Bray, "Lack of Affordable Funding Slows Major Investment in East Europe," *Wall Street Journal,* 9/27/91.

152. Denis MacShane, "Ownership and Control—The Black Hole of Democratic Theory," *Peace and Democracy News,* Fall 1990, p. 6.

153. According to Kovrig (p. 287), the Springer deal was ultimately dissolved.

154. Gati, *The Bloc That Failed,* p. 126.

155. For energy subsidy controversy see Vlad Sobell, *CMEA in Crisis* (New York: Praeger, 1990), pp. 12-6; on Czechoslovakia's role in providing machinery see Staar, p. 87.

156. "The Soviet Economy Stumbles Badly in 1989," *Joint Economic Committee Report, 1990,* p. 16.

157. van Brabant, p. 43.

158. "The Soviet Economy Stumbles," p. 46.

159. For such punditry see Helen Junz, "Integration of Eastern Europe into the World Trading System," *The American Economic Review,* May 1991. Free trade generally accrues benefits to larger and more powerful countries. After concluding free-trade pacts with the United States, Latin American nations have, for instance, seen precious few economic advantages, according to the World Bank. See "'Little benefit' in FTAs for Latin America," *Financial Times,* 1/29/92.

160. van Brabant, p. 169.

161. For an analysis of currency convertibility, see John Williamson, *The Economic Opening of Eastern Europe* (Washington, DC: Institute for International Economics, 1991).

Chapter 6

1. Interview with Zoltan Illes in Budapest, week of July 23, 1990. All quotes from Illes in this chapter are based on this interview.

2. For a good introduction to Eastern European environmental problems, see Marlise Simons's occasional pieces in the *New York Times*: "Pollution's Toll on Eastern Europe: Stumps Where Great Trees Once Grew," 3/19/90; "Central Europe's Grimy Coal Belt: Progress, Yes, But At What Cost?" 4/1/90; "Rising Iron Curtain Exposes Haunting Veil of Polluted Air," 4/8/90; "Befouled To Its Depths, Danube Reaches a Turning Point," 5/7/90; "East Europe's Nuclear Plants Stir West's Safety Concerns," 6/7/90.

3. Claudio Magris, *Danube* (New York: Farrar, Straus, and Giroux, 1989), p. 29. For another view of this river, see the piece on the historic canal connecting the Rhine and Danube by Kenneth Danforth, "Charlemagne's Dream," *Atlantic*, October 1991.

4. Hungary had been considering a dam along that stretch of the Danube since 1948. See "Unfinished Past: The Gabcikovo-Nagymaros Project: 1953 and Now," *East European Reporter*, Autumn 1985.

5. *Hungarian Observer*, May 1990, p. 4.

6. Interview with Tamas Fleischer in Budapest, week of July 23, 1990.

7. A parallel can be drawn to other ill-conceived dams—James Bay in Quebec, the Narmada Valley Development Project in India, the Balsas River dam in Mexico. See Steve Turner and Todd Nachowitz, "The Damming of Native Lands," *Nation*, 10/21/91.

8. For background on Vargha, see Mark Schapiro, "The New Danube," *Mother Jones*, April/May 1990.

9. "Special Report on Environmental Politics in Hungary," *Across Frontiers*, Summer/Fall 1987, pp. 7-14. For a taste of press coverage of the dam protests see Gabor Revisz, *Perestroika in Eastern Europe: Hungary's Economic Transformation, 1945-1988* (Boulder: Westview, 1990), pp. 125ff.

10. Interview with Judit Vasarhelyi in Budapest, week of July 23, 1990.

11. Miklos Haraszti, "The Beginnings of Civil Society: The Independent Peace Movement and the Danube Movement in Hungary," in Tismaneanu, ed., *In Search of Civil Society*, p. 80.

12. Garton Ash, *The Uses of Adversity*, p. 293.

13. Hans Magnus Enzensberger, *Europe, Europe* (New York: Pantheon, 1989), p. 96. Also see George Schopflin, "Conservatism and Hungary's Transition," *Problems of Communism*, January-April 1991.

14. Ferenc Miszlivetz, "Dialogue—And What is Behind It," *Across Frontiers*, Summer 1989, p. 30; also see "Danube Blues," *East European Reporter*, vol. 2, no. 2.

15. Garton Ash, *The Magic Lantern*, p. 56.

16. The entire Hungarian opposition did not embrace the anti-political stance. Several figures, including philosopher Gaspar Tomas Miklos, attemped candidacies in the mid-1980s but were not successful. See Gabor Demszky, "Parliamentarism in Eastern Europe: The Chances of the Independent Candidate," *East European Reporter*, Autumn 1985 and Andrew Short, "Liberal Hungary," *Across Frontiers*, Winter 1985. Also Hankiss, pp. 75-9.

17. Vera Rich, "Czechs [sic] Push Ahead with Danube Dam," *New Scientist*, 12/1/90.

18. Interview with Janos Vargha, *Technology Review*, October 1990, p. 62; for the text of this petition see "Hungarian Intellectuals Appeal to Austrian Public Opinion," *Across Frontiers*, Summer/Fall, 1987.

19. For more on the region's energy dependency, see Marnie Stetson, "Eastern Europe's Crude Awakening," *World Watch*, July/August 1991.

20. Interview with Laszlo Urban in Budapest, week of July 23, 1990. For a Western argument in favor of market incentives to control pollution, see Peter Fuhrman, "Breathing the Polish Air," *Forbes*, 6/24/91. For the more convincing retort, see David Moberg, "Markets and the Environment," *Dissent*, Fall 1991.

21. Interview with Imre Szabo, *Technology Review*, October 1990, p. 58.

22. Also see Stanley Kabala, "The Hazardous Waste Problem in Eastern Europe," *Report on Eastern Europe*, 6/21/91.

23. Interview with Zoltan Illes, week of July 23, 1990.

24. Interview with Gyongy Mangel in Budapest, week of July 16, 1990.

25. Hilary French, "Eastern Europe's Clean Break With the Past," *World Watch*, March/April 1991, p. 23.

26. Interview with Eniko Bollabas in Budapest, week of July 16, 1990.

27. Ivan Volgyes and Nancy Volgyes, *The Liberated Female* (Boulder: Westview, 1977), pp. 61, 161-3. Several helpful chapters in collections include Marilyn Rueschemeyer and Szonja Szelenyi, "Socialist Transformation and Gender Equality: Women in the GDR and in Hungary," in David Childs *et al.*, ed., *East Germany in Comparative Perspective* (London: Routledge, 1989) and Barbara Jancar, "The New Feminism in Yugoslavia," in Pedro Ramet, ed., *Yugoslavia in the 1980s* (Boulder: Westview, 1985). An excellent article by Yugoslav feminist Slavenka Drakulic, "In Their Own Words," appeared in *Ms.*, July/August 1990. Also see Peggy Simpson, "No Liberation for Women," *The Progressive*, February 1991. A book on Soviet women, Francine du Plessix Gray's *Soviet Women: Walking the Tightrope* (New York: Doubleday, 1989), raises many of the issues common to women in Eastern Europe: work, sexuality, childrearing, and so on.

28. Interview with Lynne Haney in Budapest, week of July 23, 1990.

29. Interview with Agnes Hochberg in Budapest, week of July 23, 1990.

30. Laszlo Kurti, "The Wingless Eros of Socialism: Nationalism and Sexuality in Hungary," *Anthropological Quarterly*, April 1991, p. 63.

31. Interview with Robert Braun in Budapest, week of July 16, 1990.

32. Ivan Volgyes, "For Want of Another Horse: Hungary in 1990," *Current History*, December 1990, p. 434.

33. Cited in the *Hungarian Observer*, May 1991.

34. Although it is a commonplace to note that many Hungarians are obsessed with the rights of their countrypeople living in neighboring countries, it is worth mentioning that according to one poll, only 27 percent of high school graduates even knew that there were Hungarians living outside the country. Lendvai, p. 38.

35. For background on anti-Gypsy sentiment in Hungary, see David Crowe, "The Gypsies in Hungary," in David Crowe and John Kolsti, *The Gypsies of Eastern Europe* (Armonk: M.E. Sharpe, 1991).

36. Interview with Zsuzsanna Beres in Budapest, week of July 23, 1990.

37. Interview with Tacheles members in East Berlin, week of September 24, 1990. See also "Violence by Bands of Racist Skinheads Stalks East Germany," *New York Times*, 8/21/90.

38. Interview with Tomaz Mastnak in New York City, December 3, 1991. Ali Zerdin, "After Free Elections, No Democracy," *Yugofax*, 11/16/91.

39. The prototypical shift might be Rudolf Bahro, whose Marxist critique of "real existing socialism" developed into a Green opposition to modernization when he settled in the West. Bahro, *From Red to Green* (London: Verso, 1984). For a review of contemporary options, see "Future Environments for Europe: Some Implications of Alternative Development Paths," *Environment*, October 1990.

40. Lendvai, p. 101.

41. For the "productivist" bias, see, e.g., Jean Baudrillard, "The Mirror of Production," in *Selected Writings* (Stanford, CA: Stanford University Press, 1988), pp. 98-118.

42. I am borrowing these concepts from Ronald Inglehart, *The Silent Revolution* (Princeton: Princeton University Press, 1977), particularly pp. 262-90 and his more recent *Culture Shift in Advanced Industrial Society* (Princeton: Princeton University Press, 1990).

43. Fred Block, *Postindustrial Possibilities* (Berkeley: University of California Press, 1990), pp. 189-218. Block notes that the second variant could consist of "protecting the environment, providing individuals with greater economic security, encouraging the production of community and voluntary services, and improving the quality of goods and services."

44. See Lester Brown, "The New World Order," *State of the World 1991* (New York: Norton, 1991), pp. 4-9; see also David Korten, "Sustainable Development," *World Policy Journal*, Winter 1991-92.

45. For background on Western European Greens, see Ferdinand Muller-Rommel, ed., *New Politics in Western Europe: the Rise and Success of Green Parties and Alternative Lists* (Boulder: Westview, 1989). The key document crystallizing mainstream Green thinking in the mid-1980s is The World Commission on Environment and Development's report, *Our Common Future* (New York: Oxford University Press, 1987).

46. One economist claims that the pollution in the region is not as bad as originally thought, at least in comparison to, say, Milan's air quality, the mercury content of the Thames, the dust in Athens's atmosphere, or the smoke in Madrid's air. See "Dirty Stories," *Economist*, 2/1/92.

47. John Kramer, "The Environmental Crisis in Eastern Europe," *Slavic Review*, Summer 1983, p. 204.

48. *Ibid.*, p. 210.

49. The first figure comes from Andrea Cezeaux, "East Meets West to Look for Toxic Waste Sites," *Science*, 2/8/91. The second figure is from *Our Common Future*, p. 227.

50. Hilary French, *Green Revolutions: Environmental Reconstruction in Eastern Europe and the Soviet Union* (Washington, DC: Worldwatch Institute, 1990), p. 17.

51. Hilary French, "Industrial Wasteland," *World Watch*, November-December, 1988, p. 21. The cancer rate information comes from Barbara Jancar, "Democracy and the Environment in Eastern Europe and the Soviet Union," *Harvard International Review*, Summer 1990, p. 13.

52. For the tonnage statistic, Christine Laurent, "Ceausescu's Poisonous Bequest to the Nation," *New Scientist*, 2/9/91, p. 22. For the river statistic see French, "Industrial Wasteland," p. 21. For unbelievable photographs of Copsa Mica, see *National Geographic*, "East Europe's Dark Dawn," June 1991. For a description see Georgina Harding, *In Another Europe* (London: Hodder & Stoughton, 1990).

53. Tamas Fleischer, "Economic Policy, Environmental Regulations," Ister report, mimeo, 1990.

54. John Kramer, "The Environmental Crisis in Poland," in Fred Singleton, ed., *Environmental Problems in the Soviet Union & Eastern Europe* (Boulder: Lynne Rienner, 1987), pp. 152-3.

55. *Ibid.*, p. 160.

56. Kurier Szczecinski quoted in John Kramer, "The Environmental Crisis in Eastern Europe: The Price for Progress," *Slavic Review*, Summer 1983, p. 204. Richard Darman, a US government official, recently reduced environmentalism to a similar absurdity when he said that "Americans did not fight and win the wars of the 20th century to make the world safe for green vegetables."

57. Kramer, "The Environmental Crisis in Poland," p. 150. For more background, see, e.g., Rafal Serafin, "The Greening of Poland," *Across Frontiers*, Summer 1984.

58. Fred Singleton, "Czechoslovakia: Greens Versus Reds," in Singleton, ed., *Environmental Problems*, p. 178. For Charter 77 positions, see "Charter 77 on the Ecological Situation in Czechoslovakia," *Across Frontiers*, Summer 1984.

59. *Gazeta Wyborcza*, 5/7/90. To the question, would you vote for the following groups, the response was: Solidarity (72 percent), the Citizens' Committee (64 percent), Polish ecological parties (38 percent), the official trade unions (38 percent), Solidarity's Peasant Party (31 percent).

60. After the 1990 elections, Ecoglasnost and the Green Party controlled a bloc of 32 seats in the Bulgarian Parliament; the Green Party had 23 seats in the Romanian Parliament; the Green Party had six seats in the Slovakian legislature. East German Greens, allied with Alliance '90, currently have several seats in the new German Parliament. French, *Green Revolutions*, p. 33.

61. Interview with Zsuzsanna Beres in Budapest, week of July 23, 1990.

62. R. Dennis Hayes, "Eastern Europe's Nuclear Window," *Nation*, 8/26/91.

63. The United States provided start-up money for the "Regional Environmental Centre" in Budapest though most of the funds have come in from European countries. A total of over 200 million ECU has come from the G-24's PHARE program, with the Nordic countries and Denmark providing much of this aid. See PHARE, *Indicative Financial and Aid Commitments and Near Commitments in Favour of Poland and Hungary*, July 4, 1990, pp. 6, 14. The EC provided an additional 25 million ECU for environmental protection in Poland, funding five of 14 projects prepared by the Polish Ministry of Environmental Protection. *Gazeta Wyborcza*, 6/19/90.

64. Interview with Krasen Stanchev in Sofia, week of August 20, 1990. Eighty percent of cultivatable land in Bulgaria is damaged by erosion. French, *Green Revolutions*, p. 25.

65. Zsuzsanna Beres, "The Green Party of Hungary," mimeo, 1990.

Chapter 7

1. Welcoming address presented to the Pope by the president of the Czech and Slovak Federated Republic, 4/21/90.

2. See, e.g., Jiri Dienstbier, "The Helsinki process 'from below,'" *END Journal*, no. 37.

3. "The Address of President Vaclav Havel in Oslo, Norway," 8/28/90, p. 8.

4. "The Arena I Do Not Wish to Enter," interview with Vaclav Havel, *East European Reporter*, Winter 1989/90.

5. "View from the Castle," an interview with Sasa Vondra by Jan Kavan, *East European Reporter*, Spring/Summer 1990, p. 11. See also interview with Jiri Dienstbier in *Lidove Noviny* reprinted in Whipple, ed., p. 131.

6. "President Vaclav Havel's Address," 3/15/90, p. 5.

7. "Statement of His Holiness the Fourteenth Dalai Lama at the Conclusion of his Visit," *East European Reporter*, Spring/Summer 1990, p. 17.

8. Henry Kamm, "Prague Says Moscow Has Agreed to Turn the Warsaw Pact Into a Political Grouping," *New York Times*, 6/13/90.

9. See Jiri Dienstbier, "Central and Eastern Europe and a new European Order," in Whipple, ed., pp. 122-23. Also "Havel Makes Appeal for Help But Not in the Usual Form," *Congressional Quarterly Weekly Report*, 2/24/90. For comments see Anthony Lewis, "Leveraged Investment," *New York Times*, 5/22/90; also see Anthony Solomon and John Edwin Mroz, "Prague's Plan to Aid Moscow," *New York Times*, 7/10/90. In 1991, Havel renewed his call for such a plan in "The Paradoxes of Help," *New York Times*, 7/14/91.

10. *World Armaments and Disarmament, SIPRI Yearbook 1990* (Oxford: Oxford University Press, 1990), pp. 220-21. Also see Nick Thorpe, "Swords Into Ploughshares," *World Press Review*, January 1991.

11. Quoted in Craig Whitney, "Prague Arms Trade to End, Foreign Minister Says," *New York Times*, 1/25/90.

12. Interview with Daniel Kumermann in Prague, week of June 25, 1990.

13. *Report on Eastern Europe,* 3/29/91.

14. The tank deal to Syria was put on hold in November 1991—in order to encourage the peace negotiations between Israelis and Arabs—but resumed again by 1992. For information on the Pakistan and Nigeria deals, see John Tagliabue, "Czechoslovaks Find Profit and Pain in Arms Sales," *New York Times,* 2/19/92. Also James Graff, "Confronting a Tankless Task," *Time,* 6/10/91; "Hard-Pressed Czechs Retain Arms Trade," *New York Times,* 5/3/91.

15. Peter Martin, "Economic Reform and Slovakia," *Report on Eastern Europe,* 7/5/91.

16. Interview with Miroslav Zamecnik in Prague, week of June 25, 1990.

17. Steven Greenhouse, "Slovaks Are Hurt By Arms-Sales Ban," *New York Times,* 8/29/90.

18. On other military questions, the new government did make substantial progress, disbanding the 120,000-strong People's Militia, reducing conscript service, demobilizing divisions, and destroying tanks as part of the Conventional Forces in Europe Treaty. *The Military Balance (1990-91)* (London: International Institute for Strategic Studies, 1990), pp. 44-5.

19. Quoted in Peter Grier, "Eastern Europeans Wary of Neighborhood Conflicts," *Christian Science Monitor,* 10/25/91. At the same time, an earlier statement by Defense Minister Lubos Dubrovsky to the effect that Czechoslovakia had no interest in joining NATO indicates that policy is by no means uniform. *Report on Eastern Europe,* 9/20/91.

20. For some background on this debate between CSCE and NATO, see Jiri Dienstbier, "Central Europe's Security," *Foreign Policy,* Summer 1991; Vaclav Havel, "Speech at NATO Headquarters," *East European Reporter,* Spring/Summer 1991; John Orne, "Security in East Central Europe," *Washington Quarterly,* Summer 1991; Barton Gellman, "US Commanders See New Challenge: Slowing Retreat From Europe," *Washington Post,* 10/15/91. At the beginning of 1992, Havel again proposed a CSCE structure that would rise above a "debating club." The US delegation expressed little enthusiasm. Thomas Friedman buried this information in his "10 Former Soviet Republics Join Human Rights Group," *New York Times,* 1/31/92. By contrast, Ariane Genillard structured her article around the Havel proposal—"Stronger Security Role Urged for CSCE," *Financial Times,* 1/31/92.

21. In early 1992, Dienstbier offered his plan once again at the US-sponsored conference on post-Soviet aid, but received no concrete backing. David Hoffman, "Major Powers Differ on Ways to Aid Ex-Soviet States," *Washington Post,* 1/23/92.

22. Jan Obrman, "From Idealism to Realism," *Report on Eastern Europe,* 12/20/91.

23. Stephen Engelberg, "3 Eastern European Leaders Met, But Delicately," *New York Times,* 2/17/91.

24. See Vaclav Havel, "The New Year in Prague," *New York Review of Books,* 3/7/91, p. 20.

25. Interview with Kazimierz Duchowski in Warsaw, week of April 6, 1990.

26. Jan Obrman, "From Idealism to Realism," *Report on Eastern Europe,* 12/20/91, p. 13.

27. de Rougemont, p. 106.

28. Thomas Masaryk, *The New Europe: The Slav Standpoint* (Lewisburg: Bucknell University Press, 1972), p. 78.

29. Thomas Masaryk, "Man and his Ideals," in George Kovtun, ed., *The Spirit of Thomas Masaryk (1850-1937)* (New York: St. Martins, 1990), p. 153.

30. Edward Stettner, ed., *Perspectives on Europe* (Cambridge: Schenkman, 1970), p. 135.

31. The initial reactions to the Soviet crackdown continued to borrow from the language of revisionism: "We condemn what happened a year ago, because it violates our national sovereignty and discredits socialism." "A Ten-Point Declaration on the first Anniversary of the Occupation," in Riese, ed., p. 4.

32. Jan Patocka, "Wars of the 20th century and the 20th century as war," *Telos,* Winter 1976-77; Erazim Kohak, *Jan Patocka: Philosophy and Selected Writings* (Chicago: University of Chicago Press, 1989); Richard Rorty's review of Patocka's works, *The New Republic,* 7/1/91.

33. Riese, ed., pp. 199-201.

34. Havel, *Living in Truth,* pp. 47, 69.

35. *Ibid.,* p. 155. For similar reflections in the spirit of both Masaryk and Patocka see Erazim Kohak, "To Live in Truth: Reflections on the Moral Sense of Masaryk's Humanism," in Milic Capek and Karel Hruby, eds., *T.G. Masaryk in Perspective: Comments and Criticism* (SVU Press, 1981).

36. Havel, *Living in Truth,* p. 117. For a more recent portrait of Havel, stripped of theory, see Stephen Schiff, "Havel's Choice," *Vanity Fair,* August 1991.

37. *Ibid.,* p. 62. Alex Callinicos disagrees. He portrays Havel as a "romantic neo-conservative" wholly in thrall to the market. Callinicos, p. 52. I would argue that this vulgarizes Havel's positions.

38. Havel, *Living in Truth,* p. 54.

39. Gella, pp. 133, 140.

40. Similarly, Polish intellectual Adam Michnik objects to the notion that "politics and ethics belong to different worlds...[W]e, the men and the women of the anti-totalitarian opposition movements, have a different view of politics, and our participation in it." Adam Michnik, "After the Revolution," *New Republic,* 7/2/90, pp. 28-9.

41. Rupnik, *The Other Europe,* p. 241.

42. See, e.g., Richard John Neuhaus, "Havel Living in Truth," *National Review,* 11/5/90.

43. Kolakowski, *Modernity on Endless Trial,* p. 149.

44. Michnik, "Maggots and Angels," in *Letters From Prison,* pp. 169-98.

45. *Ibid.,* p. 195.

46. Havel was not entirely bi-polar in his thinking. "Young people in Czechoslovakia," Havel wrote from the underground, "today are quite unaware that we used to have politicians in this country—even communist ones—who were normal, honorable, and stalwart people, despite their often tragic fates...it might bring home to them that politics and politicians are not necessarily objects of mockery, but can also be objects of respect." Vaclav Havel, "Thinking About Frantisek K," in *Open Letter* (New York: Knopf, 1991), p. 372. For a picture of the uncompromising wing of the Czech movement, see "Introduction," in Whipple, ed., p. 58. For an analysis of the Polish counterparts, see Andre Gerrits, *The Failure of Authoritarian Change* (Aldershot: Dartmouth, 1990), pp. 151-57.

47. Milan Simecka, "Between Danton and Robespierre," in Whipple, ed. Also Conor Cruise O'Brien, "Virtue and Terror: Rousseau and Robespierre," *Passion & Cunning* (New York: Simon & Schuster, 1988).

48. Adam Michnik, "After Communism: A Conversation with President Havel," *Gazeta Wyborcza,* reprinted in *World Press Review,* March 1992.

49. "President Vaclav Havel's Address," 3/15/90, p. 6. Misha Glenny puts it this way: "President Havel, whose influence in government and among the population is paramount, has made it clear that Czechoslovakia will not be a playground for liberal economists," Glenny, p. 36.

50. For Klaus's perspective see, e.g., "Interview with Vaclav Klaus," *The European,* 10/25/91.

51. For a recent exposition of Komarek's views, see Valtr Komarek, "Shock Therapy and Its Victims," *New York Times,* 1/5/92.

52. Leslie Collitt, "Havel Aide Says Cabinet Could Fall This Year," *Financial Times,* 7/17/90.

53. See, e.g., John Tagliabue, "Rifts Threatening Czech Reform Movement," *New York Times*, 12/20/90.

54. "Czech and Slovak Federal Republic," *Financial Times Survey*, 11/7/91.

55. "Introduction," in Whipple, ed., p. 50.

56. Gella, p. 30.

57. Turnock, p. 84.

58. Mark Wright, "Ideology and Power in the Czechoslovak Political System," in Lewis, ed., *Eastern Europe: Political Crisis and Legitimation*, pp. 139-40.

59. Not discussed in this chapter are the Moravian and Silesian movements. Moravian and Silesian Autonomists, a separatist party within the Czech lands, came in fifth in the 1990 national elections, and third in the Czech national council elections.

60. Jiri Pehe, "Growing Slovak Demands Seen as Threat to Federalism," *Report on Eastern Europe*, 3/22/91.

61. Carnogursky in particular has shifted his perspective, from imagining more independence for Slovakia only within an integrated Europe (see "An Interview with Jan Carnogursky," *The Insider*, 5/9/91) to supporting secession as a viable alternative (see "Ready for Divorce," *Economist*, 11/2/91).

62. "Plaque to Fascist Unnerves Slovaks," *New York Times*, 7/22/90; Henry Kamm, "War Criminal Gets Slovak Memorial," *New York Times*, 12/3/91. For clerical fascism in the inter-war period, see Vago in Laqueur, ed., p. 246.

63. Asked by a reporter about the anti-Semitism, Havel responded, "Well, as a matter of fact, I would like to be Jewish myself—at least I would be wiser." *Warsaw Voice*, 3/24/91.

64. *Philadelphia Daily News*, 3/11/91.

65. Ariane Genillard, "Havel Urges Referendum on Slovak Demands," *Financial Times*, 9/25/91.

66. Jan Obrman, "Further Discussions on the Future of Federation," *Report on Eastern Europe*, 9/20/91.

67. Quoted in *World Press Review*, February 1991, p. 16.

68. De Rougemont, p. 108.

69. "The Lure of Integration," *Hungarian Observer*, 5/19/90; also Tudjman, pp. 38, 63-4; also Halecki, pp. 125-44.

70. In 1990, in the first large international conference held in Albania, six Balkan foreign ministers proposed a permanent secretariat in Bulgaria.

71. Interview with Vojko Volk in Ljubljana, week of September 10, 1990.

72. See Jane Kramer, p. 85.

73. See, e.g., Marlise Simons, "East Europe's Gypsies: Unwanted Refugees," *New York Times*, 7/30/90.

74. See, e.g., Craig Whitney, "Surprise for Western Europe: Eastern Kin Come Knocking," *New York Times*, 11/15/90.

75. One measure of these extinguished hopes was the elimination of the GDR Foreign Ministry's innovative department devoted exclusively to Central and Eastern Europe. During its short lifespan, the department concentrated on furthering diplomatic contacts from below. It protested the adoption of a new West German law requiring visas for Romanians, Bulgarians, and Poles to visit Germany. It tentatively explored new East German relations with the Third World. It reached out to Third World workers in the GDR. Like many innovative experiments during the GDR's brief democratic autonomy, the department was ended by unification. Interview with Friederike Kockert of the East German Foreign Ministry, in Prague, week of June 15, 1990.

76. As many as 100,000 troops from the European theater will form a force designed to fight outside of Europe (chiefly in the Middle East). See Paul Montgomery, "NATO Agrees to Expand a Rapid Reaction Force," *New York Times*, 4/14/91.

77. See Kolakowski, *Toward a Marxist Humanism*, pp. 9-38.

Chapter 8

1. There is also the suspicion that the critical subjective accounts one wants are not available. As *New York Times* Middle East correspondent Thomas Friedman describes this phenomenon: "any protagonist in the Middle East who is ready to talk to me cannot be worth talking to; he cannot be at the center of what is happening. It's the people who won't talk to me whom I really want to meet." Friedman, p. 75.

2. Quoted in Andrei Codrescu, *A Hole in the Flag* (New York: Morrow, 1991), p. 135.

3. For this interrogative approach to Romania, see also Katherine Verdery and Gail Kligman, "Romania after Ceausescu: Post-Communist Communism," in Banac, ed.

4. Interview with Mariana Celac in Bucharest, week of July 30, 1990.

5. Mary Ellen Fischer, *Nicolae Ceausescu: A Study in Political Leadership* (Boulder: Lynne Rienner, 1989), p. 50.

6. Trond Gilberg, *Nationalism and Communism in Romania: The Rise and Fall of Ceausescu's Personal Dictatorship* (Boulder: Westview, 1990), p. 142.

7. *Ibid.*

8. Fischer, p. 1.

9. *Ibid.*, pp. 130-40.

10. See Robert King, *A History of the Romanian Communist Party* (Stanford: Hoover Institute, 1980), p. 91.

11. Ion Mihai Pacepa, *Red Horizons* (Washington: Regnery Gateway, 1987), p. 211.

12. Robert Cullen, "Down With the Tyrant," *The New Yorker*, 4/12/90, p. 100.

13. Aurelia Tanguy, "A Submissive Nation," *Across Frontiers*, Spring/Summer 1988.

14. Edward Behr, *Kiss the Hand You Cannot Bite* (New York: Villard, 1991), pp. 239-40. Also Jonathan Eyal, "Why Romania Could Not Avoid Bloodshed," in Prins, ed.

15. Gilberg, *Nationalism and Communism in Romania*, p. 143. Also see Behr, p. 240.

16. For description of this project see, e.g., Matei Lykiardopol, "The Mutilation of Bucharest," *UNESCO Courier*, January 1991.

17. There were nevertheless some important challenges to Ceausescu's rule, notably the 1977 Jiu miner strikes, the 1985 riots in the Banat, the 1986 strikes in Transylvania, and the 1987 anti-Ceausescu demonstrations in Brasov. For more individualistic protests, see Robert Sharlet, "Human Rights and Wrongs: Dissent and Repression in Eastern Europe," in Nicholas Kittrie and Ivan Volgyes, eds., *The Uncertain Future: Gorbachev's Eastern Bloc* (New York: Paragon House, 1988), p. 109.

18. Behr, pp. 253-57.

19. Fischer, p. 265. Also see William Crowther, "'Ceausescuism' and Civil-Military Relations in Romania," *Armed Forces and Society*, Winter 1989.

20. Vladimir Tismaneanu, "New Masks, Old Faces," *New Republic*, 2/5/90, p. 20. Also see Matei Calinescu and Vladimir Tismaneanu, "The 1989 Revolution and Romania's Future," *Problems of Communism*, January-April 1991; also Marc Almond, "Romania Since the Revolution," *Government and Opposition*, Autumn 1990; for some of the original speculation see Jonathan Eyal, "Rival Versions of Uprising Back Claims to Power," *The Manchester Guardian*, 1/5/90.

21. Codrescu, pp. 203-205.

22. See Calinescu and Tismaneanu, p. 45 fn.

23. Interview with Petru Clej in Bucharest, week of August 6, 1990.

24. "It is also fairly clear that most of the Securitate forces actively opposed the revolution and attempted to stop it through violent acts in Timisoara and elsewhere. But there were also individuals and, allegedly, certain units in this organization that helped bring about the fundamental changes that the revolution seemed to augur." Trond Gilberg, "Romania: Will History Repeat Itself?" *Current History,* December 1990, p. 410.

25. Chuck Sudetic, "Romanian Protestors Assert Revolution Has Been Stolen," *New York Times,* 5/14/90. Mazilu asserts that he only taught several courses at the school.

26. Interview with Cornel Nistorescu, editor of *Expres,* in Bucharest, week of August 6, 1990.

27. Interviews with Gabriel Andreescu and Velicu Radina in Bucharest, week of August 6, 1990.

28. David Binder, "Romanians Using the Secret Police," *New York Times,* 10/4/90. *Expres* estimates 6,000. See translation of article in "The Securitate (Still) Wants You," *Harpers,* September 1991.

29. David Binder, "Ceausescu's Snipers Still At Large, Ex-Officials Say," *New York Times,* 8/29/90.

30. Stephen Engelberg, "Uneasy Romania Asks: Where Are the Spies Now?" *New York Times,* 2/13/91.

31. Mihai Sturdza, "The Files of the State Security Police," *Report on Eastern Europe,* 9/13/91.

32. Kathleen Hunt, "Letter From Bucharest," *New Yorker,* 7/23/90, p. 74.

33. An independent television station wouldn't go on the air until the end of 1991.

34. For background on Iliescu and the rumor that he was Gorbachev's choice to lead Romania's *perestroika,* see Gilberg, *Nationalism and Communism in Romania,* pp. 122, 154.

35. For instances of election fraud, see "News From Romania: Election Report," *Helsinki Watch,* May 1990.

36. Interview with Petru Clej in Bucharest, week of August 6, 1990.

37. These figures come from "Romania: Aftermath to the June Violence in Bucharest," *Helsinki Watch,* May 1990. The report quotes extensively from "minority" (opposition) and "majority" (Front) reports prepared by a parliamentary inquiry.

38. That the majority were indeed miners has been verified by the accounts of several reporters who visited the mines after the June incidents. See, e.g., David Binder, "Romanian Miners Dispute Criticism," *New York Times,* 9/6/90.

39. Helsinki Watch, "Romania: Aftermath," p. 20.

40. See Vladimir Tismaneanu, "Homage to Golania," *New Republic,* 7/30/90, p. 17.

41. Interview with Cornel Nistorescu, week of August 6, 1990.

42. Simpson, *Blowback,* pp. 78-9. Also see Vago, in Laqueur, ed., p. 232. Investigations in 1952 revealed that over 30 percent of officials in the West German foreign ministry were former Nazis, with comparable percentages in the police and judiciary. See David Childs, "The Far Right in Germany since 1945," in Luciano Cheles *et al.,* eds., *Neo-Fascism in Europe* (London: Longman, 1991).

43. Simpson, p. 78.

44. In May 1991, NSF Senator Dan Iosif and NSF Deputy Claudiu Iordache began to push for a parliamentary investigation into deputies' links to the Securitate. *The Insider,* 5/30/91. Meanwhile, new citizens' groups such as Patriot, designed to counteract the influence of the Intelligence Service, are fighting to root out and destroy the Securitate's legacy.

45. Quoted from a description of the National Salvation Front in "Choosing a New Romanian Leader," *New York Times*, 5/20/90. Writers with less pretense to objectivity state their cases more baldly, as with Robert Kaplan, "Bloody Romania," *New Republic*, 7/30/90.

46. For this argument, see also, e.g., Andrzej Korbonski, "Ideology Abused," in Kittrie and Volgyes, eds., pp. 51-4.

47. Dan Ionescu, "National Salvation Front Holds Convention," *Report on Eastern Europe*, 3/29/91.

48. That July, for instance, the editor of the independent daily *Romania Libera* called for a renewal of aid. Steven Greenhouse, "Stung by Denial of Western Aid, Romanian Officials Say Aim Is Democracy," *New York Times*, 7/14/90.

49. See, e.g., "Once Blackballed Romania Joins the Aid Club," *New York Times*, 1/31/91.

50. Allegations of former Securitate agents making money from private companies were also of little importance. Engelberg, "Uneasy Romania Asks: Where Are the Spies Now?" *New York Times*, 2/13/91.

51. Jean-Baptiste Naudet, "Whose Hand was Behind the Miners' Coup in Romania?" *Le Monde*, reprinted in the *Manchester Guardian Weekly*, 10/4/91.

52. Celestine Bohlen, "Romania's Leader Vows Freer Reins," *New York Times*, 10/3/91.

53. For background on the Transylvania dispute, see Fischer-Galati, p. 9; Jaszi, pp. 306-7fn.

54. A point made by Charles Gati, "East-Central Europe: The Morning After," *Foreign Affairs*, Winter 1990/91, p. 135. Also see Henry Kamm, "Rising Verbal Attacks Shake Romania's Jews," *New York Times*, 6/19/91. The Romanian Parliament has officially honored Antonescu. Neither President Iliescu nor then Prime Minister Roman, Kamm reports, supported the measure. A mock fascist newspaper sold out its 100,000 copies in September 1991. "The danger is real," the paper's editorial read. "The proof is that you have bought this paper." *Report on Eastern Europe*, 10/4/91.

55. Interview with Manole Neagoe in Bucharest, week of August 6, 1990. Even Western scholars seem to have a blind spot concerning Antonescu's role in the murder and deportations of Jews. See, e.g., Hugh Seton-Watson's claim that Antonescu's destruction of the Iron Guard actually saved hundreds of thousands of Jews, in *The "Sick Heart" of Europe* (Seattle: University of Washington Press, 1975), p. 43.

56. Dennis Deletant, "The Role of Vatra Romaneasca in Transylvania," *Report on Eastern Europe*, 2/1/91; Michael Shafir, "The Greater Romania Party," *Report on Eastern Europe*, 11/15/91.

57. Trip to Gradinari, week of August 6, 1990.

58. Interview at Medecins du Monde in Bucharest, week of July 30, 1990.

59. It would of course be wiser to argue that all social interaction, whether in capitalist or communist societies, is based on compromises. See, e.g., discussion in Erving Goffman, *Asylums* (New York: Anchor, 1961), pp. 181-93.

60. See Judy Dempsey, "Haunted by the Ghosts of the Past," *Financial Times*, 11/11/91.

61. John Tagliabue, "Uncovering of Spies Jolt East Germany," *New York Times*, 9/15/90.

62. Stephen Kinzer, "Germany's New Custodian of Stasi Secrets Insists on Justice," *New York Times*, 1/20/91.

63. See, e.g., "Spying Comes in From the Cold War," *Der Spiegel*, reprinted in *World Press Review*, March 1992.

64. Interview with Ferenc Koszeg in Budapest, week of July 16, 1990.

65. See David Franklin, "Bounced Czechs," *New Republic*, 6/10/91.

66. See "Prague Spy Charges Raise Witch-Hunt Fear," *New York Times*, 4/2/91; Lawrence Weschler, "Jan Kavan in Kafkaland," *New Politics*, vol. 3, no. 3; Jan Kavan, "Right of Reply," *East*

European Reporter, Spring/Summer 1991; Catherine Monroy, "Czechoslovakia Asks Whether its Purge has Gone too Far," *Le Monde,* reprinted in *Manchester Guardian Weekly,* 3/15/92.

67. Dan Ionescu, "The Posthumous Ceausescu Cult and Its High Priests," *Report on Eastern Europe,* 5/31/91.

Chapter 9

1. Peter Alter, *Nationalism* (London: Edward Arnold, 1989), p. 5.

2. Clyde Haberman, "Bulgaria Convenes a Post-Communist Parliament," *New York Times,* 7/11/90.

3. In *ProQuest,* a periodical data base covering the last several years, the article distribution as of July 1991 was: East Germany (916), Poland (828), Czechoslovakia (514), Hungary (495), Romania (326), Yugoslavia (235), Bulgaria (94).

4. Ernest Klein, *A Comprehensive Etymological Dictionary of the English Language,* vol. 1 (New York: Elsevier, 1966).

5. Magris, p. 340.

6. Halecki, p. 78. Leslie Tihany adds that "as Pushkin said of the Tartars, the Turks brought their subjects neither Aristotle nor algebra. When they finally receded, they left behind devastation, backwardness, and underdevelopment." Tihany, p. 95. As Perry Anderson points out, Machiavelli was the first theorist to "use the Ottoman State as the antithesis of a European monarchy." Perry Anderson, p. 397.

7. George Logio, *Bulgaria: Past & Present* (Manchester: Sherratt & Hughes, 1936), p. 309. Also see E.L. Jones, pp. 175-92. Leland Buxton writes, "The fanaticism of the Turk is of a mild variety compared with that of most of the Christians," *The Black Sheep of the Balkans* (London: Nisbet & Co., 1920), p. viii.

8. Coles, pp. 112-3, 117, 175.

9. Richard Crampton, *Bulgaria: 1878-1918* (New York: Columbia University Press, 1983), p. 71.

10. *Ibid.*

11. Bilal Simsir, *The Turks of Bulgaria* (London: K. Rustem & Brother, 1988), pp. 4-7.

12. Ilker Alp, *Bulgarian Atrocities: Documents and Photographs* (London: K. Rustem & Brother, 1988), p. 5.

13. See, e.g., Georgi Bokov, *Modern Bulgaria* (Sofia: Sofia Press, 1981). Crampton merely lists the emigration figures and doesn't provide any commentary.

14. Simsir, p. 162.

15. See Philip Shashko, "The Past in Bulgaria's Future," *Problems of Communism,* September/October 1990.

16. Quoted in Simsir, p. 133.

17. Torsten Baest, "Bulgaria's War at Home," *Across Frontiers,* Winter 1985.

18. Staar, p. 52.

19. Ilker Alp estimates "thousands" were killed by the infantry troops on March 14, 1972 alone. He also maintains that in June 1972 "Bulgarian air-planes sprayed poisonous gas on the mountainous areas where the Turks had taken shelter and killed thousands of Turks by poisoning." Neither of these incidents have been independently confirmed, however. See Alp, pp. 147, 156.

20. *Destroying Ethnic Identity: The Expulsion of the Bulgarian Turks, Helsinki Watch,* October 1989, p. 5.

21. *Helsinki Watch* reports that "villages with predominantly Turkish inhabitants were surrounded by police and troops, often in the early hours of the morning. The villages were sealed off and ethnic Turks were forced, in some cases at gunpoint, to accept identity cards bearing their new Slavic names." *Ibid.*, p. 5-6. See also Stanko Todorov's nationalist-communist fulminations in "Name Changes in Bulgaria," reprinted in Gale Stokes, *From Stalinism to Pluralism*, (New York: Oxford University Press, 1991).

22. Misha Glenny reports that the decision was undertaken only by Zhivkov and associate Milko Balev without the advice and consent of the Party hierarchy. Glenny, p. 172.

23. *Destroying Ethnic Identity*, p. 7.

24. *Ibid.*, p. 1.

25. Quoted in "Out of Bulgaria," *Economist*, 6/17/89.

26. Quoted in "News From Bulgaria," *Helsinki Watch*, March 1990.

27. Interview with Deyan Kironov in Sofia, week of August 20, 1990.

28. Interview with Vikhr Kristev in Sofia, week of August 20, 1990.

29. Thomas Kuhn, *The Structure of Scientific Revolutions* (Chicago: University of Chicago Press, 1970).

30. *Destroying Ethnic Identity*, p. 64.

31. It is true that Bulgarian Jews suffered the least when compared to the fate of Jews throughout the region. Twenty-two percent were killed in Bulgaria compared to 90 percent in Poland, 83 percent in Slovakia, 70 percent in Hungary, 60 percent in Yugoslavia, and 50 percent in Romania. Nevertheless, the Bulgarian government permitted 14,000 Jews to be sent to death in Hitler's gas chambers, and those who remained were subjected to considerable persecution. See Lucy Dawidowicz, *The War Against the Jews, 1933-1945* (New York: Bantam, 1981), pp. 522-27 and table on p. 544.

32. Zlatko Anguelov writes in the *East European Reporter*, Spring/Summer 1991, p. 41, "Most discouraging about the present situation is that the majority of Bulgarian intellectuals appear, at least implicitly, to side with the nationalists." It is also worth noting that the Bulgarians are not the only culprits. Turks, Pomaks, and Gypsies are also heavily discriminated against in the Thracian part of Greece. See "Race in Thrace," *Economist*, 3/2/91.

33. Interview with Piotr Diertliev in Sofia, week of August 20, 1990.

34. Interview with Bojko Nikolov in Sofia, week of August 20, 1990. One recent poll revealed that 48 percent of Bulgarians view Turkey as a "serious threat." See Engelbrekt, "Movement of Rights and Freedom to Compete in Elections," *Report on Eastern Europe*, 10/4/91.

35. *Duma*, 8/13/90.

36. *Duma*, 8/16/90.

37. Interview with Philip Bokov in Sofia, week of August 20, 1990.

38. "Bulgarian Opposition Claims Victory in a Close Vote," *New York Times*, 10/15/91; Mary Battiata, "Bulgaria's Democrats Face Dilemma Over Turkish Party's Role," *Washington Post*, 10/17/91; "Ethnic Turks Hold Key to Minority Cabinet," *The European*, 11/1-3/91.

39. Interview with Miroslav Darmov in Sofia, week of August 20, 1990.

40. Interview with Krassimir Kanev, presidential counselor on the national issue and member of Ecoglasnost, in New York City, April 6, 1991.

41. Quoted in Zlatko Anguelov, "The Leader and His Movement," *East European Reporter*, Autumn/Winter 1990, p. 27.

42. Kjell Engelbrekt, "The Movement for Rights and Freedoms," *Report on Eastern Europe*, 5/31/91.

43. Kjell Engelbrekt, "Movement for Rights and Freedoms to Compete in Elections," *Report on Eastern Europe,* 10/4/91.

44. Duncan Perry, "Ethnic Turks Face Bulgarian Nationalism," *Report on Eastern Europe,* 3/15/91.

45. *Report on Eastern Europe,* 1/25/91.

46. Quoted in Duncan Perry, "The New Prime Minister and the Moslems," *Report on Eastern Europe,* 1/18/91.

47. *Report on Eastern Europe,* 5/3/91.

48. *Report on Eastern Europe,* 10/11/91.

49. Rada Nikolaev, "The New, Noncommunist Government," *Report on Eastern Europe,* 11/22/91. Shortly thereafter classes in Turkish began, along with the expected nationalist protests. *Report on Eastern Europe,* 11/29/91.

50. Even Jeri Laber's otherwise helpful overview in the *New York Review of Books* neglected to mention the Movement, Jeri Laber, "The Bulgarian Difference," *New York Review of Books,* 5/17/90. Laber works for Helsinki Watch, an organization which has done extensive work on ethnic Turks—which makes her omission all the more confusing. John Bell's "'Post-Communist' Bulgaria" in *Current History,* December 1990, at least mentions the Movement though doesn't provide much information on its background or aims. In coverage of the Bulgarian elections in the *New York Times,* the Movement received a mention only the day before the elections, Chuck Sudetic, "Election Buoys Bulgaria's Ethnic Turks," *New York Times,* 6/10/90. The election day story neglected to mention it, and only the day after the election did it become clear that the Movement had come in third. See Celestine Bohlen, "Ex-Communists Decisively Lead Bulgarian Voting," *New York Times,* 6/11/90; and Celestine Bohlen, "Bulgarian Voting Stuns Opposition," *New York Times,* 6/12/90. The major exception to this lack of coverage, as should be clear from other footnotes, was Radio Free Europe's *Report on Eastern Europe.*

51. The Movement won 94 mayoralties compared to the UDF's 64. However, the Movement captured the mayoral spot in only one major city—Kardzhali. The BSP was the clear winner on the local level with 385 mayoralties. *Report on Eastern Europe,* 10/25/91.

52. "News From Bulgaria," *Helsinki Watch,* August 1990, p. 11.

53. Crampton, p. 174.

54. Chuck Sudetic, "Vietnamese in Bulgaria: Bitter Times," *New York Times,* 8/1/90.

55. *Report on Eastern Europe,* 4/5/91.

56. Some exceptions in the Western press: Dan Pavel, "Wanderers," *New Republic,* 3/4/91; Paul Hockenos, "Free to Hate," *New Statesman and New Society,* 4/12/91; Toby Sonneman, "Old Hatreds in the New Europe: Romania After the Revolutions," *Tikkun,* January/February 1992. For a more academic treatment, see Crowe and Kolsti. Unfortunately this edited volume doesn't address the question of Gypsies in Bulgaria.

57. Luan Troxel, "Bulgaria's Gypsies: Numerically Strong, Politically Weak," *RFE/RL Research Report,* 3/6/92.

58. Simsir, p. 55.

59. *Ibid.,* p. 176.

60. Interview with Krassimir Kanev.

61. In part Bulgaria does not want to grant "Macedonians" who live in the Pirin region the special rights they enjoyed from 1944 to 1948. Pedro Ramet, "Religion and Nationalism in Yugoslavia," in Pedro Ramet, ed., *Religion and Nationalism in Soviet and East European Politics* (Durham: Duke University Press, 1989), p. 374. According to a September 1991 poll, 65 percent of Bulgarians believed Macedonians to be Bulgarian; only 10 percent did not. *Report on Eastern Europe,* 10/4/91.

62. Pavlowich, p. 71.

63. See F. Stephen Larrabee, "Long Memories and Short Fuses: Change and Instability in the Balkans," *International Security*, Winter 1990/91, p. 75.

64. Quoted in "Here Comes Reform, at a Price," *Economist*, 3/9/91.

65. Viktor Valkov, "Partnership Between Bulgaria and NATO: a Promising Development," *NATO Review*, October 1991, p. 17.

66. See, e.g., "A Road Map to Bulgaria," *Nation's Business*, March 1991.

67. Jaszi, p. 31.

68. See, e.g., Hans Kohn, *The Idea of Nationalism* (New York: Collier, 1944), pp. 3-24.

69. Quoted in Dan Beck, "The Luther Revival," in Pedro Ramet, *Religion and Nationalism*, p. 223.

70. Garton Ash, *The Magic Lantern*, p. 145.

71. For the notion of an "irreducible plurality of cultures," see the interview with Isaiah Berlin in *New Perspectives Quarterly*, Fall 1991.

72. Benedict Anderson, *Imagined Communities* (London: Verso, 1983).

73. Etienne Balibar makes this point with respect to the "true" German and the Aryan archetypes. See "Racism as Universalism," *New Political Science*, Fall/Winter 1989.

74. Rupnik, p. 22.

75. Tadeusz Konwicki, *A Minor Apocalypse* (New York: Farrar, Straus and Giroux, 1983), p. 57.

76. Tadeusz Konwicki, *Moonrise, Moonset* (New York: Farrar, Straus and Giroux), 1987), p. 101.

77. FIDESZ program, prepared in Hungary in 1990.

78. For a a useful genealogy of the concept of "Oriental despotism," see Perry Anderson, pp. 462-66 with chart on p. 472.

79. Mieczyslaw Orlowicz, *Przewodnik Warszawy* (Warszawa: Wydawnistwo PAN, 1922), p. 136.

80. An interesting interpretation along these lines is David Carlin, Jr.'s "East Meets West," *Commonweal*, 3/8/91, pp. 150-51.

81. The push toward ethnic homogeneity by both Bulgaria and Turkey was an old solution. In 1878, the Ottoman empire representative suggested a huge population transfer: "Such a large population exchange which would entail the relocation of hundreds of thousands of human beings would not have been an easy undertaking, but it would have been the most humane solution under the conditions which prevailed at that time." Quoted in Simsir, p. 158. For some, such population transfers still are the only solution. "It seems," Bilal Simsir writes in 1988, "that there is only one way left for solving radically the case of the Turks of Bulgaria: that is, to bring these fellow-Turks to Turkey. A comprehensive emigration, which admits no exception, which leaves out no single Turk, is the sole and definitive way to a solution." Simsir, p. xvi.

Chapter 10

1. Austrian playwright Franz Grillparzer (1791-1872) was describing the decline of the Habsburg empire but his quote holds true for the Yugoslavia of today. Quoted in Jaszi, p. 11.

2. See "Roads Sealed as Yugoslav Unrest Mounts," *New York Times*, 8/19/90.

3. Zvi Gitelman, "Federalism and Multi-Culturalism in Socialist Systems," in Daniel Elazar, ed., *Federalism and Political Integration* (Lanham, MD: University Press of America, 1984), p. 167.

4. The Illyrians were a pre-Christian people who inhabited the Balkan region around the 10th century B.C. For more information on the roots of pan-Slavism and pan-Yugoslavianism, see Aleksa Djilas, *The Contested Country* (Cambridge: Harvard University Press, 1991), pp. 22-4.

5. This was particularly true under Count Khuen Hedervary's regime in Croatia (1882-1903). See Jaszi, pp. 109, 371.

6. Quoted in *ibid.*, p. 16.

7. Kann, pp. 513-17.

8. Ivo Banac, *The National Question in Yugoslavia* (Ithaca: Cornell University Press, 1984), p. 416.

9. Dennison Rusinow, "Nationalities Policy and the 'National Question,'" in Pedro Ramet, ed., *Yugoslavia in the 1980s* (Boulder: Westview, 1985), p. 131. Political scientist Daniel Elazar writes in the late 1970s: "Yugoslavia is an excellent example of the use of federalism to enable different nationalities to live together." Elazar, "The Role of Federalism in Political Integration," in Elazar, ed., p. 35.

10. Pawlovitch, p. 73. The consensus view among Yugoslav experts seemed to be that the country combined elements of both confederation and federation. See, e.g., Pedro Ramet, *Nationalism and Federalism: Yugoslavia, 1963-1983* (Bloomington: Indiana University Press, 1984), p. 69.

11. Anton Logoreci, "A Clash Between Two Nationalisms in Kosova," in Arshi Pipa and Sami Repishti, eds., *Studies in Kosova* (New York: Columbia University Press, 1984). Logoreci notes that because of this repression 230,000 Albanians left Yugoslavia from 1953 to 1966.

12. Pedro Ramet, "Religion and Nationalism in Yugoslavia," in Ramet, ed., *Religion and Nationalism in Soviet and East European Politics*, p. 316.

13. Within the Yugoslav federation, Kosovo did make irrefutable advances in literacy, life expectancy, health care, and so on. See Peter Prishti, "Kosova's Economy: Problems and Prospects," in Pipa and Repishti, eds.

14. For a rundown of this complicated legal issue, see Sami Repishti, "The Evolution of Kosova's Autonomy Within the Yugoslav Constitutional Framework," in *ibid.*

15. The Yugoslav government in the 1950s began economic assistance to developing regions under the impression that regional disparities could be eliminated within a decade. This estimate was clearly inaccurate. See Turnock, p. 97.

16. Pawlovitch, p. 74.

17. Michael Scammell, "The New Yugoslavia," *New York Review of Books*, 7/19/90. For more background, see Ramet, *Nationalism and Federalism.*

18. Nora Beloff, *Tito's Flawed Legacy* (London: Victor Gollancz, 1985), p. 206.

19. Ivo Duchacek, *The Territorial Dimension of Politics, Within, Among and Across Nations* (Boulder: Westview, 1986), p. 123.

20. Quoted in Staar, p. 239.

21. Figures from Scammell, "The New Yugoslavia."

22. Pawlovitch, pp. 86-7.

23. In 1981, twice as much money went to Kosovo than Slovenia. Of a $110 million loan from the World Bank to finance small- and medium-sized projects, $50 million went to Kosovo, $30 million to Bosnia-Herzogovina, $20 million to Montenegro, and $10 million to Macedonia. Staar, p. 238. The official name for this program was the long and alliterative Federation Fund for Financing Development of Less-Developed Republics and the Province of Kosovo.

24. Helsinki Watch has written about Serbian pressure and intimidation on the Kosovo MPs who voted for the elimination of the region's autonomous status: "It was pointed out that the result was foregone anyway, and that they would lose their jobs and their sinecures, and would very likely be arrested as well if they voted against ratification." *Yugoslavia: Crisis in Kosovo,* Helsinki Watch, March 1990, p. 14.

25. *Yugoslavia: Crisis in Kosovo,* p. 15.

26. There had been isolated cases of Albanian attacks on Serbs, but these were exaggerated by Milosevic to serve his political ends. For more on Milosevic see, e.g., Sabrina Ramet, "Serbia's Slobodan Milosevic: A Profile," *Orbis*, Winter 1991; Roger Thurow, "Divisive Populist," *Wall Street Journal*, 10/10/91.

27. Interview with Zarko Puhovski in Zagreb, week of September 3, 1990.

28. Gitelman, p. 168.

29. Ivan Voivoda, presentation at the New School for Social Research, New York, 2/19/92.

30. Interview with Marko Hren in Ljubljana, week of September 3, 1990.

31. Masaryk, *The New Europe*, p. 77.

32. Of course, Yugoslavs and particularly Slovenians were not in general happy with recession. Chuck Sudetic, "Slovenia Hopes to Find New Role in Yugoslavia," *New York Times*, 7/16/90.

33. Interview with Dushitsa Sefaragic in Zagreb, week of September 3, 1990.

34. Interview with Mira Oklobdzija in Zagreb, week of September 3, 1990.

35. Djilas, p. 122.

36. See, e.g., Chuck Sudetic, "Piles of Bones in Yugoslavia Point to Partisan Massacres," *New York Times*, 7/9/90. Also Nikolai Tolstoy, "Bare Bones," *New Republic*, 12/24/90.

37. While the Belgrade government conducted "hits" on anti-Yugoslav targets abroad, the Ustasha continued to function secretly. During the 1970s and 1980s, secret Ustasha cells conducted bombings, hijackings, and even the murder of several Yugoslav diplomats. See Simpson, p. 198; Jane Kramer, pp. 100-01.

38. Glenny, p. 127.

39. Interview with Puhovski. According to Scammell, Tudjman has called for "a return to Croatia's historical borders." Michael Scammell, "Yugoslavia: the Awakening," *New York Review of Books*, 6/28/90, p. 43. The disparaging comments Tudjman made against Serbs on a May 1991 trip to London confirm this desire. See Judy Dempsey, "Politicians Ride Nationalist Tiger in Croatia," *Financial Times*, 5/9/91. See also Daniel Martin, "Croatia's Borders: Over the Edge," *New York Times*, 11/23/91. Tudjman's side of the story can be found in his op-ed, "All We Croatians Want is Democracy," *New York Times*, 6/30/90.

40. See the provocative article by Robert Kaplan, "Croatianism," *New Republic*, 11/25/91. In his book *Bespuca* ("Impasse"), Tudjman makes several extremely questionable remarks concerning Jews, occasionally calling attention to the anti-Semitism of the authors cited, only to quote them at length further on, or note that others have made similar observations. For instance, at one point, Tudjman quotes a source who writes, "A Jew is always a Jew, even in the Jasenovac camp…selfishness, slyness, lack of integrity, avarice, perfidy, and secretiveness are their main characteristics." Tudjman goes on to comment that "Prnjatovic's judgment shows exaggeration and an anti-Semitic attitude, but some other witnesses have made similar statements." The sections quoted come from Branimir Anzulovic's translation of the fourth chapter, p. 9.

41. See profile by Yves Heller, "The 'Black Legion'—Croatia's Mercenary Arm," *Le Monde*, reprinted in *Manchester Guardian Weekly*, 9/22/91.

42. Chuck Sudetic, "Croatian Serbs Declare Their Autonomy," *New York Times*, 10/2/90.

43. "Serbian Settlers for Albanian Area," *New York Times*, 3/14/90.

44. *Report on Eastern Europe*, 10/18/91.

45. It is important to mention, as Dennison Rusinow does, that "there is very little at the center by way of power, funds and favors to be redistributed or other spoils to quarrel over." Rusinow, "Nationalities Policy and the 'National Question,'" in *Yugoslavia in the 1980s*, p. 141.

46. Chuck Sudetic, "Serb Chief Warns of Land Demands," *New York Times*, 1/11/91.

47. According to a recent poll, 56 percent of Serbs are anti-communist and only 27 percent identify themselves as socialists. *Report on Eastern Europe*, 11/22/91.

48. Florence Hartman, "A lonely voice for peace in Yugoslavia's ethnic strife," *Le Monde*, reprinted in *Manchester Guardian Weekly*, 9/29/91. Draskovic has changed his position several times. Previously he supported a united Yugoslavia comprised of Swiss-type cantons. *Report on Eastern Europe*, 4/19/91.

49. *Yugoslavia: The March 1991 Demonstrations in Belgrade*, Helsinki Watch, May 1991, p. 5.

50. Interview with Sonja Licht in Belgrade, week of August 29, 1990.

51. Interview with Mitja Zagar in Ljubljana, week of September 10, 1990. Zagar is supported by Slovene economist Alexander Bajt. See interview in *East European Reporter*, Spring/Summer 1991, p. 17. When I talked again with Zagar, he was rather more pessimistic. "Democratic federation at this stage seems impossible." Interview in New York City, April 6, 1991.

52. Jaszi, pp. 123-4.

53. Croatia and Slovenia do have minor disagreements over Istria and Medjimora. See Milan Andrejevich, "Relations between Croatia and Slovenia," *Report on Eastern Europe*, 3/22/91.

54. Laura Silber, "Belgrade Plans to Resettle Serbs to Occupied Croatia," *Financial Times*, 11/22/91.

55. See the two Helsinki Watch reports that were issued as letters to Milosevic (1/21/92) and Tudjman (2/13/92).

56. Dennison Rusinow, "Yugoslavia: Balkan Breakup?" *Foreign Policy*, Summer 1991, p. 156.

57. Judy Dempsey and Laura Silber, "A Six-prong Quest for Power," *Financial Times*, 6/27/91; Judy Dempsey, "Secret Talks Over Yugoslav Borders to be Restarted," *Financial Times*, 7/10/91.

58. Timothy Heritage, "Serbs to Carve New Republic From Bosnia," *Washington Post*, 12/22/91.

59. Judy Dempsey, "Secret Talks on Dividing Bosnia Revived in Zagreb," *Financial Times*, 1/16/92.

60. Milan Andrejevich, "Montenegro Follows Its Own Course," *Report on Eastern Europe*, 11/22/91.

61. For history and assessment of rival claims to Macedonia, see Robert Kaplan, "History's Cauldron," *Atlantic*, June 1991.

62. Glenny, p. 137.

63. "Breech Birth of Two Nations," *Manchester Guardian Weekly*, 1/26/92; Chuck Sudetic, "UN Peace Plan for Yugoslavia Eroded by New Croatian Demand," *New York Times*, 1/31/92; Hella Pick and John Palmer, "Croatia Loses Interest in Truce," *Manchester Guardian Weekly*, 2/9/92; Ian Traynor, "Croatia Set to Acquire MiGs," *Manchester Guardian Weekly*, 2/16/92.

64. For the latest European statement, see "Declaration on the Guidelines on the Recognition of New States in Eastern Europe and in the Soviet Union," *European Community*, Brussels, 12/16/91.

65. Riker establishes a spectrum for federations that ranges from centralized to peripheralized depending on where the power is concentrated. William Riker, *Federalism: Origin, Operation, Significance* (Boston: Little Brown, 1964), p. 6. For the discussion of federation in this passage, I have also drawn from Ivo Duchacek, "The Territorial Dimension of Politics," and Daniel Elazar, "The Role of Federalism in Political Integration," in Elazar, ed.

66. Ethnic groups or nations were frequently forced to join both federations (as in Switzerland) and unitary states (India). Preston King, *Federalism and Federation* (Baltimore: The Johns Hopkins University Press, 1982), pp. 88-9.

67. See Zoran Pajic, "Yugoslavia and the Confederation Model," *Review of International Affairs*, 4/20/91.

68. For a proposal for confederation, see "A Confederate Model Among the South Slavic States," *Review of International Affairs,* 10/20/90.

69. See Schaeffer, *passim.*

70. Quoted in Howard LaFranci, "Conference on Yugoslav Crisis Tests EC Resolve," *Christian Science Monitor,* 9/6/91.

71. Quoted in David Buchan, "Yugoslav Crisis Thrusts Dilatory EC into Frontline," *Financial Times,* 6/29-30/91. Deputy Secretary of State Lawrence Eagleburger's business connections in Yugoslavia also contributed to the incoherence of US policy.

72. Polanyi, p. 3.

Conclusion

1. Quoted in Stettner, p. 12. Barraclough made his statement at a conference on Europe in 1969. More than two decades later, his words have even greater resonance.

2. To be more precise, economic integration began with a free-trade area (no internal custom duties or trade quotas) which then became a customs union (a common import duty) and only then turned into a common market (the free movement of capital and labor). See Dennis Swann, *The Economics of the Common Market,* (London: Penguin, 1990), pp. 11-2.

3. Prior to 1986, the Council of Ministers more or less abided by consensus: all members had to agree to a proposal before the proposal could be passed. After 1986, the Council moved to majority voting. If a single member objects to a particular proposal, as Britain has done over the Social Charter, the majority can pass the controversial program and move on to other business.

4. This idea, as Dennis Swann points out, goes back as far as German thinker Friedrich Naumann in the early part of the century. Swann, p. 1.

5. Edith Cresson, "France and the European Community," *Harvard International Review,* Summer 1989, p. 28.

6. "1992—The Social Dimension," *European Documentation,* 1990, p. 5. Furthermore, as Italian Foreign Minister Gianni De Michelis argues, inclusion of the eastern lands into the new Europe will only improve these figures, boosting Western European business with the extension of the market to 140 million new consumers. De Michelis, "Europe: A Golden Opportunity Not to be Missed" in Lawrence Freedman, ed., *Europe Transformed* (New York: St. Martins, 1990), pp. 514-15.

7. Pascal Fontaine, "Europe—A Fresh Start," *European documentation,* March 1990, p. 25.

8. Although the United Kingdom got opt-out clauses inserted in the agreements on EMU and the Social Charter, it will not likely take advantage of the compromise.

9. For a debate on this issue, see Timothy Garton Ash *et al.,* "Let the East Europeans In!" and William Pfaff, "Keeping the East Europeans Out," *New York Review of Books,* 10/24/91.

10. Quoted in *Financial Times,* 6/29/90.

11. George Brockway, "A Road Eastern Europe Could Take," *New Leader,* 11/12/90, p. 18.

12. French, *Green Revolutions,* p. 48.

13. Luigi Barzini, *The Europeans* (New York: Penguin, 1985), p. 13.

14. Hugh Seton-Watson, *The "Sick Heart" of Modern Europe* (Seattle: University of Washington Press, 1975), p. 76. Christopher Dawson writes at the height of the Cold War era: "Yet if our civilisation is to survive it is essential that it should develop a common European consciousness and a sense of its historic and organic unity." Dawson, *The Making of Europe* (New York: Meridian, 1966), p. 21.

15. "Anti-Semitism in France," *Economist*, 4/6/91. According to Alan Riding in "Bad News Pummels French Premier," *New York Times*, 6/28/91, former Prime Minister Jacques Chirac has claimed that the French worker has had enough of "the noise and smell" of Arabs and Africans.

16. See Michalina Vaughan, "The Extreme Right in France: 'Lepenisme' or the Politics of Fear," in Cheles *et al.* Douglas Johnson, in "New Right in France" in the same volume, mentions right-wing groups such as Groupement de Recherche et d'Etudes pour une Civilisation Europeenne and Defense de l'Occident.

17. The anti-immigrant sentiment is likely to increase with the westward push of economic immigrants from Poland, Romania, and the Soviet Union. See, e.g., Alan Riding, "West Europe Braces for Migrant Wave from East," *New York Times*, 12/14/90. John Tagliabue reports that 1.3 million people left the former "Soviet bloc" in 1990. "Europeans Fleeing West in Search of a Better Life," *New York Times*, 8/11/91.

18. Alexander Stille, "No Blacks Need Apply," *Atlantic*, February 1992, p. 28.

19. "The Other Fortress Europe," *Economist*, 6/1/91, p. 46.

20. See "Brother, We Just Missed the 1992 Balloon," *Economist*, 6/23/90; Keith Harper, "Working in the EC," *Multinational Monitor*, July/August 1990; "The Great Debate on Social Rights," *The European*, 9/28/90; Ivo Dawnay, "Labour gets ready for jeux sans frontieres," *Financial Times*, 6/19/91. For Euro-business's recent nostalgia for continued governmental subsidies, see "Business in Europe: Second Thoughts," *Economist*, 6/8/91.

21. *Business Week*, 1/27/92.

22. See, e.g., Sylvia Nasar, "Russians Urged to Act Fast," *New York Times*, 1/6/92.

23. See "What to do with the WEU," *Economist*, 2/2/91, and "Of Bridges, Pillars and Canals," *Economist*, 2/9/91. In late 1991, France and Germany proposed a joint army within the EC. See Quentin Peel, "Bonn Presses Euro-force Plan," *Financial Times*, 2/6/92.

24. Garton Ash, *The Uses of Adversity*, p. 159.

Selected bibliography

Abel, Elie, *Shattered Bloc* (Boston: Houghton Mifflin, 1990).

Adam, Jan, *Economic Reforms in the Soviet Union and Eastern Europe Since the 1960s* (New York: St. Martin's Press, 1989).

Albert, Michael, and Robin Hahnel, *Looking Forward: Participatory Economics for the Twenty-First Century* (Boston: South End Press, 1991).

Allen, Bruce, *Germany East* (Montreal: Black Rose Books, 1989).

Alp, Ilker, *Bulgarian Atrocities* (London: K. Rustem & Brother, 1988).

Alter, Peter, *Nationalism* (London: Edward Arnold, 1989).

Amin, Samir, *Eurocentrism* (New York: Monthly Review, 1989).

Anderson, Benedict, *Imagined Communities* (London: Verso, 1983).

Anderson, Perry, *Lineages of the Absolutist State* (London: New Left Books, 1974).

Andrzejewski, Jerzy, *Ashes and Diamonds* (London: Wiedenfeld and Nicolson, 1962).

Bahro, Rudolf, *The Alternative in Eastern Europe* (London: New Left Books, 1975).

— *From Red to Green: Interviews with New Left Review* (London: Verso, 1984).

Banac, Ivo, *The National Question in Yugoslavia* (Ithaca: Cornell University Press, 1984).

— ed., *Eastern Europe in Revolution* (Ithaca: Cornell University Press, 1992).

Baranczak, Stanislaw, *Breathing Under Water* (Cambridge: Harvard University Press, 1990).

Barzini, Luigi, *The Europeans* (New York: Penguin, 1985).

Batt, Judy, *East Central Europe from Reform to Transformation* (New York: Council on Foreign Relations Press, 1991).

Behr, Edward, *Kiss the Hand You Cannot Bite* (New York: Villard Books, 1991).

Bell, Daniel, *The Cultural Contradictions of Capitalism* (New York: Basic, 1976).

Beloff, Nora, *Tito's Flawed Legacy* (London: Victor Gollancz, 1985).

Berend, Ivan, *The Crisis Zone of Europe* (Cambridge: Cambridge University Press, 1986).

Bernal, Martin, *Black Athena* (New Brunswick, NJ: Rutgers University Press, 1987).

Blazyca, George and Ryszard Rapacki, eds., *Poland into the 1990s* (New York: St. Martins, 1991).

Bloch, Fred, *Postindustrial Possibilities* (Berkeley: University of California Press, 1990).

Bokov, Georgi, *Modern Bulgaria* (Sofia: Sofia Press, 1981).

Borsody, Stephen, *The Tragedy of Central Europe* (New Haven: Yale Concilium on International and Area Studies, 1980).

Bradbury, Malcolm, *Rates of Exchange* (New York: Knopf, 1983).

Brown, J.F., *Surge to Freedom: The End of Communist Rule in Eastern Europe* (Durham, NC: Duke University Press, 1991).

Brumberg, Abraham, ed., *Poland: Genesis of a Revolution* (New York: Vintage, 1983).

Bruun, Geoffrey, *Nineteenth Century European Civilization, 1815-1914* (London: Oxford University Press, 1969).

Bugajski, Janusz and Maxine Pollack, *East European Fault Lines: Dissent, Opposition and Social Action* (Boulder: Westview, 1989).

Bunn, Ronald and William Andrews, eds., *Politics and Civil Liberties in Europe* (Princeton: D. Van Nostrand, 1967).

Callinicos, Alex, *The Revenge of History* (University Park, PA: Pennsylvania State University Press, 1991).

Cantor, Norman and Samuel Berner, *The Modern Era, 1815 to the Present* (New York: Crowell, 1971).

Cantor, Norman and Michael Werthman, eds., *The Twentieth Century: 1914 to the Present* (New York: Crowell, 1967).

Capek, Milic and Karel Hruby, eds., *T.G. Masaryk in Perspective* (SVU Press, 1981).

Carr, E.H., *The New Society* (Boston: Beacon, 1957).

Cheles, Luciano *et al.*, eds., *Neo-Fascism in Europe* (London: Longman, 1991).

Childs, David *et al.*, eds., *East Germany in Comparative Perspective* (London: Routledge, 1989).

Chirot, Daniel, ed., *The Origins of Backwardness in Eastern Europe* (Berkeley: University of California Press, 1989).

— ed., *The Crisis of Leninism and the Decline of the Left* (Seattle: University of Washington Press, 1991).

Clarke, Roger, ed., *Poland: The Economy in the 1980s* (Harlow: Longman, 1989).

Codrescu, Andrei, *The Disappearance of the Outside* (Reading, MA: Addison-Wesley, 1990).

— *A Hole in the Flag* (New York: William Morrow, 1991).

Cohen, Stephen, *Bukharin and the Bolshevik Revolution* (New York: Vintage, 1975).

— *Rethinking the Soviet Experience* (New York: Oxford University Press, 1985).

Coles, Paul, *The Ottoman Impact on Europe* (New York: Harcourt, Brace and World, 1968).

Crampton, Richard, *Bulgaria: 1878-1918* (New York: Columbia University Press, 1983).

— *A Short History of Modern Bulgaria* (Cambridge: Cambridge University Press, 1987).

Crowe, David and John Kolsti, *The Gypsies of Eastern Europe* (Armonk: M.E. Sharpe, 1991).

Cviic, Christopher, *Remaking the Balkans* (London: The Royal Institute of International Affairs, 1991).

Dahl, Robert, *A Preface to Economic Democracy* (Berkeley: University of California Press, 1985).

Dahrendorf, Ralf, *Reflections on the Revolution in Europe* (New York: Random House, 1990).

Davies, Norman, *Heart of Europe: A Short History of Poland* (New York: Oxford University Press, 1984).

Dawidowicz, Lucy, *The War Against the Jews, 1933-1945* (New York: Bantam, 1981).

Dawisha, Karen, *Eastern Europe, Gorbachev, and Reform: The Great Challenge* (Cambridge: Cambridge University Press, 1990).

Dawson, Christopher, *The Making of Europe* (New York: Meridian, 1966).

Denitch, Bogdan, *Limits and Possibilities* (Minneapolis: University of Minnesota Press, 1990).

de Rougemont, Denis, *The Idea of Europe* (New York: Meridian, 1968).

Devetak, Silvo, *The Equality of Nations and Nationalities in Yugoslavia* (Vienna: Wilhelm Braumiller, 1988).

Devine, Pat, *Democracy and Economic Planning* (Cambridge: Polity Press, 1988).

Djilas, Aleksa, *The Contested Country* (Cambridge: Harvard University Press, 1991).

Djilas, Milovan, *The New Class* (New York: Harcourt, Brace and Jovanovich, 1982).

Duchacek, Ivo, *The Territorial Dimension of Politics Within, Among, and Across Nations* (Boulder: Westview, 1986).

Echikson, William, *Lighting the Night* (New York: William Morrow, 1990).

Elazer, Daniel, ed., *Federalism and Political Integration* (Lanham, MD: University Press of America, 1984).

Enzensberger, Hans Magnus, *Europe, Europe* (New York: Pantheon, 1990).

Feffer, John, *Beyond Detente* (New York: Hill and Wang, 1990).

Feher, Ference and Agnes Heller, *Eastern Left, Western Left: Totalitarianism, Freedom, and Democracy* (Atlantic Highlands, NJ: Humanities Press International, 1987).

Fischer, Mary Ellen, *Nicolae Ceausescu: A Study in Political Leadership* (Boulder: Lynne Rienner, 1989).

Fischer-Galati, Stephen, *Twentieth Century Rumania* (New York: Columbia University Press, 1970).

Freedman, Lawrence, *Europe Transformed* (New York: St. Martins, 1990).

French, Hilary, *Green Revolutions* (Washington, DC: Worldwatch Institute, 1990).

Gaddis, John Lewis, *Strategies of Containment* (Oxford: Oxford University Press, 1982).

Galleano, Eduardo, *Opens Veins of Latin America* (New York: Monthly Review, 1973).

Garton Ash, Timothy, *The Polish Revolution* (New York: Vintage, 1985).

— *The Uses of Adversity* (New York: Random House, 1989).

— *The Magic Lantern* (New York: Random House, 1990).

Gati, Charles, ed., *The Politics of Modernization in Eastern Europe* (New York: Praeger, 1976).

— *Hungary and the Soviet Bloc* (Durham, NC: Duke University Press, 1986).

— *The Bloc That Failed* (Bloomington: Indiana University Press, 1990).

Gella, Aleksander, *Development and Class Structure in Eastern Europe* (New York: State University of New York Press, 1989).

Gerrits, Andre, *The Failure of Authoritarian Change* (Aldershot: Dartmouth, 1990).

Giddens, Anthony, *The Class Structure of the Advanced Societies* (New York: Harper & Row, 1972).

Gilberg, Trond, *Nationalism and Communism in Romania* (Boulder: Westview, 1990).

Glenny, Misha, *The Rebirth of History* (London: Penguin, 1990).

Goodwyn, Lawrence, *Breaking the Barrier: The Rise of Solidarity in Poland* (New York: Oxford University Press, 1991).

Greene, Nathaniel, ed., *European Socialism Since World War I* (Chicago: Quadrangle, 1971).

Gwertzman, Bernard and Michael Kaufman, eds., *The Collapse of Communism* (Random House, 1990).

Halecki, Oscar, *The Limits and Divisions of European History* (New York: Sheed and Ward, 1950).

Hankiss, Elemer, *East European Alternatives* (Oxford: Clarendon, 1990).

Haraszti, Miklos, *A Worker in a Worker's State* (New York: Universe, 1978).

— *The Velvet Prison: Artists Under State Socialism* (New York: Basic, 1987).

Harding, Georgina, *In Another Europe* (London: Hodder & Stoughton, 1990).

Havel, Vaclav, *The Power of the Powerless* (Armonk: M.E. Sharpe, 1985).

— *Living in Truth* (London: Faber and Faber, 1987).

— *Open Letters* (New York: Knopf, 1991).

Hay, Denys, *Europe: The Emergence of an Idea* (Edinburgh: Edinburgh University Press, 1957).

Heilbroner, Robert, *Between Capitalism and Socialism* (New York: Vintage, 1970).

— *The Worldly Philosophers* (New York: Simon and Schuster, 1986).

Helsinki Watch, *From Below: Independent Peace and Environmental Movements in Eastern Europe & the USSR* (1987).

— *Destroying Ethnic Identity: The Expulsion of the Bulgarian Turks* (1989).

— *Increasing Turbulence: Human Rights in Yugoslavia* (1989).

— *Yugoslavia: Crisis in Kosovo* (1990).

Herlihy, David, *Medieval Culture and Society* (New York: Harpers, 1968).

Hieronymi, Otto, *Economic Policies For the New Hungary* (Columbus, OH: Battelle, 1990).

Inglehart, Ronald, *The Silent Revolution* (Princeton: Princeton University Press, 1977).

— *Culture Shift in Advanced Industrial Society* (Princeton: Princeton University Press, 1990).

International Institute for Strategic Studies, *The Military Balance (1990-91)* (London: 1990).

Isaacson, Walter and Evan Thomas, *The Wise Men* (New York: Simon & Schuster, 1988).

Jaszi, Oscar, *The Dissolution of the Habsburg Monarchy* (Chicago: University of Chicago Press, 1966).

Jelavich, Barbara, *History of the Balkans,* vol. 2 (Cambridge: Cambridge University Press, 1983).

Jones, E.L., *The European Miracle* (Cambridge: Cambridge University Press, 1981).

Kaminski, Bartlomiej, *The Collapse of State Socialism: The Case of Poland* (Princeton: Princeton University Press, 1991).

Kann, Robert, *A History of the Habsburg Empire: 1526-1918* (Berkeley: University of California Press, 1974).

Kennedy, Paul, *The Rise and Fall of Great Powers* (New York: Random House, 1987).

King, Preston, *Federalism and Federation* (Baltimore: Johns Hopkins University Press, 1982).

King, Robert, *A History of the Romanian Communist Party* (Stanford: Hoover Institute, 1980).

Kittrie, Nicholas and Ivan Volgyes, eds., *The Uncertain Future: Gorbachev's Eastern Bloc* (New York: Paragon House, 1988).

Kochan, Lionel and Richard Abraham, *The Making of Modern Russia,* 2nd edition (New York: Penguin, 1983).

Kohak, Erazim, *Jan Patocka: Philosophy and Selected Writings* (Chicago: University of Chicago Press, 1989).

Kohn, Hans, *The Idea of Nationalism* (New York: Collier, 1944).

Kolakowski, Leszek, *Toward a Marxist Humanism* (New York: Grove, 1968).

— *Modernity on Endless Trial* (Chicago: University of Chicago Press, 1990).

Kolankiewicz, George, *Poland: Politics, Economics and Society* (New York: Pinter, 1988).

Konrad, George, *Anti-Politics* (San Diego: Harcourt, Brace and Jovanovich, 1984).

Konrad, George and Ivan Szelenyi, *The Intellectuals on the Road to Class Power* (New York: Harcourt, Brace and Jovanovich, 1979).

Konwicki, Tadeusz, *A Minor Apocalypse* (New York: Farrar, Straus and Giroux, 1983).

— *Moonrise, Moonset* (New York: Farrar, Straus and Giroux, 1987).

Kornai, Janos, *Contradictions and Dilemmas* (Cambridge: MIT Press, 1986).

— *Vision and Reality, Market and State* (New York: Routledge, 1990).

Kostov, Vladimir, *The Bulgarian Umbrella* (New York: St. Martins, 1988).

Kovrig, Bennett, *Of Walls and Bridges* (New York: New York University Press, 1991).

Kovtun, George, ed., *The Spirit of Thomas Masaryk (1850- 1937)* (New York: St. Martins, 1990).

Kramer, Jane, *Unsettling Europe* (New York: Random House, 1981).

Kuncewicz, Maria, ed., *The Modern Polish Mind* (London: Secker and Warburg, 1962).

Kuttner, Robert, *The Economic Illusion* (Boston: Houghton Mifflin, 1984).

— *The End of Laissez-Faire* (New York: Knopf, 1991).

Landau, Zbigniew and Jerzy Tomaszewski, *The Polish Economy in the Twentieth Century* (London: Croom Helm, 1985).

Laqueur, Walter, ed., *Fascism: A Reader's Guide* (Berkeley: University of California Press, 1976).

Laue, Theodore von, *The World Revolution of Westernization* (New York: Oxford University Press, 1987).

Lemke, Christiane and Gary Marks, eds., *The Crisis of Socialism in Europe* (Durham, NC: Duke University Press, 1992).

Lendvai, Paul, *Hungary: The Art of Survival* (London: I.B. Tauris, 1988).

Lenin, V.I., *Selected Works,* vol. 2 (Moscow: Progress Publishers, 1977).

Leonhard, Wolfgang, *Eurocommunism: Challenge for East and West* (New York: Holt, Rinehart and Winston, 1979).

Lewin, Moishe, *Russian Peasants and Soviet Power* (New York: Norton, 1975).

Lewis, Bernard, *The Muslim Discovery of Europe* (New York: Norton, 1982).

Lewis, Paul, ed., *Eastern Europe: Political Crisis and Legitimation* (New York: St. Martins, 1984).

Lieber, Nancy, ed., *Eurosocialism and America* (Philadelphia: Temple University Press, 1982).

Lipski, Jan Josef, *KOR: Worker's Defense Committee in Poland 1976-1981* (Berkeley: University of California Press, 1985).

Lissaker, Karen, *Banks, Borrowers, and the Establishment* (New York: Basic, 1991).

Logio, George, *Bulgaria: Past & Present* (Manchester: Sherratt & Hughes, 1936).

Macesich, George, ed., *Essays on the Yugoslav Economic Model* (New York: Praeger, 1989).

Magris, Claudio, *Danube* (New York: Farrar, Straus and Giroux, 1989).

Marer, Paul, ed., *Creditworthiness and Reform in Poland: Western and Polish Perspectives* (Bloomington: Indiana University Press, 1985).

Marx, Karl, *The Eighteenth Brumaire of Louis Bonaparte* (New York: International Publishers, 1963).

Masaryk, Thomas, *The New Europe: The Slav Standpoint* (Lewisburg: Bucknell University Press, 1972).

Michnik, Adam, *Letters From Prison and Other Essays* (Berkeley: University of California Press, 1985).

Mojzes, Paul, *Christian-Marxist Dialogue in Eastern Europe* (Minneapolis: Augsburg, 1981).

Muller-Rommel, Ferdinand, ed., *New Politics in Western Europe: The Rise and Success of Green Parties and Alternative Lists* (Boulder: Westview, 1989).

Nove, Alec, *The Economics of Feasible Socialism* (London: Allen and Unwin, 1983).

O'Brien, Conor Cruise, *Passion & Cunning* (New York: Simon & Schuster, 1988).

Olszer, Krystyna, ed., *For Your Freedom and Ours* (New York: Unger, 1981).

Ost, David, *Solidarity and the Politics of Anti-Politics* (Philadelphia: Temple University Press, 1990).

Pacepa, Ion Mihai, *Red Horizons* (Washington, DC: Regnery Gateway, 1987).

Pavlowitch, Steven, *The Improbable Survivor: Yugoslavia and Its Problems, 1918-1988* (Columbus: Ohio State University Press, 1988).

Pinder, John, *The European Community and Eastern Europe* (New York: Council on Foreign Relations, 1991).

Pipa, Arshi and Sami Repishti, *Studies in Kosova* (New York: Columbia University Press, 1984).

Polanyi, Karl, *The Great Transformation* (Boston: Beacon, 1957).

Prins, Gwyn, ed., *Spring in Winter: The 1989 Revolutions* (Manchester: Manchester University Press, 1990).

Prybyla, Jan, ed., *Privatizing and Marketizing Socialism,* The Annals of the American Academy of Political and Social Science (Newbury Park, CA: Sage Publications, 1990).

Ramet, Pedro, *Nationalism and Federalism in Yugoslavia, 1963-1983* (Bloomington: Indiana University Press, 1984).

— ed., *Yugoslavia in the 1980s* (Boulder: Westview, 1985).

— ed., *Religion and Nationalism in Soviet and East European Politics* (Durham: Duke University Press, 1989).

Ramet, Sabrina, *Social Currents in Eastern Europe* (Durham: Duke University Press, 1991).

Ranelagh, John, *The Agency: The Rise and Decline of the CIA* (New York: Touchstone, 1987).

Resis, Albert, *Stalin, the Politburo, and the Onset of the Cold War, 1945-6,* The Carl Beck Papers in Russian and East European Studies, no. 701 (Pittsburgh: University of Pittsburgh Center for Russian and East European Studies, 1988).

Revisz, Gabor, *Perestroika in Eastern Europe: Hungary's Economic Transformation, 1945-1988* (Boulder: Westview, 1990).

Rhodes, Richard, *The Making of the Atomic Bomb* (New York: Simon and Schuster, 1988).

Rice, Eugene, *The Foundations of Modern Europe, 1460-1559* (New York: Norton, 1970).

Riese, Hans-Peter, *Since the Prague Spring* (New York: Vintage, 1979).

Riker, William, *Federalism: Origin, Operation, Significance* (Boston: Little Brown, 1964).

Robertson, Priscilla, *Revolutions of 1848: A Social History* (Princeton: Princeton University Press, 1952).

Rollo, J.M.C., *The New Eastern Europe: Western Responses* (New York: Council on Foreign Relations, 1990).

Rothschild, Joseph, *Return to Diversity* (New York: Oxford University Press, 1989).

Rupnik, Jacques, *The Other Europe* (New York: Pantheon, 1989).

Rybakov, Anatoly, *Children of the Arbat* (Boston: Little Brown, 1988).

Said, Edward, *Orientalism* (New York: Vintage, 1979).

Schaeffer, Robert, *Warpaths* (New York: Hill and Wang, 1990).

Seton-Watson, Hugh, *The "Sick Heart" of Modern Europe* (Seattle: University of Washington Press, 1975).

— *The East European Revolutions* (Boulder: Westview, 1985).

Sherwin, Martin, *A World Destroyed: The Atomic Bomb and the Grand Alliance* (New York: Vintage, 1977).

Simpson, Christopher, *Blowback* (New York: Weidenfeld and Nicolson, 1988).

Simsir, Bilal, *The Turks of Bulgaria* (London: K. Rustem & Brother, 1988).

Singleton, Fred, *Environmental Problems in the Soviet Union and Eastern Europe* (Boulder: Lynne Rienner, 1987).

Sobell, Vlad, *CMEA in Crisis* (New York: Praeger, 1990).

Speiser, Stuart, *Mainstreet Capitalism* (New York: New Horizons, 1988).

Staar, Richard, *Communist Regimes in Eastern Europe* (Stanford, CA: Hoover Institute, 1984).

Stettner, Edward, ed., *Perspectives on Europe* (Cambridge: Schenkman, 1970).

Stokes, Gale, *From Stalinism to Pluralism* (New York: Oxford University Press, 1991).

Sugar, Peter and Ivo Lederer, *Nationalism in Eastern Europe* (Seattle: University of Washington Press, 1971).

Swann, Dennis, *The Economics of the Common Market* (London: Penguin, 1990).

Szelenyi, Ivan, *Socialist Entrepreneurs* (Madison: University of Wisconsin Press, 1988).

Tihany, Leslie, *A History of Middle Europe* (New Brunswick, NJ: Rutgers University Press, 1976).

Tipton, Frank and Robert Aldrich, *An Economic and Social History of Europe, 1890-1939* (Baltimore: Johns Hopkins Press, 1987).

Tismaneanu, Vladimir, *The Crisis of Marxist Ideology in Eastern Europe: The Poverty of Utopia* (New York: Routledge, 1988).

— ed., *In Search of Civil Society* (New York: Routledge, 1990).

Tokes, Rudolf, ed., *Eurocommunism and Detente* (New York: New York University Press, 1979).

— ed., *Opposition in Eastern Europe* (Baltimore: Johns Hopkins University Press, 1979).

Tudjman, Franjo, *Nationalism in Contemporary Europe* (New York: Columbia University Press, 1981).

Turnock, David, *Eastern Europe: An Economic and Political Geography* (New York: Routledge, 1989).

van Brabant, Jozef, *Remaking Eastern Europe* (London: Kluwer, 1990).

Volgyes, Ivan, *Hungary: A Nation of Contradictions* (Boulder: Westview, 1982).

Volgyes, Ivan and Nancy Volgyes, *The Liberated Female* (Boulder: Westview, 1977).

Voslensky, Michael, *Nomenklatura: The Soviet Ruling Class* (New York: Doubleday, 1984).

Wachtel, Howard, *Workers' Management and Workers' Wages in Yugoslavia* (Ithaca: Cornell University Press, 1973).

Wallerstein, Immanuel, *The Modern World-System,* two volumes, (New York: Academic Press, 1980).

Weber, Max, *The Protestant Ethic and the Spirit of Capitalism* (New York: Scribner's, 1958).

Weilemann, Peter, *et al.*, eds., *Upheaval Against the Plan: Eastern Europe on the Eve of the Storm* (Oxford: Berg, 1991).

Whipple, Tim, *After the Velvet Revolution: Vaclav Havel and the New Leaders of Czechoslovakia Speak Out* (New York: Freedom House, 1991).

Williamson, John, *The Economic Opening of Eastern Europe* (Washington, DC: Institute for International Economics, 1991).

Wolf, Eric, *Europe and the People Without History* (Berkeley: University of California Press, 1982).

Wolff, Philippe, *The Awakening of Europe* (Middlesex: Penguin, 1985).

World Armaments and Disarmament, SIPRI Yearbook 1990, (Oxford: Oxford University Press, 1990).

World Bank Reports, *Poland, Reform, Adjustment, and Growth* (Washington, DC: World Bank, 1987).

World Commission on Environment and Development, *Our Common Future* (New York: Oxford University Press, 1987).

Worldwatch, *State of the World 1991* (New York: Norton, 1991).

Zinner, Paul, *Revolution in Hungary* (New York: Columbia University Press, 1962).

Index

A

B

C

D

E

F

G

H

S

T

Y

Z